J. Ellis Photography

PATRICIA MILLER is an award-winning author and journalist whose fascination with the untold stories of women led her on a ten-year journey to unearth the history of the Pollard-Breckinridge scandal. Her work on the interplay of politics and sexual morality has appeared in *The Atlantic*, *Salon*, *The Nation*, *The Huffington Post*, and *Ms.* magazine. She received a master's degree in journalism from New York University and lives outside of Washington, D.C., with her husband and dog.

Also by Patricia Miller

*Good Catholics: The Battle over Abortion
in the Catholic Church*

Additional Praise for *Bringing Down the Colonel*

"A meticulously researched and deftly written narrative about the epic struggle between a wronged woman and the powerful man who abused her. *Bringing Down the Colonel* puts a colorful cast of characters on stage in a gripping courtroom drama that folds in large swaths of American social and political history at a moment of national transition. In many ways, as Patricia Miller demonstrates, the monumental case of *Pollard v. Breckinridge* was an important catalyst for the nascent women's movement and a precursor of today's #MeToo phenomenon. An entertaining and informative read."

—Tom Sancton, author of *The Bettencourt Affair:
The World's Richest Woman and the Scandal That Rocked Paris*

"History shows how often yesterday's sex scandal is tomorrow's sexual revolution. Patricia Miller's timely and exhilarating book shows how a supposedly 'fallen' and 'ruined' woman in 1890s Washington shockingly took a powerful man to court to demand reparations. You'll cheer for the woman who spoke out, brought down the colonel, and struck an early blow against the double sexual standard."

—Elaine Showalter, Professor Emerita of English,
Princeton University

"Polite society deemed Madeline Pollard a 'ruined woman' when her long-time lover, Kentucky congressman William Breckinridge, refused to marry her as promised. Here's the surprising tale of how she sued him and roused a generation of women to throw him out of office."

—Meryl Gordon, author of *Bunny Mellon:
The Life of an American Style Legend*

"*Bringing Down the Colonel* reads as if it were ripped from today's headlines. Deeply researched, beautifully written, the story of Madeline Pollard brings alive a period when sexual mores were beginning to change from Victorian to modern. But as [Pollard's] story makes all too clear, the more things change, the more they stay the same: vulnerable women and powerful men are not that different more than a century later. [Pollard]

uses her beauty and fierce intelligence to come out ahead, with all of us rooting for her."   —Kristin Luker, Elizabeth Josselyn Boalt
Professor of Law (Emerita), University of California,
Berkeley School of Law

"Though the sexual exploitation of women has been well documented, stories of women successfully bringing down their abusers have, until recently, been few and far between. Journalist Miller reaches back into the past to resurrect one woman's compelling odyssey from victim to victor . . . A fascinating examination of a historical #MeToo episode."
                                                                                    —*Booklist*

"Miller dusts off a long-forgotten scandal that gripped the nation's capital in the late-nineteenth century [and] seamlessly weaves in the stories of other unmarried women connected to the case . . . This book will enthrall readers interested in women's and political history."
                                                                        —*Publishers Weekly*

"Ms. Miller shows how the scandal laid open previously taboo topics— adultery, illicit pregnancies, abortion and sexual hypocrisy . . . Her wide historical lens makes it a valuable, timely addition to discussions of gender and power, not to mention an eerie echo of recent news."
                                                                          —*The Economist*

"A panoramic examination of women's changing roles and of women's efforts to provide for themselves and make their way in the largely male public sphere. Good, timely history for the #MeToo moment."
                                                                          —*Kirkus Reviews*

BRINGING DOWN
THE COLONEL

BRINGING DOWN THE COLONEL

A Sex Scandal of the Gilded Age,
and the "Powerless" Woman
Who Took On Washington

PATRICIA MILLER

Picador
Sarah Crichton Books
Farrar, Straus and Giroux   New York

Picador
120 Broadway, New York 10271

Printed in the United States of America
Published in 2018 by Sarah Crichton Books,
an imprint of Farrar, Straus and Giroux
First Picador paperback edition, March 2020

The Library of Congress has cataloged the Farrar, Straus and Giroux
hardcover edition as follows:
Names: Miller, Patricia, 1964– author.
Title: Bringing down the Colonel : a sex scandal of the Gilded Age, and the
   "powerless" woman who took on Washington / Patricia Miller.
Description: First edition. | New York : Sarah Crichton Books, Farrar, Straus
   and Giroux, 2018. | Includes bibliographical references and index.
Identifiers: LCCN 2018016403 | ISBN 9780374252663 (hardcover)
Subjects: LCSH: Pollard, Madeline, approximately 1866– | Breckinridge, William
   Campbell Preston, 1837–1904. | Sex scandals—United States—History—
   19th century. | Scandals—United States—History—19th century.
Classification: LCC E664.P75 M55 2018 | DDC 973.8092/2—dc23
LC record available at https://lccn.loc.gov/2018016403

Picador Paperback ISBN: 978-1-250-23491-9

Designed by Jonathan D. Lippincott

For Anthony and Rosie

The fight is getting hotter
As fades the Summer's grass;
The boys down in the trenches
Let not their chances pass;

They drink with party bosses,
Go to all the barbeques,
Have jolly times in general
And, it's "damn old Billy's shoes";

Now, who's to be elected?
If you guess you make a "scoop,"
So, hurry up and tell us
Who's the party "in the soup"?

The country's getting restless—
That is easy to be seen—
Is it "Evan," "Bill," or "Billy"
In this burgoo soup tureen?

—*Kentucky Leader*, August 23, 1894

Contents

BRINGING DOWN
THE COLONEL

1

Gold to Be Made

On January 29, 1894, a depression formed east of the southern Atlantic coast, moved inland over the Chesapeake Bay, and traveled northward, where it collided with another area of low pressure coming from the west and exploded into one of the most severe coastal storms the region had seen in years. A fierce gale and snow pounded the eastern seaboard into the next day, whipping Atlantic City with winds that reached sixty miles an hour, and wrecking the schooner *Aberdeen* off the coast of Glouces-ter, Massachusetts. As the tempest gathered strength, a young woman hurriedly made her way from Boston down its path, as if the swirling storm were itself drawing her southward. By the time she reached New York, the full force of the blizzard had descended on Boston, burying it under snow. She took a ferry across the Hudson River to the Pennsylva-nia Railroad Station in Jersey City, dashed off a letter to her sister as she sat in the ladies' waiting room, and then boarded the Baltimore & Potomac Railroad's midnight express to Washington. She crossed paths with the storm's original landfall near Havre de Grace, Maryland, early on the morning of the thirtieth, just as the oystermen and the market duck hunters with their Chesapeake Bay retrievers would have been setting out to provision the restaurants and markets of Baltimore and Washington with those mainstays of the nineteenth-century diet.

For Jane Tucker—Jennie to her fractious family and her friends—the rushed journey southward was a desperate gamble to break free from the rut of low-paying jobs and lecherous bosses that had come to define her life as part of the first generation of women to foray into the formerly forbidden—and largely male—realm of office work. Still single and nearing thirty, like many young women of the time she realized she likely would need to take care of herself, but she had struggled to find financial and professional security. The opportunity in Washington was coming just as she felt "the bottom had dropped out of everything," as she told her mother. Her sister Patty, a successful journalist, had died the previous November, just months after being diagnosed with uterine cancer. Her aging parents had taken it hard, and her father in particular seemed "feeble and [grew] childish," deepening Jennie's guilt about leaving them alone in the family home in Maine. Then, just before Christmas, Jennie had lost her job as a secretary at the West End Street Railway in Boston, making her another casualty of the financial depression that had wracked the country since the previous winter. Adding to that, she had developed an excruciating toothache, the result of a badly abscessed tooth that had been treated three times but had so far resisted the ministrations of nineteenth-century dentistry.

Jennie had found herself questioning what her life as a working woman was adding up to, with a string of insecure jobs, paychecks that never seemed to stretch to the end of the month, and moves from one lonely boardinghouse to another. "I'm so tired of living alone," she wrote to her sister Maude. "I have not gained much by being independent in the past. It's brought more heartache . . . than anything else." She confessed she felt so despondent that she "tried to make up my mind to kill myself only I didn't have the courage."

Jennie had returned home to take stock. "I think the shock to my nerves from all the trouble since Patty's death has kind of broken me up," she told her mother. When she arrived at Castle Tucker, which is what the locals called her family's turreted mansion on the Sheepscot River, her mother was shaken by the terrible condition her normally hale daughter was in, the trouble with her tooth compounded by "bleeding piles" from the arduous train journey north.

All Jennie wanted was to spend a quiet winter at home, but her respite was short-lived. Two days after she arrived, on January 17, she received a telegram from one of her old bosses, Charles Stoll—the only one she liked and the only one who had treated her as more than a stenography-taking drudge. He asked if she was available immediately for a two-month engagement in Washington, but didn't say what the nature of the work was. As much as she wanted to work for him again, Jennie hesitated. Physically and mentally, she felt depleted. And her mother needed her to get Castle Tucker ready for the paying summer guests who came to enjoy the Maine coast, the family fortune having gone the way of the cotton markets that built it. There was also the matter of money; Jennie was flat broke and her clothes were so shabby that she had spent much of her free time the previous fall mending and reworking her "old duds" to maintain some semblance of fashionable dress.

Why, she must have wondered, would Stoll need her to come all the way to Washington to do secretarial work when the capital, like the rest of the country, was awash in unemployed stenographers and typists?

When she raised her concerns with Stoll, he dashed off a quick letter dismissing them. "Why you, of all persons, are the last to let a little sickness effect your spirits . . . Of course you have not made money—who has? Why for six months I was scared to death," he wrote. And then he said she could name her price if she agreed to come. That settled it. Jennie cabled back that she would come for fifteen dollars a week, the most she had ever made, plus her travel expenses. Stoll cabled back a quick acceptance of her terms, plus fifty dollars for expenses, and told her to go to Boston and await further instructions. The rest of the week was a rush of preparations. Not wanting to spend too much money on the new dress she desperately needed, Jennie took apart one of her sister's old wrappers—a loose-fitting, high-necked house gown that Victorian women wore belted like a robe—dyed it twice to get the color she wanted, and made what her mother called a "pretty, tasteful dress." She packed and made arrangements to return temporarily to the Beacon Hill boardinghouse where she had been living.

When Jennie arrived in Boston on Saturday morning, January 27, a thick letter from Stoll was already waiting for her. When she read it and comprehended what he wanted her to do, she shuddered. "My surprise and the feelings which first crept over me cannot be described," she wrote him back. He had explained that what he wanted her to do was "in the line of detective work" and required someone "thoroughly acquainted with human nature and able to devise and execute plans." He detailed exactly what the job entailed and how to make arrangements to come to Washington. The mission filled Jennie with trepidation, but she didn't want to disappoint Stoll. Swallowing her doubts, she cabled, "I leave for Washington Monday."

There was now no turning back. Sitting among the politicians and businessmen on the Congressional Limited Express, Jennie must have marveled at the turn of events precipitated by Stoll's letter: in a matter of days she had gone from an unemployed secretary to a player in the middle of the greatest political scandal of the day.

Stoll had written: "My lifelong friend, Col. W.C.P. Breckinridge, of Kentucky, has become complicated with a young woman by the name of Madeline Pollard . . . She brought suit against him for breach of promise last summer." Jennie already knew this. The suit had been front-page news around the country. Col. William Campbell Preston Breckinridge, a U.S. congressman from Kentucky who was known as the "silver-tongued" orator of the Democratic Party, was a revered former Confederate officer and scion of a prominent political family. The Breckinridge name was practically synonymous with the Bluegrass region of Kentucky, which, as one Louisville newspaper noted, was as famed for "the brilliant achievements of its statesmen" as it was for "the speed of its horses and the excellence of its whiskey." It had been quite a surprise to polite society in Washington and Kentucky when Breckinridge's engagement to Madeline Pollard, who was nearly thirty years his junior, was announced the previous June, less than a year after the death of his wife. As far as anyone knew, Pollard was a no one—a poor young woman from Kentucky with literary aspirations who had managed to rise in Washington's southern social circles in recent years. It was even more surprising, then, when Breckinridge turned around and married someone else. When Pollard sued him for damages over the broken engagement, what had been only whispers of impropriety turned into a full-throated scandal.

Stoll wanted Jennie to figure out what everyone was wondering: What, exactly, did Madeline Pollard want? Since Breckinridge had married someone else, the suit couldn't be used as it was deployed by many a despairing Victorian woman—to force a reluctant suitor to the altar.

And while breach of promise suits were designed to provide women with financial compensation for their dashed marriage chances, money also didn't seem to be the motive—Breckinridge was far richer in stature than in cash. As the *Washington Post* put it, "Everybody who knows the 'silver tongued' blue grass orator is aware that he is not a man of means." Mysteriously, Pollard had refused Breckinridge's offer of a modest settlement, and her lawyers hadn't even extended to Breckinridge, who was himself a lawyer, the professional courtesy of notifying him of the impending suit and giving him a chance to settle it.

Then there was the mystery of where Pollard got the money to hire two of Washington's best lawyers, who seemed to have nearly unlimited funds to prosecute the case. Somehow, a penniless girl from Kentucky was mounting a serious legal challenge to a powerful congressman, threatening a political dynasty that stretched back to the administration of Thomas Jefferson. What Stoll wanted Jennie to do was to get close to Pollard and determine "the real motive and purpose of the suit." He hoped that if they could figure out what Pollard really wanted, and who was backing her, they could prevail on her to take a settlement. It wasn't just his friend whom Stoll hoped to spare from the trial. The filing of the suit, he told Jennie, had "created such a sensation in the country" that every household was certain to "be filled with the details" of the trial, and "the effect upon society, and especially the young people of the country, cannot be for good."

And if the suit couldn't be prevented from coming to trial, Stoll wanted Jennie to "be in a position" to give Breckinridge's legal team a day-to-day appraisal of "the movements of the other side" and the contours of any testimony that might be introduced—in other words, he wanted her to spy on the opposition.

There was a catch, however. Pollard had entered the House of Mercy, a home for "fallen" women in Washington. Jennie would have to devise some "pitiful tale" to get in, Stoll wrote, and live in the institution to befriend Pollard. The idea of "lying and living a lie day after day" filled Jennie with trepidation. At the same time, she sensed an opportunity to turn around her own flailing life and give it the purpose it lacked. "If I could be the means of bringing about a settlement of a frightful scandal like this, and prevent the harm which must surely result from such a trial, and could also feel that I had helped a friendless woman to re-trieve a terrific blunder, I might truly think that I had lived to some purpose," she told Stoll.

Jennie also hoped the unconventional mission would open new pro-fessional opportunities for her and finally put her on a sound financial footing. "I have undertaken quite a thing here and if I succeed I shall doubtless make a good thing out of it," she wrote to her mother, saying that despite the challenges and her own misgivings, "the gold is too scarce to let a good chance slip to make it."

2

A Bright and Brainy Woman

The telegram that arrived for Madeline Pollard on July 9, 1893, was addressed to her simply at "The Farm, Charlottesville, Va." Everyone in the city knew the place. It had been called The Farm since before the Revolutionary War, when it was the only homestead amid the virgin forest of what would become Charlottesville. And it remained The Farm long after the rough colonial farmhouse had been replaced by a red brick neoclassical mansion built by the same master craftsmen who constructed Mr. Jefferson's university not far away.

Madeline was visiting Julia Churchill Blackburn, of the Churchill Downs Churchills, and the widow of the former Kentucky governor Luke Blackburn. Blackburn was herself a guest of Julia Ann Farish, the widow of Thomas Farish—the owner of The Farm and a former Confederate officer who narrowly escaped being hung on his own front lawn as a spy during the Civil War when he tried to sneak home in civilian clothes to visit his family. The other guest rounding out the party was Nancy Hines. She was the wife of Thomas Henry Hines, who actually had been a Confederate spy, renowned for his daring escapes and for plotting with Luke Blackburn to foment unrest in northern cities during the war. Hines was at this point a retired chief justice of the Kentucky Court of Appeals.

Madeline found herself among this august group of Confederate wives and widows because Col. W.C.P. Breckinridge had, on a Friday evening back in March, asked Julia Blackburn to serve as a social chaperone for Madeline, as, he explained, he planned to marry her once a suitable period of mourning for his late wife Issa had passed. Now their engagement—and Madeline's ascent to Bluegrass royalty—was public knowledge. It had been announced in the *Washington Post* social column a little more than two weeks ago and subsequently reported in the *New York Times*. Like many of the Bluegrass elite, the Breckinridges came to America in the early 1700s as part of a wave of Scotch-Irish Presbyterians who immigrated first to Pennsylvania before following the spine of the Appalachians south in search of virgin land. The Breckinridges settled near Staunton, Virginia, in the Shenandoah Valley. Economically and socially ambitious, they quickly became part of the local gentry, in no small part because Congressman Breckinridge's grandfather John Breckinridge in 1785 married Mary Hopkins Cabell of the prominent Cabell family, whose roots reached back to the British gentry who founded Virginia.

But John Breckinridge felt constrained in late eighteenth-century Virginia—which was crowded with ambitious, well-connected men and short on cheap land—despite receiving a four-hundred-acre farm outside Charlottesville as his wife's dowry and being elected to the Virginia House of Delegates when he was twenty. In 1793, he joined the emigration of Virginians to Kentucky and moved his family to Cabell's Dale, a six-hundred-acre farm near Lexington, on what was still the frontier of white settlement. Breckinridge's foresight brought the family land and wealth (eventually he would own thirty thousand acres) and, according to the family biographer James Klotter, what he really sought: "greater prestige for unborn generations of Breckinridges."

Much of this prestige came from an energetic role in the political life of the new state of Kentucky and, eventually, on the national stage. Within thirteen years, John Breckinridge "serve[d] the commonwealth as attorney general, Speaker of the Kentucky House, United States Senator, and the first member of the cabinet from west of the [Appalachian] mountains," recounts Klotter. While in the Kentucky legislature, John Breckinridge conspired with Jefferson, then vice president, to introduce the Kentucky Resolutions of 1789, which opposed the Alien and Sedition Acts and what Jefferson and Breckinridge saw as a dangerous consolidation of federal power. As a U.S. senator, he helped Jefferson negotiate the Louisiana Purchase and was rewarded with an appointment as his attorney general.

In the generations that followed, members of the Breckinridge family became fixtures in the political and social elite of the South. "They were governors and senators and members of Congress, and presidents of colleges and eminent divines, and brave generals . . . There were four governors of old Virginia. They were members of the cabinet of Jefferson and Taylor and Buchanan and Lincoln. They had major-generals and brigadier-generals by the score; and gallant officers in the army and navy by the hundred," wrote the biologist Charles Davenport in lauding the family as an example of superior genetics. Or, as the *Lexington Herald* later put it, the "Breckinridges of Kentucky . . . have been in American public life ever since there was an American public life."

This was the world that William Campbell Preston Breckinridge was born into, his very name "a reminder of past glories to be emulated, of men and women to be honored," Klotter notes, as well as an advertisement of kinship connections going back generations. Not only had his grandfather John elevated the family into the Tidewater elite with his marriage to Mary Cabell, but his father, Robert, a nationally prominent Presbyterian minister, had married Ann Sophonisba Preston, a grandniece of Patrick Henry. She was the daughter of Francis Preston, who was one of John Breckinridge's cousins, which was typical of the highly consanguineous marriages of the southern aristocracy and which allowed the founding families to consolidate their power in society. (One of William's daughters complained that the "Prestons and Breckinridges have intermarried so often that trying to unravel the relationship is as difficult as solving a Chinese puzzle.")

William, who was called "Willie" by his family, kept up the family tradition of advantageous marriages. After graduating from Centre College in 1855 and receiving his law degree two years later, he married Lucretia Clay, the granddaughter of "the Great Compromiser" Henry Clay, Kentucky's most famous statesman. Unfortunately, she died a little more than a year into their marriage, days after giving birth to a son, who also died. Less than two years later, shortly after the start of the Civil War, Willie married seventeen-year-old Issa Desha, the granddaughter of the Kentucky governor Joseph Desha.

The war divided the Breckinridge family as it did the state of Kentucky, which still thought of itself as a western state, perched between North and South. Willie's father, Robert, was an outspoken opponent of slavery, one of a handful of prominent southern emancipationists who in the decades before the war promoted the never very popular nor practical idea of gradually ending slavery by having the government compensate owners for their slaves and sending them back to Africa. Robert remained staunchly loyal to the Union. President Abraham Lincoln counted on the influential minister to keep Kentucky from joining the Confederacy, saying, "I think to lose Kentucky is nearly the same as to lose the whole game. Kentucky gone, we cannot hold Missouri, nor Maryland . . . We would as well consent to separation at once."

Willie's brothers Joseph and Charles sided with their father and joined the Union army, while Willie and Robert Jr. joined the Confederates. Willie was a somewhat reluctant Confederate. From conversations with relatives already fighting and such family acquaintances as Jefferson Davis and Robert E. Lee, he feared the war would be "a bloody repulse." He also was loath to defy his beloved father. His mother had died when he was young, and he remembered Robert as "a loving, kind, indulgent father" who was "as tender as a mother." But in his political heart he agreed with his towering, fierce cousin John Cabell Breckinridge, the former vice president and senator who had been expelled from the Senate as a traitor after joining the Confederate cause. Now a general, Breckinridge had opposed Abraham Lincoln in the 1860 presidential race as the pro-slavery Southern Democratic candidate and carried most of the South, arguing that the Constitution gave the southern states the right to set their own course on slavery.

Willie stalled for more than a year after the war started until the threat of Union arrest forced him to act. "I shall never forget your kindness to me," he wrote to his father before he slipped off early one morning in July 1862 on one of his father's thoroughbreds to help raise the Ninth Kentucky Calvary.

By December, twenty-five-year-old Willie Breckinridge had been elected colonel of the regiment. He spent part of the war riding with Gen. John Hunt Morgan's feared raiders in Kentucky and Tennessee, harassing Union forces and living off the land. "Morgan on the loose was an object of terror to the countryside," remembered one woman who was a wide-eyed child when Morgan's troops neared her family's farm in Indiana, "ransacking country stores and farmhouses, taking anything he wanted . . . burning and destroying everything before him." Eventually Breckinridge's battalion ended up in Georgia, where he took part in some of the closing battles of the war outside Atlanta and became part of the small contingent of troops that escorted the fleeing Confederate president Davis southward.

At the end of the war, in early May 1865, Willie and his cousin Gen. John C. Breckinridge, who was now the Confederate secretary of war, were among the handful of men present at the last Confederate council of war at Armistead Burt's estate in South Carolina. There it fell to young Colonel Breckinridge, Gen. Basil Duke, and three other brigade commanders to convince Davis that the cause was lost. After each man spoke his piece, it was Duke who finally told Davis that the soldiers themselves thought "the war was over." After Davis staggered to his feet, General Breckinridge helped him from the room, and the Confederacy was no more. Willie took advantage of the general amnesty granted to officers of his rank and below and returned to Lexington, while his cousin fled south through the Florida Keys to Cuba and eventually took refuge in Canada.

After the war, Willie took over the influential *Lexington Observer and Reporter* as editor. Within two years, however, his and Issa's growing family brought him back to the practice of law. Their first child, a daughter named Ella, had been born just before he left for the war. His mother's namesake, Sophonisba, whom everyone called Nisba, was born the year after his return. Two sons, Desha and Robert, followed. The next two children died in infancy. Curry, born in 1875, would be Willie and Issa's last child. Even as his law practice grew, he kept his hand in public life, working for the Democratic Party, making a failed bid for district attorney, and building a reputation as an orator. After a particularly stirring speech at the state Democratic convention, the party newspaper noted he had "all the elements of a solid and substantial popularity": "purity of life and character, a lofty and chivalrous bearing, a matchless eloquence, and a cherished Kentucky name."

In 1884, Willie Breckinridge, whom most people called "Colonel Breckinridge" or simply "the Colonel" (or affectionately, but not to his face, "ol' Billy Breck"), decided to put that cherished name to use and seek the seat in Congress that Joseph Clay Stiles Blackburn—Julia Blackburn's brother-in-law—had vacated to run for the Senate. Willie was elected easily, taking his place in the constellation of Breckinridges and Blackburns and Clays that defined the Bluegrass region.

Breckinridge ascended immediately to the powerful House Ways and Means Committee, thanks to fellow Kentuckian John Carlisle, who was elected Speaker of the House. A compact man, he still had the bearing of a cavalry officer and a "thick growth of silver-gray hair, a long beard, and large, 'brilliant' blue-gray eyes" that together with his large head "gave him the appearance of a silver-maned lion." He was, declared his Civil War comrade Basil Duke, "the most gifted and attractive orator I ever heard."

Religion and morality were favored topics of Breckinridge's speeches. This wasn't surprising. As a young man, notes the historian Klotter, he "vacillated between the law and theology" and even spent one year at the Danville Theological Seminary. As his reputation as a speaker grew in the latter half of the 1880s, he addressed the Evangelical Alliance of the United States, the Eastern Presbyterian Church, and the Washington Bible Society, where he spoke about "the Bible, book by book, and its relation to the history of man." He was the featured orator at the dedication of a monument to the Pilgrims in 1889, where he expounded on the importance of "monogamic marriage" and the "sanctity of home." He was particularly concerned with the strict moral code that constrained women's sexual behavior, which, like many in Victorian America, he exalted as essential to a well-ordered society. He told an audience at the Bourbon Female College in Paris, Kentucky, in 1872 that female chastity was "the foundation, the corner-stone of human society" and that "pure homes make pure government." In 1882, at the Sayre Institute in Lexington, he lectured the young women to remain pure and warned them to avoid "useless hand-shaking, promiscuous kissing, needless touches and all exposures."

But it was the Great Tariff Debate of 1888—"two days of oratory in which the best gladiators of the House participated," as the historian Allan Nevins has described it—that made Breckinridge a star. Other than the question of gold or silver currency, tariffs were the biggest

political issue of the day. The Democrats generally opposed high tariffs on imported products as impediments to free trade and also
because they didn't want to see the federal government swollen with
revenue that it would be tempted to spend. The Republicans supported
high tariffs as a means of protecting farming and manufacturing interests from import competition and as a way of raising revenue for what
they deemed badly needed infrastructure improvements for the country
at a time when there was no income tax, just internal revenue taxes,
mainly on tobacco and whiskey.

When President Grover Cleveland called for tariff reform in 1887,
Breckinridge traveled around the country promoting the Democrats'
tariff reform plan, casting tariffs as a tax on consumers that would
dampen trade and foster a corrupting surplus. "The money in the Treasury is not the money of the Government, it is the money of the people,
wrung from them by a false and wrong policy of taxation," he told a large
audience in Philadelphia, who arose "almost en masse and applauded
for several minutes" when he finished, before demanding an encore,
which, the *New York Times* reported, Breckinridge obliged, making "another brief address."

When the Democrats' reform measure came to the floor of the House
in May 1888, "the galleries were filled" in anticipation of an oratorical
showdown, says Nevins. When Breckinridge rose to speak, "a bouton-
nière in his coat," applause shook the House chamber; it was several
minutes before he could begin. "The surplus continues to grow; the evil
effects of it are daily exhibited; schemes without number to squander
the public money; to distribute it among the States, to cultivate a habit
in the American people of looking to Washington as a great alms-
giver can be defeated only by your action on this bill," he exhorted his
colleagues.

It wasn't just his ability to simplify a complicated subject that made
Breckinridge a star. At the time, writes the historian Robert Wiebe, the
tariff and related issues like currency were assuming an "eternal quality
that set them apart as touchstones of public morality," as they encapsu-
lated fears about far-off, unseen forces that increasingly controlled the
daily lives of Americans in a rapidly commercializing nation. Breckinridge was now speaking for morality both private and public.

•

By 1893, W.C.P. Breckinridge was as well known and well liked as any politician in the country. He had been mentioned as a possible Speaker of the House and was eyeing Joe Blackburn's Senate seat; his future seemed limitless. "Colonel Breckinridge is an idol," the *New York Herald* would declare. "His imposing appearance, his dignified, almost fatherly, bearing, his courtly manners, his earnest, warm hearted friendliness, his sparkling appreciative eyes, his ready intelligence, broad cultivation and quick, harmless wit make him a universal favorite."

On the June day in 1893 that Madeline Pollard arrived at The Farm in Charlottesville, she appeared to be on the cusp of pulling off a re-markable social coup in marrying Breckinridge. Here was the daughter of a saddler who died so broke that his family couldn't afford to bury him. Her mother had to take a chattel mortgage on what furniture they had in order to feed Madeline and her six brothers and sisters. Since the age of twelve, Madeline had been shuttled from home to home of a suc-cession of aunts. One of her cousins remembered her as a "remarkably bright girl," but she spent the better part of her teens trying unsuccess-fully to find a relative to pay for her continued schooling at a time when secondary education was a luxury, especially for a girl.

Now, having broken news of the betrothal, the *Washington Post* was lauding Madeline in an article headlined "A Bright and Brainy Woman" as a "well-known writer." The *Post* gushed that "she early displayed an extraordinary intellect, and is one of the most brilliant women who has ever grown up in [Lexington]." It noted her literary bent and said she had worked as a reporter for the *Lexington Gazette* and done "literary work" in New York. Although "she was poor," said the *Post*, she was "very ambitious, and those who knew her felt that someday she would make her mark in the literary field."

The *Post* also mentioned Madeline's one brush with notoriety to date: When she was employed as a clerk in the Interior Department, and the death of the Union general William Tecumseh Sherman (who was reviled in the South for his "March to the Sea," which ravaged the land from Atlanta to Savannah) was announced, Madeline exclaimed, "At last, the devil has got his own!"

"The remark made her famous at the time," reported the *Post*; it also "was the cause of her losing her situation."

The paper said Madeline was about twenty-five and gave her name as Madeline Breckinridge Pollard, which suggested that she was a member of the Breckinridge clan—which many people in Washington assumed, as she clearly was close to Congressman Breckinridge. What the *Post* didn't yet know was the extent of that closeness.

•

Madeline Pollard had been Colonel Breckinridge's mistress for nearly a decade. The relationship had begun when she was still in school and he was running for Congress, married to his second wife, and the father of five. Willie always assured Madeline that he would marry her if he ever became free to do so, so when his wife Issa died in the summer of 1892, Madeline assumed she would become the next Mrs. W.C.P. Breckinridge once an acceptable period of mourning passed. After all, they had taken every precaution to ensure that her reputation stayed intact. She lived in a convent school the first two years she was in Washington, and told a woman she considered a friend that Breckinridge "was as careful of me and my reputation as if I had been his daughter."

Madeline knew that protocol dictated that they couldn't marry for a year or two, so she was happy to bide her time in the knowledge that their relationship finally would be legitimized. But throughout the spring of 1893, she became increasingly disquieted. Gossip linked Willie to his distant cousin Louise Scott Wing. A friend of her landlady's told her he had met the couple at a diplomatic reception, but when Madeline confronted Willie, he denied he intended to marry anyone but her. He seemed intent, however, on having her leave Washington—for Europe or New York. She'd go, she said, but only if they announced the engagement. But Breckinridge refused to do so, claiming it was out of consideration for his grown children, who would be shocked at the news of his hasty remarriage.

Still, news of the engagement leaked out. For her part, Madeline hadn't been exactly circumspect and had mentioned it to at least two or three friends. On June 18, the *Cincinnati Commercial Gazette*, just across the river from Kentucky, published the following tidbit: "There is an apparently well authenticated rumor that Hon. W.C.P. Breckinridge of Lexington, Ky., the silver-tongued orator, is to marry Mrs. Madeline Breckinridge Pollard." The mistake about her marital status aside, Madeline may have been happy to finally have the news public. That is, until days later, when the *Kentucky Leader* published a denial from Breckinridge of any such engagement.

It was then that Madeline decided to release news of their engagement to the *Washington Post.* "I am sorry to have announced our engagement before you wished it, but you have driven me to do so," she wrote to Willie as she prepared to depart Washington for Charlottesville. "I had no thought of putting it into print, but after the *Cincinnati Gazette* printed it and it was denied in an undignified way in the Lexington *Leader*, I gave the announcement to the *Post.*"

Now, here Madeline was with Julia Blackburn and her friends pretending that nothing was amiss, even as increasingly acrimonious letters and telegrams flew back and forth between the couple. Willie, in Lexington and about to embark on a speaking tour of the Southeast, begged Madeline to lie low and let him handle matters. Madeline threatened to come to Lexington to ask his daughter Nisba what they should do about the situation. Breckinridge wrote back on June 27 pleading with Madeline to "control" herself. "I cannot go to Charlottesville, nor you come to Lexington. It would result in an open scandal," he told her. "As matters now are, your character and reputation are safe."

What Madeline did not know was that a parallel drama was playing out in Kentucky. Louise Scott Wing's brother, Dr. Preston Scott, a well-respected Louisville physician, was telling people there that Breckinridge was going to marry his sister, whom, indeed, Breckinridge had been courting all spring. On July 1, Scott had summoned Breckinridge to his home to confront him about the Pollard engagement announcement. A reporter from the *Commercial Gazette* got wind of the brewing scandal and tracked Breckinridge there. Breckinridge "denied that there had ever been a possibility of him marrying Miss Pollard." He told the reporter that Louise "has not yet promised to accept me" and that "anything you might say on the subject would injure my suit," so the reporter kept the story under wraps even as gossip continued to percolate throughout Lexington and Louisville.

After Breckinridge's letter of June 27, Madeline threatened to make public the details of their relationship if he wouldn't confirm the engagement. The telegram that reached her at The Farm on July 9 was the response she had been anticipating from Breckinridge for days: "Written [Maj.] Moore. See him before you make publication."

Major William Moore was the superintendent of the Metropolitan Police Department in Washington. He had helped Breckinridge quietly settle matters a few years earlier when the colonel's troubled son Robert got caught passing bad checks to support his gambling and drinking habits. Now, Breckinridge turned to Moore to serve as an intermediary with Madeline.

Shortly after receiving the telegram, Madeline made the two-hour train ride to Washington to meet with Moore. If she had hoped he would offer some kind of assurance about the marriage, she was sorely let down. In fact, when she got to Washington, she found the following in the July 13 edition of the *Lexington Gazette*, which, like many politically important out-of-state papers, was available in the busy hotel newsstands of the city: "Col. W.C.P. Breckinridge, about whose marriage with Miss Madeline Pollard, of Washington, a great deal has been written and said, told a friend in this city a day or two ago that there was no truth in the report." It called the rumors of the engagement to Madeline "mortifying to Col. Breckinridge."

Madeline returned to Charlottesville and on July 15 wrote a blistering letter to Breckinridge, accusing him of having "said what was false" in denying the engagement and having "repudiated your solemn promise to marry me." In light of his public denials, she insisted that he send her immediately "a clear statement, over your signature, that the report of our engagement is true." She went on to say that if he failed to "admit and confirm your promise to marry me . . . I will, without further communication with you, without delay, and without fear of consequence to you or to me, seek redress." She gave him until the following Saturday to respond.

The next day, Sunday, July 16, the *Louisville Courier-Journal* reported the "engagement is announced of Hon. W.C.P. Breckinridge, of Lexington, and Mrs. Louise Scott Wing" and said the "marriage will occur during the first week of August." When Breckinridge denied that announcement as well, Dr. Scott showed up at the offices of the *Courier-Journal* on Monday and "rather testily" announced that Breckinridge would marry his sister at his home the following day and "insisted upon publication to that effect."

On Tuesday, July 18, W.C.P. Breckinridge did indeed marry Louise Scott Wing in her brother's front parlor in Louisville.

•

The news of the Breckinridge-Wing nuptials "created a sensation in the capital," according to the *New York Times*. And it wasn't just in Washington that tongues were wagging. In Kentucky, "a great deal of gossip was indulged in by society people and friends of the Scott family," reported the *Cincinnati Enquirer*, which mentioned rumors that "the marriage was only hurried up because it was feared that Miss Pollard might give trouble."

While the dueling marriage announcements certainly fueled the gossip, there was more: the ceremony had all the hallmarks of a shotgun wedding. It was obviously hastily arranged, coming on a Tuesday evening just one day after Dr. Scott's visit to the *Courier-Journal*, and it wasn't in a church, which was odd for so prominent a Presbyterian churchman as Breckinridge, who was an elder. It was also "quiet in the extreme," reported the *Courier-Journal*, with only family members and a few friends on hand to see Louise, in an "exquisite bridal robe of white chiffon," marry Breckinridge in a brief ceremony performed by a minister cousin of his, brought in for the occasion because no local clergy was available on such short notice. The whole affair was so rushed that the wedding supper was served at seven and the newlyweds caught the 8:10 southbound limited to Tennessee for their honeymoon at the Four Seasons Hotel in Cumberland Gap.

Even more tellingly, the *Courier-Journal* noted archly, Louise had "spent the past three months in Atlantic City, where she had been quite ill." She had spent last winter's social season in Washington, advised the paper, "but became of rather delicate health and was not able to go in society as much as her friends would have liked." Louise's sudden ill health, and her equally sudden disappearance from society, suggested that she was, or had been, pregnant.

Despite the rumors, it was an advantageous marriage for Breckinridge. Wing, who had just turned forty-eight, was tall, slender, and graceful, with "clear-cut" features and a "captivating and pleasing" manner, said the *Courier-Journal*. And she was the widow of Edward Rumsey Wing, who had died some twenty years earlier while serving as ambassador to Ecuador. As such, she had excellent social connections and was well known in Washington diplomatic circles.

For Madeline, the news that Breckinridge had married the well-situated Wing was humiliating, devastating. But she had warned Breckinridge she would seek redress if he did not fulfill his promise to her, and that's exactly what she intended to do.

By the end of July, Washington was again abuzz. Madeline's brother John Dudley Pollard, a Kentucky newspaper editor, had joined Madeline in Washington. To the nineteenth-century mind, that could only mean one thing—violence. The resort to violence to protect a woman's honor was unexceptional at the time, especially among southerners. Just the previous spring, a young clerk named Henry Delaney had been abducted at gunpoint from behind a drugstore counter in Sturgis, Kentucky, by the parents of Abbie Oliver, whom, according to the local paper, he had "ruined about eight months ago." When he refused to marry Abbie when she became pregnant, Mr. and Mrs. Oliver took the matter into their own hands. They drove the couple to nearby Morganfield, secured a marriage license, and presided over if not a shotgun wedding, then at least a pistol-point one. Unfortunately, the impromptu wedding party was intercepted on the way home by four of Delaney's friends, who also were armed. Abbie was shot in the ensuing melee and died the following morning, but at least her honor was restored.

With Breckinridge due back in Washington for a special session of Congress, residents of the capital braced to see how Madeline's honor would be avenged. By early August, Breckinridge was being escorted around the city by two police detectives, detailed courtesy of Major Moore because "he had reason to believe that either Miss Pollard herself or her brother designed to shoot him."

Breckinridge spent Saturday, August 12, in Philadelphia with Vice President Adlai Stevenson I launching the USS *Minneapolis*, the navy's newest cruiser. He and his new wife, Louise, returned to Washington by train, reaching the Cochran Hotel in time for dinner. As the couple was leaving the dining room, a nervous-looking aide from the marshal's office handed Breckinridge a pack of legal papers. Breckinridge glanced at them, showed them to his wife, and sauntered over to the elevator. "He betrayed no sign of nervousness and was as courtly as ever in his demeanor," noted the *Washington Evening Star*. The nonchalance likely was feigned. Breckinridge already had been tipped off by a well-placed friend that a lawsuit naming him as defendant had been filed earlier in the day in the Supreme Court of the District of Columbia. Madeline Pollard wasn't going to have her brother shoot W.C.P. Breckinridge for jilting her; she was suing him for fifty thousand dollars for breach of promise to marry.

Breach of promise was a Victorian-era legal convention that allowed women to sue for damages from a broken engagement. Breach of promise suits recognized that marriage was a woman's primary vocation, and if her chances to marry were quashed—either because they passed her by while she waited for her fiancé to make good on his promise, or the broken engagement raised questions about her morals—she suffered a real financial loss. Such suits frequently were scandalous; the intimation was that a woman had given her virginity to the man under the expectation of marriage and now had neither her virginity nor a wedding band to show for it.

But Madeline's suit was explosive. She revealed that she and Breckinridge had maintained an illicit relationship for the past nine years—through all of his five terms in Congress—and that she had borne two children by him. Furthermore, she accused Breckinridge, then "a married man of 47 years of age, and a distinguished lawyer and orator," of taking advantage of her "youth and inexperience" and by "wiles and artifices and protestations of affection" seducing her when she was a seventeen-year-old student. She said Breckinridge had "made her acquaintance by accosting her on a railway train" when she was traveling home to visit her sick sister in April 1884, saying that he knew her family. After he "completed his seduction of her . . . she became pregnant, and . . . bore a child begotten by the defendant" and then a second child later on. Madeline charged that Breckinridge repeatedly vowed to marry her if he were ever able to, and in August 1892, after his wife died, he "promised the plaintiff to marry her."

She said he repeated that promise most recently in May 1893, after she became pregnant a third time, to "repair the injury that had been done to her and to place her under the protection of his influence, name and family." Despite these repeated pledges, Breckinridge "disregarded his promise" and "wrongfully and injuriously married another person." For her part, Madeline said she had "remained unmarried at the request of the defendant" and "being deeply in love with him she was induced by his protestations of affection to remain under his domination and control," abandoning her "desire and intentions" to "make a career for herself."

The charges were shocking, given that Breckinridge was such a well-respected figure. What was even more shocking, and novel, however, was what Madeline had to sacrifice to bring the suit. She had to reveal herself as a "ruined" woman—a woman who had acquiesced to sex outside marriage. Few things could be more injurious to a woman in late nineteenth-century America. A woman's chastity was the bedrock of her social capital. Its loss, the specter of the "fallen" woman, haunted society. "Victorian Americans obsessively feared that their unmarried daughters would be sexually disgraced," says the historian Robert Ireland. Such sexual disgrace meant certain and complete ostracization: no one would hire you or let you a room in a respectable boardinghouse, to say nothing of invite you into their home or marry you. "The fallen woman," wrote Kate Bushnell of the Woman's Christian Temperance Union in 1886, summing up society's view, "is an exposed criminal . . . and she becomes a castaway."

Madeline's decision to come forth was especially surprising because she could have walked away from her relationship with Breckinridge with her reputation more or less intact and because it appeared she had little to gain financially from the suit. It was, as Charles Stoll told Jennie Tucker, "a complete riddle," as Pollard had "published to the world her life of shame in order that she might prosecute a suit for damages against a man who is known to her to have absolutely nothing out of which a judgment can be made." He told Jennie he couldn't understand why "any woman, whose reputation has not already been destroyed" would "voluntarily offer herself and all that she has, and can ever have, as a sacrifice."

It seems that in taking on Breckinridge, and sacrificing her own reputation to do so, Madeline wasn't challenging just a powerful politician, but also entrenched notions about women and sex.

3

A Bastard Catch'd

Late nineteenth-century attitudes about women and sex might have seemed eternal, but they were of course part of an evolution in how western society regarded marriage and sex—and sought to control the latter outside the former. In the early American colonial world of the 1600s, courtships occurred under the watchful eye of the whole community, which had both religious and practical reasons for ensuring that sex was channeled toward marriage—to prevent sin and the birth of illegitimate children who would be a charge on a still-fragile society. While the Puritans were strict moralists with firm prohibitions against sex outside of marriage, the reality was a bit fuzzier. There was in Plymouth Colony "a steady succession of trials and convictions for sexual offenses involving single persons," notes the historian John Demos, most commonly for "fornication" between young adults, but also for public masturbation and bestiality.

Some couples—like one in New England who in 1644 slipped out of a gathering and subsequently were "seen upon the ground together"—were caught in the act. Most instances of fornication, however, were revealed because a baby arrived too soon after the wedding. Many New England churches followed the "seven months" rule, which considered any child born within seven months of the wedding to have been conceived outside of wedlock. While Puritans generally are associated with harsh moral judgments, they actually gave couples a fair chance to repent their sin. In a ritual observed throughout churches in the early colonies, the couple would have to publicly confess to the crime of for-nication, express contrition, and accept punishment, which could be a fine, a whipping, or both. In Plymouth Colony, one Thomas Cushman was fined five pounds "for committing carnall coppulation with his now wife before marriage." Throughout New England in the 1600s, say the historians John D'Emilio and Estelle Freedman, "a fine of nine lashes awaited both parents of a child born too soon after marriage."

Once the couple admitted the transgression, they would be readmit-ted back into the church, and by extension, the community, in good standing. It was more important to have them as productive members of society than to continue to shame them. The Puritans were remark-ably evenhanded in punishing fornication. After a brief period in the earliest days of settlement when men were more likely to be punished, men and women were punished at the same rate. Furthermore, women had significant leverage over men when it came to enforcing commu-nity standards regarding premarital sex. If an unmarried woman uttered a man's name while in the throes of labor, the local authorities took her word, as related by the midwife, as authoritative and the man was "judged the 'reputed father.'" Such assignments of paternity were taken so seri-ously that they were often enough to get a reluctant groom to the altar rather than face a paternity suit that he would almost certainly lose.

Despite the occasional offenders, this community-based system of sexual control was remarkably effective. According to David Hackett Fischer, in "Massachusetts during the seventeenth century, rates of prenuptial pregnancy were among the lowest in the West."

However, with each succeeding generation the fervent religiosity and community cohesion of the early Puritans faded, and alternative sexual folkways crept in, particularly from the British Isles and Dutch- and German-speaking countries. By the mid-1700s, it wasn't uncommon in much of New England and parts of the mid-Atlantic region for courting couples to be allowed to spend nights together in bed "bundled" up in their cloths, or with the young lady in a "bundling bag" sewn up or tied at the bottom in a tradition traced to the working classes of Wales, Scot-land, Holland, and Germany. A Rev. Bingley visiting Wales in 1804 described the practice: "The lover steals, under the shadow of night, into the bed of the fair one, into which (retaining an essential part of his dress) he is admitted without shyness or reserve. Saturday or Sunday nights are the principal times when this courtship takes place, and on these nights the men sometimes walk from a distance of ten miles or more to visit their favorite damsels."

Whether it was called bundling, questing, sparking, or tarrying, some form of this night courting was known from Europe to Afghanistan—where it was called *namzat bezé*—to Borneo, according to the physician and historian Henry Reed Stiles, whose 1871 study of premarital courting traditions was banned in Boston. Often, some type of light was involved to signal a young woman's availability. In his travels through the upper Mississippi Valley region in the late 1680s, the French baron de Lahontan reported that in Native American villages, a young warrior would steal into the hut of his sweetheart with a sort of match that he lit at the communal fire. "If she blows out the light he lies down by her; but if she pulls her Covering over her Face, he retires," wrote de Lahontan. This was the opposite of the custom in Borneo, noted Stiles, where a young man would wait until the "family is supposed to be fast asleep" and slip into the room of "the girl he desires to make his wife" to make court. If the girl asked him to "'light the lamp' (a bamboo filled with resin), then his hopes are at an end." There were "districts in New England where the bundling light"—usually a candle in the window—"was a beacon to the farm lad" on Saturday night, according to the folklorist A. Monroe Aurand, Jr., who speculated that such signals were later adopted by "women of a shady reputation," giving rise to the term "red-light district."

What all these customs had in common besides tacit parental approval was the recognition that some form of premarital intimacy among young adults was not only likely, but also beneficial in creating a lasting relationship and was acceptable as long as it was directed toward marriage. In the New World, where, according to Stiles, bundling "prevailed among the young to a degree which we can scarcely credit," the courting couple would sit up by the fire until the rest of the family had gone to bed, then "having sat up as long as they think proper, get into bed together also, but without putting off their undergarments, to prevent scandal." Bundling was a way for a courting couple to have some privacy in tiny, crowded colonial homes, which didn't have much in the way of comfortable furniture, as well as to accommodate suitors who had to travel a distance to woo their intended. Why sit up all night on a hard bench by the fire, burning precious firewood and candles, reasoned the pragmatic colonists, when a young man could "pursue his wooing under the downy coverlid of a good feather bed?"

Bundling also served another important purpose, particularly as the eighteenth century progressed. Young adults in the heady years leading up to the American Revolution were more independent-minded than their parents and grandparents. Part of this was the revolutionary rhetoric that filled the air, with liberty and the pursuit of happiness replacing older values of restraint and self-sacrifice. Part of it was the simple economic fact that many of the farms of the original colonies had been so divided and subdivided among several generations of sons that there was precious little land left to pass along, diminishing the control that parents had over their children. This pre-revolutionary generation was headstrong; they stayed out late "frolicking" and "night walking" in large, raucous groups that met up to shuck corn or piece a quilt. The Reverend Jonathan Edwards of Northampton, Massachusetts, complained in 1738 that the youth of his parish would "very frequently get together in conventions of both sexes, for mirth and jollity, which they called frolics; and they would often spend the greater part of the night in them." These frolics, he noted in a sermon, often led to "frequent breakings out of gross sin; fornication in particular."

Apparently the reverend was correct, because starting around 1700, the colonies' formerly low rate of premarital pregnancy began to creep up. This increase occurred from the bays of Massachusetts to the tidewater of the Chesapeake, where, in a more diverse and disorderly society, it was already higher—some one-fifth of births in Somerset County, Maryland, in the late 1600s were the result of premarital conceptions. According to Daniel Scott Smith and Michael Hindus's landmark study of extant church records, fewer than 10 percent of women gave birth to a baby who was likely conceived before they were married in 1680. That number climbed to more than 20 percent between 1720 and 1760—at least for white women. Records weren't kept of births for the enslaved black population because, according to the historian Robert Wells, "the only social condition that mattered was that the children of slaves were also slaves."

At the same time, the local courts were turning their attention from prosecuting ecclesiastical matters to the commercial interests of the growing colonies. In the first half of the eighteenth century, nearly two-thirds of cases that came before the court in New Haven, Connecticut, involved fornication. After about 1750, however, such prosecutions practically disappeared, leaving the policing of the increasingly exuberant population of young adults to their families. Within this context, bundling was a compromise. It ensured that any premarital sexual activity that did occur happened under the watchful eye of parents instead of in some field or hayloft. While in the ideal the relationship wouldn't be consummated until after marriage, premarital pregnancies weren't particularly tragic in an agrarian economy where people married fairly young and children were an extremely desirable commodity as family laborers. For some, premarital sex functioned as a means of "fertility testing" to ensure that a woman could get pregnant, a version of the old Scottish Highland custom of "hand-fasting" in which two clan chieftains "agreed that the heir of one should live with the daughter of the other as her husband for twelve months and a day." If the woman became pregnant during that time, "the marriage became good in law, even although no priest had performed the marriage ceremony" according to *A History of the Highlands, and the Highland Clans*. If she did not, the arrangement was ended and the woman was returned to her family "at liberty to marry or hand-fast with any other," while the disappointed chieftain was free to find another trial bride for his son.

This casual attitude about premarital pregnancy was an extension of European courtship rituals, in which premarital sexual experience was unexceptional and often commenced with the betrothal or the expectation of one, the marriage ceremony itself being a formality. The demographer Peter Laslett noted that throughout most of Europe before the late nineteenth century, "a high proportion of all spouses at all times and in all places had sexual intercourse before marriage." As the Reverend Bingley said of Wales, it was common for the consequence of bundling "to make its appearance in the world within two or three months after the marriage ceremony had taken place. The subject excites no particular attention among the neighbors, provided the marriage be made good before the living witness is brought to light." Only the landed gentry, who had to worry about their heirs inheriting substantial estates, enforced expectations of premarital virginity in women, but they were a minority of the population. Even the Puritans recognized the special status of premarital sex within the expectation of marriage, says John Demos. While the standard fine for fornication in Plymouth Colony was ten pounds or a whipping for individuals who weren't betrothed, it was only fifty shillings (each) for those who were engaged.

It was fairly easy for parents in small, close-knit colonial communities to police any pregnancies that did result from bundling and make sure they resulted in marriage. Any man who wouldn't live up to his obligations could be excommunicated from the church or shunned from the community, a devastating punishment in a world where drifting single men were viewed with suspicion. If social pressure didn't work, there were legal options. In addition to paternity suits that were initiated by women, fathers could sue men for seduction to recoup their financial losses due to being deprived of their daughter's services during her pregnancy. Even a woman who didn't get married because she was jilted by her lover or too distant from him in social class to enforce the expectation of marriage often didn't have any trouble finding a husband in short order, her advertised fertility and a cash settlement from the father of her child having both erased her shame and made her a desirable bride. As the colonial historian Laurel Thatcher Ulrich notes, "There is no evidence that in rural communities women who bore children out of wedlock were either ruined or abandoned." It was a world in which the sexual appetites of both men and women were taken for granted and accommodated and in which both parties were held equally responsible for breaches of protocol.

Bundling had its detractors, especially ministers, for whom the flagrant disregard for the proscribed morality was galling. In a 1729 sermon, the famed Puritan minister Jonathan Edwards denounced "such liberties in company-keeping" that are "commonly winked at by parents" as "shameful and disgraceful." But even some in the rising colonial elite admitted that bundling had benefits. In an unpublished 1761 essay written at the time he was courting Abigail, John Adams decried the stuffy courtship practices of "Persons of Rank and figure" who concealed their daughters "from all males, till a formal courtship is opened." He thought it was a good idea for young women to get to know young men "privately," and wrote, "Tho Discretion must be used, and Caution, yet on [considering] the whole of the Arguments on each side, I cannot wholly disapprove of Bundling."

By the time of the Revolutionary War, bundling and premarital sex had become so common that about one-third of all brides were already pregnant when they got married, according to Smith and Hindus. In one Massachusetts parish, sixty-six of the two hundred covenanted members of the church who married between 1761 and 1775 confessed to having premarital sex. The experience of midwife Martha Ballard in the Maine town of Hallowell in the 1780s and 1790s was typical. Just under 40 percent of the first babies she delivered were conceived out of wedlock, some of them the children or grandchildren of town leaders. However, thirty-one of the forty women were married by the time her services were needed—some just barely. "Was called . . . to go and see the wife of John Dunn who was in Labour," she wrote in her diary on August 25, 1799. She recorded that Mrs. Dunn was "safe delivered . . . of a fine son" at 7:30 Sunday evening, having been "married last Thursday." Ballard's own son Jonathan got a woman named Sally Pierce pregnant out of wedlock: "Sally declard [sic] that my son Jonathan was the father of her child," Martha wrote of the delivery in her diary, which she knew would be used as evidence in court when Sally sued Jonathan for paternity. A month before his trial and four months after the baby was born, Jonathan married Sally.

The colonial world was undergoing its own revolution, though that made it less likely that Jonathan would marry Sally. Better roads and growing towns and cities, as well as the war itself, created a more transient population, which made it harder to enforce local expectations about marriage following a premarital pregnancy and more likely that a young woman would be abandoned. The percentage of truly illegitimate births, which had been low, started to rise in the last decades of the 1700s, reflecting this changing society. This possibility of abandonment, and a rash of babies without paternal support, gave "rise to profound and widespread anxiety" about the sexual exploitation of young women, says the historian Richard Godbeer. It was this anxiety—the result of the "disintegration of the traditional, well-integrated rural community" at the dawn of "economic and social modernization," conclude Smith and Hindus—that fostered a profound change in attitude about premarital sex. If local communities could no longer police premarital sex, then young adults would have to respond to a riskier sexual marketplace by "constraining their sex drives."

The rise in nonmarital pregnancies attracted the attention of ministers and moralists, who fretted about what it meant to the moral health of the young nation and called for an end to bundling. In 1781, the Reverend Jason Haven shocked his congregation in Dedham, Massachusetts, when he denounced bundling, "a favorite custom" about which only "mirth and merriment" had been heard, from the pulpit. "The females blushed and hung down their heads. The men, too, hung down their heads, and now and then looked out from under their fallen eyebrows, to observe how others supported the attack," remembered one parishioner, who noted that afterward the "custom was abandoned."

Other cultural forces helped prompt a change in attitude about premarital sexual experimentation. Seduction novels became wildly popular among an increasingly literate American audience, introducing the trope of the virtuous maiden who is seduced and abandoned by a libertine and dies, either literally or figuratively, of shame. Two of the best-selling books of the era, Samuel Richardson's *Pamela: or, Virtue Rewarded* (1740) and *Clarissa: or, The History of a Young Lady* (1748), focused on the importance of chastity and the dangers of seduction. In *Pamela*, a young housemaid refuses to surrender her chastity to her persistent master. He is reformed by her rectitude and marries her. While Pamela is rewarded with "virtuous domesticity," Clarissa dies in disgrace after she runs off with a charming rake named Lovelace who traps her in a brothel and despoils her. In addition to melodramatic tales of despoiled maidens, widespread reports of sexual assaults by British troops during the Revolutionary War also reinforced the idea of women as vulnerable to sexual predation. A woman's virtue increasingly became intertwined with the honor of the young nation, which was itself striving for legitimacy.

Bundling, and the casual attitude about premarital sex it represented, now came under attack as immoral and dangerous. A popular 1785 ballad called "A New Bundling Song; or, A Reproof to Those Young Country Women" ridiculed "sparks courting in a bed of love" as a "vulgar custom" admired by "many a slut and clown":

> A bundling couple went to bed,
> With all their clothes from foot to head,
> That the defense might seem complete,
> Each one was wrapped in a sheet.
> But O! this bundlin's such a witch
> The man of her did catch the itch
> And so provoked was the wretch,
> That she of him a bastard catch'd.

Now, premarital sex was portrayed as the road to illegitimacy and ruin instead of the gateway to marriage. The "Bundling Song" was so influential, says Stiles, that even decades later its publication was remembered as a watershed. After that, "no girl had the courage to stand against it, and continue to admit lovers to her bed," he said. Other widely circulated poems and moral tracts like "The Forsaken Fair One" warned young women that if they dabbled in premarital sex, they not only risked impregnation and abandonment, but also would be irrevocably stained and cast out by society. In a 1791 essay in *Massachusetts Magazine*, an anonymous author referred to a "ruined female" who had "fallen from the heights of purity to the lowest grade of humanity." Now, a woman who had sex before marriage was "ruined" and, unlike her colonial sisters, "fallen" and unredeemable in the eyes of society. In this way, the responsibility for managing premarital sex was transferred from the community—and men and women more or less equally—to women, and shame was the means of enforcing their compliance with this new, more restrictive regime. "By the late 1700s," notes Godbeer, "moralists regularly portrayed women as the guardians of sexual virtue."

In the first decades of the 1800s, premarital sexual restraint became more important than ever as young men delayed marriage to get enough education and experience to compete for jobs in an urbanizing and industrializing country. Now, a premarital pregnancy could derail their path to the expanding middle class. With a revolution in transportation and many young men on the move, young women found themselves at even greater risk of abandonment. A seemingly earnest suitor might take liberties and then disappear on a steamboat to New Orleans, a packet boat up the Erie Canal, or, eventually, a train to Cincinnati before anyone was the wiser. By the time Washington Irving published his satirical *Knickerbocker's History of New York* in 1809, he was already mocking bundling as a "superstitious rite," a relic of New England's "primitive" past, albeit one that populated the coast with "a long-sided, raw-boned, hardy race of whoreson whalers, wood-cutters, fishermen, and peddlers; and strapping corn-fed wenches."

By 1828, the *Yankee* could report that, unlike in earlier eras, "to have had a child before marriage would now be fatal to a woman . . . No man would have the courage to marry her; no woman of character would associate with her." The lusty colonial sexual ethic had been eclipsed by a bourgeoisie standard of sexual morality that elevated female purity and shunned those who violated it. A woman who had fallen from virtue, the *Middlesex Washingtonian* could say with confidence in 1844, is "an object of disgust and loathing—a very worm, that creeps along the byeways of life, shunned and abhorred by all the virtuous and the good."

At the same time, the production of household goods like candles, soap, and cloth moved from the home to the factory, and middle-class women became more and more symbolically domestic, the "angels of the home" whose proper, virtuous role was in the domestic sphere, while men competed in the public world. The new strictures on women were effective in terms of managing premarital pregnancy. By 1840, about 20 percent of brides were pregnant when they got married; over the next forty years, that would fall to only about 10 percent.

Attitudes about gender and sexual desire were readjusted to fit this new reality. Women were now viewed as having innately less sexual desire than men, which better positioned them to control sex. The most popular sexual advice book of the mid-1800s, William Acton's *Functions and Disorders of the Reproductive Organs*, assured readers that "the majority of women (happily for them) are not very much troubled with sexual feelings of any kind." The vigorous participation of women in the religious revivals that swept the nation during the Second Great Awakening in the decades prior to the Civil War reinforced the idea that women were more morally virtuous than men. At the same time, men came to be seen as naturally more sexually aggressive and licentious than women and in need of an outlet for their sexual desire, which women who were "ruined" both conveniently provided and justified. The Victorian double standard was born.

Having raised the value of a woman's chastity to that of a "priceless jewel," as the *Middlesex Washingtonian* called it, society now had to grapple with the question of how to compensate otherwise respectable women for its loss, without appearing to condone promiscuity. Throughout history, various cultures took differing approaches to this conundrum. In the Bible, a man who takes the virginity of a woman "who is not engaged" must pay her father fifty shekels of silver and marry her. Under Welsh medieval law, a woman of age who "goes with a man clandestinely, and taken by him to bush, or brake, or house, and after connection deserted" was owed a "bull of three winters" if her family filed a complaint. The catch, however, was that the bull was to have "its tail well shaven and greased and then thrust through the door-clate" and the woman was to stand on the other side of the threshold and "take his tail in his hand." If she could hold on to the bull, she could have it as compensation for her *wynet-werth* (face-shame), but if she couldn't, all she would get was "what grease may adhere to her hands."

Under western common law, seduction lawsuits could be filed to compensate fathers—and originally, masters—for the loss of a woman's labor if she was impregnated illicitly, thus having been "seduced" away from her work. Women themselves weren't allowed to bring suit, as seduction was viewed as a property matter and women had no property rights. The Victorian feminist Caroline Dall bitterly complained that "in the eyes of this law, female chastity is only valuable for the work it can do."

As the American marriage market became more autonomous and women more vulnerable under the double standard, the courts stepped in to enforce promises of marriage under breach of promise suits. Here, women could file themselves, since the suits were based on the common law understanding of a betrothal as a contract. In the colonial era, breach of promise suits were equally likely to be brought by a man or a woman if one party torpedoed a carefully negotiated marriage agreement, which usually included a dowry from the wife's family and a portion of land or other inheritance from the groom's. In 1661, for instance, John Sutton sued Mary Russell for two hundred pounds for "engaging herself to another by promise of marriage wheras shee had engaged herselfe by promise of marriage unto the said John before." He lost when Mary testified that she had "heard such thinges concerning said Sutton as might justly discourage her" from marrying him. Courts would continue to hold that discovering that a potential partner was unchaste after an engagement had been made was grounds to break the contract.

An 1818 case, *Wightman v. Coates*, established breach of promise suits as a special recourse for women who had been jilted. Maria Wightman sued Joshua Coates after he failed to make good on what she said was a longstanding engagement and married another woman. In a decision finding for Wightman, Massachusetts chief justice Isaac Parker wrote that women had more reason to resort to breach of promise suits and that juries had more reason to apportion them generous damages because their life prospects were "materially affected by the treachery of the man to whom she had plighted her vows." Parker also said that breach of promise suits were necessary to protect the interests of society in men making good on marriage promises, particularly in a culture with a rigid double standard, writing that "the delicacy of the sex, which happily in this country gives man so much advantage over woman, in the intercourse which leads to matrimonial engagements, requires for its protection and continuance the aid of the laws."

Breach of promise suits became largely a female recourse as the nineteenth century progressed. Like the bull with the greased tail, however, there was a catch: they applied only to virtuous women, including in some instances those who had sex with their fiancés under the understanding they were to be married. A woman who was otherwise already ruined couldn't expect consideration from the court because she had no chastity to defend. As Justice John Dillon wrote in *Denslow v. Van Horn*, an 1864 case in which the court ruled that evidence of a woman's past sexual indiscretions should be given to the jury, a "woman who falls from virtue, no matter how artful the deception, or how distressing the circumstance, is, by the severe edict of society, dishonored." The Pennsylvania Supreme Court put it more harshly in dismissing the

1875 breach of promise suit of a prostitute: "It is enough to say that the law will not enforce a contract of marriage in favor of a party who is not fit to be married at all."

Madeline Pollard was asking the courts to discard this thinking and to award her damages for a broken marriage promise even though she was by definition a "ruined" woman—she had entered into a sexual relationship with Breckinridge that was explicitly outside of marriage. She asserted, however, that she was "without sexual fault" otherwise, and "being a woman of good repute in all respects, notwithstanding her relations to the defendant," Breckinridge should be held to his promise. In a revolutionary request, she was asking the court to ignore the double standard that considered "ruined" women beneath society's consideration.

4

The Left-Hand Road

Madeline Pollard's breach of promise suit made headlines across the country that August 1893. "A Sensational Suit," said Washington's *Evening Star*. "A Congressman in Trouble," reported the *New York Times*. "Was Wicked of Him: Breckinridge of Kentucky Sued for Breach of Promise," said San Francisco's *Morning Call*. "The Breckinridge-Pollard case was discussed wherever the publication of the filing of the suit had been read," said the *Chicago Daily Tribune*. "Nothing in recent years has created such a social agitation . . . as the sequel to the brilliant Congressman's recent marriage," said the *Cincinnati Enquirer*.

The Breckinridge-Pollard scandal was a welcome diversion from what had been relentlessly downbeat news since February, when a run on gold and the bankruptcy of the Philadelphia & Reading Railroad kicked off a cascading financial panic that blossomed into the worst depression the country had ever seen, with frenzied days of bank runs and stock market plunges. Banks called in loans and businesses failed: two dozen a day in May alone. Within the year, six hundred banks and fifteen thousand businesses would be gone. The great railroads, the very heart and lungs of the industrial revolution, went bust one after another like faltering bulbs on the string of newfangled electric Christmas-tree lights that would soon debut at the White House: the Philadelphia & Reading, the Northern Pacific, the Union Pacific, the legendary Erie Railroad, and the Atchison, Topeka & Santa Fe.

Unemployment stood at close to 15 percent; there were one hundred thousand people out of work in New York City and seventy-five thousand unemployed in Chicago. In Detroit, they planted potatoes in vacant lots. The destitute stood in line at soup kitchens in the cities and roamed the countryside begging to exchange their labor at some menial task for a meal. The head of one Midwestern relief committee warned that "famine is in our midst."

"Men died like flies under the strain," remembered Henry Adams, who himself was "suspended, for several months, over the edge of bankruptcy" in the summer of 1893. August, the very moment Madeline filed her suit, "was the worst month," says the historian Hal Williams. "Mills, factories, furnaces, and mines shut down everywhere. Hundreds of thousands of workers were suddenly unemployed." Even Thomas Edison, "the symbol of the country's ingenuity," had to lay off 240 of the 355 employees at his Menlo Park laboratory in New Jersey. Just a month earlier, Frederick Turner had advanced his bold thesis that the closing of the American frontier had taken with it something fundamental to the American character—the drive and grit and sense of boundless possibilities that made the country. Indeed, the unspoken fear was that America's best days might be behind it, that something essential had been lost, that the current financial uncertainty might stretch into the distant future. The Panic of 1893, says Williams, was the seminal event of the decade; everything that happened afterward would in some way be a response, as it "reshaped ideas, altered attitudes, uprooted deep-set patterns."

Now, according to the *Evening Star*, the Breckinridge-Pollard scandal had displaced "the financial situation which had engrossed the public," as the "prominence of the person charged with the offense makes the case interesting from one end of the country to another." With reporters clamoring for a statement the evening the suit was filed, Breckinridge wasted no time in trying to paint Madeline as a scorned woman out for revenge. He told the press, "These charges are the result of vindictiveness, vexation and perhaps of intention to blackmail" and asked his supporters to "suspend judgment" until he had a chance to make his case.

His allies joined in to paint him as the victim of a scheming fallen woman. His esteemed Confederate comrade Gen. Basil Duke, who, like Breckinridge, was one of "Morgan's men," professed to be shocked at the charges. "Miss Pollard is not the woman that he would engage himself to. She is not his style in any sense," he told a reporter as the city's political class—the lawyers and judges and tax collectors and journalists—gathered in the lobby of the Galt House in Louisville and "discussed the matter with as much interest as if they had just received a telegram announcing the noted Congressman's death." Duke said, "I am satisfied that the whole matter is a trumped-up charge. I believe it to be only a case of blackmail. Miss Pollard's life will show that she is an adventuress."

Despite the fact that he said he hadn't been in touch with Breckinridge except "indirectly," Duke previewed what was to be Breckinridge's strategy in refuting the explosive charge that he had seduced Madeline when she was a teenager. "In regard to the seduction part of the story, Miss Pollard is thoroughly able to take care of herself. She is nearly thirty years of age, I believe, and she is used to the world and its ways." Duke was claiming that Madeline was nearly thirty, which would put her age closer to twenty-one when she met Breckinridge nine years earlier, rather than the twenty-six she claimed to be.

Another "prominent gentleman" painted a picture of Madeline as a scheming social climber from "humble circumstances" to a reporter from the *Cincinnati Enquirer*. He claimed that after her dismissal from the Interior Department for her remark about Sherman, she "resorted to her wits for a living," which was a shaded reference to trading sexual favors for sustenance. He said that she "constantly claimed to have in the press, ready for publication, various books" and came to the attention of the well-known *Harper's Magazine* editor Charles Dudley Warner, who wrote *The Gilded Age: A Tale of Today* (1873), the book that gave the era its name, with Mark Twain. "Mr. Warner commended her to the social recognition of his friends in New York. She played her cards with considerable skill," he said, charging that Madeline had "three styles of visiting cards" printed—"Madeline Vinton Pollard," "Madeline Breckinridge Pollard," and "Madeline Blackburn Pollard"—and that she would use different cards "depend[ing] upon the popularity of the assumed names in the company she happened to be in." He concluded that "with her antecedents and considering her past schemes and methods . . . I do not see how her claims can be recognized in the court . . . Colonel Breckinridge's character and standing should not be destroyed by the scheme of a woman who has long been recognized as daring and unscrupulous."

It also didn't take long for reporters to learn about the most embarrassing aspect of Madeline's past. When she was a teenager hungry for an education, she consented to marry a friend of her uncle's who agreed to pay for her schooling. James Rhodes was nearly fifty, but he had a steady job and he was her means of getting to the Wesleyan Female College. It was a desperate deal, but Madeline was a desperate girl at the time.

•

Madeline was born Madeline Valeria Pollard, the third of seven children of John Dudley Pollard, who went by J.D., and his wife, Nancy. J.D. was a saddler by trade, but as Madeline recalled, he was "well educated, a constant student and a most omnivorous reader." In addition to stocking saddles, bridles, and harnesses in his shop on Clair Street in the state capital of Frankfort, he also sold the popular New York weeklies like *Frank Leslie's Illustrated Newspaper*, monthlies like *Harper's Magazine*, and all the Cincinnati and Louisville daily newspapers. This would have made his shop across the street from the Franklin County Courthouse a hub for local politicians, reporters, and merchants. J.D. also held some minor political offices. He was doorkeeper of the state senate in 1863 and in 1865 was appointed as a local police judge, a sort of justice of the peace who handled low-level civil disputes and misdemeanor crimes, by Governor Thomas Bramlette.

Mattie, as she was called, remembered their house being "full of books, papers, and periodicals," reflecting her father's love of learning and reading. She was a bright child, and he delighted in teaching her, especially about history. "I could tell you about the great men and women, who they were, why they were great, in whose reign or administration they had lived," she recalled. She also learned Latin and memorized poems and "whole scenes from Shakespeare."

By fall 1865, Pollard had resigned his position as a police judge with no other explanation than he was "about to Engage in a business that will necessarily call me from home," sold the contents of his shop, and moved his family to nearby Bridgeport, where his wife had family. From there, the family moved to Crab Orchard, a small town about fifty miles south of Lexington, in the summer of 1866. Around that same time, he began styling himself as J.D. Pollard, Esq., and Madeline remembered that in Crab Orchard he "always held some public office . . . and practised law." It's not clear how Pollard obtained a legal education. At the time, there were no formal credentials required for lawyers. Degree-granting law schools wouldn't become standard for two decades, and bar associations were just getting off the ground; the Kentucky Bar Association wasn't formed until 1871. Traditionally, most lawyers learned the profession by "reading the law" with an established lawyer, which Pollard doesn't appear to have done, but that didn't mean someone couldn't study law on their own—Abraham Lincoln had done just that. Ten years earlier, Lincoln told a young man, "If you are absolutely determined to make a lawyer of yourself the thing is more than half done already . . . I did not read with any one. Get the books and read and study them in their every feature, and that is the main thing."

The Pollard family was never well-off, but Madeline remembered a happy home, with her mother's "refined influence" and her father spending his leisure hours with the family and "being interested in every detail of our lives." Mattie was clearly his favorite, and she adored him. "I was constantly with him and my love for him is known by everyone who even slightly knew me," she remembered. Pollard was an active member of two fraternal associations: the Independent Order of Odd Fellows and the Masons. These fraternal organizations, which stressed personal development and mutual reciprocity, were important to ambitious nineteenth-century men, creating a brotherhood that transcended religious and class barriers and offered the promise of success and stability in the rapidly industrializing nation. Pollard joined the IOOF in 1845 in his home state of Pennsylvania and became a member of the Kentucky lodge in 1850, when he moved to Kentucky. He was an earnest and active member and moved up through the ranks of the organization, becoming a grand patriarch, the highest of the order's three degrees, in 1861 and a representative to the Grand Lodge of the United States in 1862. In 1865, he was elected grand master of Kentucky and distinguished himself by visiting every lodge in the state—on foot.

J.D. also was active in local politics, first as a member of the

Kentucky American Party, which was a short-lived, anti-immigrant Know-Nothing Party, and then as a member of the newly formed Republican Party. In 1876, he was a delegate to the Republican National Convention in Cincinnati that nominated Rutherford B. Hayes. It was during the June convention, according to a friend, that J.D. "took cold." He returned home to Crab Orchard and died five days later at the age of fifty-two, a stark reminder, according to one of his fellow Odd Fellows, "that the King of Terrors lays his cold and icy hand not only on those whose hairs are whitened by lapse of years, but as well on the middle aged."

His death devastated his family emotionally and financially. Pollard may have been well regarded, but he owned no property and left no estate. One local woman remembered that in the wake of J.D.'s death, the family was "almost on the verge of starvation." The Odd Fellows paid for J.D.'s burial, erected a handsome monolith on his grave commemorating his service as grand master, and took up a collection for the family. With no means of support and only Edward, the oldest child, able to fend for himself, Nancy Pollard had to disperse the family. She took the oldest girl, Mary, who was known as Mamie, and baby Earnest, who had just turned one, to live with her sister Mary Stout in Bridgeport. The three children born in succession after Madeline—Rosalie, John, and Horatio—were sent to the Masonic Widows and Orphans Home in Louisville. Right after the funeral, still reeling from the shock of her father's death, Madeline found herself on a train to Pittsburgh with her father's sister, her aunt Valeria, for whom Madeline had been named, bound for a new life in the North with a family she didn't know. At the time, she thought she was about twelve years old, which would mean she was born around 1864. Later, when she asked her mother, Madeline was told that she was born on November 30, 1866, and that's the date she used as her birthday going forward.

Madeline lived with her aunt and her uncle, William Cowan, who was a bookkeeper, and their six children in the Hazelwood section of Pittsburgh, a leafy but fast-industrializing hamlet along a deep bend of the Monongahela River about five miles south of where it meets the Allegheny and forms the city's famous "Point." She attended public school with her cousins, who remembered her as well behaved and very bright.

She never adjusted to being away from the people and places she knew, however, and in August 1880 she left Pittsburgh to rejoin her mother in Kentucky. Madeline realized belatedly that she didn't understand the "advantages of a Northern education" and returning home put her at a significant disadvantage when it came to her schooling. While universal grammar school was well established at the time, public high schools weren't outside the cities and larger towns of the Northeast and Midwest. Pittsburgh had one, but few places in the South did. Most southern girls who received any kind of secondary education did so at private women's "seminaries," which combined an academic curriculum that could range from delusory to surprisingly advanced, including math, the sciences, Latin, and rhetoric, with the skills expected to make a young woman an agreeable and accomplished wife: the ability to speak a foreign language (especially French), music and art lessons, and fancy embroidery. Women's seminaries were expensive; most cost several hundred dollars per semester. Madeline, who at this point was harboring ambitions to be a writer, hoped that her aunt Mary, who was fairly well off and had paid for her sister to go to school, would also send her to school.

Unfortunately, that wouldn't come to pass. As Madeline tells it, one day in October, as the family was sitting on the front porch, a phrenologist came along and asked for some water. Phrenology, the discernment of personality traits through the measurement and shape of the skull, was all the rage at the time. The phrenologist was handsome and, thought Madeline, "charmed with my young, widowed auntie." Under the impression that Madeline was her daughter, he examined her head and "poured forth such a volume of talents and accomplishment" that Madeline trembled. Unfortunately, when her aunt's daughter Laura made an appearance, he pronounced her talents only ordinary. "The die was cast and my doom was sealed," remembered Madeline. Whether this specific incident was the turning point, as Madeline thought, or just emblematic of family tensions exacerbated by the arrival of another dependent niece—or just too many Pollard women living under the same roof—Aunt Mary refused to send Madeline to school, and Madeline left Bridgeport after a few months.

Madeline next went to live with her mother's oldest sister, Aunt Lou, and her husband, John, about five miles outside Lexington. She soon found that Aunt Lou "jealously guards every penny" and was even less likely to pay for her education, so she ended up doing what so many dependent nineteenth-century women did: working for her aunt as a housekeeper and governess. Three years went by in a slog of housekeeping and lessons for her cousins. In her spare time, she took horseback rides and read. She started calling herself Madeline Vivian Pollard, having seen the name "Vivian" in a book and deciding that she liked it better than Valeria. Madeline was learning that names, as well as identities, could be malleable.

One afternoon in the summer of 1883 she was out riding her favorite horse, a pretty gray mare, when the bridle broke. An "old, gray-faced rough-looking customer" who happened along fixed it for her. It was James Rhodes, who knew her uncle from the war and tended the gardens at the Eastern Kentucky Lunatic Asylum near Lexington. He saw Madeline home, stayed a few days to visit his old comrade, and quickly became besotted with the young woman. After a while, Rhodes asked Madeline to marry him. At first she turned him down, saying she didn't intend to get married until she had finished her education, but then he said he would send her to school if she would marry him. To Madeline it must have seemed the only way to escape her fate as the poor relation. Rhodes expected them to get married; he envisioned her teaching school and supporting him in his old age. Madeline saw it as more of a loan, intending to pay him back once she got a job. Regardless, a deal was struck and a letter to the effect was drawn up.

Madeline entered the Notre Dame Convent, a secondary school for girls in Reading, Ohio, on September 1, 1883. Her stay proved short-lived. The nuns read her letters and discovered her unconventional arrangement with Rhodes. Fearing she would be kicked out, Madeline telegrammed Rhodes to meet her and snuck out early one morning while the sisters were at mass. Given her hasty exit, rumors abounded. Her departure proved fortuitous, however, because she then convinced Rhodes to send her to a better school—Wesleyan Female College in Cincinnati.

Wesleyan had been a pioneering institution in the advanced education of women at a time when "the liberal education of women was largely an experiment." When it opened in 1843, it was only the second women's college in the country. These early women's colleges were designed to improve on women's seminaries by providing an academic liberal arts education for women and granting degrees, although many, like Wesleyan, had only a three-year program and fairly lax admissions standards. Wesleyan had been popular with the daughters of wealthy planters before the war, when it had an enrollment of some five hundred students. It was famous for having graduated Lucy Ware Webb Hayes, the popular wife of President Rutherford B. Hayes and the first First Lady to go to college. By 1884, it was past its heyday. Now-impoverished southerners could no longer afford to send their daughters, and competition from the first real women's colleges, like the academically rigorous Vassar and Smith Colleges, founded in 1861, and Wellesley College, founded in 1870, eclipsed the early women's colleges. Still, it was a coup for Madeline to finagle herself into Wesleyan.

Madeline was supposed to enter Wesleyan at the start of the new term in January 1884, but she was impatient to get started and headed to Cincinnati on her own at the end of November. She looked up Rankin Rossell, a friend of her cousin Nellie's who was a clerk at Shillito's, a popular downtown dry goods store, and had him escort her to Wesleyan, with the promise that Rhodes would be along the next day to pay her tuition. On November 20, 1883, Madeline officially entered Wesleyan as a sophomore studying literature, Latin, French, rhetoric, arithmetic, and elocution.

At first Madeline struggled academically—her lack of formal education showed—but she worked hard to catch up. "I never saw a person who studied with such avidity as she did," remembered the Reverend Brown, who was then the president of the college. Apparently it didn't take her long to come up to speed, because in the winter of 1884 she won a dramatic victory in a debating contest "before a large and brilliant audience." What many in the audience remembered best about the evening was Madeline's theatrics: whenever her opponent scored a good point, Madeline would "pluck a flower from a bouquet and gracefully toss it to her, to the applause of the audience." Socially, however, Madeline struggled in an environment of privileged, more cosmopolitan young women. She was remembered as a "poor, ambitious, delicate girl" who was unfashionably dressed and had a "nervous temperament" and a flair for the dramatic. One of her classmates remembered that Madeline had a habit of "always looking downward," yet she had the feeling that she was "ever watchful."

A picture taken at that time shows a serious, slender young woman with long, dark hair in a plain dress that ends just at her ankles—the length that denoted a young woman not yet of age. Her best friend, Wessie Brown, the daughter of the president of the school, found her socially awkward, especially around men. "She had never lived in a city," she recalled, and said that Madeline had "considerably less experience of the ways of the world than the average young woman who came to college." It appears, though, that she was eager to master her new circumstances. Another classmate recalled that Madeline "always seemed anxious to raise her social position." She said Madeline "seemed to push herself forward. She insinuated herself in the good graces of people in good society, and by her charming manners made them her warmest friends."

Despite her relief at finally getting an education, Madeline was haunted by her deal with Rhodes. In January, she wrote a long letter to Wessie telling her about the agreement and her fear that she would have to marry Rhodes. "When I think of the debt of gratitude as well as the debt I owe him I almost die of pain. How can I marry the old wretch when I hate him so?" she wrote. "I must crawl out from under these miserable clutches." Rhodes, whom Madeline said was her guardian, sometimes visited her at the college on the evenings when the girls were allowed to receive guests in the school's front parlors. Rossell, the young store clerk who had escorted her to Wesleyan, also visited. By the holidays, he had become smitten and was talking marriage. Once, Madeline found herself juggling her young and old suitors on the same night in a game of musical front parlors.

As winter turned to spring, Madeline received a telegram telling her to rush to her mother's home in Frankfort. Her younger sister, Rosalie, was seriously ill with consumption. On the morning of April 1, 1884, Madeline boarded a southbound train to Lexington to make a connection to a westbound train to Frankfort. Just after she had changed trains and gotten settled in her seat, a man got up and approached her. "Your face is very familiar. Do I know you?" he asked. She stood and told him that she thought he did not, but that she knew him. "I know you are Col. Breckinridge," she said. She had met "the star of Kentucky"—W.C.P. Breckinridge, the noted lawyer and newspaper editor who was running for Congress. At forty-nine, he was still a striking man, with clear blue eyes and a thick head of hair only beginning to silver. He asked about her family and said he knew the Horines, her mother's family. It was an amazing moment for Madeline; her father had particularly admired W.C.P. among the great men of the Bluegrass. Breckinridge asked if he could call on her in Frankfort. Still standing and still in awe of a man who had, to her, literally just walked off a pedestal, Madeline said her mother and aunt would be pleased to have him call.

It would be the only bright moment Madeline had for months. She continued on to Frankfort, where she found her sister dying of tuberculosis. She remained in Frankfort until Rosalie died in early June. After the funeral, she made her way back to Wesleyan. The spring term was just ending, but she planned to stay through the summer and make up the work she had missed. She couldn't wait to tell Wessie about meeting Breckinridge. Wessie recalled Madeline being elated about meeting him and that a "man of his standing should come to her and address her." She said, "We heard a great deal of this incident." So much, in fact, that she and her classmates teased Madeline about it, calling her "Madeline Vivian Breckinridge Pollard." When she was away from school, Wessie even addressed a letter to Madeline by that name, which caused a great deal of consternation with the local post office, which refused to deliver the letter on the grounds that there was no such person at the school.

Madeline was receiving other, more unwelcome letters at the same time. Rhodes was pressuring her to make good on her debt to him. It seems that his funds were starting to run low and some of his friends were advising him that Madeline was taking him for a ride. He demanded that she either marry him or pay him back and threatened to "compel" her to marry him. Madeline was in a panic at the thought that she could be forced to make good on their contract in the flesh. She needed legal advice, and she could think of only one person to turn to: Breckinridge. Despite their brief meeting, she remembered his warm words about knowing her family, so in July she wrote him a letter outlining her plight and asking if she could be forced to marry Rhodes.

On Friday, August 1, around four in the afternoon, a servant brought a calling card up to Madeline. Her face flushed when she read it. W.C.P. Breckinridge was in the drawing room. She said she hadn't expected him to reply to her letter in person. Breckinridge said he was in Cincinnati on business and, having nothing else to do in the late afternoon, took a streetcar from the Burnet House to Wesleyan to answer her in person. When Madeline came down to the drawing room, she was dressed in black, still in formal mourning for her sister. After they exchanged greetings, Madeline settled on a divan; Breckinridge sat on a chair across from her.

What happened next would be a matter of dispute, even years later. They would both agree that Madeline explained the particulars of her situation with Rhodes and asked if she could be legally forced to marry him. Breckinridge would claim he laughed at the idea of a girl being compelled to marry anyone in that day and age. But then, he claimed, Madeline started sobbing and told him she had already given Rhodes "higher proof" of her intention to marry him—meaning she had slept with him. Hearing this, Breckinridge claimed that he told her she had no choice but to marry him, but she said she could not. "I do not want to be like Aunt Lou, with a houseful of children and a half-educated woman," she said. "I want to be educated to make money as a writer."

Pollard would deny ever having said that she and Rhodes were sexually intimate. After they talked for a while, Madeline claimed that Breckinridge suggested that they "get up some kind of relationship"—pretend they were related—so they could go out that evening and continue the discussion. She said he was holding a handbill for a local concert and suggested they go to that. Breckinridge, on the other hand, claimed it was Madeline who wanted to go to the concert, saying there was a famous clarinetist performing on Vine Street. Both would agree that Madeline asked for permission from Orvid Brown, the son of the president of the college, who was in charge while his father was gone. He said that Breckinridge led him to understand "he was a relative of Miss Pollard's," so he assented to the outing. Breckinridge said he would be back later, returned to his hotel, and had supper.

It was dusk when Breckinridge returned. There were a handful of people, mostly professors and their wives who lived at the school, sitting on the front porch, hoping to catch either a breeze or a glimpse of the famous Kentuckian. But the intense, liquid heat of the day had only congealed into a dense, breezeless warmth, which made it all the more surprising when Breckinridge pulled up in a carriage with a closed cab—an open carriage would have been much more comfortable on a stifling night. The wife of one professor even "protested about a student going off that way with a married man." Madeline said she was surprised to see the carriage, as there had been no mention of driving. "Are we going in a closed carriage on so warm an evening?" she said she asked. She said Breckinridge said he had throat trouble and the night air was bad for him. Breckinridge said he decided to drive because he wasn't exactly sure where on Vine Street the concert was and merely engaged the first carriage in line at the hack stand near his hotel.

They started in the direction of the concert hall. After they had driven for about fifteen minutes, Madeline said Breckinridge claimed to have a headache and asked if she minded if they drove into the cool of the foothills rather than going to the concert. Breckinridge remembered complaining of a headache, but said when they came to a fork in the road that it was Madeline who suggested they skip the hot, gaslit concert hall and instructed the driver to take the left-hand road leading into the countryside. As they drove, Breckinridge said Madeline told him about her ambition to be a writer. She said she preferred living the life of George Eliot to "being an ignorant Kentucky country woman, raising a house full of children and churning butter." They drove for close to an hour. Madeline remembered that Breckinridge said she should take off her hat because it was so hot; he remembered her leaning forward and placing it on the front seat. She said he took her hand and, when she objected, told her he was old enough to be her father and that "such an act on his part was entirely proper." He said he put his arm around her and, finding no resistance, started to kiss her. Madeline said he then attempted to take "further liberties" with her, which she didn't "fully understand but vigorously resisted." She said she "wrenched" herself away from him, and after that he "tried to take her mind off his bad actions" by talking of "when he was a little boy and how much he loved his first wife."

As they drove back to Wesleyan, Madeline said Breckinridge

explained that she was too young to understand that his "conduct had not been improper" and told her she was "foolish and prudish." He said it was near ten o'clock when they returned; Madeline thought it was closer to midnight. He claimed to have pressed some money into her hand—ten dollars—as he dropped her off. She said there was no money involved, but that she returned home "nervous and excited."

•

Now, ten years later, going public about her relationship with Breckinridge would open Madeline's whole life and her unconventional past up for examination. The arrangement with Rhodes in particular didn't portray her in the most favorable light. Rhodes, it turned out, wasn't the "uncouth farmer" that Madeline had made him out to be, but a member of "one of the best families of the Bluegrass," and the family was still angry at the "cruel manner" in which Madeline had used Rhodes, who died heartbroken—and broke—over the relationship. The husband of her old friend Wessie Brown leaked to the press Madeline's long-ago letter to Wessie about Rhodes, serving up a humiliating look not only at Madeline's desperate arrangement but also her peripatetic upbringing and her teenage romantic angst. Soon, the papers were reporting that she had "a penchant for rich and gay old men and had several in her string."

History didn't suggest that Madeline's suit would turn out well. Sixteen years earlier, in 1877, a woman named Mary S. Oliver, a "lady clerk in the Treasury Department," sued the former senator Simon Cameron for fifty thousand dollars for breach of promise. She acknowledged that the two had begun a relationship in Washington while Cameron's wife was still alive, but she claimed that after Mrs. Cameron's death, the now-widowed senator promised to make her his wife after the two had an "improper meeting" at the St. Charles Hotel in New Orleans in 1875. Over the course of four years, however, he failed to make good on his promise. Oliver did have a colorful personal history—and by her own admission wasn't a virgin when she met Mr. Oliver, who may still have been married—so it was easy for Cameron's lawyers to paint her as a scheming woman out to make a buck. Nonetheless, her attorney argued that as she had letters from Cameron attesting to his marriage pledge, it was for the jury to "say whether or not he had made the promise." Cameron's attorney said the letters were forgeries and vilified Oliver for having the temerity to "disgustingly and without shame" testify about the details of the affair. He said that when a woman "departs from her sphere, then she descends to the depths of the devils."

Neither the press nor those in the courtroom seemed to take Oliver's case seriously. "Mrs. Oliver was easily shown to be one of the characterless adventuresses who infest the capital and seek a living through dubious relations with public men," said the *New York Times*. After a two-week trial, the judge gave the jury such a ridiculously perfunctory charge it became legend in Washington legal circles. "Gentlemen of the jury, take this case and dispose of it," he said as the courtroom burst into laughter. When the jury asked if they could review a transcript of the proceedings, the judge refused to give it to them. There was little surprise when, after a few hours' deliberation, the jury found for Cameron. No one even bothered to fetch Oliver for the verdict; she came back to find the court adjourned and spectators streaming out of the courtroom.

5

The Wanton Widow

History suggested consequences more dangerous than being laughed out of a courtroom for women who challenged powerful men on issues of public morality; sometimes they found that more than just the loss of their reputation was at stake. Such was the case of Maria Halpin.

In 1868, Halpin was a young widow living in Jersey City in the shadow of rapidly urbanizing Manhattan. Her husband, Frederick, the son of a British émigré engraver of some prominence, had died three years earlier of tuberculosis. Her son, Frederick, was six; her daughter, Ada, was four. It was a perilous time to be a widow with young children. The Civil War, which had ended a few years earlier, left many women on their own and looking for work—twenty-five thousand in Boston alone, according to one estimate. Employment opportunities for women were limited and, according to a pioneering study of the women's labor market by Virginia Penny, most jobs that were available to women at the time paid "a mere pittance, scarce enough to keep body and soul together." The average wage for a working woman in New York City in the mid-1860s was "about $2 a week and in many instances only 20 cents a day," according to a government report, at a time when board ran about $3 a week. The majority of the 533 jobs for women that Penny painstakingly curated in *The Employments of Women: A Cyclopaedia of Woman's Work* (1863) represented only a handful of occupations: servant, governess, teacher, factory worker, seamstress, milliner, and trades such as bookbinding and cigar rolling, which traditionally employed women.

At the time, the overwhelming majority of women who worked for wages were servants, mostly "girls of all work"—the sole servant who assisted the lady of the house from dawn to dusk with the heaviest of household tasks for a roof over her head and about $1.25 per week. Before she wrote *Little Women* and gained a measure of financial security for her genteelly poor family, Louisa May Alcott tried "going into service." She had already "tried teaching for two years, and hated it." She tried sewing but "could not earn my bread in that way, at the cost of health." She "tried story-writing and got five dollars." Too "proud to be idle and dependent," she figured service would be "healthier than sewing and surer than writing." She worked, she recalled, like a "galley slave": she cooked and cleaned, scrubbed the hearth, mended socks, blackened boots, "dug paths, brought water from the well, split kindling, made fires, and sifted ashes, like a true Cinderella." She quit after seven weeks, with "grimy, chill-blained hands" and the paltry sum of four dollars in her pocketbook for "the hardest work I ever did."

Teaching was more respectable and might net a woman fifty cents more a week. But that was only for the six months or so that school was in session. Most teachers made less than fifty dollars per year, a salary that was geared toward young women living at home who taught for a few years before they married, not a woman living independently or with children to support.

Factory work was both grueling and poorly paid, as the ever-increasing influx of immigrants drove down wages and working conditions. That left sewing, the last resort for women who needed an income but were too respectable to work in a factory or had young children at home. Women were paid a per-garment "piece rate" sewing for the ready-to-wear garment industry that sprang up as mechanization transformed the production of clothes from something women did at home to a centralized manufacturing process controlled by men who subcontracted sewing out to women, who worked for a pittance either in their homes or in sweatshops. In 1870, the *New York Times* profiled a widow supporting two young children by sewing fourteen hours a day, seven days a week making "vests at 18 cents apiece for a wholesale house." She made eight dollars per month, three dollars of which went to the tiny attic she rented. She told a reporter in January that "she had eaten meat only once since Thanksgiving, and then it was given to her."

Maria had experience working as a seamstress and lived near her in-laws in Jersey City, so she was able to leave Frederick and Ada with them and get a job at Stewart's, the first department store in the city, a six-story, cast-iron monument to retailing straddling Ninth and Tenth Streets on Broadway in lower Manhattan. While well-heeled Victorian ladies prowled the lower floors of the "Iron Palace," with its "tasteful frescoes" and "gilded chandeliers" and "graceful Corinthian columns," for camelhair shawls, silk capes, merinos from Scotland, and the latest housewares in a "gayly dressed, restless, ever-changing throng," Maria would have labored on the top floor with some nine hundred other seamstresses employed in Stewart's in-house factory. A visiting reporter from *Godey's Lady's Book* described a "flock of women and girls" sewing away at long worktables that sat 250 making "finished garments, cloaks, sacques" and "hundreds of dozens of sheets, pillow-cases, towels and napkins, dozens of blankets, counterpanes, etc."

Within a few years, Maria had risen to what she would tell a friend was a "responsible position" at Stewart's, perhaps as one of the "careful matrons" who, as *Godey's* described, supervised the workers. Unfortunately, Stewart's was known for paying the "lowest market rate" for employees, and with even the best-paid women of the time making one-third to one-half of what men made, it's doubtful she obtained even a measure of financial security.

Sometime around 1870, Maria moved to Buffalo, New York, with Frederick in search of better opportunities, possibly with some of her late husband's family, leaving Ada with her in-laws. Buffalo was a busy, thriving city—the tenth largest in the country at the time. Maria got a job making mourning collars, an essential part of the elaborate Victorian mourning dress that she herself had recently worn, with Flint & Kent, an up-and-coming dry goods store that was the Buffalo equivalent of Stewart's.

By 1872, Maria had been promoted to sales clerk. It was an extraordinary opportunity for a woman at the time. Traditionally retail clerks were men; only a fraction of the 320 or so sales clerks at Stewart's were women. The explosion in retailing at the time created a tremendous demand for clerks, and, as it was quickly realized, women were better at selling things to other women. With women still largely barred from office jobs, department store clerking was by far the most genteel, semiprofessional job available to native-born white women like Maria (department stores wouldn't hire immigrant, black, or Jewish women as clerks). Women clerks were expected to dress fashionably, be knowledgeable about the latest styles and trends, and project a refined persona that mirrored the mannerisms of their customers. Many rejected the English term "shopgirl," with its connotations of "inferior class position, poor taste in dress and speech, and possibly low moral state," says the department store historian Susan Porter Benson, in favor of "saleslady."

By 1873, Maria was the head of the cloak department at Flint & Kent. The cloak department was one of the busiest in the store, and Maria felt she had "the confidence and esteem" of her employers. An acquaintance remembered her as "ladylike, intelligent and fine appearing." Tall and slender, she spoke fluent French, thanks to some Huguenot-descended relations she'd spent time with as a child, and possessed, according to one local man, "unusual intelligence, modesty, neatness and business tact." Like all women moving into formerly all-male workplaces in the second half of the nineteenth century, however, Maria walked a fine line no matter how ladylike she was. In the eyes of society, a woman who was self-supporting "no longer owed her sexuality to one man alone," notes historian Sharon Wood. The very act of working, as well as the traversing of public spaces alone, "implicitly compromised her sexual reputation." The fact that women were poorly paid engendered the suspicions that they were easily compromised. As one Buffalo department store clerk noted even thirty years later, "You have to dress well or you can't keep your place, and there's always somebody ready to be your 'friend' and put up for your clothes. Still most of the girls keep straight, though I know lots of folks think they don't."

Maria walked that line as well as any woman of her time. By 1873, she had what was by any measure an excellent life for a woman who had been a struggling widow five years earlier. She had a good job; she was living in a fashionable boardinghouse, Mrs. Randall's on Swann Street; and she attended the equally fashionable St. John's Episcopal Church. With a "remarkable sweetness of manner and a liberal share of personal magnetism," Maria "drew about her the better class of people, and numbered among her friends some of the very best" of Buffalo's citizens, according to one local man who remembered her.

It wasn't surprising, then, when a friend of Mrs. Oscar Folsom, one of Maria's customers, "persistently sought" to make Maria's acquaintance. His intentions seemed "honorable" according to Maria—he had followed the proper procedure of seeking an introduction through a mutual acquaintance—and his character was, by all accounts, very good. He had been Oscar Folsom's law partner and was just finishing up a term as the sheriff of Erie County. Maria was in her early thirties at the time, and her suitor was thirty-six, so remarriage, which would have put her on sounder financial footing, probably seemed like a very real possibility. Maria and her suitor saw each other for a few months, and he paid Maria what she called "very marked attention." One evening in mid-December 1873, Maria was on her way to the Tifft House, the city's most prominent hotel, to call on her friend Mrs. Johnson, when she ran into her beau. He asked her "to go with him to dinner, which invitation I declined because of my prior engagement," Maria said, but "by persistent requests and urgings he induced me to accompany him to the restaurant at the Ocean House, where we dined." After dinner at the Ocean Dining House and Oyster Hall, said Maria, he "accompanied me to my rooms at Randall's boarding house . . . as he had quite frequently done previous to this time, and where my son lived with me." It was there in her rooms "by the use of force and violence and without my consent," she later asserted in an affidavit, that Grover Cleveland raped her.

Maria said that after Cleveland had "accomplished my ruin," he told her he had been determined to "secure my ruin if it cost him $10,000, or if he was hanged by the neck for it." Perhaps it was her independence, her temerity to go about unescorted in public, to earn her own wages, which suggested she was available sexually. Cleveland later spoke of wanting his wife to be a "sensible, domestic American wife"—clearly he didn't approve of working women. Maria said she "told him that I never wanted to see him again, and commanded him to go away."

Six weeks later she changed her mind and summoned him back to Swann Street. Maria was pregnant and in despair and nearly hysterical at the thought of what an illegitimate pregnancy would mean for her. "What the devil are you blubbering about? You act like a baby without teeth," she said Cleveland told her. "What do you want me to do?" he asked, as if he didn't know. What Maria wanted him to do was what was "honorable and right." She wanted Cleveland to marry her.

It's an indication of how devastating unwed pregnancy, and the social rejection that would follow it, was to a nineteenth-century woman that Maria's biggest concern was getting her rapist to marry her. To her, it likely seemed the only practical solution. It would have been nearly impossible for Maria to prevail in court on rape charges. According to Mary Block, a historian of rape law, the courts at the time "made it virtually impossible for a mature, healthy woman to prove she had been raped." While nineteenth-century law defined rape as "the unlawful carnal knowledge of a woman by a man, forcibly and against her will," courts tended to adhere to the old common-law standard of rape. This held that in order for a sexual encounter to be classified as rape, a woman had to physically resist the act the entire time and had to give "hue and cry"—to call out during the rape and report it immediately afterward. If at any time during the rape she gave up fighting and didn't use "utmost resistance," she was considered to have acquiesced to the act, and it was considered "seduction"—which in most states was still a civil action reserved for men—not rape. As Block notes, in effect, "consummation meant consent."

It was also a time when, according to Block, "there was a general assumption that men used a certain amount of force and women showed a respectable degree of resistance in the course of an ordinary seduction." Damning pieces of evidence, like torn underclothes or physical injuries, were dismissed as evidence of "overly zealous seduction." In one 1868 case, a judge wrote that "notwithstanding the defendant treated the girl roughly at first, and actually threatened to kill her, yet if she afterwards freely consented to the sexual intercourse, being enticed to surrender her chastity by means employed by him, then the offense is seduction."

Myths about rape still held sway, including the belief that a woman couldn't become pregnant as a result of rape because "without an excitation of lust . . . no conception can probably take place" or that it was "impossible" for a man to rape a healthy woman because she could use her limbs and "the force of her hands to prevent the insertion of the penis into her body," as Samuel Farr wrote in *Elements of Medical Jurisprudence*, which purported to be the first forensic treatise on rape law. In 1868, Dr. Horatio Storer, an influential gynecologist who was a vice president of the American Medical Association, wrote that "ordinarily it is impossible for a man without assistance to gain access to the penetralia of an unwilling woman," likening it to an "attempt to sheathe a sword in a vibrating scabbard."

As chastity became central to the definition of a respectable woman in the nineteenth century, women found it was their sexual conduct, not the actions of men, that was really on trial. Any indication that the woman "was willing to socialize alone with her attacker . . . or that she put up little resistance could be taken as consent, even if she believed to the contrary," writes the historian Barbara Lindemann. If Maria had tried to take Cleveland to court, it likely would have been her independence and her decision to go about the streets unescorted at night that was on trial. Nor would a rape conviction have done anything to provide for her and the child she was expecting or to restore her reputation. Only marriage could do that.

On the day she confronted Cleveland about her pregnancy, Maria said that he "promised that he would marry me." However, Cleveland, according to the historian Horace Samuel Merrill, cherished his freedom and grew "irritated, rude and rebellious" if it was threatened. He was also, according to the biographer Allan Nevins, a "man's man" who "noticeably kept his distance from the belles of the city" and was "happiest in a hotel lounge; in a friend's room full of tobacco smoke, glasses, and cards," in the back room of a saloon, or "on the duck-marshes with a gun, or on the Niagara River with a rod." Apparently Cleveland had no intention of giving up his much-loved bachelor lifestyle to be roped into a marriage not of his design, because he showed no sign of making good on his promise.

Lacking a male relative in Buffalo to pressure Cleveland to take responsibility, Maria turned to her pastor, the Reverend Charles Avery of St. John's, and told him "the circumstances of her intimacy with Grover Cleveland"—although it's unlikely she told him that she had been raped. He probably assumed that she had been seduced under the promise of marriage, which, as the historian Michael Grossberg notes, "was excusable and understandable" in an otherwise respectable woman. At the time, states were moving to criminalize seduction as "the act of a male person in having intercourse with a woman of chaste character under promise of marriage, or by the use of enticement or persuasion." New York was the first state to criminalize seduction in 1848. The main purpose of seduction laws, however, according to the legal scholar H. W. Humble, wasn't to punish men, but "to compel an unmarried man who has had intercourse with a virtuous woman under promise of marriage to keep his promise."

With the understanding that Cleveland had seduced Maria, Avery said, "He must marry you," and agreed to talk to Cleveland on Maria's behalf. When Avery confronted Cleveland, however, he heard a different story. Cleveland didn't deny that he had been intimate with Maria, but he told Avery that he was unsure if he was the father of the child she was carrying, intimating that Maria had been intimate with another man. Avery said he agreed that marriage "would be impossible" given the "very doubtful paternity" of the child—no upstanding man could be expected to marry a woman whose chastity was suspect. Seduction statutes specifically protected only women "of good repute," not "lewd women." Having determined that Maria's purported unchasteness removed any obligation of Cleveland's to marry her, Avery said he got Cleveland to "agree to provide for the child" and ended his involvement, convinced that Cleveland had acted "nobly."

Now Maria was utterly defeated and utterly ruined. No longer able to hide her pregnancy, she gave up her job at Flint & Kent and her comfortable rooms at Randall's boardinghouse. She sent her son, Frederick, back to Jersey City. She entered St. Mary's Lying-In Hospital, a charitable institution run by Catholic nuns for the care and seclusion of unwed mothers. It was there, on September 14, 1874, that her son was delivered by Dr. James King, an obstetrician whom one local described as Cleveland's "friend, employé and father confessor." Maria said Cleveland insisted on naming the baby Oscar Folsom Cleveland after his former partner and good friend Oscar Folsom.

Oscar was taken away from Maria shortly after his birth and brought by Dr. King to the home of his sister-in-law Minnie Kendall and her husband, William. Minnie was pregnant and expecting shortly. King pressured Minnie to take Oscar, telling her, she said, he "would pay me . . . and told me several times that I could call him my twin baby." The Kendalls finally consented, and Oscar was left with them. "All of his clothing was marked M.H.," Minnie Kendall recalled. "They told me to call him Jack, and to take all his clothing and replace it with new, and give them back the marked clothing." This she did. "We virtually had the child hid, and largely at the request of Dr. King. We moved once to hide the traces of the child if any existed," she said.

Maria was frantic and heartbroken. "I begged Cleveland on my knees to let me have sight of my baby," she said, but he relented only once and let her see Oscar at his lawyer's office for a few minutes to prove he was being well cared for. Cleveland installed Maria in a seedy boardinghouse on East Genesee Street. She was "very much depressed and broken down," according to her neighbor Mrs. William Baker, and she began drinking and railing against Cleveland. The threat of scandal and exposure must have been too much, because after a year, Oscar was returned to Maria. As Minnie Kendall recalled, "They came to me in a hurry one day, apparently alarmed, and told me to take the baby and get its things all together quick and go in a hack and give it to its mother." Dr. King warned Kendall not to tell Maria where she lived and had the driver take a circuitous route to and from Maria's home so that Minnie didn't know where she was. Afterward, said Kendall, King repeatedly told them not to "tell what we knew about Maria Halpin's child, and used all manner of means to intimidate us." Shortly after Minnie dropped off Oscar, their house was "broken into and all the baby's trinkets stolen," including a little knit cap that Maria had made for Oscar that "had a picture of a man inside which looked just like the picture of Cleveland" and had "Baby's papa" written on the back.

Kendall said Maria was "overjoyed" to have Oscar back, but she continued to drink and make threats against Cleveland. Cleveland told friends he was concerned she was neglecting the baby and was "apprehensive that she might attempt some injury to him or herself." Mrs. Baker said he sent Maria letters "in which he demanded that she give the baby up and threatening to take it from her by force." When that didn't work, Cleveland "appealed to the Chief of Police, Col. John Byrne, to keep her under surveillance," apparently with the idea of using Maria's purported neglect of Oscar to get him away from her. Byrne sent two detectives to Genesee Street, but they reportedly found they "could do nothing with her." Cleveland then turned to a retired judge, Roswell Burrows, to try to reach some kind of agreement with Maria. Burrows told Maria that if she would leave town and surrender Oscar to the local orphanage, Cleveland would pay for his care and establish her in a dressmaking business in Niagara Falls. Maria finally agreed, and on March 9, 1876, left Oscar at the Buffalo Orphan Asylum. That wouldn't last. She pined for Oscar, and on April 28 she spirited him from the orphanage and ran off.

Cleveland next turned to John Level, who was the overseer of the poor in the city, and, according to the biographer Denis Lynch, an "old crony" of Cleveland's from the days when he and a little posse of political friends hung out at Level's livery stable. Cleveland persuaded Level to use his authority as overseer of the poor to sign an order granting him custody of Oscar, while, according to Lynch, "avoiding a court proceeding, and the attendant publicity." On the night of July 10, Robert Watts, one of Byrne's detectives, and Dr. King drove up to the Genesee Street lodgings. With "the assistance of Mr. Baker Mrs. Halpin was forced into the carriage and driven to the Providence Insane Asylum." Watts, who was paid some fifty dollars for his services, said it took all his strength to overpower Maria. "It was a hell of a time," he told a friend. Mrs. Baker said that Maria "was drunk at the time, and we understood that Mr. Cleveland wanted her put in an asylum to wean her from liquor, but there are those who say he made her condition an excuse to get her out of the way."

Drunk or not, Maria was sent to the insane asylum, according to Dr. William Ring, the attending physician, "without warrant or form of law." When Ring examined Maria, he determined that she was "boozy" but "not insane." Since there was "no authority for committing an intemperate person to the asylum," Ring advised Maria to stay long enough to dry out; according to Ring, she spent about a week at the asylum. She hired M. A. Whitney, one of the leading lawyers in Erie County, to institute proceedings against Cleveland for "abduction and false imprisonment." Whitney investigated Maria's assertion that Cleveland "had plotted the abduction and hired the man to carry it out" and "was on the eve of taking legal measures for redress," he said, when Simeon Talbott, Maria's brother-in-law, arrived from Jersey City.

Talbott was "anxious to avoid public scandal" so that "innocent parties" wouldn't have to bear the weight of "Maria's shame." He showed up at Whitney's office with Maria and an agreement "in the handwriting of Grover Cleveland," according to Whitney, that "stipulated that upon the payment of the sum of $500 Maria Halpin was to surrender her son, Oscar Folsom Cleveland, and make no further demands of any nature whatever." Under pressure from Talbott, Maria signed the agreement, left Buffalo, and never saw Oscar again. He was adopted by Dr. King.

•

Maria Halpin would have been just another "ruined" woman lost to history if Grover Cleveland hadn't experienced one of history's most meteoric political rises, benefiting time and again from a divided opposition party and a climate that favored a little-known political outsider free from the corruption of machine politics. From being what one local politician described as a "fair lawyer in the host of average lawyers" in Buffalo in the 1870s—albeit one with a reputation for prodigious hard work and integrity—Cleveland won an upset victory to become mayor in 1881 after being drafted by local officials casting about for a reform candidate. While in office, he earned a reputation as a crusader against corruption after he vetoed an exorbitant street-cleaning contract that epitomized the graft that had overtaken the governments of many cities.

By this time, he was the Cleveland of caricature, a heavyset walrus of a man, right down to his mustache. He was, according to the historian Merrill, a fundamentally conservative, parochial man who was "remarkably unreceptive to new ideas" and who had little taste for travel or culture to broaden his worldview. His hallmarks were a narrowly legalistic approach to the law and a "frustrated, uneasy retreat into conservatism" when challenged. His basic political philosophy came down to spending as little taxpayer money as possible while giving businesses and industry a free hand to make as much money as possible.

In 1882, Cleveland was elected governor of New York State, carried into office by pro-reform Democrats who wanted a governor who was fundamentally honest but not particularly imaginative; they didn't want him championing any newfangled social legislation or giving in to public agitation to regulate increasingly monopolistic business concerns. He vetoed a popular bill that would have reduced the rush-hour fare for New York's elevated railroad to five cents after the "much-despised Jay Gould" merged two railroad companies and doubled the peak fare to ten cents. He vetoed a bill that would have limited the number of hours that horse-drawn streetcar conductors could work to twelve from the usual fourteen to sixteen, calling it "class legislation." He wasn't a particularly savvy politician, displaying a distinctly rigid, sanctimonious streak, but it often served him well in the eyes of the public, who, says Merrill, saw in his unwillingness to compromise a "refreshing moral correctness." When he lurched into a battle with Tammany Hall, the infamous political machine that controlled New York City, over political appointments, he nearly split the party and unwittingly torpedoed two important reform bills, but what the public remembered was his willingness to confront the feared Tammany Tiger.

Within two years, "Grover the Good" was the Democratic nominee for president of the United States and a favorite to win after an influential group of Republicans known as the "mugwumps" deserted Republican nominee James Blaine, who had been implicated in shady financial dealings with the railroads. But Cleveland's momentum came to a halt less than ten days after he accepted the nomination in July 1884, when an upstart Buffalo paper, the *Evening Telegraph*, broke the story of the Halpin affair, which had lived on in rumor long after Maria departed the city, under the headline "A Terrible Tale." The accusation that Cleveland had ruined a respectable woman—she was seduced under the promise of marriage, it was reported—had taken her son from her, drove her to drink, and then tried to dump her in an insane asylum, was potentially devastating to any candidate, never mind Grover the Good.

By the first week of August, the story of the scandal had been printed in papers across the country. In an era of partisan newspapers, it was largely ignored or downplayed by Democratic-leaning papers like the *New York World* and trumped by Republican-leaning papers like the *Chicago Daily Tribune*, but it was obviously having an effect. The *New York Evening Post* editorialized: "We do not believe that the American people will ever elect a notorious libertine and profligate to the office of the President of the United States." Cleveland's backers tried to diffuse the story by claiming that only a candidate's public actions, not their private life, should be considered as qualification for office. "The issue of the campaign is not one of personal character," the *World* editor Joseph Pulitzer told one audience.

A week after the initial story appeared, the influential *Boston Journal* published an independently reported confirmation. Rumors began circulating of other women Cleveland had taken advantage of. There were reports that the Democrats might ask Cleveland to step down in the face of a "serious stampede" away from him. Cleveland famously instructed his campaign managers to "tell the truth" after the story broke, but a wholesale denial would have been pointless; too many people in Buffalo knew the story. "I don't think there is an intelligent man in the city who questions the substantial truth of the terrible story," one local Methodist minister wrote. On August 5, a "defense" of Cleveland was published in the *Evening Post*. Cleveland's allies admitted that he had "formed an irregular connection with a widow" twelve years ago but asserted that "she was a person of intemperate habits, and that the paternity of a child born subsequently was doubtful." The article not only backdated Maria's Cleveland-induced drinking problem to suggest she had been dissolute all along, but also absolved Cleveland of any responsibility for sending Maria to the asylum. It claimed that Roswell Burrows had charge of the matter and hired Watts, who supposedly found Maria "suffering from delirium tremens and threatening to kill the child," so she was taken to the "inebriate Asylum for treatment."

Charles McCune, the editor of the city's leading paper, the *Buffalo Courier*, and a longtime backer of Cleveland's, started spreading the rumor that Oscar Folsom, who had died in a buggy accident the year after his namesake was born, was Oscar's father and that Cleveland hadn't spoken out to protect him. Privately, Cleveland was furious that someone was besmirching the name of his friend. "Is he fool enough to suppose for a moment that if such was the truth (which it is not, so far as the motive for my silence is concerned) that I would permit my dead friend's name to suffer for my sake? . . . This story of McCune's must be stopped," he wrote to a friend. Publicly, however, Cleveland didn't deny the rumor, a classic example of what the historian Merrill calls his willingness to let political associates do his dirty work while he kept his reputation for personal integrity.

With reports circulating that influential mugwump Henry Ward Beecher was reassessing his support of Cleveland—which was more than a little ironic because Beecher himself had been caught up in an epic scandal involving a parishioner with whom he was intimately involved—Cleveland tapped Horatio King to keep Beecher from bolting. King was a friend of Beecher's who was also a Cleveland political appointee; Cleveland had made him judge advocate general of the state National Guard. King assured Beecher he would investigate the charges against Cleveland and headed to Buffalo to do "a little bit of detective work." According to the *Chicago Daily Tribune*, King's "investigation" consisted of "call[ing] on some of Gov. Cleveland's friends." When he returned to New York, he assured Beecher that Cleveland was "the victim of outrageous slander" and that "Cleveland's character is as free from stain as the whitest lily." He blamed the Reverend George Ball, who had first brought the story to the *Evening Telegraph*, asserting he was on the payroll of the Republicans.

On August 8, King released the results of his "investigation" in a sensational *New York World* interview:

> The facts seem to be that many years ago when the governor was "sowing his wild oats," he met this woman, with whom his name has been connected, and became intimate with her. She was a widow and not a good woman by any means. Mr. Cleveland, hearing this, began to make inquiries about her and discovered that two of his friends were intimate with her at the same time as himself.
>
> When a child was born, Cleveland, in order to shield his two friends, who were both married men, assumed the responsibility of it. He took care of the child and the mother like a man, and did everything in his power for them, and he provided for them until the woman became a confirmed victim of alcoholism and made it impossible by her conduct for him to have anything to do with her. He never separated the mother and child, nor did he do anything to injure the woman. He was throughout

the affair a victim of circumstance. He accepted responsibilities that not one man in a thousand has shouldered and acted honorably in the matter.

It was a devastating story that cut to the heart of contemporary assumptions about "bad" women and a man's right to sow his wild oats. King was asserting that Maria had been simultaneously sexually active with Cleveland and two of his friends. King said that after the baby was born, Maria "made a habit of visiting every man with whom she had been intimate and demanded money." According to King, Cleveland took responsibility to protect his married friends' "hearthsides" from any "unpleasantness." King had turned Cleveland from the villain who had abandoned the woman he impregnated into a hero protecting Victorian homes from a predatory woman.

It strained credulity to believe that Cleveland had become intimate with Halpin only to find out afterward that she just happened to be sleeping with two of his friends. Furthermore, unlike the *Telegraph* and *Journal* stories about the scandal—which were corroborated by Maria's neighbor Mrs. Baker; Minnie Kendell, the woman who cared for Oscar; Dr. William Ring, the doctor who attended her at the Providence Insane Asylum; M. A. Whitney, the lawyer Maria hired; and Messrs. Flint and Kent themselves, who confirmed that Maria was "much esteemed" and "bore an unblemished name" when she worked for them—King offered no proof of any of his assertions. He provided no names of the other men who were supposedly involved with Maria, other than to say that the likely father was "dead and the child is his perfect image in manner and looks"—in other words, Oscar Folsom. "It is perhaps worthy of note that Grover Cleveland is the only authority cited by Gen. King," wrote an incredulous John Creswell, the editor of the *Telegraph*. "He does not let us know who told him that Gov. Cleveland is so close in his associations that he and two dear friends at the same time held relations with a woman who left the paternity of her children doubtful . . . he does not cite a witness to [make] the shameful allegations he makes against the mother of the son of Grover Cleveland." King also never explained, as Maria herself would later note, how such a "vile wretch" as he portrayed her to be managed to fool everyone—her neighbors, employers, and fellow congregants at St. John's—into thinking she was a respectable woman.

Nonetheless, it made national headlines when Beecher proclaimed himself satisfied with King's investigation. He declared the Halpin story "vile slander" and said that although Cleveland "committed an error," he "acted a generous and very honorable part," and Beecher said he would support him enthusiastically. Several days later, a *New York Times* headline proclaimed the charges had been "Swept Away" after two more thinly sourced "investigations" by pro-Cleveland loyalists determined that beyond the "primary offense" of an "illicit connection" with Halpin, Cleveland had acted "honorably."

The *New York Mercury* completed the smear when it published a story titled "Wicked Maria Halpin," a largely fictional account of Maria's life that recast the decorous salesclerk as the village siren. The article claimed she grew up "plump, pretty and decidedly attractive" and was "a magnetic girl" with a "free, jolly disposition," who "attracted a large circle of admirers from the towns and villages around." The article was riddled with biographical errors, including Maria's maiden name, which was Hovenden, not Crofts; the claim that she was an orphan; and the number of children she had with her late husband. But that didn't diminish its impact or its contribution to what was quickly becoming the accepted portrait of the "widow Halpin" who, proclaimed the *Mercury*, "Lured [Cleveland] from Virtue."

Maria tried to get her side of the story out, giving a brief statement to the *Telegraph* in which she asserted that Cleveland was Oscar's father "and to say otherwise is infamous." She called the attempt to link her to Folsom "cruel and cowardly," and said she "had but a very slight acquaintance" with him. She said it didn't seem possible "that an attempt would be made to blacken my name" after the years of "shame, suffering, and degradation forced upon me by Grover Cleveland." But many papers didn't run her statement—the *New York Times* never even referred to her by name.

Maria herself had by mid-August gone into hiding, after being smuggled out of New Rochelle, New York, where she had been living with her aunt Harriet and her uncle James Seacord as a "quiet, decorous, unobtrusive housekeeper," under cover of night and onto a train bound for New York City.

Cleveland again pressured Maria's family to intercede. In mid-August, Maria's brother-in-law Simeon Talbott received a letter from Cleveland "urging [him] to make a statement showing that he had always treated Mrs. Halpin well" and promising, said Talbott, "anything I could wish in case he was elected." Cleveland told Talbott that the "published reports in the press that two other men were intimate with Mrs. Halpin were wholly unauthorized by him, and were not true." Talbott said Cleveland promised to have the record "corrected" if he would make "the required statement," but this time he refused to play ball, saying he learned after Maria's "trouble" that "Cleveland was a notorious libertine." Talbott also said that the Democrats had offered Maria ten thousand dollars to make a statement exonerating Cleveland but that she "said she would die before she would make" such a statement. "She says she would rather tell the truth for the Republican cause than take any sum from the Democrats," he said.

In late September, Maria's now-grown son Frederick was summoned to the Hoffman House in New York City, a favorite Democratic meeting place, by William C. Hudson, a former political reporter and Democratic operative who was close to Cleveland. Hudson, said Frederick, prepared a statement that he wanted Maria to sign asserting that she had received "uniform kindness and courtesy" from Cleveland and that she "always had a high esteem for Mr. Cleveland." Frederick said Maria refused to sign the statement because it was "not true."

Despite a lack of a statement from Maria, by mid-September Cleveland felt the tide had turned in his favor. He wrote to his former law partner Wilson Shannon "Shan" Bissell on September 11 that "the scandal business is about wound up" and he thought "the matter was arranged in the best possible way." At the end of the month, Maria officially became a laughingstock when she was made the subject of one of the most famous political cartoons in history: Frank Beard's cartoon of Cleveland determinedly blocking his ears to baby Oscar's wails of "I want my pa," as Maria hides her face in shame. Soon Republicans all over the country were pushing baby carriages in political parades chanting, "Ma, ma, where's my pa?" Maria's personal nightmare had become the stuff of political farce.

On October 22, Henry Beecher addressed a "vast audience" at the

Brooklyn Rink and gave Cleveland his full-throated endorsement and bemoaned the "ghouls who have been scattering scandal," blaming the Republican Party and "credulous clergymen" for listening to a "harlot and drunkard." In a desperate last effort to expunge her reputation as a "harlot" as the election neared, Maria swore out and released two affidavits on October 28 and 29. She said she would "gladly remain silent" but felt she had a duty to her family and friends to make a public statement refuting the charges against her "character and actions." Maria attested that her "life was as pure and spotless as that of any lady in the City of Buffalo" up until the time she met Cleveland. She defied Cleveland or his backers to "state a single fact or give a single incident or action of mine to which anyone could take exception." She confirmed that the story of her ruin as published in the *Telegraph* was largely true and that there "never was a doubt as to the paternity of our child."

In her affidavit of October 28, Maria said that the "circumstances under which my ruin was accomplished are too revolting on the part of Grover Cleveland to be made public." Apparently she changed her mind, because the following day she swore out a second affidavit in which she attested that Cleveland "accomplished my ruin by the use of force and violence and without my consent." Maria's accusation of rape received little press coverage. In fact, two days later the *New York World*, which was controlled by Cleveland ally Joseph Pulitzer, ran what it purported to be an interview with Maria in which she disavowed any statements against Cleveland and said he was a "good, plain, honest-hearted man, who was always friendly to me and used me kindly." The language sounded much like the language in the statement Cleveland had repeatedly tried to get her to sign. Maria herself had said back in August, "Me make a statement exonerating Grover Cleveland? Never! I would rather put a bullet through my heart."

Four days after the second affidavit was published, Grover Cleveland was elected president of the United States. His victory was taken as a vindication of his forthrightness in dealing with the Halpin incident. But Cleveland won one of the closest presidential elections in history because of an historic political blunder by Blaine, who had the momentum going into the final week of the campaign. On October 29, Blaine was campaigning in heavily Irish Catholic New York City when a clergyman named Samuel Burchard, who was introducing him at a rally, denounced the Democratic Party as the party of "rum, Romanism, and rebellion"—booze, Catholics, and Confederates. The Democrats cranked out handbills denouncing Blaine as anti-Catholic and handed them out the following Sunday in front of Catholic churches throughout the city, "blowing hitherto undecided Catholic voters off the fence and into Democratic shelters," according to Merrill.

Blaine's "black Wednesday" continued when he attended a lavish "prosperity dinner" at Delmonico's that evening that was packed with millionaires and robber barons—Jay Gould, Andrew Carnegie, Charles Tiffany—at a time when factories across the country were closing down. The dinner was savaged the next day in the press as the worst kind of Gilded Age excess. A week later, Blaine lost New York State, the most critical swing state, by 1,149 votes. It cost him the election. Triumphant Democrats responded to the "Ma, ma, where's my pa?" taunt with the rejoinder, "Gone to the White House, ha, ha, ha!"

Once in the White House, Cleveland married a woman whose respectability was unquestioned because he had personally supervised it since she was a child: twenty-one-year-old Frances Folsom, the daughter of the late Oscar Folsom. He had acted as her informal guardian since Oscar's death; she called him "Uncle Cleve." When she was still a child and Cleveland's sister asked if he was ever going to get married, he said, "I'm only waiting for my wife to grow up." He had courted her since she was a teenager, sending her roses every week when she was in college. It was "Frank," as she was known, whom he spoke of wanting to make a "sensible, domestic American wife." She was married to the forty-nine-year-old Cleveland in the Blue Room of the White House in an ivory wedding gown.

Meanwhile, Maria Halpin went down in the history books as a whore. King's slander of the wanton widow Maria was codified in Allan Nevins's Pulitzer Prize–winning biography *Grover Cleveland: A Study in Courage.* Nevins wrote that Maria—"tall, pretty and pleasing in manner"—"accepted the attentions of several men." When "a son was born to her . . . whom she named Oscar Folsom Cleveland, she charged Cleveland with his paternity." According to Nevins, "Those closest to [Cleveland] believed that Mrs. Halpin was uncertain who was the father;

that she fixed upon him because she hoped to make him marry her." But Cleveland himself told Simeon Talbott that King's story about Maria's multiple lovers wasn't true. He even told his friend Bissell when he was bragging about having the whole scandal wrapped up that "King's intrusion made me trouble," suggesting that he wasn't happy about the outlandish tale King concocted.

Nevins also repeated the explanation from King's investigation that Cleveland "did not question [Maria's] charge because the other men in the scrape were married." Yet during the 1884 Democratic National Convention, Cleveland reportedly told fellow New York politician Alfred Chapin about his "woman scrape"—probably because he knew the Halpin rumors would dog him if he got the nomination—and apparently never suggested it was anything other than what it appeared: he had gotten a woman pregnant. More important, as the Cleveland biographer Denis Lynch notes, one other man in Cleveland's circle of chums also was unmarried—his junior law partner Shan Bissell. "If a scapegoat was to be chosen, no one more suitable could have been found than Shan Bissell, the youngest of the lot, with the least to lose, and one of the gayest bachelors in town," Lynch wrote.

As a final vindication of Cleveland, Nevins offers the assessment of the Reverend Kinsley Twining that after the "preliminary offense," Cleveland's "conduct was singularly honorable, showing no attempt to evade responsibility, and doing all that he could to meet the duties involved, of which marriage was certainly not one." Twining was a Congregationalist minister who conducted another of the sham investigations that in 1884 exonerated Cleveland, this one for the *Independent*, a weekly Congregationalist magazine that formerly was headed by Henry Beecher. Kinsley was the book review editor of the *Independent*, and his investigation appears to have been about as thorough as King's—not very.

Nevins never mentions Maria's rape allegation. What's most important about the whole Halpin incident, according to him, is how a mere "transient weakness" on the part of Cleveland "also throws light upon his latent strength." For women, such a "transient weakness" would be ruinous; but for men, apparently, it was redemptive.

The idea that Cleveland took responsibility for Oscar to protect his friend Folsom was popularized in the 1894 novel *The Honorable Peter*

Stirling. In it, a fictionalized Cleveland assumes responsibility for his law partner's illegitimate child to "spare the feelings of his partner's daughter, to whom he is betrothed." As Lynch notes, the idea that Cleveland needed to take responsibility for Oscar to spare Folsom makes no sense: "Cleveland and Folsom had not been partners for nearly four years" when Oscar was born and "Cleveland owed nothing to Folsom." Oscar Folsom was alive and well when little Oscar was born and perfectly capable of making arrangements for him if he was his son. Frances Folsom was only ten at the time, so her betrothal to Cleveland was still over a decade away.

The idea that Cleveland needed to protect Oscar Folsom to prevent scandal also grossly misinterprets the sexual politics of the time. If Maria Halpin had been having an affair with Folsom—and there is no evidence that she was—she would have been considered a woman of ill repute by definition because she was sleeping with a man she could not marry. As such, she had no social capital. If she had become pregnant by Folsom, she would have had little recourse and would have been unlikely to make a fuss. The best she could have expected was for Folsom to make some provision for the child—many a philandering nineteenth-century husband quietly supported an illegitimate child. A more significant scandal would have occurred if it became public knowledge that Cleveland, an up-and-coming politician, had relations with a respectable woman and failed to marry her when he was able to do so, consigning her to life as a "fallen" woman—hence the motive for squirreling little Oscar away.

Popular historians compounded the legend of the wanton widow when they picked up on the unfounded assertion of the Reverend Ball that Cleveland and his friends in a club called the "Jolly Reefers" had drunken orgies to assert they passed Maria around like a plaything. Despite the rather satiric-sounding name, the truth of the Jolly Reefers was much tamer. As one of the founding members told *Forest and Stream*: "Half a dozen of us floated down the river from Buffalo one day fishing for bass . . . Someone suggested that we float over to Grand Island and eat our dinner on the grass. Before we finished our meal we began to discuss the organization of a permanent fishing club . . . We became the 'Jolly Reefers.'" They changed the name, he said, after their wives criticized it because it suggested an "extravagant picture of sociability."

They built a clubhouse on the island that became known as the Beaver Island Club, a proper Victorian sportsman's club where the members fished and hunted duck. They took fishing so seriously that they had "regular fishing days at which every member was expected to be present" and elected a commodore for each outing. An orgy it was not. Members recalled seeing Cleveland there "leading the chubby little girl, 'Frankie' Folsom, by the hand."

No one seemed to question why Maria would risk her comfortable, and hard-won, life to have simultaneous affairs with three men when the consequences would be ruinous or why no evidence was ever produced linking her to other men, especially Folsom. Why would she, as Nevins asserted, name the baby Oscar Folsom Cleveland if it would advertise her sexual connection to two men? It seems just as likely that Cleveland concocted the name to obscure Oscar's paternity, perhaps figuring it didn't matter since he planned to give the baby away anyway and hide his parentage. If Maria was as dissolute as the portrait of her suggested, why hadn't she taken the money offered by the Democratic Party? Why would she make a false accusation of rape against Cleveland if all she stood to gain was more shame?

All that mattered was that a powerful man declared Maria a wanton woman after using his position and privilege to strip her of everything she had—her reputation, her job, her home, and her children. And in Maria's story was a warning for Madeline Pollard about what she stood to lose.

6

Not So Easily Handled

It seemed likely that Madeline Pollard would meet much the same fate that Maria Halpin and Mary Oliver did: she would be dismissed in the court of public opinion before she ever got a chance to make her case. With his illustrious family name and deep political and social connections, Breckinridge seemed unassailable. He also was friendly with many reporters thanks to his stint as editor of the *Lexington Observer and Reporter*, and like other congressmen, he controlled much of the political patronage in his district, meaning that the livelihoods of many were dependent on his good graces.

Several elements of Pollard's suit gave people pause, however. One was that the charge of blackmail—or any kind of financial motive—didn't add up. "Col. Breckinridge's friends say the money could not be collected for the simple reason that he does not possess it," noted the *Washington Post*. As Charles Stoll told Jennie Tucker in his brief to her, Breckinridge had offered Madeline "a liberal allowance for such length of time as might be necessary to fit her for some honorable vocation." Stoll also assumed that if Madeline could be persuaded to take a lump-sum settlement, Breckinridge had "many warm, devoted friends" who would be happy to lend him the money to keep the matter out of court. But Madeline didn't seem interested in a settlement at all.

Another was the reputation of the attorneys representing Madeline—Jere Wilson and Calderon Carlisle. "No members of the

legal fraternity are better known" in Washington than Wilson and Carlisle, said the *Post*. Wilson was a former congressman and brilliant litigator who had been "identified with nearly half of the most important
cases fought in District courts during the past five years." Carlisle was
primarily an international lawyer, having successfully represented the
British legation in the high-profile Bering Sea seal-fisheries dispute between the United States, England, and Russia before the Supreme
Court. He came from a well-known Washington legal family and was a
bona fide "cave dweller," which was what the locals called the oldest
Washington families for their devotion to antiquated social forms. He
was also a "club man" and a regular on the high-society social circuit.

Ironically, Mary Oliver had tried to hire Carlisle's father, James
Mandeville Carlisle, who was at the time one of the city's leading lawyers,
to take her case but had to settle for out-of-town lawyers, which was a
major strike against her credibility in her breach of promise suit. It also
was reported that Wilson and Carlisle had the evidence and witnesses
to back Madeline's charges, as "men of their reputation would not un-
dertake a suit of the grave character of this without a careful scrutiny of
the grounds on which it was to be brought," noted the *Philadelphia Press*.

In addition, one of Madeline's classmates from Wesleyan wrote to
the *Cincinnati Commercial Gazette* and affirmed that everything Madeline claimed about Breckinridge's visit to Wesleyan could be "corroborated by a number of students, boarders and professors," and that she
herself was sitting across from Madeline when a servant handed her
Breckinridge's calling card. She said that Breckinridge came back around
seven that evening and they went to the "hill-tops and did not return till
near morning" and the next day Madeline "showed a sum of money."

Four days after the suit was filed, the public heard from Madeline
for the first time when a reporter from the *Washington Evening Star*
tracked her down to a boardinghouse in an out-of-the-way neighborhood.
By that time, the Duke interview as well as the interview about her set
of multiple calling cards had been reprinted in papers around the country. Madeline received the reporter in the parlor wearing a "stylish ecru-
colored" dress. She said she was reluctant to talk to the press on the
advice of her attorneys. "My position is public enough without making
it any worse," she said, but then continued, "I am not by any means all

the sorts of a woman I have been described. When I go on the stand I think that many people will change their views about me and my position in this whole affair."

Madeline made it clear that she didn't intend to settle and planned to testify in court. "Anyone can see from the character of the lawyers who have undertaken my case that I have a good case. They would not have taken it if it had not been such," she assured the reporter. Still, she understood the precarious position she had put herself in by going public. "What could I say that would not be open to misinterpretation?" she asked. "The publicity I have already had thrust upon me has not been pleasant or welcome, and the less you say about me in the *Star* the more I shall like it."

As others had, the *Star* reporter described her as "not exactly a beautiful girl"—although tall and slender "with an excellent form"—but one with "something extremely attractive and winning about her." It was, he decided, "when she begins to speak that one realizes the charm. She has a clear, musical voice, and talks earnestly and with the best use of language." He said that Madeline showed "education and breeding" and was "the last person one would ever take for an adventuress." He concluded, "She does not even look the part well enough to play it in amateur theatricals."

Madeline appeared to have more credibility than Mary Oliver and more willingness to go public with her story than Maria Halpin, who had been irrevocably smeared by the time she tried to take a stand against Cleveland. But the "Star of Kentucky" was at the apex of his political career, and few believed that a penniless girl from Kentucky could end that.

•

Politically, Willie Breckinridge entered 1893 in an enviable position. Breckinridge's political fortunes had risen with those of the "Bourbon Democrats," a faction of conservative Democrats who, according to the historian Heather Cox Richardson, originated in aristocratic southerners who held themselves out as "bastions of old tradition and culture" against the federalizing influence of Reconstruction. Eventually the Bourbons came to encompass the entire pro-business, laissez-faire wing of the

Democratic Party that came to power with Cleveland's election in 1884 on a platform of limited government, "home rule"—shorthand for states' rights—and low taxes. The Bourbons shared a near-religious faith in the power of the free market and an evangelical belief in a constitutionally limited federal government that, in the words of Cleveland, could not "interfere, beyond the very minimum of absolute necessity, with the economic and social privileges of individuals and businesses."

Breckinridge's affinity with northern business interests may seem odd, but he was a leading advocate of the "New South" movement, which hailed "cheap resources, business opportunities, railroad developments, and commercial enterprise" as the way forward for the region, according to the historian C. Vann Woodward. "They might look like Southern colonels, with goatee and moustaches, and speak like Southern orators, retaining those trappings of the olden days," noted the historian Edward Prichard, but their agenda was essentially a "surrender" to Eastern financial interests.

Breckinridge made a name for himself as a leader of the Bourbons. In 1890, when Republicans were in the majority, House Speaker Thomas Reed moved to revitalize a Congress that had taken on "a helpless, inept air" due to years of Democratic obstruction through arcane parliamentary tactics like the "disappearing quorum," in which Democrats would participate in a debate on a bill but then refuse to answer the roll call, robbing Republicans of the quorum needed to vote. On January 29, early in the second session of the Fifty-First Congress, when the quorum again disappeared, Reed instructed the house clerk to record the names of those "members present and refusing to vote" and declared a quorum. As pandemonium broke out, Breckinridge sprang to his feet and roared, "I deny the power of the Speaker and denounce it as revolutionary," as the Democrats chanted, "Czar! Czar!" at Reed.

Republicans proceeded to pass a slate of landmark bills that session under the leadership of "Czar Reed," including the McKinley Tariff Act, the Republicans' attempt to modernize the tariff schedule by raising some tariffs (notably on crops to aid beleaguered farmers), lowering others, and adding key manufacturing inputs to the "free list" on which no duties were paid. They also passed the historic Sherman Antitrust Act to rein in the monopolies and trusts that even the Democrats admitted were resulting in an unhealthy concentration of wealth and power, and the Sherman Silver Purchase Act, which doubled the amount of silver the Treasury purchased as backing for currency, moving away from the gold standard that the Bourbons held dear. They passed a long-awaited bill to provide pensions to disabled Union veterans. They even came close to passing a federal civil rights bill to oversee voting in the South, where African Americans were being rapidly disenfranchised through Jim Crow laws and voter intimidation.

Republican efforts to address so many problems at once, however, created a backlash. Voters in the South rebelled against the attempt to monitor voting rights, which the Democrats labeled the "force bill," conjuring up visions of bayoneted federal troops reinvading the South. Democrats denounced the increase in federal appropriations for things like pensions, dubbing the Fifty-First Congress the "Billion-Dollar Congress." They sent speakers around the country to drum up fears of skyrocketing consumer prices under the McKinley Tariff Act. In some places they "paid peddlers to sell household goods at inflated prices, with signs that blamed the McKinley law," according to the historian Hal Williams. They campaigned against recently passed state laws to prohibit the sale of alcohol or require children to attend school as examples of unnecessary government intrusion into private life and individual liberties. The 1890 midterm elections were a rout; the Republicans lost nearly eighty seats in the House and with them their majority. And two years later, Frances Folsom Cleveland was proved right when she told the servants at the White House in 1885 to leave the furniture just as it was because "we are coming back just four years from today."

Breckinridge was an early backer of Cleveland's bid to become the first president to serve nonconsecutive terms, and with the Democrats back in power was now a key ally and "close friend of President Cleveland," according to the *Cincinnati Commercial Gazette*. There had been "much gossip connecting his name with a cabinet position under Cleveland." Breckinridge and Cleveland had a natural affinity, as they "shared common traits as sons of ministers, as Presbyterians, and as men with similar views on the nature of mankind," notes the Breckinridge biographer James Klotter. Both revered the tenets of Jeffersonian democracy, believing that government was naturally corrupting and that the strength of the country lay in a hardworking, self-sufficient populace that didn't look to the government to solve its problems. When he vetoed a popular bill to provide government-funded seed to drought-stricken farmers in 1887, Cleveland wrote: "I do not believe that the power and duty of the general government ought to be extended to the relief of individual suffering . . . though the people should support the government, the government should not support the people."

Jeffersonian Democrats like Breckinridge and Cleveland believed in a weak, decentralized government because they viewed a properly functioning society as largely self-ordering. Underpinning this belief was a fundamentally patriarchal, hierarchical worldview in which everyone knew their place and fulfilled their assigned role: employers and laborers, whites and blacks, men and women. Just as Cleveland dismissed a law to reduce sixteen-hour workdays for streetcar conductors as "class legislation," Breckinridge asserted in one of his famous tariff speeches that the labor strikes increasingly plaguing the country weren't a symptom of the need for great protections for working people, but of a "system [that] must be wrong," of a disequilibrium between employers and the "laboring people" that prevented them from being "content." Of course, this worldview also suggested that anyone who stepped outside his or her proper role—such as a woman who left the domestic sphere—deserved society's censure, not its protection.

With the Democrats in control of both the House and the Senate for the first time since the war, Breckinridge was now an acknowledged party leader and was rumored to be in consideration for the speakership. While he declined to challenge Georgia congressman Charles Crisp for the job, one paper noted that it "looks very much as if Congressman Breckinridge . . . will be the real leader on the floor of the house." In addition to demonstrating a "thorough command of parliamentary maneuver," Breckinridge, it said, had "made the best impression on the public of all the Democratic Representatives." There also were rumors he would seek a Senate seat when Senator John Carlisle resigned to join Cleveland's cabinet as treasury secretary. Breckinridge also was more in demand than ever as a speaker. He was selected to deliver the dedication address at the opening of the Chicago World's Fair, the biggest event of the decade, although his appearance was scuttled when controversy arose over the fact that he had, as a good Bourbon Democrat, opposed a congressional appropriation for the fair. By March 1893, Breckinridge was boasting that things in Washington were "running very smoothly" with the Democrats in charge, likening the "conservative and business-like" Cleveland administration to one of the "best regulated families."

Then, on May 3, "Industrial Black Friday," the stock market crashed. There had been rumblings all winter that the economy was in trouble. Many of the railroads·had overexpanded in a fit of competitive euphoria and were heavily leveraged; crop prices had plummeted; exports were declining; and the banking system, lacking a central bank, was struggling to absorb the shocks as credit tightened. After the Philadelphia & Reading Railroad went under, panicked investors rushed to buy gold, which streamed out of the Treasury. The nation's gold reserves dipped dangerously low. The Bourbons blamed the Silver Act because the government notes that were used to buy silver could be redeemed for either silver or gold. They also were philosophically opposed to silver because it inflated the value of the dollar, putting more money in circulation, which tended to help farmers and other small businessmen who were often strapped for capital. They considered gold-backed currency "honest money," but it also helped keep the money supply constricted and interest rates high, which favored eastern financial interests. Cleveland staked his presidency on his belief that the answer to the financial crisis was the repeal of the Silver Act, which is why Congress had been called back to Washington in August 1893. Breckinridge was supposed to put his oratorical firepower behind the repeal with a speech in Congress on August 22, a little more than a week after Madeline filed her suit. It should have been another star turn for the "silver-tongued" orator. For two days people packed the galleries waiting for him to appear, but to no avail. Breckinridge had ducked out of the city and gone to his daughter Ella's home in Staunton, Virginia, to avoid the curious crowds. "There is one distinguished member of the House of Representatives whose mind just now is occupied with other thoughts than the ratio of gold and silver. There are some double standards even more difficult to maintain at parity," the Republican *Philadelphia Times* said with glee.

Breckinridge couldn't stay away for long. On August 28, he returned to Washington to help pass the repeal of the Silver Act. With the repeal bill off to the Senate, a late-summer hush settled on the capital. Undoubtedly Breckinridge thought interest in the scandal would die down. Friends wrote him letters assuring him of vindication and of their "undiminished confidence" in him and his "spotless honor." A lawyer he consulted advised him to enter a brief formal plea and predicted Breckinridge "would not be further annoyed about the matter for a year; possibly longer; possibly never."

Then a bombshell dropped. On September 2, the *Cincinnati Enquirer* published excerpts from a letter that Julia Blackburn had sent to Gen. Basil Duke the day after his remarks about Pollard were published. She told him that if he knew the facts of the case, he wouldn't be so quick to defend Breckinridge. She said that Breckinridge not only had "told her of his engagement with Miss Pollard," but had "placed Madeline under her chaperonage, and had specially requested Mrs. Blackburn's kindest consideration for Miss Pollard on the grounds that she would soon be Mrs. Breckinridge." As a result, Blackburn "permitted Miss Pollard to share all the social recognition she herself received" and was "indignant beyond expression" when she found out the true nature of their relationship. She was so indignant, said the *Enquirer*, that despite her "womanly modesty," she would "not hesitate to respond to a summons for her presence in court."

Breckinridge had made a powerful enemy. Along with the Clays and the Breckinridges, the Blackburns were one of the most consequential families of the Bluegrass. Julia Blackburn had met Madeline in 1890 when she boarded with a Mrs. Fillette, whom Julia's sister Emily Zane had met in Europe. A fast friendship developed between the widowed Blackburn and the young woman from her home state. Julia's only child, a daughter, had died in infancy, and it's possible she saw herself as something of a surrogate mother to Madeline, whom she was concerned for as an "unprotected" girl—meaning she had no male relatives to look after her interests. She also knew Madeline's aunt Mary Stout, the Bridgeport aunt who had taken in Mrs. Pollard and Madeline's sister Mary after J.D. Pollard died.

There, too, was a bit of a sacred connection between Julia and Madeline. Julia's late husband, Dr. Luke Blackburn, had been a public health pioneer, one of the first to recognize the importance of quarantine and basic sanitary procedures in fighting the epidemics of cholera and yellow fever that periodically ravaged the South. When "yellow jack," as yellow fever was called, broke out in the Mississippi River port city of Hickman, Kentucky, in 1878 during a massive epidemic, he rushed to Hickman to try to halt it before it spread inland. Blackburn put out a call for volunteers to assist him. Madeline's oldest brother, Edward, who was nineteen at the time and a trained telegraph operator, volunteered, along with three doctors, several nurses, and a pharmacist. Edward filled in for the local telegraph operator who had died, and was for days the town's only link to the outside world before he, too, succumbed to yellow jack. "He sat with his hand on the key and worked until unconsciousness came," Madeline told Julia, and "when death was very near, he went from his bed to the instrument and sent a message for another operator to come." It was Luke Blackburn himself who closed Edward's eyes and who "brought what was left of his last words" to the Pollard family, said Madeline.

Ultimately the epidemic was halted, although most of the volunteers perished. The incident was a turning point in Blackburn's career, which had been marred by ultimately unproven but circumstantially damning charges that he had plotted to infect northern cities with yellow fever during the war by shipping trunks of infected clothing and blankets across the Mason-Dixon Line. The "Hero of Hickman," as he was known thereafter, received a diamond-studded medal and a gold-headed cane from the grateful citizenry and cruised to election as governor.

It didn't take long after their introduction for Madeline to become a regular visitor at Julia's flat in the fashionable Portland, the city's first luxury apartment building, where she lived with her widowed sister, Emily. Julia enjoyed the company of the bright young woman who called her "the Duchess." Madeline read to her and told Julia about the Sunday school she ran at the local penitentiary—Julia was well known herself for having organized such classes at the Kentucky penitentiary when her husband was governor and made reforms at the infamous "Black Hole of Calcutta," a filthy, overcrowded prison with open sewers, unheated cellblocks, and rampant vermin.

In January 1893, Julia paid Madeline the ultimate compliment by inviting her to be a co-hostess at an afternoon tea that she and Emily were holding, one in a daily round of receptions that occupied much of the time of both official and unofficial Washington. Such receptions were inevitably packed and surprisingly democratic affairs, with congressmen rubbing shoulders with visiting dignitaries and the latest literary sensation, and someone's cousin in from Cincinnati chockablock with a legendary Civil War general. One congressman's daughter, visiting from Indiana, remembered for the rest of her life meeting General Sherman at a reception, with his "keen, penetrating eyes—kind eyes, but with grains of gunpowder lurking in them."

On that day in January, Madeline stood with Julia and Emily and the other hostesses in the receiving line and then poured coffee and tea for guests, an honor reserved for unmarried young women who needed to show off their hosting skills. As with all such occasions featuring prominent society ladies like Julia, the event was meticulously detailed in the society columns of the Washington papers, including the names of the sixty-five guests and the "toilettes" of the hostesses: "Mrs. Zane received in a gown of shrimp pink bengaline and flowered brocade," while Mrs. Blackburn wore "black satin flowered in pink." For Madeline, seeing her name in the society columns of the *Washington Post* and the *Evening Star* alongside those of the Blackburns and Lees and Breckinridges—Willie's brother Gen. Joseph Cabell Breckinridge was a guest—signaled that her climb from poverty and obscurity into the inner circle of the southern aristocracy was complete.

Now her friendship with Julia was proving critical. Julia's condemnation of Duke's remarks relit interest in the scandal and gave new gravitas to Madeline's charges. If it weren't for "those utterances of Mrs. Blackburn the problem would be much more easily handled," Breckinridge's law partner John Shelby wrote to him gloomily from Lexington. Stuck in Washington dealing with legislative matters, Breckinridge had outsourced much of the scandal management and preparation of his defense to an ad hoc team that included Shelby; his son Desha; former congressman Phil Thompson, who was a close friend and lawyer; Charles Stoll, who, despite being the only Republican in the bunch, was a longtime friend; and Maj. William "Sam" McChesney, a local political operative who was his late wife's uncle and served as a fixer of sorts for Breckinridge.

In 1888, McChesney had warned Breckinridge that "a scandalous report . . . calculated to do you great injury" was being circulated. Supposedly Senator Joe Blackburn told someone that a couple of years ago, a young Kentucky woman from a "good family" came to Washington and pestered him to help get her a government job. He told her to see Breckinridge, as he was her congressman and as a matter of courtesy had first dibs on such appointments. She refused, and when he asked why, she burst into tears and said that she already had seen Breckinridge and he had offered to get her a position "upon certain conditions; and these conditions were that she should submit to [his] desires."

As a result of McChesney's warning, Breckinridge was able to run damage control. He got Blackburn to send a letter to one of the men who was repeating the story that, while not exactly denying it, at least denied that he had ever talked to the man who was repeating it, and saying the story was "not true in many essential particulars." The other senator from Kentucky, James Beck, who happened to be the former law partner of Breckinridge's cousin John Cabell Breckinridge, also came to Breckinridge's defense. He said that Blackburn told him the young woman said that Breckinridge "had not treated her well (or properly)," but he thought that Blackburn "may have in a joking way intimated that Col. B. had said something improper to her." Having passed the whole thing off as a joke, Beck assured one of the men who had heard the rumor that Colonel Breckinridge was a "man of honor, morality, [and] integrity" and that "no man has a higher standing in Washington." With the elite men of Breckinridge's circle closing rank, the story that Breckinridge was trading political patronage for sexual favors was snuffed out.

Now, McChesney was again helping Breckinridge manage another scandal. "It seems that the publication in reference to Mrs. Blackburn has done you more harm than all the rest, and something should be done at once to counteract its effect," he warned Breckinridge. For men like McChesney, counteracting unfavorable stories usually involved reaching out to other influential men and friendly reporters. Shortly after, a correspondent from the *Kentucky Leader* reported that he had learned "on the best of authority that the letter to General Duke from Mrs. Luke P. Blackburn . . . was never written," even as Breckinridge and his team fumed in private about how the letter—which Shelby had seen— got leaked.

Breckinridge's team also previewed his defense to the *Leader* and the *Courier-Journal*. Breckinridge would "deny absolutely every one of" Pollard's charges and "his denials will be supported by the strongest sort of proof that he was never engaged to Miss Pollard," who would be shown to be "utterly depraved where morality is concerned." Breckinridge would take the stand in his defense and "vigorously deny that he is the father of Miss Pollard's children."

It was this charge, that he had fathered children—whose fate was unknown—with Pollard that "has touched womankind so that they have rallied to Miss Pollard's support," reported the *Leader*. The abandonment or murder of unwanted, often illicit children either at birth or shortly thereafter was rarely discussed, but haunted Victorian society. In Philadelphia alone in the nineteenth century, "thousands of dead newborns were found in alleys, ash heaps, privies, rivers and so on"—tiny ghosts of women's shame. In 1868, the *New York Times* railed against the "horrible crime of infanticide" that prevailed in the "great cities" after a young servant named Hester Vaughn, who was convicted of crushing her newborn's skull, became a cause célèbre among suffragists concerned about the rampant sexual predation of young women on their own in the cities. The *Albany Law Journal* reported in 1876 that the "laws of infanticide must be a dead letter in the District of Columbia" because, according to local officials, "hundreds" of "dead bodies of infants, still-born and murdered . . . have been found during the past year, scattered over parks and vacant lots."

Some of these abandoned, or aborted, or smothered, or strangled infants were the unwanted children of married women, a crude form of birth control, but many were, as Susan B. Anthony asserted in 1876, the castoffs of "seduced deserted unfortunates, who can no longer hide the terrible secret of their lives." It was concern—and a certain prurient curiosity—about what happened to Madeline's baseborn children that drove much of the female interest in the story.

Breckinridge's team gave another, more hard-nosed version of the defense to C. E. Sares, a reporter from the *New York World*, the widely popular and sensational tabloid, who had come to Breckinridge's Lexington law office looking for a scoop. According to the *World*, the "chief effort of the defense will be to prove that Miss Pollard was unchaste . . . before Col. Breckinridge formed her acquaintance" and that "she had been discovered in compromising relations with two or three young men before she left for school." They would also show that Pollard was "a mature woman and not a giddy young school-girl when he met her on the train." In other words, Breckinridge hadn't ruined an innocent girl; Madeline Pollard was already "ruined" when Breckinridge met her.

Even just a few years earlier, the story might have ended there, with the assertions that Madeline was unchaste releasing Breckinridge from culpability. It was hard to push back on such an entrenched narrative. The newspapers already were squeamish about publishing the details of the affair and rarely interviewed women about such matters, which meant the overwhelming majority of voices weighing in were men's. Luckily for Madeline, however, upstart media outlets were reshaping the landscape of what stories, and voices, the public heard, as tabloids like the *World* pushed aside old strictures about propriety in search of audiences eager for sensational news.

On September 17, the six hundred thousand readers of the *World's* popular Sunday edition opened their papers to find the multipage, self-penned story of Madeline's life. She wrote it sitting at a desk in her room at the boardinghouse, as a reporter watched as her hands "glided to and fro over the paper with wonderful rapidity." Madeline said she decided to take her story directly to the public, sensing that if the allegations made against her were allowed to stand "in the weary interval which must elapse before the case can be tried in court," she would have no chance to prevail. "It is because I am determined in the few ways left open to me to redeem my life that I feel an irresistible impulse to tell the story of my life," she wrote, noting the "atmosphere of falsehood and deception in which I have been forced to live for nine years by my infatuated devotion to Col. Breckinridge."

Madeline denied that she was the desperate orphan of a lowly saddler, telling the story of her happy childhood as the daughter of a respected local merchant who was both a Mason and an Odd Fellow. She told of how she "very much wanted to study for a degree for music or a literary course" and how she met Rhodes and came to an agreement to borrow money for school, and said, "Though my wish to pay back the money was as strong as his wish that I should marry him, we both perfectly understood each other." She denied that she had been sexually intimate with Rhodes or any man other than Breckinridge. "With this man alone have I ever been guilty of a single impure thought or act," she wrote. "The miserable reward of my fidelity is a sermon in itself to show how low the highest devotion the human soul is capable of may fall."

Madeline acknowledged that she had "claimed to be engaged in literary work when I was not . . . for I disarmed suspicion and curiosity with whatever weapon was necessary." She denied, however, that she had three sets of calling cards or misrepresented herself to Julia Blackburn or anyone else. She said that more than five years ago, "Mr. Breckinridge and I decided that I should take his name for my middle name, drop Valeria and say my father admired John C. [Breckinridge] and had me christened Breckinridge . . . Tiffany and Brentano made my cards, and they have records of the plates."

Most important, she upended the traditional narrative of the predatory fallen woman by asserting that she and Breckinridge had a long-term, companionate relationship. "Mr. Breckinridge knew each day the events of my life," she said; they were in constant contact, and her life was "full of work with him": "I read books, papers, magazines, speeches and whatever he was interested in, with him and for him, and we discussed together whatever plans he had and he always gave me the rough draft of his speeches and proof of paper or magazine articles. I undertook anything he wished me to, and found my greatest pleasure in doing intellectual work for him. I always sat in the gallery to hear his speeches on the floor, and signed to him if his voice was too weak or if his attention waned. He never made a speech that there was not a message direct to me in it."

Madeline also appended her original statement to her lawyers, filling in the details of her life and giving readers a firsthand account of how a powerful, older man seduced a young woman and held her in his thrall for nearly a decade. She told of meeting Breckinridge on the train and of the carriage ride in which Breckinridge had attempted to take liberties. She told how she had agreed to meet Breckinridge the following morning at the Cincinnati public library because he had yet to give her any concrete advice about her situation with Rhodes and because "he had succeeded in fascinating me so that I believed his assurances that I had nothing to fear from him." Once there, he told her "he could not talk with me there, because the rules prohibited conversation, and suggested that I go with him in the [street]cars to the house of a friend" who lived on George Street. When they arrived, they sat in the front parlor talking until a woman came in and announced that "the upstairs room was ready." Breckinridge asked her to go upstairs "pretending that it was for the purpose of talking over my matter." Madeline said she "had not the faintest comprehension of the character of the house to which he had taken me, but I steadily refused to go with him." She said Breckinridge then left the room, "locking the door after him." He returned with the woman, who "endeavored to persuade me to go to the upper room with Col. Breckinridge, but still I refused, and after being detained there for a long time he took me away, doing and saying everything in his power to re-establish his fascination and control over me."

She said Breckinridge persuaded her to leave Wesleyan and go to the Sayre Institute in Lexington, "stating that the school was as good as the one in Cincinnati, and that I would then be near, where he could advise me and keep me out of any difficulty with Mr. Rhodes until my education was finished, when he would assist me to procure a situation as a teacher." Pollard said Breckinridge sent a false telegram to her at Wesleyan summoning her home to Frankfort, and "that afternoon I left on the train with him." They arrived in Lexington on Saturday evening. They took a streetcar to a cottage on Short Street where Breckinridge said a friend lived, and he "suggested that it was better I should stay there than at a hotel because I was a girl alone." Madeline said a "mulatto woman came and opened the door and let us in." Breckinridge then "resumed his course of conduct towards me, and being controlled by his fascination and now overcome with his persistence, he accomplished my seduction and ruin."

She told how Breckinridge kept her at the house until Monday, leaving to go to his home, which was three blocks away, and coming back in the evening. On Monday morning he learned that Rhodes had been at his Lexington office inquiring about Madeline because Rhodes had gone to visit her at Wesleyan and found that she wasn't there and that Breckinridge had been to see her. Breckinridge then hustled her onto a train back to Cincinnati, where he visited her and again took her to the house on George Street, until "as a result of this course of conduct by him I became pregnant." Madeline said she returned to Lexington in late August and enrolled at the Sayre Institute. She lived in a boardinghouse run by two respectable women for six months, "doing what I could to conceal my condition." In mid-February 1885, at Breckinridge's direction, she went to Cincinnati to "secure a room in some secluded place." Madeline took a room "over a mattress store and opposite a livery stable," with Breckinridge paying her expenses, and took her meals "at the Vienna Bakery." On April 1, she went to the Norwood Foundling Asylum, which was run by the "Black Cap" Sisters of Charity, an order of Catholic nuns, and she "remained there in a private room, with my face veiled" under the name of Louise Wilson. On May 29, when Madeline was "exactly eighteen years and six months of age, a female child, begotten by Col. Breckinridge . . . was born to me."

Madeline said that she wanted to keep the baby and go away somewhere where no one knew her, but that Breckinridge "begged in every way that I should not leave him, and promised me most solemnly that if I would not do so and would leave the child at the asylum, and if he were ever free to do so, he would marry me and give me his protection and his name and in some proper way care for his offspring." She complied and returned to Lexington in August 1885 and reentered Sayre. For the next two years, "Col. Breckinridge wrote me passionate love letters" and "he having completely won my love . . . I was faithful and obedient to him in all things."

When she became pregnant for a second time in 1887, she came to Washington "by his invitation" and gave birth to a second child in February 1888 at the home of a midwife, which she again gave up, and "he renewed his promise, so many times made, that if he were ever free to do so, he would marry me." Madeline said her "only explanation for maintaining for eight years my guilty relations with Col. Breckinridge was our mutual devotion." She said she had "several times wished to leave him, not because I had ceased to love him, but because I wished to end a life of deception, but he always overcame my desire by his protestations of affection and his begging me not to leave him."

Madeline's account in the *World* was a compelling story and unlike anything that had been written by a disgraced woman for public consumption. Taking her story directly to the public was a stroke of genius that leveraged a growing popular press willing to print sensational material and humanized the trope of the "fallen" woman. Madeline's tale was an instant media sensation and reprinted in papers around the country. At the same time, the impenetrable facade around Breckinridge cracked a bit, as stories about his rumored past exploits with women began to seep out. "I have been told many things about Colonel Breckinridge which I have never heard before," said one astonished member of the Cleveland administration who had known Breckinridge for eight years.

A week later, Madeline entered the House of Mercy, a home for fallen women run by Episcopalian nuns, saying she planned to devote herself to a life of charity work. "My purpose in entering the institute was to compose and discipline myself and to devote myself for the remainder of my days to the work of educating and uplifting fallen women," she told a reporter from the *Post*, who found her a woman of an "intense nature," refined manners, and "brilliant" conversation. "It is the quality of her mind that first impresses one who meets her," he wrote, noting how impressed he was with her sincerity in committing to help other disgraced women—as well as how comely she looked in the "well-fitting but severely plain dress of dark blue serge" that appeared to be the dress of the house.

Entering the House of Mercy also allowed Madeline to reframe the purpose of the suit, which had been widely reported as revenge for Breckinridge's discarding of her for Wing. "Revenge!" she scoffed. "Not at all. I have no such feeling. I thought it unjust that I should bear all the burden alone." The suit, then, wasn't about a ruined woman looking to even the score. It was about challenging the double standard that created ruined women in the first place.

7

What Shall We Do with Our Daughters?

On the September day that Madeline Pollard entered the House of Mercy, Jennie Tucker still hadn't even heard of the institution and didn't know that she would play a role in the infamous Breckinridge-Pollard scandal. She was in Chicago, attending the World's Columbian Exposition, where she surely would have visited the Maine State Building, a great granite octagon full of "relics and historic treasures," and perhaps the Kentucky State Building, "a southern colonial mansion," with "cool parlors and verandas." She would have strolled the Midway, six hundred feet wide and sprawling over eighty acres, with its exhibits of cultures from around the world—a Javanese village up against a replica of a Donegal castle, a feudal German landscape giving way to the streets of "Old Cairo," with its mosque and camel drivers and "Little Egypt" doing her belly dance as scandalized mothers hurried their children past. She would have most certainly ridden the Ferris wheel, "260 feet above terra-firma," and thrilled at the mechanical and scientific exhibits: the giant Yerkes telescope, the intramural railway with its trains gliding above the crowds, and the "caged lightning," as the journalist Marian Shaw called it, of the first large-scale electricity exhibit, as the fairgrounds lit up at night with "8,000 arc and 130,000 incandescent lamps."

Jennie had to borrow the money to attend the World's Fair from her mother, since she had lost her job with Stoll the previous spring, but she couldn't pass up the opportunity to visit the biggest attraction of the era.

It seemed like everyone was going to the fair, and that wasn't far from the truth—some twenty-seven million people attended the World's Fair between May 1 and October 30, 1893. "I am very glad I did go," she wrote to her father, "for I have seen so little of the world that it was a great treat and an education in a way." By October she was back to reality, back to her old employer in Boston, the West End Street Railway, and back to counting pennies. "It has been hard to get along until pay day," she wrote to her mother as she gloomily repaired yet another torn hem on a dress that had seen better days.

It hadn't always been that way for the Tucker family. Jennie had been born into the mercantile elite of Maine. Her family made a fortune in the shipping business founded by her grandfather, conveying bales of cotton from the South to New England and Liverpool on a fleet of four-masted schooners in the years before the Civil War, one of many northern families that prospered from the labor of enslaved African Americans. Jennie's father, Richard Tucker, followed his father into the business, first captaining the *Othello* on its transatlantic runs and then working as an agent for the Tucker family vessels out of Charleston, South Carolina. In 1857, Captain Tucker married sixteen-year-old Mary Geraldine Armstrong and the following year returned home to Wiscasset, Maine, and purchased a federal-style brick mansion on a bluff overlooking the Sheepscot River and set about remaking it in high Victorian fashion. He added a dramatic three-story glass-enclosed piazza to the front and a large two-story addition to the back and painted the whole house, including the two turrets that flanked the piazza, a creamy white, which gave the house the effect of a bonsaied Italianate castle, earning it the moniker Castle Tucker. Tucker bought furniture and carpets and art, and a full-size billiards table, from the best stores in Boston, shipped them up the coast, and had everything hauled up Windmill Hill in wagons to what was now a thirty-three-room mansion.

Jennie was the fifth of five children born in the house. She was a tomboy, all boldness and confidence. She loved to skate and sled in the Maine winters and swim and sail in the summer. She adored horseback riding and was keen to shoot anything the boys were shooting, from bows and arrows to revolvers. She was also a daredevil, climbing trees with abandon. "I used to climb to the topmost branches, and swing there, to the horror of my girl friends but the envy of my boy friends," she remembered. Her schooling was erratic; she missed a whole year when she was twelve because she was "sick." When she was thirteen, she was sent away for a year to the Moses Brown School, a boarding school in Providence, Rhode Island, that she called the "Quaker jail" because the food was bad, the girls were mean, and she was stuck inside all the time.

From 1880 to 1882, the family lived in Boston to avoid a tax that had been levied in Wiscasset, and Jennie attended public school. It was then that many of the seeds of contention that troubled the family sprouted. The cotton trade and the Tucker shipping business never recovered from the Panic of 1857 and the Civil War. Jennie's father had invested in a number of "high-maintenance, high cost, and low- or no-return enterprises," from a pilot boat business, to a gold mine, to a new propulsion system for ships that never came to fruition. He traveled frequently to attend to his floundering businesses: Halifax for two weeks here, Europe for a few weeks there. His young wife, Mary, was left at home to care for the children and try to make ends meet. The marriage frayed, and the pressures seem to have gotten the best of Mary, who had seen her own family go bankrupt; she was committed for a time to the McLean Asylum for the Insane.

Around that time, in 1882, Jennie was sent away to school again, this time to St. Joseph's Academy in Emmitsburg, Maryland, which her mother had attended when it was a popular seminary for well-off girls before the Civil War. It would be Jennie's last experience as a privileged, carefree Victorian girl. She studied rhetoric and composition, math, mythology, philosophy, French, music, and fancy needlework, which was her best class. Right before Christmas in 1883, blissfully unaware of the family's deteriorating financial state, she wrote to her father, "I am very much anxious for a watch of some kind. I should like to have a gold one, but if I can't have that, one of the silver chatelaine watches would be very acceptable."

By 1884, Jennie and her parents were back at home in Wiscasset. Her brothers as well as her two older sisters had already left home to fend for themselves—Maude as an actress and Patty as a journalist. "The old folks have numerous fights & each have disagreeable spells," she wrote to Maude. "I don't think I can stand them another winter."

She filled her days with housework and pursuits typical for an unmarried daughter of a well-off family: she painted china and did embroidery. Jennie spent part of 1886 visiting her sister Patty, who was a well-known columnist for a Denver paper. She took vocal lessons at the Denver Conservatory of Music, joined a reading club, and went to balls—and her dance card usually was full. By the time she returned home, however, reality was catching up with Jennie. She was nearly twenty and had no marriage prospects; her parents, like many in the shaky postwar economic climate, couldn't afford to support her indefinitely. She wasn't alone. All across the country, marriage patterns were changing. Both men and women were getting married later; for women the mean age of marriage was twenty-three, up from twenty in earlier times. In New England, women weren't getting married until twenty-five on average. And more women weren't getting married at all. By 1880, nearly a third of the women living in New England and the mid-Atlantic area hadn't gotten married by their thirtieth birthday.

There were several reasons young women weren't getting married. Both young women and young men were in less of a rush to get married. New forms of entertainment and recreation in cities—amusement parks and dance halls and theaters—and new ways to get there, like streetcars, made young adulthood a time for fun and exploration. As one writer explained in *The Nation*: "Married life has lost in some measure its advantage over single life." Young adults also became pickier about their marriage partners. Increasingly, marriage was based on compatibility and romance, not economic need. Even for women who wanted to get married, marriage was becoming more elusive, especially on the overcrowded East Coast, as more and more men set out to seek their fortune in the West and left behind them a trail of would-be wives. The *New York Times* created a panic about a generation of spinsters when in 1868 it estimated that there were 250,000 "surplus" women on the East Coast. In 1881, the *Washington Post* noted "the popular belief regarding the number of superfluous women" even though the U.S. census showed an excess of one million men—just not where the single women were. The following year, an essayist in the *North American Review* suggested that "if women do not marry, and cannot find work, the question must arise whether the Chinese practice of laying a wet cloth on a new-born female child must be legalized." In 1883, the suffragist Lillie Devereux

Blake told a congressional committee what the numbers made obvious: that marriage was "no longer a career for women, nor a means of support for them."

Increasingly, society fretted about what to do with these "surplus" women. Some male authorities said the problem was too much education and not enough focus on domestic skills. "Girls are being prepared daily, by 'superior education' to engage, not in childbearing and housework, but in clerkships, telegraphy, newspaper-writing, school-teaching etc.," complained Nathan Allen in the *Journal of Psychological Medicine*. In 1883, the suffragist and social reformer Mary Livermore addressed the subject of "superfluous" women in her popular and widely reprinted lecture "What Shall We Do with Our Daughters?" She rejected the idea that unmarried women were somehow extra or useless. "Who are the women whom the social scientists insult with the adjective 'superfluous,' at whom misogynists sneer as 'old maids,' and whom sociologists brand as 'social failures'?" she asked. "A glance at them reveals the fact, that in many instances they are the most useful women in society," she said. What single women needed, said Livermore, was not less education, but more, as well as "fair remuneration" for their work and an opportunity to enter the "higher fields of labor"—the professions like law and medicine jealously guarded by men.

Jennie unwittingly found herself at the cutting edge of the debate about "surplus" women. Her family could no longer support her. By 1888, out of money and other options, her mother had begun quietly taking summer boarders, a haunting reminder of her own family's downfall, when her mother ended up running a boardinghouse to make ends meet after her father's death. With no jobs available near home, Jennie did what young women around the country were doing: she made her way alone to the city to work, something that would have been unimaginable for a woman of her social status just a decade earlier. She worked for a time at R. H. Stearns, the best department store in Boston, doing fancy embroidery. Then she returned home and gave lessons in needlework and took custom embroidery orders. The continued encroachment of factories was making the needle trades less profitable than ever, so she turned toward what was about to become the biggest advance in employment opportunities for women in the nineteenth century: office work.

Traditionally, offices had employed male clerks who worked mainly as copyists, laboriously writing out in longhand copies of letters that their bosses had scribbled out in draft. The dual introductions of stenography and typewriters revolutionized office work right as the industrial boom created an explosion in the number and kinds of businesses that needed clerical help. "Five years ago the typewriter was simply a mechanical curiosity," noted *Penman's Art Journal* in 1887. "Today its monotonous click can be heard in almost every well regulated business establishment in the country." Who better to fill the suddenly insatiable demand for office workers than the thousands upon thousands of educated "surplus" women? They could be had cheaper than men and, unlike male clerks, there was no expectation that they were looking to move up in the business. The *National Stenographer* reported the existence of exactly "six women shorthand writers" in Manhattan and Brooklyn in 1874. By the early 1890s, there were more than five thousand. "In every large down-town building in New York there are now employed dozens, and in some cases, hundreds of women," effused the 1890 catalog for the Albany Business College, one of the many secretarial schools that had sprung up to train office workers for jobs that paid upward of five dollars an hour, making office work by far the best-paying job available to most women.

Employing women in public spaces, however, ran up against long-standing prohibitions against respectable women mingling with strange men. In 1854, the U.S. Patent Office hired three women copyists, including thirty-three-year-old Clara Barton, and put them to work in its Washington office until Interior Secretary Robert McClelland ended the practice the following year. "I have no objection to the employment of the females by the Patent Office . . . in the performance of such duties as they are competent to discharge, and which may be executed by them at their private residences," he said, "but there is such an obvious impropriety in the mixing of the sexes within the walls of a public office, that I am determined to arrest the practice."

When Dr. Isabel Barrows became the first woman to take shorthand for congressional committees in the early 1870s (to supplement her practice as the country's first woman ophthalmologist), her boss told her to sign her vouchers "I.B." so that no one would know there was a woman working on Capitol Hill. That worked fine until the day she was told to report to the sergeant at arms to take the oath of allegiance to the United States. When "the gentleman whose initials are I.B." was called, there were "surprised whispers and a few loud guffaws" as Isabel stepped forward. The sergeant at arms "paled a bit" but plowed forward. "I.B., will you raise your right hand," he said. Isabel did and was duly sworn in "as a roar of laughter rose to the dome of the Capitol."

A few years later, when another pioneering stenographer named Nettie White became the first woman to take shorthand for the Committee on Military Affairs, she brought along a friend "to accompany her to keep her as well as the 'Members' in countenance," quite aware of the danger to her reputation of going alone into a room full of men. The inference was that any woman who would mingle with strange men must be sexually available—or might become so for the right inducement.

Indeed in 1864, only three years after the U.S. government again began employing women in offices because of the shortage of male clerks during the Civil War, the "Treasury courtesan" scandal rocked Washington when female clerks in the Treasury Department complained of widespread sexual harassment by their supervisors. A special congressional committee was formed to investigate the charges. One man testified that his sixteen-year-old daughter had been forced to work by her supervisor Mr. Gray until ten o'clock at night six nights in a row and said that he propositioned her, telling his daughter "if she would go with him (Gray) to a certain hotel in this city and submit to his (Gray's) wishes, he (Gray) would raise her salary to $75 per month." Jennie Germon, who worked for the National Currency Bureau, testified that her supervisor "came to me in the office and asked me to come to his private residence," which she did the following Saturday night, and they "went to a private bedroom, and both occupied the same bed until morning."

The discomfort caused by employing women in public offices had to do with the difficulty people now faced in distinguishing between "good" and "bad" women, notes the historian Cindy Sondik Aron, as "all female clerks (innocent or guilty) now behaved in ways that would previously have been defined as improper: they approached and asked favors of strange men, [and] they conversed and formed friendships with men to whom they had not been properly introduced." For a time when women first entered the workforce and public spaces, attempts were made to keep them separate from men, with segregated offices and special ladies-only tearooms, waiting rooms in train stations, and reception rooms in hotels. But the sheer need for office workers and the logistical difficulties of segregating women eventually overcame the reluctance to place women in the same physical spaces as men. When the revolution finally came, noted one historian of clerical work, it came "rather quietly, on high-buttoned shoes." In 1870, fewer than 5 percent of stenographers and typists were women; by 1880, 40 percent were, and by 1890, nearly 65 percent of all office workers were women.

It was in 1890 that Jennie did what thousands of other women were doing—she enrolled in secretarial school: Hickox's School of Shorthand and Typewriting in Boston. By the spring of 1891, she had graduated and was excited to take her first job, in the office of a shoe factory paying ten dollars per week. But instead of using the shorthand she had so laboriously perfected, Jennie found herself copying page after page of tiny numbers in longhand, a task that bothered her eyes and one that she apparently fumbled, because the job didn't last.

Next, she got a job at the West End Street Railway, where she more than got to use her shorthand. West End operated the electric street-cars that were transforming cities like Boston, creating an affordable urban public transportation system and giving rise to a new nether land of neither city nor country called a suburb. Streetcars were fast and efficient—a little too much so. Nearly every week the speeding street-level cars were involved in an accident with a hapless pedestrian or horse-drawn vehicle. Jennie's job was to take the shorthand reports of the accident testimony. It was grueling work, ten hours a day, six days a week; one day she took the testimonies of twenty-five men. This "office is an awfully hard place," she told her mother. She grew weary of not only the pace of the work but also the gory accident reports, although eventually she did develop a sort of gallows humor about it. "I suppose you have noticed in the paper that we've killed another man," she wrote home. "It does make such a lot of work to have a death; if they would only be satisfied to get their legs or arms cut off, it would save me a lot of work. This poor fellow's head was smashed almost flat."

Nonetheless, Jennie loved city life. She had lots of acquaintances in

Boston and rarely lacked for company. She visited friends on her day off, went to the theater every chance she got, acted in a few plays, and frequented the bargain counters of the Boston department stores looking for the latest fashionable update to her wardrobe. She was so busy that her mother complained that she was "going all the time" and accused her daughter of being "morbidly restless and seeking excitement." Jennie did have a restless nature, or maybe she just wanted more than what life offered a ten-dollar-a-week working girl.

In May 1892, she took a new job at the W. A. Boland Company that she hoped would be easier work for the same money. It was short-lived. By the fall, Jennie had decided to try her luck in New York City. She got a room in a respectable boardinghouse after making inquiries at the local Young Women's Christian Association and signed on with an employment agency. Her first job was with a life insurance company. It lasted for exactly one week. "I stood it as long as I could and then I just got out," she told her mother, because "the man I had to work for was a regular fiend." She didn't say exactly what had transpired, only that he was "the ugliest man I ever struck," so it's not hard to imagine what happened.

Just when it seemed like she would never find a job that didn't involve grueling, monotonous work or a lecherous boss, she got the call to work for Charles Stoll. She knew at once the job was different. "I have at last 'found location,'" she wrote home triumphantly. "I am perfectly delighted with my position." Stoll, she said, was "a real southern gentleman" and was "the kindest and nicest man to work for." He treated Jennie as an equal; he actually took her to lunch, which, she said, "seems so nice after the hard times I've had." The pay was more than she had ever made—fifteen dollars per week—and the hours a luxurious 9:30 to 4:30. When Stoll needed her to work late, traveling with him on the L train or the ferry taking shorthand as they went along, "he always makes it up in some kindness or other," she said. She also had real responsibility and autonomy. Stoll traveled frequently, and she handled his mail and attended to whatever she could in his absence. Before long, she was managing the office. Flush with success, Jennie donned her very best dress and sat for a photograph at New York's most fashionable portrait studio and sent it home—proof that she had finally made it.

Unfortunately, Jennie's dream job didn't last much longer than the others did. By March 1893, with the whole country reeling from the financial panic, she wrote home that she was worried about her job. "The money market has been very high and this also effects Mr. Stoll's business," she told her mother. The blows, when they came, came close together. By the end of April, all that she had left of her job was a glowing letter of recommendation from Stoll. At the end of May, she learned her sister Patty had cancer. By October, Jennie was back from the World's Fair and again working for the West End Street Railway. It seemed as if her life had circled back upon itself. "I do hope Patty will get through all right, for it does seem as if she had so much more to live for than you or I," Jennie wrote gloomily to her sister Maude. "Somehow we don't get much fun or happiness out of life and haven't as much of a desire to hang on to life wereas [sic] she has . . . I am sure I don't care a cuss whether I live or die."

By January, even her job at West End was gone and Patty was dead. Jennie was in mourning not just for her sister, but for how her own life had turned out. She was unemployed and in debt. "I hardly know what I want to do," she wrote forlornly to her mother. It's no wonder that when the request came from Stoll, no matter how unconventional the assignment was, it seemed that Jennie had little to lose.

8

For the Likes of Me

Congressman Breckinridge made his first public appearance since the scandal broke when he spoke in Congress on September 28, 1893, in support of a bill to repeal the last vestiges of federal oversight of southern polling places—the Democrats' revenge for the so-called force bill. He appeared confident—unconcerned about the galleries crowded with curious onlookers who pointed when he rose to speak. "Mr. Breckinridge never was heard to better advantage," noted the *Post*. "His tones were never mellower nor more magnetic, his picturesque, highly colored periods rolled out with rhythmic plentitude, crowding one after another, his white locks tossed above flashing blue eyes." But he could not escape the scandal hanging over him. When he dismissed a Republican colleague who opposed the bill, Congressman Henry Johnson shot back, "There are other things the gentleman might like to dismiss; but the people will not dismiss them."

There was mounting evidence that the scandal was beginning to erode Breckinridge's political support. One Frankfort, Kentucky, paper reported there was "growing opinion that the Congressman is guilty"; the *Frankfort Call* demanded his resignation. There were rumblings from home that several challengers were looking to form political "clubs," which were what the loosely organized campaigns run by supporters were called, to challenge him in the Democratic primary amid reports that he was hamstrung in Congress because of the scandal. "I did not believe the tide would turn so soon," he wrote to his son Desha, even as he assured supporters that he was as influential as ever in what he said was the "most important session to the Democrats that we have ever had since before the war"—their big chance to turn the tide on the Republicans' expansive vision of the federal government.

The Pollard scandal was only the most visible of Breckinridge's woes. Behind the scenes, his family also was in turmoil. In July, just as the situation with Madeline was coming to a head, Breckinridge received word that his twenty-three-year-old son, Robert, had been arrested in Lexington after nearly killing a man in a fight. "Keep Bob locked up until I get there," he cabled to John Shelby and rushed home to deal with his younger son, who had long been the most problematic of his children—Robert's main occupations being drinking and gambling. Breckinridge was constantly paying off his gambling debts. Bob had "no apparent aim in life or desire to do anything," he complained to his daughter Nisba, saying that all he did was "sleep all morning, ride with some girl all afternoon and go somewhere at night." In the fall of 1891, Bob became locally "notorious," according to his father, when he got in a knockdown fight with the son of a well-known Lexington preacher "over the hand of a Blue Grass beauty for a certain dance" at the Governor's Ball, as the *New York Times* reported, noting that the "prominence of the parties . . . makes this the sensation of the hour."

Breckinridge pushed his son to go to work, but by the spring of 1892 he wrote to Nisba that Bob had been "more or less under the influence of liquor since about February" and had "bought poison & was going to kill himself" after he got caught forging checks in his father's name. "We are making a mighty effort to save Robert," he wrote, as he used his connections and a cash inducement to get the captain of the British steamer *Hilston* to take Bob on as an apprentice in hopes a long sea journey would shock him out of his dissolute life. "This is the damnedest mess I ever got into," Bob lamented to his father in a note he sent back by tugboat as the *Hilston* departed for Calcutta. Bob returned home in March 1893, but by July was again in jail for a drunken brawl. Breckinridge again got Bob released and again signed him up to work on a ship—this time an Australian steamer departing from New York in mid-August. Bob read about the Pollard suit in the newspaper the day before his ship left. "Lock father up and keep him until I get there," he telegraphed to Shelby, no doubt with a grin on his face. Days later, he jumped ship in Savannah and disappeared on a freighter headed to New Orleans.

Then there was Breckinridge's new wife, Louise. Just the previous winter she had been thrilled to be on his arm as he escorted her to functions around Washington. Her letters gushed with her delight at finding love so unexpectedly after a long period of widowhood: she told Breckinridge to always refer to her as the "Happiest Woman in Washington." Yet, by September, just six weeks after their wedding, Louise was decidedly unwell. In mid-September, Breckinridge told Desha she had suffered a "right serious attack" and was "still confined to bed." In late September, Breckinridge wrote that Louise was still indisposed. As the fall slipped into winter, it became increasingly apparent that what was ailing his wife wasn't physical. "She does not sleep well, has little or no appetite, and her nervous system is out of gear," Breckinridge wrote to Desha just after the New Year, admitting that he was "a little anxious" about her condition.

It wasn't only Louise whom Breckinridge was worried about. He also was increasingly concerned about Nisba. She was his favorite—the child of his heart. But she also was unwell and had been for some time—physically as well as, it seemed, spiritually. She appeared lost and deeply unhappy, and he didn't know how to help her. "I am somewhat nervous about Nisba," he wrote to Desha, "so much so that I have gotten a little superstitious and for the first time in my life receive a telegram with a slight tremor." Everything that meant anything to Breckinridge was in jeopardy—his career, his reputation, the upward trajectory of the storied family name—but the one thing he couldn't stand to lose was Sophonisba.

•

Sophonisba Preston Breckinridge was born on April Fool's Day 1866, which was also Easter Sunday, an odd mix of the sacred and profane that was appropriate for a woman who would spend a good part of her life traveling between two worlds. She was named after her father's mother, Ann Sophonisba "Sophy" Preston Breckinridge, who, like many women of her era, died in her forties after giving birth to the last of a large brood—in her case, at forty-four, after the birth of her eleventh child. Her name, Sophonisba would later tell friends, meant "keeper of her husband's secrets," but it was her father's secrets that would come to define, and eventually haunt, much of her life.

Nisba always felt like a bit of an outsider in her own family. As a child, she remembered being puzzled as to how someone as "common" as she was could be related to the well-bred southern ladies around her—her mother and her elegant grandmother Mary Curry Desha. By "common" she meant that she "liked all kinds of people and was not particular in my choice of amusements." She remembered "playing with a crowd of boys" in the street outside the family's house or sitting on the curb for hours just watching the world go by—that is, until Grandma Desha led her by the ear back into the house, scolding Nisba for being a "common child." Grandma Desha still held to the antebellum standards of what made a proper lady; she told Nisba that you could "tell a lady by the button holes she made" and said that she "had never known a Breckinridge woman who could make a decent button hole." She attempted to remedy this shortcoming with regular lessons in the "essential domestic arts" for her granddaughter. In her estimation, no girl was really "finished" until she could "sew a complete layette."

Introverted and serious, with a long, somber face, Nisba stood out in a family of quick-witted, sociable southerners; they teased her that she "missed the point of every joke." While she excelled at school, she thought herself "dull," especially in comparison with her older sister, Ella, who was the epitome of southern womanhood—vivacious, charming, and attractive, with a cloud of young men flocking about her. The brightest spot in her childhood was her father. Willie was devoted to the baby girl who was born after he returned from the war. He called her his "peace baby," and having missed his oldest daughter Ella's early years, he threw himself into taking care of Nisba. "I had left Ella to others . . . but this would never be done to you. I put you to sleep; I walked you when you were sick," he reminded her later on.

It wasn't just love that drove Breckinridge to be an exceptionally involved father. Nisba's mother, Issa, was a delicate woman, made more so by repeated childbearing. In the North, women were already using crude contraceptives, abortion, and sexual abstinence to effect a dramatic decline in the number of children they bore in a lifetime—from an average of about eight children in 1800 to just four by 1900. But in the South, especially among the elite, childbearing patterns remained much as they had been, with early marriage and frequent pregnancies. Issa was seventeen when she married Willie in 1861; she gave birth to Ella a year after her wedding. The Civil War gave her a three-year break from childbearing, but after Willie returned home in the spring of 1865, she had five babies in seven years, and a final baby, Curry, in 1875. "There was no doctrine of birth control or spaced child bearing prevalent at that time," recalled Nisba, and the quick succession of children overwhelmed her mother. Issa spent long periods in bed and was a loving but ghostly presence to her children, best remembered as a frail belle playing the piano with a gardenia tucked in her hair.

It was Willie who often got the children up and dressed in the morning. "My father was wonderfully skillful in caring for us," said Nisba, remembering how "patient and kind" he was. He taught Nisba how to tie her shoes, and in a mark of the sensitive, pensive demeanor that would be her hallmark, she recalled being overwhelmed by the thought that she would have to put them on in the morning and take them off at night for the rest of her life. "I seemed overwhelmed with tragedy and wept both loud and long," she said.

From her earliest childhood, Nisba basked in her father's company and approval. Willie often brought Nisba with him to his law office. "I learnt my letters off the backs of my father's law books," she remembered. He made it clear he expected her to excel at school, offering a reward for perfect report cards, which she got. To her, it was simple: "I loved my father and wanted to please him." Nisba posed a conundrum to her father, however. It was clear from an early age that she was the most intellectually gifted of the Breckinridge children—Ella was the social butterfly, Desha the charmer, Robert the troublemaker, and Curry the coddled youngest, who had difficulty learning to read and struggled in school. But Nisba was a girl in a culture with sharply defined roles for women, especially those of the patrician class. Even as middle-class women in the North left their homes to teach for a few years before marriage or join one of the many charitable associations doing good works in the community, white southern women of all but the lowest class remained confined to the domestic sphere, and young women were heavily chaperoned. Nisba and Ella entertained in the parlor with their father sitting watchfully in the corner on a damask-covered rosewood divan—although if there was dancing, he was known to break into the "Highland Fling." When they got older and went to Ashland and other local estates for dances, there was always a servant in attendance. The "coveted and forbidden joys of buggy riding" with young men were not for the Breckinridge girls, remembered Ella in a memoir of her coming-of-age. "We went in our father's carriage, driven by an old-time negro retainer quick to note, reprove, and report any undue friskiness on the part of his cargo."

Nisba, reserved and bookish, had no problems with her father's rules, but the ever-popular Ella and Willie clashed frequently over her testing of the limits of what was allowed for a proper southern girl. "Long before it was time for me to 'come out' I was leaking out," Ella said, and her father packed her off to boarding school. Later, when she was being courted by a young man her father didn't approve of because he was the "son of a rich and indulgent mother" and Willie didn't think he would be able to support a wife, Ella snuck around behind her father's back and met her suitor at a friend's house. When Willie found out, she was promptly married off in a heavy black silk dress, "sleeves up to my wrist, whale boned collar up to my eyes," that her father not only insisted on but personally bought the material for when Ella dithered over obtaining the dress that was de rigueur for proper southern brides—even in June. "I looked a million years old in it," she remembered, "but my father was satisfied that he had made the ceremony legal beyond question." No one would question the respectability of the Breckinridge girls.

Despite the strictures placed on southern girls, politics and public service were in the air Nisba breathed. The ghosts of her relatives paraded through history, from her great-grandfather Breckinridge, who was Thomas Jefferson's confidant, to her grandfather Desha, who was the governor of Kentucky; senators and visiting dignitaries were regulars at the dinner table; and Ashland, the estate of Henry Clay, was "a favorite playground." That her family was known in Washington and beyond was a matter of course. When her father introduced her to Secretary of State James Blaine, she thought it natural that he should say, "She looks somewhat like both the Deshas and the Breckinridges." As children, remembered Ella, it wasn't fairy tales they begged for but "stories of Sam Houston, of Andrew Jackson, of Zachary Taylor, and the battle of Buena Vista; for anecdotes of Harrison, the praying politician, and of the 'Tippecanoe-and-Tyler-too' campaign with its cunning little log cabin emblem . . . One of our favorite stories was the one about Preston Brooks breaking his cane over the head of the seated Charles Sumner."

The family didn't lack for strong female role models. "Grandma Black Cap," John Breckinridge's widow, was a legendary figure in the family. After John died of tuberculosis at age forty-six, leaving his young widow alone in the wilds of Kentucky with a big farm and a big family, she refused to bend to convention and remarry. She donned the black widow's cap she would wear for the next fifty years and ruled over Cabell's Dale with "a sword in one hand and a Bible in the other." Nisba's grandma Desha, her mother's mother, was not only charming and imperious, but also the family's "ready reference bureau," said Ella. She knew everything, from "which art gallery some famous painting hung in" to "which family every flower belonged." A true southern lady, she rarely left her home "but kept in touch with worthwhile, interesting people" and had an "uncanny judgment about the value of new writers." She helped James Lane Allen, considered Kentucky's first important novelist, get his start.

For Nisba, then, the seeds of the conflict that would come to consume her young adult life were laid early, in a family that cherished its role in the shaping of the country and valued strong, intelligent women, but held fast to society's constraints on maintaining women's respectability. The role of Breckinridge women had long been to solidify the family's position through marriage and give birth to the next generation of statesmen. But Nisba was born into a postwar world that already had irrevocably changed by the time she was a young woman. With the ranks of men thinned by the war and the fortunes of many elite southern families decimated, a young woman's neat progression from her father's home to a husband's by her late teens or early twenties could no longer be ensured. Even more than the North, the South was gripped by widespread fear about a generation of spinsters and old maids "hang-[ing] like a locket around the neck of some long-suffering male relative," as Ella put it.

The Breckinridges had experienced the postwar financial vicissi-tudes firsthand. Willie ended up being responsible for his wife's sister Mary, who went by "Mollie," and her mother, Mary—Grandma Desha—when Issa's father, John Randolph Desha, a successful doctor with con-siderable land holdings in Kentucky and Arkansas, went bust during the Panic of 1873, "when a great number of planters from the south experi-enced financial disaster," as Nisba remembered. For a time Mary and Mollie ran a dame school—a private grammar school—out of their home, as did many southern women trying to scrape together a living the only way they could. "If we cannot teach, or make shirts, we must starve," one North Carolina woman complained to a friend in 1871. Eventually, Mary and Mollie were forced to move in with the Breckinridges. Still unmarried by her mid-twenties, Aunt Mollie faced life as the dependent spinster aunt, reliant on Willie's kindness for everything from the roof over her head to the clothes she wore. Mollie, however, was an energetic woman, remembered Ella, and even though "it was humiliating for a lady to admit she needed money," never mind "go out and try to make it," Mol-lie got a job as a teacher in the Lexington public schools. "It is impossi-ble . . . to realize the storm of criticism this simple act provoked," said Ella, "but apologetically and timidly first one young woman and then another followed her example and found the joy of having a little money and consequently a little independence."

Money, or the lack thereof, was the constant worry thrumming be-neath the Breckinridges' lives. "We were very poor," Nisba later wrote of her childhood. Ella remembered that their "dresses were like the annals of the poor—few and simple." In addition to supporting his wife's family and the children "coming in swift succession," Willie had to foot the bill for what Nisba remembered as "long visits from very many relatives." Among the impoverished relations who showed up on the Breckinridges' doorstep was former Confederate general John Cabell Breckinridge and his family, who lived with his cousin after he returned from exile in Canada. Both Nisba and Ella remember their house overflowing with aunts and uncles and hobbledehoy cousins. One freckle-faced cousin of an especially peripatetic family put his foot down and refused to pack when it was time to leave. "We will be coming back pretty soon, so I think I'll just stay," he said, and "stay he did for years," Ella recalled.

The reality that Willie Breckinridge understood all too well was that, ready or not, young women like Nisba were being thrown headfirst into a new world in which they might well be required to take care of themselves. "You ought to look squarely in the face that if I die, you will have to make your own living," Willie warned Nisba when she was eighteen, adding, "If I live you may have to do so anyway."

Recognizing Nisba's potential, Willie had worked, he said, to give her "brain a fair chance to show its power." When Nisba was fourteen, he used his position as the attorney for the Agricultural and Mechanical College of Kentucky (later the University of Kentucky) to get the school's charter changed to allow the admission of women and sent Nisba off to college. (Younger freshmen weren't uncommon at the time, as many students didn't go to high school and college admission requirements hadn't been standardized.)

At Kentucky A&M, Nisba encountered professors who didn't think women should be there and a less-than-exciting curriculum. She also wasn't allowed to receive a degree, just a certificate. After three years she began pressing her father to let her go to a new college in the Northeast that seemed, she said, to have been "established for me or the likes of me"—Wellesley College, one of what would become known as the Seven Sisters colleges that were founded to give women access to an education on par with that provided by the all-male Ivy League colleges. They represented a true revolution in education for women, offering a rigorous academic curriculum and accredited four-year degrees.

Willie balked at sending his beloved daughter so far from home, but she was persistent, and the family knew Henry Fowle Durant, the founder of Wellesley, so eventually he consented. It was an extraordinary gift to his daughter. At the time, fewer than 2 percent of American women went to college, but educational opportunities for women were exploding as four-year women's colleges replaced seminaries and the land-grant movement created new coeducational public universities. Higher education for women was still controversial, however. Doctors warned that too much education would harm young women because it would overtax their brains and draw vital energy away from their reproductive organs. "The system never does two things well at the same time," warned Dr. Edward Clarke in his widely read 1873 book *Sex and Education*, which helped popularize the idea that a young woman's bodily energy was needed exclusively for the "development and perfectation of the reproductive system." Clarke gave harrowing examples of young women who were perfectly healthy until they went away to school and studied too hard; inevitably they became pale and anemic and had irregular periods. Even if they left school, it was often too late; the damage to their reproductive mechanism was irreversible. They became semi-invalids; if they married, they couldn't conceive; if they conceived, they couldn't nurse because their breasts had failed to develop. He predicted a steady increase in the number of "permanently disabled" female college graduates and a looming shortage of healthy wives.

Willie apparently was undaunted by this. Maybe it was because as a young man at Centre College he had sat side by side with his three cousins—Mary, Caroline, and Jane Young, the daughters of the college's president—who did the same work he did but were denied degrees (all three eventually received degrees in 1905). Nisba thought it was because "his college life was spent in contact with girls of collegiate attainments and vigorous intellectual interests." There was, however, a different, and far bigger, cultural gulf that Nisba would have to cross to attend Wellesley: it had enrolled its first two black students the previous year, in 1883, and the daughter of the Confederate colonel Willie Breckinridge would have to live among them and treat them as equals. And no family better illustrated the deep contradictions that already were inherent in America's history regarding slavery and race than the Breckinridges.

Kentucky pioneer John Breckinridge was an ardent proponent of slavery and owned nearly seventy slaves, making him one of the largest slave owners in Kentucky at the time. "Purchase all the negroes you possibly can bring here," he advised his brother William, who was emigrating to Kentucky, in 1797. "It would be an important thing to you if you could turn your goods into slaves." Breckinridge didn't just establish much of his fortune on the labor of enslaved African Americans; he contributed to the entrenchment of chattel slavery by ensuring its continuation in a border state at a critical time and to its defense through a states' rights frame.

In the late 1790s, as the citizens of Kentucky agitated for a constitutional convention to make more democratic the state's founding 1792 constitution, which didn't allow for the direct election of the governor or state senators, Breckinridge took a leading role in opposing a new constitution, both to maintain the landed gentry's control of the government and to forestall calls for emancipation of slaves in the state. He wrote a widely distributed pamphlet called *No Convention* under the pseudonym "Algernon Sidney"—after the English republican political theorist whose *Discourses Concerning Government* helped lay the groundwork for the American Revolution—that mocked those who wished to free the slaves as well intended but naive, having "surely mistaken the price necessary to carry so important a work into execution." He cautioned, "Let us not liberate others at the probable expense of our own freedom"—a warning to other members of the aristocracy that if the democratic rabble could "by one experiment emancipate our slaves," as Breckinridge wrote to a fellow slave owner, they could just as easily "extinguish our land titles."

When voters nevertheless called for a constitutional convention in 1799, Breckinridge worked to ensure the selection of pro-slavery delegates—all but one of the delegates owned slaves—including himself, and took the lead in framing a new constitution that protected slavery in Kentucky, although he lost his bid to prevent the direct election of the governor and senators. At least one historian has argued that if the surprisingly strong but poorly organized anti-slavery forces, which included a young Henry Clay, had prevailed, "Kentucky would have been made a free state and the causes of the civil war destroyed in the germ."

It was the Kentucky Resolutions that Breckinridge introduced the previous year, in 1798, as a member of the state legislature that declared that acts of the federal government beyond those powers specifically designated in the Constitution were "void, and of no force." While Breckinridge altered Thomas Jefferson's original draft to remove the phrase "where powers are assumed which have not been delegated, a nullification of the act is the rightful remedy," a single Kentucky Resolution of 1799 did use the term "nullification" regarding joint action by states to protest a federal act. Together, these resolutions, says the historian James Klotter, "would form a stepping-stone" to the theory of nullification that the southern states used as a "theoretical basis" for secession.

Yet John's son, the Reverend Robert Jefferson Breckinridge—Willie's father—was a leading opponent of slavery in Kentucky, despite the fact that he himself owned slaves. Beginning in 1830 with a series of high-profile articles called "Hints on Slavery" in the *Kentucky Reporter*, Breckinridge denounced slavery and proposed the gradual emancipation of slaves in the state. "Domestic slavery cannot exist forever," he warned. "It may terminate in various ways—but terminate it must." He argued that the very constitution that his father had framed to protect the rights of slaveholders gave the state legislature the power to modify laws applying to unborn enslaved individuals "to allow for the gradual prospective emancipation of the descendants of female slaves."

Robert Breckinridge's sentiments were so controversial they cost him his seat in the state legislature and ended his political career. He joined with Henry Clay in the Kentucky Colonization Society to promote the idea of transporting freed slaves to a colony in Africa established for that purpose; to them, this would solve the problem of free black people living among white people, which was one of the objections to ending slavery. In 1833, he emancipated eleven of his slaves and provided "considerable money and supplies" to send them to Liberia.

Breckinridge remained prominent as an emancipationist throughout the 1830s and 1840s, as northern abolitionists looked to Kentucky as a key battleground over slavery, hoping that if it abolished slavery, even gradually, other border states would follow and tip the balance toward abolition. In 1849, when the state called a constitutional convention to address the simmering issue of slavery, Breckinridge stumped the state with Clay promoting his "Platform of Emancipation," which called for a constitutionally mandated system of gradual, compensated emancipation. Despite a number of prominent slave owners in their ranks, the emancipationists—who were painted as tools of radical northern abolitionists by supporters of slavery—were defeated; the new constitution further codified the status of slaves as property.

Despite his moral condemnation of slavery, Breckinridge remained a slave owner until the Fourteenth Amendment freed Kentucky's slaves. Yet throughout the Civil War he was, according to Klotter, "a leading spokesman for the North in wartime Kentucky." The influential clergyman publicly rallied support for Lincoln and the Union even as he disagreed bitterly with Lincoln's Emancipation Proclamation, which he warned would only make southerners dig in and "fight harder."

While Robert Breckinridge believed that African Americans should be treated fairly, he adhered to a rigid racial hierarchy and never countenanced the idea of "amalgamation"—the mixing of races. He was harshly criticized by famed northern abolitionist William Lloyd Garrison as "unchristian" and promoting the "spirit of negro hatred" for his assertion that black Americans could never be fully equal to whites or integrated into society.

It wasn't only African Americans who Robert Breckinridge believed were inferior to native-born white Protestants. He came to national prominence in the 1830s as a vituperative anti-Catholic who helped lay the philosophical foundation for the anti-immigrant Know-Nothing Party, which briefly replaced the Whig Party in the mid-1850s before it evolved into the Republican Party. When he was pastor of the Second Presbyterian Church of Baltimore, a city that had a large and growing Catholic population, he cofounded the *Baltimore Literary and Religious Magazine* with his brother John to warn the country about the rising danger of "Papism," an "aggressive, exclusive and intolerant" religion that he said should be "extirpate[d] . . . from the face of the earth." He considered Catholics the "most degraded and brutal white population in the world." He suggested that Protestants might need to "take arms in their hands and put down by force" the rising Catholic menace and so demonized a local Carmelite convent, which he suggested was holding women against their will, that it prompted three days of rioting, as crowds tried to storm the convent but were repelled by the city guard. Breckinridge was so convinced of what he believed to be the subversive influence of Catholics in the culture that he refused to preach in a church where an organ was used, believing it "had been for centuries one of the particular devices of the Papists to seduce mankind into attendance at their superstitious and idolatrous worship."

Given the Breckinridges' conflicted views on race and slavery, perhaps it's not surprising that Willie Breckinridge was an amalgamation himself, combining his father's relatively progressive views on race—for a southerner of his time—with his grandfather's belief in the primacy of states' rights. He was never a slave owner like his father and grandfather—he was young and in debt before the war—although his wife Issa did bring one slave, a woman named Clacy, into the marriage. As Ella told it, when Clacy was twelve, Grandfather Desha "took her by the hand, led her into the house and gave her as a first present to the hour-old" Issa. Clacy stayed with the family after the war as a servant, largely running the household for the frail Issa, to whom she remained devoted. "She bossed everyone in the place," remembered Ella, "except Grandma [Desha]."

If anything, Issa Breckinridge was a more enthusiastic Confederate than her husband. She "almost despised" her Unionist father-in-law, Robert, according to the Breckinridge biographer Klotter, and wasn't subtle about it. When she asked President Lincoln for a pass through Union lines to visit Willie during the war, he wrote back and told her she could have it only if Rev. Breckinridge "sees fit to ask it in writing." She refused to ask Robert and got her pass only when Willie asked a general friend to intercede. Eventually she found Kentucky under Yankee domination so unbearable that she decamped to Canada with other prominent Confederate wives, leaving young Ella with her parents. Willie "accepted the verdict of the Confederate failure," as Nisba put it, and reconciled with his father as soon as he came home, but Issa refused to make peace. She shunned the elderly Robert and wouldn't let him meet his grand-children until after Desha was born in 1867.

For his part, Willie lost his very first election when he ran for district attorney in 1868 because he supported allowing African Americans to testify in court. "I am aware that this avowal will most likely defeat me in this canvass," he told one audience, and chided them for letting "prejudices blind your judgment." But while he believed in basic civil rights for African Americans, and helped several up-and-coming young African American attorneys with their law careers, he didn't believe the federal government had the power to intercede to ensure those rights. Politically, he had followed his cousin John Cabell Breckinridge, who caused much consternation when in 1849 he diverged from the family's Whig leanings to become a free-trade, anti-monopoly "loco-foco" Democrat and eventually embraced the theory of nullification regarding the primacy of states' rights that could be traced to John Breckinridge.

By way of making sense of the contradictions in her father's life, Nisba would later say that "he was always for fair play" and he especially

"favored the development of educational facilities for women and negroes." So it was in early September 1884 that Willie Breckinridge accompanied Nisba north to Wellesley College. No sooner had they arrived
at College Hall to register Nisba for classes when they saw a "handsomely
dressed couple of the negro race with an attractive daughter likewise
approach the door." One of the other parents turned to Willie and said,
"Well, Colonel, maybe you won't like to have Nisba here after all." Willie
appeared nonplussed. "She got on all right with the boys; I think she will
get on all right with the colored," he said. In private, he wrote to Nisba
that she should view the situation as "temporary" and treat it with "for-
bearance." Her mother told her that it was "hard for people raised with
our prejudices to ever treat them as equals," but said that she trusted
Nisba to "treat them properly." Issa was relieved, however, when Nisba
wrote that she saw "nothing of the colored girls."

Willie and Issa were at a crossroads that fall, though it's not clear
if either of them knew it. The marriage had always had its strains. Issa
was a "proud, even haughty woman," notes Klotter, and this, plus her
treatment of her father-in-law, Robert, had caused friction in their marriage, as did their strained financial situation. Breckinridge was away
from home frequently, traveling most of the week between various circuit courts. The winter before Nisba left for Wellesley, he had announced
his candidacy for the seat in the famed "Ashland" Seventh Congressional
District vacated by Joe Blackburn's election to the Senate, so the spring
had been filled with campaigning. When he was home, there was often friction, especially over Ella, whom he found disrespectful, and
he frequently felt "uncomfortable at their house," says Klotter.

Given that no additional Breckinridge children were born after 1875,
when Issa was only thirty-two, and her long bedridden bouts and marked
frailty—which some southern women cultivated to avoid childbearing—
it's likely that sexual intimacy between the couple had ceased, or at
least become extremely limited. Issa hinted at the growing estrangement
between them in a letter she sent to Willie that fall of 1884: "I have loved
you Willie—twenty-four years—loved you at first with the love of a whole
heart." But, she said, "I [fear I] will grow less lovable—more cold in manners as I grow older."

Now, Willie was losing Nisba, his favorite child, who had been the
companion to him that in some ways his wife never was. "You know you

are your father's idol," Issa wrote to Nisba after she left for school. Issa seemed contemplative, telling her daughter to make the most of the opportunity she had been given, and noting how "the days, weeks & months fly—years," as if she was assessing her own life and its disappointments. Willie seemed resigned to the loss. "I know it is inevitable that you will drift away from me," he told Nisba.

Just a month before he took Nisba to Wellesley, Breckinridge was at another college with another young woman very close in age to his daughter. Maybe she seemed much like Nisba, a mix of naïveté and an intelligence beyond her years; maybe she reminded him of his first wife, Lucretia, who, he told her, was his great love. Who knows what calculus of longing and loss was making itself felt that August in Cincinnati, of promises made that couldn't be kept. Within months Willie Breckinridge would be elected to Congress, and his life would change forever. In some ways, it already had.

9

The Needle, the School Room, and the Store

After a brief bout of homesickness, Nisba conquered Wellesley. It was paradise for her, with an all-woman faculty and challenging classes; it made women think they could be whatever they wanted. With a mind that one friend likened to "quicksilver—ever active, amazingly fluid," Nisba took the top rank in all her classes. She was "the most brilliant student in the class . . . no one else grasped the essentials of a subject so quickly as she or expressed herself with as much clarity and accuracy," said her classmate May Estelle Cook. With the whiff of Bluegrass glamour that trailed in her wake, she immediately stood out from her classmates from New York and New England and Ohio. They found her southern accent charming and reveled in her "keen Southern wit." She also had, said Cook, "an ease and grace of manner which was a revelation to most of her college mates." Nisba's appearance also was distinctive, with her "slender face with fine aristocratic features, her wonderful dark eyes that emphasized her pallor, her crown of dark hair" piled atop her head. When Nisba was elected president of the freshman class, it was confirmation that the reluctant southern belle had blossomed in northern climes.

Her father was thrilled with her success. "We hear pleasant and sweet things of you—of your beauty . . . your brains," he wrote. And, as if something else was on his mind, he praised her for being "dutiful" and "pure" and told her not to be "selfish in the gratification of your desires."

Nisba's time at Wellesley sped by. She was elected class president two more times, and the academic accolades continued. In her spare time, she attended lectures, taught Sunday school, and delighted in sleigh rides in the New England winters. Her parochial southern world broadened. She went from a girl who told her mother "my own food I could not swallow" when she was seated at a table with the African American guests of the college president to someone who successfully stood up for a black student named Ella Smith when some of her classmates tried to keep Smith from inviting black guests to the junior prom. She said the experience helped her work through "the problem of racial relationships" and presaged a divergence from her family on issues of race. Nisba also got her first exposure to feminist ideas and wrote home to her mother about wanting to wear the new, looser styles of a working girl, no more "heavy dresses and things tight about the waist." Above all else, she wrote, "I ache to get out and work."

As college drew to a close, the question of what she would do weighed heavily on Nisba. She wasn't alone in her dilemma. "The great contradiction in the revolution in woman's higher education was that it prepared the first college graduates for a world of opportunity that did not really exist," notes the historian Ellen Fitzpatrick, as there were virtually no professions open to women. Nisba excelled at math, and Willie had counseled her in her freshman year to make a career in the sciences, telling her that "in chemistry, botany and such sciences there is a great field of profitable and honorable work for women." The botanist Carrie Harrison recently had gained prominence as the assistant curator of the Smithsonian's National Herbarium, and Breckinridge clearly saw an opportunity for his daughter to make a respectable career in the sciences working for a government agency or a university. Such work, he told her, was "less onerous and more attractive than the needle, the school room and the store." These jobs—sewing, teaching, and, more recently, clerking in stores—had defined women's work for generations. And now Nisba had a chance to break free from this dreary trinity.

But science held no appeal for Nisba. She felt the family pull toward public service and involvement in the affairs of the nation. She wanted to do what her father had done and her great-grandfather and countless cousins and uncles: become a lawyer. The path forward, however, was largely unpaved. It was at the time one of the hardest professions for women to crack. The 1890 U.S. census would find precisely 208 women lawyers in the United States (as well as 124 women engineers, 39 women chemists, and 22 women architects). Even becoming a doctor was easier, thanks to the proliferation of schools of osteopathic and homeopathic medicine that were happy to admit women. There were just over 4,500 women physicians at the time, although few were MDs.

The first woman to graduate from law school was Ada Kepley in 1870. Twenty years later, as Nisba was preparing to graduate from college, only a handful of law schools admitted women. It was the state bar associations, however, that proved the biggest hurdle. Many states restricted admission to the bar to white males, and even in states without statutory prohibitions, judges scoffed at the idea that women could practice law, so refused to admit them to the bar. Many held that women didn't have the intellectual capacity for law, while others expressed fear that women would use their "feminine wiles" to influence juries. Married women were told they couldn't be admitted to the bar because under the doctrine of coverture their legal rights had been folded into those of their husbands, so they had no legal person with which to represent clients.

When Myra Bradwell passed the Illinois bar exam in 1869 with high honors, the judge who needed to certify her admission to the bar refused to do so. An appeals court turned down her challenge, saying that women "were designed by God for domestic responsibilities." Bradwell fought all the way to the U.S. Supreme Court, which also ruled against her, saying the idea that a woman could have a career independent from her husband was repugnant and that women's "natural and proper timidity and delicacy" made them unfit for civil life. Many judges argued that barring women from the practice of law was for their own protection. One judge who said that women shouldn't be allowed to "mix professionally with all the nastiness of the world" that found its way into courts apparently saw no irony that the cases he mentioned as being unfit for women's delicate sensibilities—"sodomy, incest, rape, seduction, fornication, adultery, pregnancy, bastardy, illegitimacy, prostitution, lascivious cohabitation, abortion, infanticide"—usually involved women.

Nonetheless, a handful of women did gain admission to the bar; Ada Hulett was the first woman admitted to a state bar, in 1869. After a five-year fight, the Washington, D.C., attorney Belva Lockwood became the first woman admitted to the bar of the U.S. Supreme Court, in 1879. Even when women did gain admission to the bar, however, they struggled to establish viable law practices because they were effectively shut out of government and corporate work, like the lucrative railroad general counsel positions that bolstered the practice of male lawyers such as Willie Breckinridge. In 1888, the year that Nisba graduated from Wellesley, there were only two women practicing law in nearby Boston.

In the short run, the biggest obstacle that Nisba faced was her father. Nisba asked him if she could study law in his office, but by the end of her junior year she still didn't have an answer. "I wish you would be very clear on the subject before I see you in June as to what you want So-phonisba to do," she wrote to him. Later, she rather plaintively promised to be a "good girl" if he let her study law. Apparently Willie was fine with his daughter working quietly in a lab somewhere but not in a high-profile profession like law.

Nisba received her bachelor of science degree in June 1888; her father gave the commencement address. She returned with him to Washington, having made up her mind to study law. No one could have been better situated to break into law than Nisba. She had a degree from a prestigious university, a famous family name, and a father in the profession. She was already on the radar of some women's rights leaders. The suffragist Alice Stone Blackwell told Mary Clay, who, along with her sister Laura, founded the Kentucky Equal Rights Association, that she should recruit Nisba. "She would be a valuable acquisition, I think, being a bright girl & a college graduate," she said. Even Susan B. Anthony, who had formed an unlikely friendship with the Breckinridges when they stayed at the same Washington hotel one winter, reportedly teased Nisba about becoming a lawyer, her "penchant for a professional career" striking Anthony as "a step in the right direction."

"I had expected to study law," Nisba remembered, but her "mother's health was frail, and the family expenses were high." The sole law school in Washington open to women, the Columbian Law School, only had evening classes, when she "could be of service at home." So instead, her father took her to see a family friend who was the superintendent of schools for the District of Columbia. By the fall of 1888, Nisba was exactly where she never wanted to be: teaching school and keeping house for her family. "I had promised myself to be a lawyer and had never thought of teaching," she later wrote. She blamed herself for her predicament. "I had reasoned in such a stupid way and instead of going to [the University of Michigan] where progressive women like Miss Laura Clay went, I went to Wellesley and devoted myself to Latin and Mathematics," she lamented.

It's not clear, however, that Nisba's assertion that her family needed her at home was based on actual exigencies. Nisba said she "did a good deal of the housework." Her older sister, Ella, however, still lived at home—she wouldn't marry until the following year—and she was hardly overburdened with domestic responsibilities. By Ella's own account, the only time she stayed home was when she had a cold. She went to an "incredible number" of packed afternoon receptions at the homes of Senate and cabinet members, "seeing all sorts of queer people and consuming unbelievable varieties of creamed oysters, sandwiches and salads." Then there were the "at homes" of prominent Washington hostesses and the "small, intimate" teas hosted by First Lady Frankie Cleveland. She frequented "fashionable" literary readings and was an inveterate theatergoer, almost always stopping afterward at Harvey's for "welsh rabbits," a glass of beer, and people-watching. There were out-of-town-jaunts to White Sulphur Springs, picnics to Cabin John Bridge, twilight walks around the Mall, and army and navy cotillions. "I fear in my scamper after pleasure I sometimes left undone those things I should have done," Ella noted of her apparently not-too-essential responsibilities at home.

While helping her mother socially would have been a key duty for a young woman like Nisba, the Breckinridges rarely entertained. Technically, as the wife of a congressman, Issa was obliged to pay social calls each season to all the wives of higher officials—from the president and his cabinet to the Supreme Court, the Senate, and ranking House members—as prescribed by Madeleine Vinton Dahlgren, the doyenne of official Washington, in her book *Etiquette of Social Life in Washington*. Their wives, in turn, were expected to call on Issa, and she was expected to have occasional receptions. As Issa's frailty excused her from most of these obligations, Nisba wasn't needed on that front, and Ella relished her role as the family's designated reception-, wedding-, and funeral-goer. It seems that Nisba had fallen prey to what the social reformer Jane Addams called the "family claim," in which educated Victorian daughters who had been taught to be self-sacrificing were diverted from their post-college ambitions by their families' assertion that they were needed at home. Often, noted Addams, such claims were an excuse to camouflage their parents' discomfort about sending their daughters into the public sphere or allowing them to work for wages.

Nisba remembered those first years after graduation when she taught math at Washington High School as "hard years." The conditions in the school were poor and she didn't particularly relish teaching, although she was glad to be earning money for her perennially cash-strapped family. "The salary was a real contribution to the family income and I greatly enjoyed my first earnings, which I gave to Mama," she remembered. Nisba found herself stymied in ambitions small as well as large. Having accepted her fate as a teacher, she decided to get a bicycle because the high school was a distance from the family's rented townhouse on Capitol Hill. A woman riding astride a bicycle was still considered scandalous; just a few years earlier, President Cleveland had issued an edict forbidding the wives of his cabinet members from riding one. Nisba took a few lessons, but when Desha complained that "it was hard enough to have a sister earn her living; it was too much to have her ride a bike," she gave it up, quick as always to defer to her younger brother, who constantly reminded her that men knew better.

There were some bright spots. The always adventurous Aunt Mollie joined the family in Washington after spending two years teaching in Alaska, reportedly the first white woman to do so. She loved the equality for women she found on her journey west—she was especially pleased to find that hotels and train stations had no separate waiting rooms for women—but was dismayed at what she considered the immorality of white men and Alaska Native women marrying or, worse yet, cohabitating. "I don't expect Sodom and Gomorrah were any worse" than Sitka, Alaska, she wrote to the family.

Willie got Mollie a job in the Interior Department, and she once again found herself at the cutting edge of employment opportunities for women. After the Patent Office's ill-fated foray into hiring women clerks in the 1850s, it took the manpower shortage of the Civil War to bring women back into the government. The Treasury Department hired women to trim sheets of currency so that young men could have "muskets instead of shears" in their hands. As the federal government grew by leaps and bounds after the war, hiring women was an economical way to round out the workforce while providing jobs to needy war widows. "The truth is that these ladies were put into the Departments of Government as clerks because they were cheaper," said one senator. Women clerks received only about three-quarters of what men made, but the average salary of nine hundred dollars a year was by far one of the best-paying jobs available for women. Like Mollie, many female clerks came from formerly well-off families that had fallen on hard times—not a small number from the "war smitten and impoverished South." Also like Mollie, many had worked previously as teachers, but, as one civil service applicant put it, teaching jobs "pay such miserable prices that it is almost starvation."

For Mollie, older than Nisba and more self-assured, with no immediate family to answer to, Washington was a revelation. The city was already gaining a reputation as a "special center" for professional women and women in public life, according to Ellen Hardin Walworth, who was on her way to becoming a noted historic preservationist. "The women who are leaders in literature, art, Science, and patriotism congregate here," she wrote. Indeed, even flighty Ella remembered the incredible procession of women "heroines and pioneers" she regularly saw about the city: Clara Barton, "gentle and benign," who "came to Washington to seek national recognition for the Red Cross"; Frances Willard, the head of the Woman's Christian Temperance Union, which was at the time the most powerful women's organization; and the suffragists Elizabeth Cady Stanton and Dr. Anna Shaw. Susan B. Anthony was in Washington the better part of most winters for the annual meeting of the National Woman Suffrage Association and to lobby Congress for women's suffrage, making the Riggs House on the corner of Fifteenth and G Streets her headquarters. It was there, before they rented their first house in Washington, that she became friendly with the Breckinridges.

Like most Democrats, Willie didn't support suffrage, but would none-theless share his legislative knowledge with Anthony, helping her "plan her conferences with other members of the House of Representatives" and make "final arrangements for a hearing before some committee," Nisba said. Knowing that Issa was a woman "who had all the rights she wanted," Anthony would "share with Mama her knowledge and skill in the areas of fancy work or sewing" as she and Willie plotted legislative strategy.

Mollie quickly became a mainstay among the women's organiza-tions that were exploding in Washington in the early 1890s. From the District Woman Suffrage Association, to the Woman's National Press Association, to the Colored Women's League of Washington, to Pro Re Nata, an organization established to teach women about parliamen-tary procedure so they could run all the organizations they were founding, Washington was a city of women organizing and networking like never before. In 1890, Mollie founded Wimodaughsis ("union of women") with Susan B. Anthony's niece Lucy Anthony. It was soon the city's premier women's club, offering lectures on everything from political science to art and night classes in practical skills like typing and shorthand to help working girls get ahead. Under Mollie's energetic direction and fundraising, Wimodaughsis rented its own building with meeting rooms and offices with the objective of giving women the same networking opportunities that men had at the large downtown hotels; the National Woman Suffrage Association, the District suffrage and temperance organizations, and the women's press club had offices there.

As with her experience in Alaska, however, it proved difficult to excise the southerner from Mollie Desha. She got into a nasty fight with Anna Shaw and the other northern suffragists on the board of Wimodaughsis when she tried to block an African American woman from taking a typ-ing class because her enrollment would entitle her to attend the club's social functions. Mollie said the southern women she recruited would never countenance "colored and white ladies [being] placed on the same social footing," and she was afraid black women would bring "col-ored men to the entertainments," which, to her, was self-evidently im-possible. "I feel I have been treated outrageously," she told the *Washington Post* after she and a number of her friends quit the organization when the board voted it had neither the legal nor the moral right to deny admission to black women.

Undaunted, Mollie poured her energy into another organization, as she had, the *Washington Post* noted with some admiration, "the executive ability of a Yankee." The journalist Mary Lockwood had just written a scathing letter in the *Post* after the newly formed Sons of the American Revolution denied admission to women. "Were there no mothers of the Revolution?" she asked incredulously. Mollie was "determined that the contribution of women should not be ignored," said Nisba, as her great-grandmother Katherine Montgomery had ridden dispatches for Gen. George Washington through the wilds of Virginia during the Revolutionary War, once escaping pursuing British soldiers through a "daring feat of horsemanship."

Over the summer of 1890, Mollie met with Lockwood, Ellen Hardin Walworth, and Eugenia Washington, sometimes in the Breckinridges' front parlor, plotting a new patriotic organization especially for women. Nisba had experience with parliamentary procedure from her tenure as class president and helped her aunt draft the constitution for what became the Daughters of the American Revolution and served as its first recording secretary. Within a year, DAR was one of the most influential women's organizations in the country, counting among its members Caroline Harrison, the popular wife of President Benjamin Harrison, whose imprimatur "brought in members by the thousands," as one Washington woman remembered.

Helping her aunt found DAR was about the only good memory that Nisba had from 1890. First, a typhus epidemic swept through the overcrowded Washington High School, which sent Nisba into a panic. Then an influenza epidemic struck; Willie was deathly ill for two weeks on a trip to Florida. One Saturday morning in the spring of 1890, as Nisba was doing the family's shopping at the Eastern Market, she collapsed at one of the stalls and had to be carried home. She was "quite ill for some time." She recovered, but not fully. Never very robust, and weighing a mere ninety pounds, she became "a semi-invalid." She gave up her teaching job and languished around the house. When asked to update her Wellesley classmates about her life and doings, she wrote: "One word suffices abundantly to tell what I am doing: Nothing, nothing, nothing.

Keeping house for my family, and teaching my sister three hours a day make up the meager list of my performances."

Her ill health did have one benefit. Concerned over his daughter's well-being—and, according to her, persuaded by her tears—Willie finally agreed to let her study law. By early 1891, she was studying law in his Lexington office. Then, when a friend of the family's, Clement Griscom, who was president of the Red Star steamship line, offered to take Nisba and Curry to Europe with him and his wife, Willie decided that a long European tour would be good for Nisba's health. The sisters left in late April 1891. The plan was for them to do some sightseeing, then spend the winter in Switzerland, where Nisba wanted to study law with a noted professor. "I am glad that you are studying law . . . You can succeed at anything," wrote Willie in July 1891, although he reminded Nisba that the main thing was for her to "get stout and strong."

Apparently worried that her education had something to do with her broken health, Nisba wrote to her friend Marion Talbot, the head of the Association of Collegiate Alumnae, and asked for a study the organization had done on the health of women college graduates. It held few answers: the survey of some seven hundred women found that 78 percent were in good or excellent health. What was probably ailing Nisba, as Jane Addams could have told her, was her untapped potential. "I have seen young girls suffer and grow sensibly lowered in vitality in the first years after they leave school," Addams wrote, not from overwork or too much education, but from the lack of work. "She finds 'life' so different from what she expected it to be . . . and does not understand this apparent waste . . . [of] this elaborate preparation . . . She is restricted and unhappy."

By spring 1892, Nisba and Curry were in Paris. By her own account, Nisba was crabby and annoyingly pious; she spent most of her time with her nose in law books. Her father wrote from Lexington, "The law practice here is not what it was years ago," noting that if it were, he'd be tempted to go back to law full-time. "I believe I went into public life solely from a sense of duty and stay in it for the same duty, but perhaps this is self-delusion and I am like others," he wrote. It was apparently financial pressures that made him reconsider public service. His prediction that Ella's suitor, Lynman Chalkley, wouldn't be able to support a wife turned out to be correct. Lynman struggled to find work as a lawyer, and Breckinridge found Ella, pregnant with her first child, living in a filthy, crowded hotel. He paid for Ella and Lynman to move to a "more wholesome" location. Robert, as usual, was in trouble. Willie found himself paying ninety dollars here, one hundred dollars there to cover Robert's debts and eventually paid to pack him off to India. Then there were the expenses that didn't show up on any ledger. On February 14, 1891, right before Nisba left for Europe, William Tecumseh Sherman died, and a certain unreconstructed clerk praised his death. As a result, she lost the job Breckinridge had gotten her at the Interior Department. Willie was keeping up a grueling lecture schedule to make ends meet. He told Nisba that if she added up all the days he was away speaking, "you will find that I was occupied more days than I was really absent, which is doing pretty good for a fat fellow my age."

If there was one bright note, it was that he and Issa seemed to have found a contented companionship as empty nesters. With their house in Lexington rented out, Ella married, and Robert, Nisba, and Curry gone, they stayed in a boardinghouse and enjoyed the freedom to come and go as they pleased. Willie wrote to Nisba about cozy late suppers of fried chicken and tomatoes at corner cafés. They gushed over their first grandchild, Preston Breckinridge Chalkley, Ella's little boy. For the first time, Issa accompanied Willie on some of his trips as he lectured throughout the Midwest about tariff reform. Willie wrote to Nisba besotted by the beauty and fecundity of the countryside they passed through and said he was glad to have a chance to see less-prosperous parts of the country, as it "gives me a better idea of the distribution of wealth and power of America."

Still, Issa was bothered by frequent headaches, and Willie noted that she hadn't been "entirely herself" for some time. In March 1892 they suffered a crushing blow when little Preston choked to death on a piece of food. By June, Nisba and Curry were making plans to come home, and Willie wrote that Issa seemed "better today than she had been for several months." A week later, she had a serious attack of dysentery. By June 30, she seemed better, but Willie was still rushing home from the office. On July 5, he wrote, "I hardly know exactly what to write . . . Your mother is comfortable . . . but her stomach refuses everything." On July 14, she rallied enough to write her daughters a brief letter, signing it, as both she and Willie always did, "With a heart full of love." Later that day, Issa Breckinridge died at the age of forty-nine, most likely from cancer, which had been slowly consuming her for more than a year.

•

Nisba returned home to a shattered family. Her mother was dead. Her brother Robert had jumped ship and disappeared. Ella and her husband were still reeling from Preston's death. Her father, undoubtedly suffering from a mix of grief and guilt, emptied the Capitol Hill townhouse and took up residence in a boardinghouse. Desha was at the University of Virginia, having finally "made up his mind to go work at his law," according to his father. After failing at running a lumber mill, he sauntered down to Charlottesville apparently unconcerned with either his domestic duties or the family's finances.

Nisba continued to search for some way to be in the world. Her father seemed on the mark when he told her she had "veracity, courage, affection, high principles and unusual loftiness of character and purpose," but was also "nervous, excitable, [and] intense." Before her mother's death, she had been planning to go to the University of Michigan Law School, but Issa's passing put that on hold. Her friend Helen Shafer, one of her former professors who had become the president of Wellesley, recommended her for a fellowship with the College Settlements Association, which would let her work for a year in one of the settlement houses that were being founded in the gritty areas of the big cities to tackle the social problems caused by urbanization—as well as to give educated young women like Nisba something to do in the new field of social work. By working to solve social problems, said Jane Addams, who had recently founded Hull House in Chicago, women like Nisba, who had the "advantages of college, of European travel, and of economic study," could replace the family claim with a "social claim" of public service. Willie, however, wasn't big on his daughter going to live in some seedy neighborhood. "Bowery boys can be found everywhere," he told her dismissively, and she didn't pursue the fellowship.

As she drifted through the fall of 1892, rattling around the family's nearly empty house, Nisba did find one friend with whom she could share her hopes and thwarted desires: Madeline McDowell, the daughter of another prominent Lexington family. Madge was more social and outgoing than Nisba—she had already turned down two marriage proposals—but like Nisba she was ambitious and restless with the life of a southern belle. She provided a much needed shoulder to lean on after Issa's death, when, Nisba said, the "day to day was often so exhausting."

Nisba seemed stalled professionally and personally. She'd had two romances, one with Thomas Hunt Morgan, her classmate at the Agricultural and Mechanical College, who would go on to become a pioneering geneticist, but they didn't blossom. "Neither really loved me, though each for the moment thought that he did," she would later lament. Now twenty-seven, it didn't seem that marriage was in the cards for Nisba.

When the Pollard scandal broke, it only added another layer of uncertainty and angst to Nisba's unsettled life. The accusations against her beloved father understandably hit Nisba hard, and, combined with her poor health, threatened to overwhelm her. Two weeks after Madeline filed her suit, Desha wrote to his father that he was worried about his sister, saying she seemed "more pulled down than she had been in a long time."

Neither Willie nor Desha likely understood the full weight of what was dragging Nisba down. Unbeknownst to them, three years earlier, in the fall of 1890, Aunt Mollie had told Nisba and her mother that Willie was having an affair with a clerk named Madeline Pollard, gossip that she apparently had picked up at the Interior Department, where she and Madeline both worked. "But when she tried to warn my mother and then tried to warn me, we refused to listen," remembered Nisba. "He was devoted, he was endlessly kind, and there could not be in our minds any question of his fidelity." Instead of heeding her warning, they cut Aunt Mollie out of their lives. When the scandal broke, Nisba must have known that everything Mollie had said was true—that her father had been having an illicit relationship with a young woman who was the same age she was; that the person she looked up to more than any other, who was her guidestar, whose judgment she had deferred her own ambitions to, was a cheat and a liar and had most certainly been selfish in the gratification of his desires.

A month after the scandal broke, on September 20, she wrote to Madge about how disappointed she was to not be able to go to law school, which she had hoped she could do with her friend, or if not, "do some work along the same line in Social study." She had been offered a fellowship to study sociology under the eminent economist Richard Ely at the University of Wisconsin but turned it down because the funding was too low—only $150. "I shall do some work on getting other good chances," she told her father. By mid-January, Nisba had decided to go to the University of Michigan, but as always, finances were a concern. She wrote to her father she would need about one hundred dollars, which "seems a great deal with your other expenses." The sudden death of her friend Helen Schafer derailed those plans. Nisba went to Oberlin, Ohio, for the funeral and to spend time with Schafer's family.

Willie was relieved that she wouldn't be going to Michigan. "I am very anxious about Nisba. More so than I have ever been," he wrote to Desha on January 22. He said that it "absolutely pained" him to think of her going to Ann Arbor and that he wished she would go to Staunton, where Ella and Lynman had finally established a household. "Yet I hate to say this because she has been so self-sacrificing and I am under so many obligations to her," he wrote. On January 27, Nisba wrote to her father that she felt as he did about going to Michigan, but she seemed completely adrift. "To tell the truth Papa, I don't know just yet what to do," she wrote, saying that although she was "very well and able to work," she felt "dazed."

Her father had no answer for her. In Washington, Willie was now consumed with preparations for the trial. If there was one thing that had seemed to be on his side—besides his fame and popularity—it was time. The Supreme Court of the District of Columbia, where the suit had been filed, was chronically backlogged. When Madeline filed suit in August, it was widely predicted that the court wouldn't get to it for at least a year—it took two years for Mary Oliver's suit to come to trial. Breckinridge thought he had plenty of time to prepare a defense. But the courts were reorganized right before Thanksgiving, and cases began moving much faster through the system. Even then, Enoch Totten, the savvy defense lawyer Breckinridge hired, predicted the case wouldn't come to trial "until some time in the summer, probably next fall." He recommended holding off on the taking of depositions so as to not tip their hand to Pollard's lawyers. But Totten was proved wrong, and by late January 1894 Breckinridge's team was scrambling to pull together a defense for a trial that looked likely to happen sometime in March.

Breckinridge, however, was almost completely hamstrung by a lack of capital. While it was common knowledge that he wasn't a rich man, few realized the depths of his money problems. He had been "in the red" quite literally for years, with the red ink indicating an overdrawn account showing up regularly on the monthly balance sheet of his congressional checking account. By the fall of 1893, Breckinridge was in debt to merchants and tradespeople, large and small. He owed Miss Lydia Fox, a stenographer, $20.80 (about $500 today) for thirteen days of work the previous winter and spring. "I wrote to you some little time ago enclosing my little bill," she wrote delicately, "but not hearing from you, think my letter must have miscarried." He owed Brooks Brothers $38; they had sent the bill twice. He owed the Hoffman House in New York City $77.27; his check had bounced and the hotel had "sent several letters in regard to the matter, but as of yet have not received any reply," wrote the manager. He owed the Belt Electric Line Company of Lexington $26.68 for five months of his light bill. He had bills outstanding from a plumber and the Hygienic Ice Company of Washington, D.C., from 1892. He got a letter from a Lexington lawyer seeking collection on behalf of Mr. J. B. Spencer, a "very worthy liveryman," saying it would be "a great hardship on Mr. Spencer, who is of small means, to lose the amount of this bill."

Breckinridge's congressional salary was $5,000 (about $125,000 today), but it "was not adequate for the support of a family like ours," remembered Nisba. The impossibility of living on a congressional salary in Washington, where it "would take the best part of a Congressman's salary to pay his board and whiskey bills," according to the journalist Frank Carpenter, was a constant refrain at the time. And Issa had insisted on accompanying her husband to Washington when very few congressmen kept their families there, because of the expense. The Breckinridges also liked to live well. In the early 1870s, they had six live-in servants, including the housekeeper Clacy, the parlor maid Easter, the laundress Adelaide, and a cook and a yardman, although by 1880 they made do with Easter, a cook, and a part-time yard man. There were summer trips to Old Point Comfort in Virginia for Issa and the girls and the family's annual pilgrimage to Boston to visit Nisba at Wellesley. There was Nisba's tuition at Wellesley and Desha's at Princeton, as well as stints at private secondary schools for Robert and Ella, and the cost of Herr Muller, the shy, bespectacled German tutor Willie had hired for the children back in Lexington because he wanted them to have "the advantages he had enjoyed from having a German governess." In addition to a substantial salary, Breckinridge kept a part-time law practice that was fairly robust and he made several thousand dollars a year lecturing. It seems that his money-management skills and the need to keep up appearances, as well as the fact that he was supporting Pollard, were a big part of the family's money problems.

With the trial drawing close and funds limited, it was clear by late January that the defense team would have to pursue a more aggressive, creative strategy. It was Stoll who came up with the idea of sending someone into the House of Mercy to spy on Madeline. "I am thoroughly convinced that an unprofessional is the best in this case and will make an effort to secure some satisfactory person," he told his old friend. So the telegram was sent, and Jennie Tucker found herself on the midnight train to Washington.

10

A House of Mercy

It was early on the morning of Tuesday, January 30, 1894, that Jennie's train snaked its way southward from Baltimore, crossed the Anacostia River, and entered Washington, a broad, low city that still seemed like a mirage in the dawn mists on what had been the nearly empty tidal flats of the Potomac just seventy-five years earlier. One visitor to Washington City in 1827 found it so sparsely populated, amid a handful of government buildings and the "wide formal avenues" that Peter Charles L'Enfant had optimistically laid out, that he thought it "look[ed] as if some giant had scattered a box of his child's toys at random on the ground." When the pioneering ophthalmologist and stenographer Isabel Barrows arrived in 1867, she found "a great, sprawling country village" where "clouds of dust rose up from passing wagons" and "cows and geese wander[ed] the paths while pigs rooted in the streets."

In the years since, Washington had grown in leaps and bounds alongside the federal government and was now the capital city that L'Enfant had envisioned, with grand public buildings and a population closing in on a quarter million. Even then, journalist Frank Carpenter thought the city still had a "fairy-tale sense of instability about it," as if "it has sprung up in a morning, or rather a whirlwind had picked up some great town, mixed the big houses up with the little ones, then cast the whole together in one miscellaneous mass, keeping intact only the city streets."

It wasn't just the physical city that had been transfigured; so, too, had its inhabitants. Beginning in the 1880s, Washington became a fashionable city for the wealthy who had nothing to do with politics, especially the nouveaux riches who had Gilded Age fortunes to spend but not the pedigree to break into the old-name high societies of Philadelphia or Boston or New York. As word of the "capital's various charms" spread—its permeable high society, its mild winters, its fine paved boulevards perfect for promenading the smartest horses and equipage, its "beautiful homes with large ballrooms"—it became a magnet for the nation's "rootless rich," says the historian Kathryn Allamong Jacob. By 1884, *Century Magazine* could assure its readers that "it is the fashion to go to Washington in the winter as to Newport in the summer." The change turbocharged the city's social scene, as both new money and old, official Washington and this unofficial big-spending populace, partook in an annual bacchanal of luncheons and receptions and dinners and balls known as "the season," which stretched from December until June. In February 1892, upon his return from a sojourn in Europe, Henry Adams lamented the changes that had taken place in the provincial city he knew, where a handful of diplomatic families like his and old-line cave dwellers controlled a fairly parsimonious social scene that ended promptly at Lent: "Houses had been opened up and there was much dining; much calling; much leaving of cards." Julia Foraker, who first visited the capital as the daughter of a congressman and came back as the wife of a senator, described a "brilliant" social whirlwind in the 1890s, when the "rich, spectacular New York-crowd-with-the-names" came to town, "took big houses [and] gave extravagant parties."

Frank Carpenter, the Washington correspondent for the *Cleveland Leader* who wrote the popular "Carp's Washington Letters" column, reported, "There is enough silk worn here every winter to carpet a whole state; there are pearls by the bushel, and diamonds by the peck." Carp was especially amused by the craze for extravagant, color-themed entertainments complete with towering sugar-spun sculptures and "monumental floral decorations" to match; he himself attended a red luncheon, a violet dinner, a pink tea, and an orange reception. His wife attended Mrs. Dr. Nathan Lincoln's "pink and gold" Valentine's luncheon that featured a life-size sculpture of a white swan filled with maidenhair fern perched on pink silk and lace, "above which poised a big heart of pink

carnations pierced with a golden arrow." After finishing their lunch and
their heart-shaped ices, each guest pulled a pink ribbon on a pink Jack
Horner pie and "found attached to it a bisque Cupid holding a gold heart."

The winter Jennie wound her way into Washington, the florists and
caterers were quieter than usual. The whole country seemed to be holding its breath, waiting to see what happened with the economy, "drifting in the dead-water of the *fin-de-siècle*," as Adams put it. Cleveland
had gotten his repeal of the Silver Act after a protracted battle in the
Senate, but still the economy sputtered, businesses failed, and unemployment rose. There was in the capital itself "a vast army of unemployed,
and men pleading for food who have never before been compelled to seek
aid," the *Washington Evening Star* reported. For the moment, however,
Jennie undoubtedly was preoccupied not with the economy but with the
question of how, exactly, she was going to get herself into the House of
Mercy. Stoll had told her to make up a "pitiful tale," but Jennie knew
that she would have to come up with more than just some sad story to
fool the nuns. "Don't you know that the 'pitiful story' must fit the particular conditions?" she asked Stoll, chiding him for not finding out more
about the home. She said she supposed it was like the Young Women's
Christian Association homes that had been established in cities to provide refuge for single working girls. If this was the case, she told Stoll,
she would be "delighted," as she had "always wanted to study the practical workings of such charitable institutions, and see whether they
really accomplish the desired purpose."

Jennie's train pulled into the Baltimore & Potomac's foreboding
neo-Gothic station on the northeast corner of the Mall a little after
7:30 a.m., just as the hansom cabs and drays and streetcars would have
been clattering to life, filling the streets with an early-morning clamor:
the clip-clop of hooves and the clang of trolley bells. As she exited the
depot, she passed the ladies' waiting room, where a bronze star in the
floor marked the spot where President James Garfield had been assas-
sinated twelve years earlier, adding to the slightly haunted feeling of the
place. Following Stoll's directions, she went one block north to Pennsylvania Avenue and the St. James Hotel. After she checked in and had
breakfast, she took the green cars of the Pennsylvania Avenue streetcar
toward Georgetown. She disembarked near Washington Circle and

found herself standing on K Street in front of a light gray, three-story brick building with a large gilt cross over the front door and a polished brass plaque that read "House of Mercy." The house had an iron gate in front and "carefully curtained windows" that, she told Stoll, "gave it that no-one-ever-allowed-to-look-out appearance." If Jennie could have seen around back, she would have realized that this was no YWCA home. The backyard was ringed by a six-foot-high brick wall that had been inlaid with broken glass bottles—with the jagged edges facing up to foil escape.

Afraid that she would lose her nerve, and "overcoming a strong desire to turn and run," Jennie pulled the bell with a "nervous but determined jerk." A middle-aged nun answered the door. Feigning a faltering voice, Jennie asked for the matron of the house. "You mean Sister Dorothea," said the nun, who took Jennie's card and escorted her to a plainly furnished parlor. The rattle of keys announced the arrival of Sister Dorothea, a sad-faced nun in a long black habit and small white cornette. She asked Jennie what she wanted. Jennie told her that she had come from Boston on account of her health and needed a place to stay until she was well enough to earn money to pay for a boardinghouse. At that, Sister Dorothea led Jennie to her private office. "My child," she said sternly after closing the door, "you evidently do not understand the character of the house you have come to; you should have gone to the Young Women's Christian Association. This, my dear, is a home exclusively for fallen women. We do not take anyone into the Home who has not committed this sin. The Home is carried on wholly for the purpose of reclaiming these poor creatures."

A feeling of consternation swept over Jennie as she realized that the story she had prepared wouldn't do, and if she was "going to tell a lie now, it must be a big one." She took a breath and began. "Sister, I know the character of this house, and because of its character came here," she said. "I want to have the example of my fallen sisters to help me lead a better life. I, too, have sinned." Out spilled the story of an orphaned girl who had fallen prey to lust and the imaginary physician who made her promise to leave Boston and begin life anew. The nun was sympathetic, taking Jennie's hand and holding it kindly as she spun her story. Jennie was so nervous that she wasn't sure if she would laugh or cry, so she buried her head in her handkerchief and was relieved when it was the latter, the real-enough tears only adding to the performance. When she finished her story, however, the nun looked doubtful. She told Jennie that she would be glad to help her but feared that Jennie "could not stand it at the Home." She told Jennie that the girls were "coarse, rough, ignorant girls, and that it would not be possible for one who had been brought up as she could see [Jennie] had been to live in close contact with them."

Sister Dorothea said that the girls who came to the House of Mercy were required to stay for one year, during which time they would be expected to learn sewing and housekeeping skills that would fit them for some useful work. She said despite her reluctance to take Jennie on, "this resolve on your part is so brave that I am going to make a concession to you." She said that Jennie could come for a one-week trial and "after that if you conclude that you can endure the life here, I shall ask you to promise to stay with me for a year." The rules, Sister Dorothea said, were very strict and Jennie would have to follow them like the other girls. She must wear the uniform of the other "inmates," could not go out unless attended to by one of the sisters, and must have no communication with the outside world. Jeannie blanched, thinking of her plans for a post office box to get her dispatches to Stoll, but seeing no other way, she agreed to the sister's terms. She told her that she had some arrangements to make and would return that afternoon.

When she got back to the hotel, Jennie wrote to Stoll and told him she had gotten in. She gave him an outline of what transpired and told him of Sister Dorothea's "appalling proposition" that she commit to a one-year internment. "I feel as if I was going to my own funeral," she wrote. "I only hope it will not be as difficult to escape as it was to get in." She closed her letter with a warning. "If you hear nothing from me at the end of three weeks," she told Stoll, "you must devise some way of getting me out."

●

By late morning, Jennie once again stood before the House of Mercy, this time with a "miserable sinking feeling" in her heart. Her own dread aside, she was dying to find out if Madeline Pollard was still in the house. She didn't have to wait long. Before she joined the others, and after the front door was locked behind her, Sister Dorothea came to speak with her. She warned Jennie that there was another young woman living there "in a false position" as "a teacher, and not as an inmate of the Home, which in reality she is." Sister Dorothea said that the woman went by the name of Miss Dudley and that she couldn't tell Jennie her real name, but she was a "notorious woman." She went on, apparently distressed by her visitor. "It was a great mistake to permit her to come here at all," she said, but when her order took over the house last October, her predecessor had already given her permission to stay. "I have told her lawyers repeatedly that I would not keep her; but they have put me off . . . As the woman claims she has not a cent in the world, I cannot turn her into the street." She warned Jennie not to talk to "Miss Dudley," as she "seems determined to tell her miserable history to everyone who will listen to her. She goes on in the most minute and disgusting details."

Now Jennie had no doubt whom she was talking about, and her mind was already turning over the possibilities as she followed Miss Grey, one of the staff in charge of the girls, to the dormitory. It put Jennie in mind of "the woman's ward of a prison": a "large, bare, whitewashed room, with rows of narrow iron bedsteads, with just enough space between each for a small chair." There she changed into a "very ugly blue gingham dress" that still had molasses drippings down the front from its previous inhabitant, an apron of the same dye-pot blue, and a white cap. As she dressed, Miss Grey took her clothes and locked them up, which caused a pang as Jennie realized if she had to leave in a hurry, she would be out on the street in the "dreadful clothes" without her hat or coat. But she did manage to conceal a chamois pouch around her neck with some money and stamps in case of an emergency and a little diary for her shorthand notes of what she discovered. She decided she was safe enough for the time being, "unless I lose my mind before getting out, which is not altogether improbable, considering my surroundings," she scribbled in her diary.

Dinner didn't improve her assessment of her surroundings. She sat at a long table with the other girls and ate in silence, as was the custom. Supper was bread and butter and tea. "The tea certainly was 'wet,' but there was nothing else attractive about it," she lamented. Afterward, she went with the other girls to a plain sitting room, with a bare floor, a large table, and a few wooden chairs. Jennie had her first chance to assess the other inmates. She was surprised at how young they were; she guessed most to be about seventeen or so. They were mostly lower-class girls. "None of them seem to have had any education," she noted. "Some are very coarse and common in every way; but as a rule they are not vulgar, simply noisy and untamed."

Jennie shouldn't have been surprised at the age or the social class of the girls. Homes for fallen women like the House of Mercy were designed to intercept working-class girls who had an out-of-wedlock pregnancy before they began what was believed to be the inevitable downward spiral to a life of prostitution. Some girls were sent by their parents and others by the courts. They were roughly modeled after the network of homes for penitent prostitutes and wayward girls established by the Catholic Sisters of the Good Shepherd throughout the Mississippi Valley and major East Coast cities before the Civil War. A surge of interest by middle- and upper-class reformers in quashing prostitution in the booming postwar cities resulted in the establishment of a wave of facilities for fallen women in the 1880s and 1890s, including homes run by the Salvation Army and the Florence Crittenton Homes established by the "millionaire evangelist" Charles Nelson Crittenton. This burst of philanthropic activity reflected anxieties about working women alone in the big cities, both as victims of male sexual predation and as possible temptations to respectable husbands and sons.

While the first homes for fallen women were run by Catholic nuns, Episcopalian clerics and laypeople became interested in the issue when the church created a counterpart to the Church of England's White Cross Army, which promoted "social purity"—a single standard of morality for men and women that eschewed premarital sex and prostitution. Creating new institutions to disseminate moral education and protect working girls before they could be led astray by the temptations of the city or the exigencies of a low wage became a fashionable cause. New York's Bishop Henry Potter was especially prominent in these efforts, and his daughter Virginia and the heiress Grace Hoadley Dodge established a widely copied Working Girls Society to provide moral uplift to working girls by giving them a place they could come after work to take classes and learn middle-class values, especially the civilizing

effects of domesticity and the expectation of premarital sexual abstinence. By 1890 there were eighteen such clubs in New York alone, offering classes and lectures on household affairs, the "grandeur of womanhood
and motherhood," the "influence of women over men," and "purity and
nobility of character" to some two thousand young women.

In 1884, the Women's Auxiliary of the Washington Episcopal Diocese founded the House of Mercy as "a house of refuge and reformatory
for fallen and outcast women." At the time, Washington had only one
other home for unwed mothers, St. Ann's Infant Asylum, founded by the
Daughters of Charity and incorporated by an act of Congress signed by
President Lincoln in 1863 to provide for "deserving indigent and unprotected females during their confinement in childbirth" and for the care
of "foundlings"—abandoned, usually illegitimate, infants. In 1887, the
District got a third home for wayward women when the local chapter of
the Woman's Christian Temperance Union, under the leadership of its
president Sarah La Fetra, opened its Home for Fallen Women. The
WCTU, at the time by far the largest women's political organization in
the country, had added social purity work to its mission of banishing liquor two years earlier following the scare over "white slavery" caused by
the publication of the sensational "The Maiden Tribute of Modern Babylon" exposé in England, in which reformer William Stead showed how
easy it was to purchase a virgin working-class girl to enslave in a brothel.
The WCTU also started campaigning around the country to raise the
age of consent, which was ten or twelve in most states, to age eighteen
to combat what it decried as the widespread sexual exploitation of young
women by older men.

Different homes had different specializations. St. Ann's took unwed
mothers for their "lying in" until they gave birth and kept their children,
as well as the infants that were routinely left on their doorstep with pleading
notes pinned to them. "Please accept this little outcast son of mine,"
read one found on a baby at a similar asylum in New York City. "I would
not part with my baby were it in any way possible to make a respectable
living with him, but I cannot." The WCTU home specialized in trying
to reclaim prostitutes and other denizens of the street from their lives of
sin. The House of Mercy confined unwed mothers for one year after they
had given birth to "rehabilitate" them. By the time Jennie arrived in 1894,

it had space for twenty-five girls and, like St. Ann's Infant Asylum, received a regular appropriation from Congress as part of a network of semi-official female penal institutions focused on policing women's sexuality.

The House of Mercy attempted to instill middle-class sexual morality through plain living, hard work, and the cultivation of domesticity—a taste for "fancy dress" and "excitement" was believed to be a major risk factor for women's moral downfall. Girls were taught sewing and housekeeping skills so that they would have some means of support after they were released. Ideally, in the minds of those who ran the institutions, they would become servants in private homes where they would have proper supervision. They believed that jobs in the public world—working in stores and factories—were the cause of most women's downfall in the first place. The production of domestics also conveniently helped address the "servant problem" that plagued middle- and upper-class women like those on the home's Board of Lady Managers. These women reluctantly had to hire immigrant and African American women for servant jobs they would prefer to see filled by native-born white women, who increasingly eschewed domestic work because of its grueling nature and the lack of personal time.

Unfortunately for the girls being groomed as domestics, they were most likely being sent right back into the proverbial lion's den. Mary Conyngton, who undertook a pioneering federal study of fallen women early in the twentieth century, found that a "disproportionate number of the fallen women had been domestic servants." And, she wrote, the fact that "the home and domestic service furnish the majority of the inmates [of homes for unwed mothers] is the more striking since the superintendents [of such homes] held strongly to the established opinion that domestic service is the safest occupation for women."

As an Episcopalian, Jennie obviously had been exposed to religious reformers' progressive ideas about these "fallen" women, which held that it wasn't inherent immorality but unfortunate circumstances and despair that drove women to "dissipation and degradation." She told Stoll she had been "taught to sympathize with erring sisters," echoing the language used by one WCTU purity activist, who spoke of "the necessity of suspending judgment in the case of an erring sister." In fact, Jennie told

Stoll when she agreed to take the job, if she found "that this woman was really ruined by your client, and that she had given her life for him, and had been deserted and abused by him, I shall as certainly espouse her case as the sun shines."

Now, Jennie was finally going to meet the woman the whole country was talking about and find out the truth for herself. She stayed in the sitting room playing games with some of the other girls until Sister Dorothea summoned her for another chat. When she returned, she found Miss Dudley playing checkers with one of the girls. When Jennie, whom Sister Dorothea introduced as "Agnes," according to her pseudonym of Agnes Parker, came in, Miss Dudley got up and insisted that she finish the game. She sat nearby cheering her on and complimenting her knowledge of checkers. After the game, Jennie shared a copy of *Harper's Magazine* she had bought on the train with Miss Dudley, who immediately turned to the table of contents and began pointing out the names of the authors she said she knew: William Dean Howells, whom she said she met when she was studying at Cambridge, and Charles Dudley Warner, whom she said she knew "very well indeed" and had been to his home in Hartford, Connecticut. "She seemed to be on very intimate terms with all these literary people, and seemed anxious that I should realize how well she knew them," noted Jennie.

As Miss Dudley spoke, Jennie cataloged her as if she were some nineteenth-century explorer studying an elusive specimen. She was, Jennie scribbled in her notes, about five feet, five inches tall; thin with square shoulders: "Her face is almost repulsive in its coarseness; her eyes are too far apart, gray in color, with heavy black brows. Her nose, which is particularly ugly, is turned up, with very large, round nostrils; her cheeks are fat and round, giving her a doughy, expressionless profile; while her mouth is decidedly coarse, her upper lip being very thick and extending over the under." Her best feature, noted Jennie, was her "very abundant" hair of a "bronze brown" that was coiled in braids at the back of her head. She was, Jennie thought, "between thirty and thirty-five years." In the dark blue dress and white cap of the home's teachers, Jennie thought she looked like "a neat but rather coarse-looking housemaid."

When Miss Dudley became animated and spoke, however, Jennie described the same almost-magical transformation that others had: "When she smiles, her face loses much of its hardness. Her voice is decidedly soft and musical. There is a particular, indescribable something in it that is attractive." Nonetheless, Jennie's overall impression was of a studied, almost schoolmarmish carefulness—she thought that Miss Dudley pronounced each word with a labored exactitude and sat "bolt upright," as if to "impress you with her determination to appear to be doing the perfectly correct thing."

Miss Dudley told Jennie she had done some writing of her own, so Jennie tried to press her for details, but Sister Dorothea sent Jennie off to bed. It was a long, restless night. Jennie had "no idea beds could be made so hard," and she couldn't settle with the rustle of strange bodies all around. Jennie was awakened at dawn by the clanging of a large bell. She donned her spartan uniform in the gloom of the gaslight and then waited in line with fifteen other girls in a "cold, cheerless" hallway for her turn to wash in cold water at one of four basins. Then it was off to chapel for prayers, followed by a breakfast of coarse oatmeal, bread, and "a rather doubtful article which was called coffee."

Jennie arrived at her sewing class to find Miss Dudley substituting for the nun who usually taught it. They spent the morning sewing and talking. Miss Dudley told Jennie that her father was an Englishman who died young and left the family poor. She said she went to live with an aunt and uncle, who also died, and that she then went to live with another aunt and uncle outside Lexington, where she had two thoroughbreds of her own to ride "and generally had whatever she wanted." She said she had a governess and tutor, the latter being a charming old German gentleman with whom she rode around her auntie's grounds as she conjugated Latin verbs and studied botany. Her only dissatisfaction was with her grandfather, who refused to rise when she entered the room, which she considered such an unbearable breach of etiquette that she "stood all the time she was in the room with him."

Afterward, as Jennie stewed over her lunch of liver and mashed potatoes—she detested liver—Miss Dudley ate the better fare served to the sisters and teachers at a table waited on by the girls. Jennie soon learned that Miss Dudley ate her breakfast in bed and had a private room, with "the luxury of a bureau, wash-stand, table, rocking-chair and book-shelves." That evening there was music and singing in the sitting room. Miss Dudley sang in a "small, weak voice" but told Jennie she had once had a "wonderful voice" and had studied music in hopes of becoming a famous singer, but lost her voice in an attack of diphtheria. By the time she turned in for her second night of tossing and turning on a bed that felt like "the soft side of a pine board"—the thin mattress was stuffed with corn husks—Jennie was sure that she had heard nothing but "fairy tales" of Miss Dudley's life. Now, she was burning with curiosity as to "her real story."

February 1, Jennie's third day in the home, was bright and warm. After the morning chores were finished, she went out into the yard with one of the other girls to get a better look at her surroundings. It was then that she saw the brick wall round the yard with its fearsome-looking glass projectiles. As she calculated whether she could climb over it, she felt for the first time like a "real prisoner." When Sister Dorothea asked her if she would like to send a letter to the doctor she mentioned to tell him she had arrived safely—which, by prearrangement with one of her old housemates in Boston, would be forwarded to Stoll—Jennie slipped in a little shorthand note confirming that Pollard was at the home and reiterating to him that if he heard nothing from her in three weeks he should put their extraction plan in motion.

By suppertime she was so hungry that she could "hardly keep back the tears" when she sat down to her meal of bread and weak tea. So it caught her attention when she heard one of the girls telling Miss Dudley that "the biscuits have arrived." She turned to Jennie and explained that she had taught the girl to call her to dinner with that phrase because when she was a child living in Paris, they often had to wait for biscuits from a nearby bakery before dinner could be served. When they came, she said, the "French waiter would throw open the door of the saloon and announce 'the biscuits have arrived, Monsieur, Madam.'"

After dinner, Jennie sidled up to Miss Dudley and shared some of the same sad story she told Sister Dorothea, hoping to inspire an exchange of tales of woe. Miss Dudley became "quite confidential, and admitted that her own life had not been all that it should have been" and promised to tell Jennie her story before she left. Then they bantered about ideas of what they would do when they left the home. Jennie suggested they go West and "begin life anew." Miss Dudley said she wanted to go to Germany and study and that "she would write and make a great name for herself, and that she would come back to this country so famous one day that no one would dare sit in her presence." They mused about taking a flat together in New York City, where Miss Dudley said they could live "the pleasantest sort of Bohemian life" and throw after-theater supper parties with all the writers and artists she knew.

Jennie came upon Miss Dudley looking "vexed and disappointed" the following afternoon after a trip to her lawyer's office. She fumed about the man who she said had ruined her and seemed to Jennie "very bitter and full of revenge." She told Jennie the man was "thirty years older than she, and that she had given him the best years of her life." She said that she "worshipped him, and that he made her believe that he loved her; but that he was a coward." Her bad temper spilled over to the other girls. Jennie watched her thoughtlessly dismiss a "sort of a household drudge" who had spent an hour polishing her brass inkwell, and harshly scold a girl who had "vexed her by some little impertinence."

Jennie spent the following day in bed, "too ill to get up." Miss Dudley visited her and told her more of her story, about how she was an "innocent little thing" when she met the man who ruined her and how she "gave him all her girlhood and never had beaux." She also told Jennie how he made her give up her children and "how she had discovered his infidelity to her" and did not "believe his wickedness possible."

By this point, Jennie had decided she couldn't bear it in the home any longer; she felt her "strength giving out," probably because, with the exception of Sunday dinner, she would tell Stoll, she hadn't had "a meal that I could eat." She also learned that some of the girls had overheard her conversation with Miss Dudley about her wayward life, and Sister Dorothea wanted her to promise not to talk to her anymore. Jennie told Sister Dorothea that she had decided to leave after her week was up. "I am getting out of prison," she scribbled with relief in her diary. She had been helping with the home's books and told Sister Dorothea she would come back and work in the office, hoping with that excuse and the friendship she had struck up with Miss Dudley she could carry on her detective work from the outside.

After breakfast on Tuesday, exactly one week after she had walked through the front door of the House of Mercy, Jennie sat with Miss Dudley looking over the "rooms to let" section in the newspaper while she waited for Miss Grey to retrieve her street clothes. It was then that Miss Dudley leaned over, and "in a sort of stage whisper," told Jennie that her real name was Madeline Pollard.

•

Jennie fled the House of Mercy with Madeline's voice still ringing in her head. It had taken all her composure to maintain a "marble calm" when Madeline told her who she really was and to pretend that she was only vaguely aware of the scandal that had engulfed her employer and fascinated the nation. Madeline urged her to get a copy of the *World* and read her story and vowed that the upcoming trial was going to be "a very bitter fight." As she said her goodbyes, Jennie promised to send word to Madeline of her new lodgings so they could keep in touch. Then, she headed straight for the dining room of the National Hotel, where she ordered herself a hearty meal that an astonished waiter watched her eat "like an Arctic explorer" back from the North Pole. "I was simply starved," she wrote to Stoll from the hotel. "It was in every way a dreadful experience." She was eager to assure him that she hadn't left the house "due to a lack of courage" but because after their conversation was overheard, "the sisters objected to me having anything to do with Miss Pollard" and she "could gain nothing by remaining there"—although, in truth, she had decided to leave even before that happened.

Stoll, who, unlike Jennie, understood from the start that the House of Mercy was no YWCA home, knew what he was putting her through. "I think a cold chill must have passed down her back when she got an inside view," he wrote to Breckinridge after he got her letter saying she had finagled her way into the home. He seemed to think what Jennie was most worried about was not getting her things back if she left precipitously. "They are going to take all of her belongings away . . . so that some scheme will have to be worked out to get them back" if she left early, he told Breckinridge. It wasn't her belongings she was worried about getting back; Jennie appeared genuinely terrified that she would get stuck in the House of Mercy, with its spartan meals and weak tea, corn-husk mattresses, and jagged glass wall, and what she told Stoll was the "contemptuous authority" of the staff: "It is like a jail there, and one is watched every minute."

For her suffering she had precious little to show. Stoll hadn't given her any background on the case and had instructed her not to read Madeline's *World* autobiography because, he told her, he didn't want her to "fix [her] mind in a certain channel, which may prevent you from reaching that correct conclusion, as to her character." Based on other avenues of investigation he was plotting at the time, it seems he thought all he had to do was get some woman to befriend Madeline and she would blab her heart out about who was really behind the suit. Without the details of Madeline's life, however, Jennie had no way to suss out fact from fiction or to delve more deeply into areas of inconsistency. When that evening Jennie got a letter from Stoll with some specific points of the case they were trying to clarify, she told him she would have liked to have the information before she entered the home, but, "I did the best that could be done with the material I had to work with." What she could tell Stoll was that a settlement was "out of the question," as she thought Madeline took pride in the idea of the trial and was un-fazed about any newspaper notoriety it might bring. She also told Stoll that Madeline had "a certain quick wit" and, in her estimation, was "a very good actress."

Madeline's backstory did appear to be cobbled together from bits and pieces of the lives of elite folks she met along the way. It was Breckin-ridge who had a governess and his children who had the idiosyncratic German tutor. She told Jennie about a young Yale student who fell madly in love with her while she was studying in Cambridge. His "parents were Kentuckians and great friends of hers" and they were "worried about their boy, because he was getting wild and drinking," and his mother implored her to use her influence to try to save him, which was clearly a recasting of the Breckinridges' desperate battle to save their son Robert. Who knows where she got the story of the Paris biscuits from, but the only Paris she had been to was Paris, Kentucky. She appears to have been a biographical magpie, collecting bits and pieces of other people's lives to weave into the one she felt she should have had—and to create a per-sona that allowed her access to the world she wished to inhabit. Yet her story about her relationship with Breckinridge, her innocence when it began, the children she sacrificed, and how he betrayed her all appeared to be true in its essentials.

It's also not wholly clear that Madeline wasn't on to Jennie. She came to Jennie one day and told her she had "a strange dream" that Jennie was Nellie Bly, the famous investigative reporter who had gone undercover at Blackwell's Island Insane Asylum to reveal the horrendous conditions there. "I thought you were one of those dreadful reporters, and that you had come here to take down every thing I said to you," she told Jennie. "I thought to myself, how much I have been talking to this dreadful woman." Jennie laughed it off, but inwardly she "knew it was not a dream." Regardless, she seemed to think that her nascent friendship with Madeline was intact. But Madeline's "dream" clearly was a suspicion tinged with a warning—Jennie had been very inquisitive, and it would have been very unusual for someone of her class to commit herself to a place like the House of Mercy. Still, she wrote to her mother, "Mr. S's associates seem to think I've done mighty well for them," and plowed optimistically into the next stage of her spy saga.

Madeline Pollard said she was a seventeen-year-old student when Col. W.C.P. Breckinridge "accosted" her on a train and later took "liberties" with her during a carriage ride. (Photograph from *The Celebrated Trial: Madeline Pollard vs. Breckinridge*)

Congressman William Campbell Preston Breckinridge was a former Confederate officer and the scion of a legendary Kentucky political family who rose to become one of the most powerful men in the Democratic Party. (Photograph by C. M. Bell, courtesy of the University of Kentucky Archives)

Madeline Pollard "startled the whole country" when she sued Congressman W.C.P. Breckinridge for fifty thousand dollars for breach of promise to marry in August 1893, exposing herself as a "ruined" woman and launching a sensational scandal. (*New York World*, August 13, 1893)

Madeline Pollard as she appeared during the five-week trial in the spring of 1894 that challenged a system of sexual moral-ity based on shaming women and excusing men for predatory behavior (Photograph by C. M. Bell, Library of Congress)

Jane "Jennie" Tucker in New York in 1893 after she left home as part of the first generation of working women, only to find herself embroiled in the Breckinridge-Pollard scandal when she was hired to spy on Madeline in a home for "fallen" women (Photograph by Edward Dana, courtesy of Historic New England)

Jennie (second from left) and her brothers and sisters in front of Castle Tucker in Wiscasset, Maine, before the family fell on hard times (Photograph by J. C. Higgins, courtesy of Historic New England)

Jennie Tucker loitered along this Pennsylvania Avenue streetcar route in Washington in 1894 in hopes of catching Madeline on a passing trolley. (Getty Images)

Julia Maria Preston Pope Churchill Blackburn violated all the rules of southern propriety when she agreed to testify on Madeline's behalf, confirming that Col. Breckinridge had told her of their engagement. (Courtesy of the Filson Historical Society)

Mary "Mollie" Desha became a power-house among women leaders in early 1890s Washington and used her influence to turn popular opinion against her brother-in-law W.C.P. Breckinridge. (Photograph by C. M. Bell, Library of Congress)

THE COLONEL

Repeats His Oft-Told Tale

Of How He Was Led Astray By a School Girl.

No Man Could Have Had Less Excuse Than He,

And For Ten Years He Has Suffered Tortuous Agony.

Judge Wilson Opens the Cross-Examination For the Plaintiff—Testimony in Detail.

PUT THE GIRLS OUT.

Judge Bradley Clears the Court-Room for the Pollard Case.

Grumbling Maids and Matrons Ousted from Choice Seats.

Trial Resumed with Another Wrangle Over Four Irving Books.

(By Associated Press.)

WASHINGTON, March 12.—Refreshed by two days of consultation and planning the Pollard-Breckinridge legal forces bristled with law books and portentious looking documents this morning as they arrayed themselves along the two rows of desks in the criminal court-room. Jurors, too, were smiling with just provocation, for directly across the court-room and facing them sat a group of fashionable young women backed by a row of solemn matrons, all guided by that fountain of curiosity which springs eternal in the female breast.

WHOLE COURT IN TEARS.

Miss Pollard Reaches the Climax of Her Tragic and Pathetic Story.

SENSATIONS IN QUICK SUCCESSION.

Adjournment Came with the Plaintiff Witness Sobbing and Every Eye Moistened.

"ONE OF THE TRAGEDIES OF LIFE."

Of Miss Pollard's Threats to Shoot, Two at Least Were Made After the Secret Marriage.

Even as Breckinridge asserted that he couldn't be expected to marry a "fallen" woman and women themselves were excluded from the courtroom, Madeline captured the sympathy of the nation with the story of her seduction by a powerful older man and the children she was forced to give up. (*Cincinnati Enquirer*, April 3, 1894; *New York World*, March 21, 1894; *New York World*, March 12, 1894)

The Breckinridges: Rev. Robert Jefferson Breckinridge (*top left*) was a noted southern opponent of slavery, but his son Willie Breckinridge (*top right*) fought for the Confederacy as a colonel in the Ninth Kentucky Calvary. Willie's daughter Sophonisba (*bottom left*) graduated from Wellesley College at a time when few women had a college education but struggled to carve a professional path for herself. Desha Breckinridge (*bottom right*) sailed into the law career his sister Nisba longed for but spent much of his father's trial picking fights and trying to provoke duels. (Robert Breckinridge: Library of Congress; Willie Breckinridge: photograph by James Mullen, Library of Congress; Sophonisba Breckinridge: photograph by Pach Brothers, courtesy of Wellesley College Archives; Desha Breckinridge: photograph by James Mullen, Library of Congress)

The cover of one of several books on the "celebrated" case of *Pollard vs. Breckinridge*, which fascinated the nation as women streamed into the workforce, raising new questions about how to protect their respectability

In 1901, Sophonisba "Nisba" Breckinridge became the first woman to receive a Ph.D. in political science from the University of Chicago, launching her career as a leading feminist social scientist. (Library of Congress)

Nisba's best friend, Madeline, married Desha Breckinridge. Madeline McDowell Breckinridge converted Desha to her progressive politics and became a leader in the fight for woman's suffrage. (Library of Congress)

The campaign to deny Breckinridge the Democratic nomination was spearheaded by the women of his hometown of Lexington, Kentucky, attracting nationwide attention.

(Photograph by Lafayette Studios, courtesy of the University of Kentucky Archives)

The powerful and popular Breckinridge's loss was like the fall "of an archangel," said the historians James Klotter and Hambelton Tapp. (*Cincinnati Enquirer*, September 6, 1894)

11

A Good Woman

Two days after she left the House of Mercy, on February 8, Jennie got lucky and ran into Madeline downtown at the Boston Store. Madeline was shopping in preparation for her departure to Cincinnati, where the first round of depositions would be taken the next day. She seemed "a little icy," but Jennie followed her around the department store nonetheless as she picked out undergarments and a new purse, and then down the street to Morez et Cie, a fashionable millinery shop where Madeline bought a fetching little hat for nearly half the thirty dollars Jennie calculated she had in her pocket. Jennie was curious as to where she got the money, as Madeline appeared completely broke at the House of Mercy. "The day my suit was filed, I hadn't even my car fare," she told Jennie. Sister Dorothea had told her that Madeline had no money when she arrived seeking refuge one evening and that Miss Talcott, who was in charge of the house then, "had gone about among Madeline's lady friends and collected money for her because she did not have a cent for the little necessities of life." Madeline explained to Jennie that she had gotten the money from her brother, who received an unexpected windfall, although Jennie didn't buy that explanation. Regardless, there clearly was no shortage of funds to pay for the trial expenses. Madeline bragged to Jennie that she had a private stateroom for the trip to Cincinnati so she "would not have to be stared at," as well as a nine-hundred-mile train pass.

Meanwhile, the Breckinridge team was scrambling to cover day-to-day expenses, which now included Jennie's room and board since she had relocated to a boardinghouse on Connecticut Avenue. Stoll had to advance William Worthington, the stenographer in Breckinridge's law office who was acting as an intermediary with Jennie, thirty dollars for Jennie's expenses because Breckinridge hadn't come through with the requested funds. Breckinridge repaid Stoll with a check postdated to his next congressional paycheck because he said he didn't have "the money to square just now without straining." Desha wrote to his father, "How are you for money? I am dead broke and I fear you are too," explaining that one witness needed seventy dollars for travel expenses. As the result of their straitened finances, the defense was relying on the shoestring detective efforts of Desha and Sam McChesney, who were managing an ad hoc crew of party loyalists dispatched to investigate Pollard in various cities, as well as intelligence that came in over the transom from Breckinridge's network of kin and political allies. A few of the leads proved potentially useful. Breckinridge's brother Robert wrote to tell him that he had overheard a story from a local doctor that Col. A. M. Swope had "tried to employ him to produce an abortion on Miss Pollard." But much of the intelligence was a stew of hearsay and rumor: a thirteen-year-old girl known as "Mad Poll" whose father was a Frankfort harness maker supposedly entertained men at the Galt House in Louisville; Pollard's aunt Mary Stout allegedly ran a secret brothel in a stable behind her house. The team ended up spending a considerable amount of time chasing leads that ended up being dead ends.

Stoll wanted to systematize and professionalize the investigation by hiring proper detectives to investigate Madeline's life and to direct Jennie's efforts. Not shy about manipulating women for his own ends, he wanted to hire a female detective to befriend Madeline's mother and get into her house, "letting her get sick on their hands and having to stay with them ten days or two weeks if necessary" to see if they could get Mrs. Pollard "to talk very freely." Stoll got a proposal from the local office of the famed Pinkerton Detective Agency that would cost between $1,500 and $2,000. But when he attempted to move ahead with the plan, Robert Pinkerton, who managed the East Coast operations of the firm his father founded, told Stoll that he would need him to personally guarantee the account because the Philadelphia office "did some work on the same case . . . and there is a balance still due on that account." Stoll, who like most of Breckinridge's friends was donating his time to the case, apparently was unwilling to go into debt for his friend, and the Pinkerton plan didn't come to fruition.

•

Madeline Pollard and her lawyer Calderon Carlisle arrived in Cincinnati on the morning of February 9, had a late breakfast, and made their way to the downtown law office where the depositions would be taken. Carlisle was in his early forties, tall, thin, and well dressed, his wavy hair slicked back, every bit the club man. Madeline was dressed in a double-breasted dark-blue coat with fashionable leg-o'-mutton sleeves over a black dress, tan gloves, patent leather high-button shoes, and her new hat, a saucer-shaped black velvet affair with a feather plume.

Charles Stoll and Desha Breckinridge, who had been dispatched to handle the Cincinnati depositions, met them at the law office to take the depositions of the three women doctors who, Pollard said, attended her after she gave birth at the Norwood Foundling Asylum in Cincinnati the first time she was pregnant. Breckinridge's strategy, as he told one of his supporters, wasn't to deny a relationship with Madeline but to prove the "absolute falsity of all the more serious charges": that he seduced Pollard when she was a girl, that he was the father of her children, and that he introduced her into society. The first two got to the heart of the case against him; the latter was a point of pride for Breckinridge, who was eager to refute the widespread notion it was he who had given Pollard a toehold into Washington's upper-class society.

The three doctors were Dr. Belle Buchanan; Dr. Mary Street, who was now married and retired and went by Mrs. Logan; and Dr. Kate Perry, who also was married and now Mrs. Cain. All three were graduates of the Pulte Medical College, a local homeopathic school of medicine. Both Dr. Buchanan and Dr. Perry recognized Madeline as a former patient. Dr. Buchanan testified that Dr. Street brought Pollard to the practice she shared with Dr. Perry sometime around February 1885, although she was unsure of the exact dates, and that she treated her for a "disorder consequent upon child-birth." Madeline said

in her autobiography that her first delivery was difficult. Dr. Perry testified that she recognized Madeline as Louise Wilson, who was introduced
to her as a widow who had suffered a miscarriage but who she later
found out was unmarried. When it was Dr. Street's turn to be deposed and
she was brought into the room, however, she didn't recognize Madeline
at all. "The name Louise Wilson means nothing to me. I don't know you,"
she said when she was introduced to Madeline.

For his part, Stoll was convinced that Street did know Madeline but
had pretended not to recognize her because, as he told Breckinridge,
"she and the Buchanan woman had performed an abortion on Louise
Wilson, who I am satisfied is Miss Pollard."

The taking of depositions next moved to the Norwood Asylum, the
charity home for unwed mothers where Madeline said her first child was
born in 1885. Madeline and Carlisle went there in December seeking
proof of her stay but hadn't been able to find any record of a Louise
Wilson, the name Pollard said she used. When Carlisle examined the
records, however, he did find an Alice Burgoyne who gave birth on a
nearby date, which Pollard then said was the name she had used but forgotten in the haze of all the aliases she had used over the years. Sister
Augustine, who was the nun in charge of the asylum, said in her deposition that she never saw Madeline before she came in December, although
she noted there were some one hundred girls there every year and most
used aliases. She said that Madeline asked her what had happened to the
baby she left there and that Madeline "went into hysterics" when she
told her the baby born to the woman named Burgoyne died in July 1885.

Sister Augustine also said Madeline didn't seem familiar with the
home. However, as the *Cincinnati Enquirer* reported, at one point Madeline went directly to a bookcase and "took therefrom a copy of Washington Irving and found among the leaves a card she had placed there
when an inmate." Madeline explained that she had left a three-volume
set of Irving's works at the home as a gift for the sisters and found in one
of the books a Christmas card that she had used as a bookmark. Sister
Augustine then pressed Madeline as to why she wanted to ruin Breckinridge, telling her that "she must be a bad woman to make such a show
of herself before the world." Madeline replied: "Oh no. I was a bad girl,
but I am a good woman."

Despite this heated exchange, the Cincinnati and Kentucky papers reported that the depositions had been "decidedly in favor of Colonel Breckinridge." Madeline returned to Washington irritable with how the depositions had gone. "She could not bear to talk of it," Jennie reported. While working on the bookkeeping at the House of Mercy, Jennie had overheard that Madeline was going out on a walk and followed her. She tried to talk Madeline into dropping the suit, since she wasn't expecting any money anyway. "I cannot give this up now; it is part of my life," she told Jennie. "This man has ruined my life . . . and he shall suffer what he has made me suffer."

Jennie had used Madeline's time out of town to befriend her brother Dudley in the hopes of gaining some useful intelligence. She spent two afternoons sightseeing with him, visiting Capitol Hill—where she had him point out Breckinridge on the House floor—and the Washington Monument and the Botanical Gardens, all the while pumping him for information about Madeline's age and her motivations. She found him "unsophisticated" and "not half as bright as his sister" and ended up convinced that Madeline didn't confide in him.

There was more urgency than ever to Jennie's work. During a preliminary hearing on February 17, Breckinridge's lawyers had asked Judge Andrew Bradley, who was scheduled to hear the case, for a postponement until late March because Enoch Totten, Breckinridge's lead attorney, was ill and recovering in Florida. Pollard's lawyer Carlisle objected, accusing the defense of obstruction and failing to prepare for the trial. Bradley refused the postponement, noting that Breckinridge had other lawyers, and set the trial date for March 8. Less than a week later, Totten wrote to Breckinridge and said he was still unwell and was "by no means able to undergo the labor of such a trial." It was a devastating development for Breckinridge. Totten was not only "rather the best lawyer here," as Breckinridge told a friend, having long defended the Pennsylvania Railroad against lawsuits, but the person who "understood the case better than anybody else."

The loss of Totten brought home the reality that the Breckinridge team was large but not particularly deep in the expertise needed. Phil Thompson hadn't practiced law before the District courts for years, Desha was a newly minted lawyer who hadn't done much more than take depositions, and Shelby and Stoll were primarily corporate lawyers, although Stoll could be devastating on cross-examination. Even as he cast about desperately for another lawyer on short notice, Breckinridge made one last desperate plea to Totten. "I am in a hole," he wrote, begging him to come back and at least be present in the courtroom. The letter went unanswered. Florida apparently not being salubrious enough for his health, Totten had decamped to Cuba.

On February 15, the taking of depositions moved to Lexington, where a long list of witnesses had been called. For Breckinridge, this was the most critical component of the defense, as many of the witnesses were expected to testify about Madeline's supposedly immoral behavior as a young woman. With Congress in session, he remained in Washington, however, and sent Desha, Stoll, and his partner John Shelby to take the depositions. The first witness of significance was Catesby Hawkins, a carpenter from Frankfort, who testified that some years ago when she was a teenager, Pollard attended a Christmas party at a Squire Tinsley's where there was much drinking of whiskey and wine. He said there was "a mock marriage between Miss Pollard and Alex Julian," and afterward they were "taken upstairs and put to bed," although he couldn't say if Julian remained there all night. He said the "talk in the neighborhood was that [Pollard] was very fast."

Next to testify was Mollie Shindlebower, who was "formerly a sporting woman"—a prostitute. She said that when she was in her teens, she went to live with Madeline's aunt Mary Stout in Bridgeport after her parents died and that Madeline once visited for three months. Shindlebower said Madeline's behavior "caused frequent family disturbances" because she "received many young men for visitors whose reputation was bad" and took buggy rides with them until ten or eleven o'clock at night. She said Madeline "bore the reputation of being wild and fast" and that she suspected that "Miss Pollard had attained a woman's estate"—lost her virginity—because her brother once "made an indecent remark" that she "did not rebuke."

John Brand then testified that he had met Pollard at the home of Lena Singleton in Lexington in 1883. He alleged that Singleton was "the mistress of James Rhodes" and kept a known "assignation house"—a place where a proprietress rented rooms with no questions asked, whether it be illicit lovers or sporting women and their clients. He claimed that once when he came to the house, "Miss Pollard ran out of the room and disappeared," and that he saw her at the house after that "in conversation with James Rhodes," who told him "he was educating Miss Pollard." Brand also claimed that when Pollard was working at the office of Howard Gratz, the publisher of the *Lexington Gazette*, "he would frequently take Miss Pollard out buggy riding," bringing her "several miles into the country," but had to "quit taking her riding" because he was afraid of his wife, who "was a jealous woman."

The deposition of Madeline's old Wesleyan classmate Wessie Brown, who was now Mrs. Robertson, was taken the same day in Cincinnati. She testified that soon after Madeline came to the school "she told her that her father was a great admirer of W.C.P. Breckinridge" and that after her absence to attend her sister's funeral, Madeline told her that "W.C.P. Breckinridge had introduced himself to her on a train, and that she seemed much elated that so prominent a man should notice her so kindly."

There was only one witness the next day, but his testimony caused "a sensation of great magnitude," reported Louisville's *Courier-Journal*. The *Courier-Journal* had been invited by Stoll to cover the Lexington depositions in retaliation for Carlisle allowing a reporter from the *Cincinnati Enquirer* to cover some of the Cincinnati depositions and leaking the contents of others, which meant that the public was able to follow the opening rounds of testimony more or less in real time—and that the battle for public opinion already had begun. Dr. T. M. Lewis testified that Col. Armstead M. Swope had in early February 1885 requested to meet with him and told him that "he had become seriously compromised in his relations with a young lady by the name of Pollard, who used to live in Crab Orchard." He didn't mention the woman's first name, but told Dr. Lewis that "he had been a frequent caller upon the young lady in Lexington," and as a result of an encounter one night in the parlor, which Swope intimated that she had initiated, "she was in a delicate condition." Swope supposedly asked Lewis to "produce an abortion" for Pollard, which he refused to do. Swope later told the doctor that "the child had been born and now had a good home."

The sensational charge that Swope, the well-known former Internal Revenue collector and Union officer who had been killed in the infamous

Swope-Goodloe duel of 1889, had tried to procure an abortion for Pollard swept through Lexington and reverberated in Washington like a "bombshell." It was quickly replaced by even more sensational testimony from an even more prominent witness: Julia Blackburn, who was so annoyed at Breckinridge that she had agreed to give a deposition, going against every ideal of southern propriety to do so. Her deposition was "intensely favorable to Miss Pollard," reported the *Cincinnati Enquirer*, which had been leaked a copy of the testimony that had been taken two weeks earlier at Julia's apartment in Washington.

According to Blackburn, Madeline and Breckinridge called at her flat on the evening of Good Friday, March 31, 1893, and insisted on seeing her. Breckinridge "came into the parlor and said he had come to ask my protection of Miss Pollard" because "he expected to make her his wife as soon as the proper time had elapsed after the death of the late Mrs. Breckinridge." She said that Madeline called him "Willie" and put her arms around him and that in general their manner was what she "would take to be that of engaged people."

She said that after that first meeting, Breckinridge came back on his own and said he could tell that Julia "looked shocked" when he announced his engagement. It wasn't the age difference that bothered Julia, although she said Breckinridge acknowledged that the engagement probably appeared "absurd" because he was "quite old enough to be [Madeline's] father." She herself had had a whirlwind courtship with a widower nearly twenty years her senior. She met her beloved husband, Luke, in the spring of 1857, when she was twenty-four and touring Europe with her sister and he was forty-one and taking a trip to recover from the death of his wife Ella. They were married the following November. What bothered Julia was Breckinridge engaging himself to marry so soon after his wife's death. "This seems to me to be a very poor return for so much devotion as you received—you have forgotten your wife so soon," she said. Breckinridge told her that he had "discovered Miss Pollard's feelings toward" him, and "being a man of honor there was nothing left for me to do." Blackburn found this excuse, which belonged in an early nineteenth-century romance novel, absurd and told him that he took "a very high view of the case" that most men would not.

Blackburn also said that Breckinridge had sung Madeline's praises, telling her "she was a woman of a great many talents"—she "sang and played and drew" and was a prodigious reader, "devouring everything that came out." She said, "He said she was one of the most magnetic and agreeable women he had ever known." She also claimed, as she had in her letter to Basil Duke, that it was largely on Breckinridge's recommendation that Madeline became "a recognized friend" of hers and was "seen many places with her on public occasions."

Breckinridge, who attended the deposition, was "appalled" at Blackburn's testimony, according to the *Enquirer*. He apparently had hoped "the memories of old time relations" between the Blackburns and the Breckinridges would "preclude any vigorous attempt on her part to prove that the statements of Miss Pollard are predicated on facts," but instead she had thoroughly "scored the Congressman." Breckinridge personally handled the cross-examination in an attempt to get Blackburn to admit that it wasn't he who had introduced Pollard to her but her landlady, Mrs. Fillette, and that Madeline's character had come into question because she had allowed Charles Dudley Warner to stay overnight at Fillette's house when she wasn't there. In fact, as Blackburn admitted, Fillette had taken the unusually harsh step of "withdrawing" her introduction to Madeline sometime the previous winter, predicting there would be a "terrible denouement" regarding the young woman. But Blackburn refused to be cowed. She "wheeled in her chair" and with eyes flashing "turned every query of the defendant to the strength of the plaintiff" and then "stated with much vigor that she thought he had not acted right in the matter, and that Miss Pollard had been irreparably wronged."

The spectacle of two of the Bluegrass's finest dueling it out in the "star-chamber," as the *Enquirer* termed it, as well as Blackburn's robust defense of Madeline, ensured that her deposition was front-page news. Breckinridge was practically apoplectic, especially since the leaked version of the deposition conveniently omitted much of his cross-examination, which he promptly provided to friendly newspapers. He complained to a friend that "Blackburn put things into my mouth which the plaintiff said when I was not present and she colored everything against me." He called the attorney who prepared the deposition a "shyster" and claimed the testimony had been "doctored."

Increasingly, Breckinridge looked to pin the blame for his predicament on others, including, as he told one friend, "a gang in Lexington who are my enemies." Breckinridge had earned the enmity of one of the most powerful political interests in the state: the Blue Grass Hemp Trust. Hemp, which was widely used in the making of rope for ship riggings, was one of Kentucky's key agricultural products and was a particularly important crop for the Bluegrass region. Bluegrass hemp, however, was facing stiff competition from imported hemp, even as overall demand sagged as steam replaced sails. Still, as a Bourbon Democrat, Breckinridge opposed protective tariffs—even for an industry based in his own district. He also blamed "those who have been disappointed in getting [political] appointments," and in letters to friends, rehashed obscure, internecine battles over postmaster and tax collector positions going back a decade. "That my enemies are using this poor woman I am perfectly certain," he told a friend.

The Kentucky depositions resumed on February 20. The first witness was Alex Julian, who had been a crush of Madeline's when she was a young woman. Julian denounced Catesby Hawkins's testimony about the "mock marriage" at Squire Tinsley's as "unqualifiedly false" and asserted that Hawkins wasn't even at the party. He said that after the consumption of some eggnog on Christmas morning in 1881, when the company was "feeling good," he performed a mock marriage between Madeline and Owen Tinsley, the squire's brother. He said that afterward someone made a joke about people going to bed after being married, and that he and Madeline, who was "very drunk," went upstairs and lay on a bed, but came back downstairs when they heard people asking about them. What Breckinridge had hoped he would testify to was what he had reportedly told his friend Omar Thomas: "that he had pulled up the plaintiff's clothes and was about in the act of entry when he was interrupted." Under questioning, however, all he admitted to was kissing Madeline one afternoon while they sat near a bridge and a few other times. When he was asked what he thought about her morals, he said, "I mean no disrespect to the people of my community when I say that I thought her to be as pure and chaste as other girls living in my neighborhood."

Following Julian, a man named Taylor Parrent testified that he had refused to rent a portion of a house in Bridgeport to Madeline's mother "on account of the reputation borne by Miss Madeline Pollard." Then Dr. James Robertson testified that he had known the Pollard family in Crab Orchard, where he "had attended Mrs. Pollard when her youngest child . . . was born in 1865." He said that the little girl known as Mattie "was about three years old" then, which would mean that Madeline was born around 1862 and was in her early twenties when she met Breckinridge.

Mrs. Ketchum and Mrs. Hoyt, the two ladies who ran the boarding-house in Lexington where Madeline lived when she attended the Sayre Institute, testified on February 22. The Breckinridge team hoped to get Ketchum to say that Colonel Swope had visited Madeline at the house, but she testified that Swope had never visited Madeline, only Rhodes once or twice a week, always in the parlor, and that they "generally quarreled all the time." She said that Madeline's behavior was "above reproach" when she lived in the house, and that when she first came in September 1884 she was still a schoolgirl in short dresses. She also testified that Madeline left in February 1885—which is when Madeline claimed she left because she was pregnant—and didn't return until the fall of 1885, when she had started wearing long dresses, the mark of womanhood. She did say that while Madeline was away, she heard a story that "Col. Breckinridge had called on Miss Pollard in Cincinnati, and that she had gone driving with him in a closed carriage." When she asked Madeline about it, she laughed it off and said, "Why, that was my uncle, Henry Oliver, of Cincinnati. He is the very image of Colonel Breckinridge and is so often taken for the Colonel. The very idea!"

Ketchum also testified that at one point when Madeline was living in the house, Col. Breckinridge came to board there for several weeks, "saying that he had an important case in court and he did not care to stay at the hotel, which was not convenient."

That afternoon Rankin Rossell, the clerk at the Cincinnati dry goods store Shillito's, testified that one November afternoon in 1884 Madeline came in and introduced herself, saying that she knew of him through her cousin Nellie Oliver. She asked him to take her to Wesleyan College and introduce her to Dr. Brown, the president, whom he knew, and told

him that her guardian Mr. Rhodes would be along the next day to pay
her tuition. He said he called on Madeline at the school frequently after
that and that their "friendship led to an engagement to marry, which was
made during the Christmas holidays" of 1884. Rossell claimed that
when he called on Madeline at Wesleyan "she would throw herself
into his lap" and that he would kiss her. He said he broke off the engagement because she "permitted him to take liberties with her," although he said he did not think she was a "bad" girl, just "forward in
her actions."

The two witnesses who testified the following day were the most
critical for Breckinridge. Building on John Brand's testimony that Madeline frequented Lena Singleton's assignation house, Breckinridge hoped
to prove that while she was living in Lexington with Mrs. Ketchum and
attending Sayre, Madeline was living "a double life, one in high and the
other in low society," as the *Morning Transcript* put it. Dr. R. D. Greene
testified that he had been summoned in 1882 or 1883 to an assignation
house in Lexington to treat Rhodes and that he returned several times
thereafter and that Rhodes pointed out a young woman "he said he
was educating" and at another point told him "the young woman was a
Miss Pollard and that he was engaged to marry her." He said he later met
the same young woman at the house of Mrs. Ketchum.

Then Hiram Kaufman, who worked at the lunatic asylum with
Rhodes, testified that Rhodes invited him to go with him to see "his girl"
at Singleton's house, where he was introduced to Madeline. He said
they got drunk on beer, and "Miss Pollard later retired to a room with
Rhodes." He also claimed to have seen Pollard out buggy riding with
John Brand and that on "one occasion he had seen Brand and Miss Pollard coming out of one of the rooms" at Singleton's assignation house.

William Wood, a carpenter from Lexington, testified that he, too,
had been engaged to Madeline, having met her in the spring of 1882 at the
farm of her aunt Lou Keene outside of Lexington. He said that she used
to sing and play the piano for him on Sunday afternoons and that they
"soon fell in love" and he "purchased a handsome plain gold ring," which
he had engraved with their names. He said Madeline broke off the
engagement after five or six weeks when he told her he couldn't afford
to take her on a bridal trip to Europe and refused to return the ring,
claiming it had been lost.

The Breckinridge team felt they had scored a victory with the last set of depositions. Desha wrote to his father that the depositions "prove every thing we have started out to prove, except direct proof of her having sexual intercourse with any man." But it soon became apparent that the old scripts weren't working as they had expected. For one, just by showing her face at the depositions, Madeline had countered the image of the shame-faced adventuress. "At no time in the course of the examinations does she betray any sense of nervousness or of trying to bear up in the playing of a part," noted the *Morning Transcript*. In fact, it said, she "gives one the impression of one who has been seared with pain until there is no more sense of suffering." Just as important, it noted, in an opinion echoed by the *Enquirer*, "in every word and action she betrays the breeding of a lady, of the polished society woman."

If they had hoped to shift public opinion by smearing this decorous lady with sensational depositions, they had miscalculated. All they accomplished, said the *Enquirer*, besides increasing the "already absorbing interest" in the case, was to demonstrate that "Miss Pollard's life has been romantic and remarkable." Importantly, ideas about engagements were changing as marriage became more about love and less about economics. A woman who had one or two before she settled down was likely to be seen as popular and flirty, not necessarily debauched. Furthermore, the more sensational depositions were immediately discredited. Alex Julian had denounced Catesby Hawkins as a liar under oath. Kaufman's deposition had the "glamour of improbability," said the *Enquirer*, while Dr. Greene had crumbled under cross-examination, "growing so very hazy and inaccurate that his evidence was largely speculative." Mollie Shindlebower, the former prostitute who testified to Madeline's wild ways, was caught in a mini-scandal of her own. She reportedly lured a tourist to her hotel room and attempted to blackmail him by threatening to "claim he attempted to take advantage of her," although the Breckinridge people claimed it was a setup to impugn their witness.

Breckinridge had ignored the advice of one of the lawyers he had contacted about taking Totten's place: don't rely on prostitutes or the men who frequent them as your key witnesses—they lack credibility. Breckinridge was so eager to discredit Pollard that he took whatever he could get in terms of testimony. One local wrote to the *Enquirer* saying, "The character of the Immaculate Son of God could be smirched" with such witnesses.

An even bigger problem with the rush to smear Madeline was the backlash it provoked. When Breckinridge's people began investigating the reports of the mock marriage, Squire Tinsley, who hosted the party, wrote to Breckinridge as "your friend and admirer" to tell him that the report was "false." He later met personally with Breckinridge to tell him that the story was incorrect. Regardless, Breckinridge's lawyers pressed ahead with the Hawkins deposition. When Tinsley asked to give a deposition to correct the record, they refused to allow him to testify. A furious Tinsley sent a letter to the *Courier-Journal* that was reprinted around the state averring that Hawkins's testimony was an "unmitigated, contemptible lie." He said that Hawkins was never at his house, and the "alleged mock marriage was a mere joke and a farce which has been distorted into a scandal." As a result of the insult to Tinsley, a man many considered "one of the most sober and highly respected residents" of Frankfort, locals were "severe in their denunciations" of Breckinridge, according to the *Courier-Journal*.

Likewise, the attempt to pin Madeline's first pregnancy on Colonel Swope, a dead man who couldn't defend himself—much like Cleveland's allies blamed the late Oscar Folsom—"aroused a storm of indignation throughout the Blue Grass," said the *Enquirer*. Dr. Lewis's testimony was largely discounted when Swope's brother William said that it was a matter of record that his brother had been in Mexico during the fall of 1884 and hadn't returned to Lexington until December 10, which didn't give him much time to have made Madeline's acquaintance and frequently called on her if he was seeking an abortion for her in early February 1885. "I can not find anybody who ever saw them together, or who knows that they were acquainted with each other," said William. Furthermore, he said that his brother was in Europe in the fall of 1885, when Dr. Lewis claimed Swope told him about the child being born.

Breckinridge was increasingly desperate to link Madeline to another man. He believed that during the summer she worked for the *Lexington Gazette*, which was in 1887, right before she came to Washington, "she was on illicit relations with H. [Howard] Gratz," the *Gazette*'s publisher, who was a widower with grown children. He also contended that "there was an engagement to marry" between Madeline and Gratz. According to the local gossip, the engagement was short-circuited when Mrs. Captain Morgan—Nellie Morgan, the wife of Rhodes's former supervisor at the state asylum—sat next to Mrs. Judge Morton—Mary Morton, who was Gratz's daughter—at a luncheon and spilled the beans about Madeline's relationship with Rhodes. Gratz, according to the *Morning Transcript*, "was heartbroken and wanted . . . to marry her anyhow, but was prevented" from doing so by his children. Now, Breckinridge hoped to prove that Gratz was likely the father of the child that Madeline said was born in February 1888. He planned to assert that a riding accident Madeline had in late June of that year, which caused several broken ribs, would have ended any pregnancy resulting from their spring liaison, even though Desha consulted a physician who told him that the timing of the accident meant "such a fall would have had no such effect on the embryo."

Breckinridge told Shelby he believed that if Gratz was "approached right . . . he can be of great service," so Desha and Stoll scheduled him for a deposition. But Gratz pleaded to be excused because he was going to be married and didn't want the publicity. He said that "he couldn't prove anything of any consequence, except that he was engaged to [Madeline]." Despite the fact that his confirmation of the engagement appeared to belie Madeline's contention that she always had been faithful to Breckinridge, they let Gratz off the hook and canceled the deposition.

Throwing caution aside and now writing directly to Jennie instead of using Stoll as an intermediary, Breckinridge pressured her to try to find out something about Madeline's relationship with Charles Dudley Warner. He said Warner "was in her room at the Elsmere"—a hotel in Washington where Madeline briefly stayed—"pretending to be writing." But Jennie had been unable to get anywhere near Madeline. "You don't know how discouraged I've been," she wrote to Stoll. Breckinridge told her not to give up, reminding her that it was a "delicate and difficult undertaking." He stressed that any little piece of information she got could be the key to the defense, likening it, perhaps a little too aptly, to the strand that fabricates a rope by which a "sinking ship" is winched "to the shore."

As what many were describing as the "trial of the decade" drew near, it seems that W.C.P. Breckinridge increasingly was aware that no rope may be at hand, at least not in the form of another man he could pin Pollard on. There was only one last thing he could do to prepare for the trial. His wife, Louise, it appears, was now mentally unhinged. On top of the widespread impression that her marriage to Breckinridge had been of the shotgun variety, the Blackburn deposition had made it clear that while Louise was swooning around Washington last spring imagining herself as the next Mrs. W.C.P. Breckinridge, her Willie was still running around with the woman who had been his lover for the past nine years. She had been made a fool of and was now displaying what Willie told Nisba was an "unnatural state of mind" caused by "these constant newspaper attacks." He confided to his daughter, who was at Ella's house in Staunton, that he was afraid to leave Louise alone in the house he had rented on Q Street while he was in court dealing with this "unfortunate and malignant trial," but said, "I do not know where to turn to find somebody to be with her." He said he knew it was "more than I ought to ask," as Nisba had "done so much and done it so heroically . . . that I am utterly without excuse to ask more of you," but ask he would. "Do you think you would have the strength to come down and be with her?" he wrote to Nisba the day before the trial started.

So as the world tilted on its axis toward the twentieth century, with speeding streetcars and electric lights and telephones blurring the old distances and darknesses, with new questions being asked about old ideas, Nisba Breckinridge made her way to Washington.

12

Miss Pollard's Ruin in Lexington

Thursday, March 8, dawned unseasonably warm in Washington, as if nature herself was trying to hurry the city past the dreary winter of 1894. President Cleveland's promised silver bullet—the repeal of the Sherman Silver Act—still hadn't revived the economy. Unemployment remained high, morale was low; the administration seemed paralyzed, "mired in outdated doctrine," with Cleveland perceived as "rigid and uncaring," according to the historian Hal Williams. There were rumors from the west that a businessman named Jacob Coxey who believed he possessed the "reincarnated spirit of Andrew Jackson" was gathering an army of one hundred thousand unemployed men to march on Washington to demand jobs. Unrest and uncertainty were in the air. "Everywhere," said Williams, "older assumptions gave way to newer patterns and nagging doubts."

The opening of *Pollard v. Breckinridge* brought an air of fervid expectation to the Greek-revival building on Fourth and D Streets that was still called Old City Hall even though the city government hadn't had offices there since 1863. The anticipation was due in no small measure to the expected sensational nature of the testimony, which would be a welcome break from the relentlessly downbeat financial news. There was also the specter of seeing a prominent moralist defend what appeared to be indefensible. But the real attraction was seeing Madeline Pollard take the stand and testify to things that no woman had talked about in public—her ruin by a powerful man. Already there was a sense that the trial might be about more than just the facts of the case.

Now that it was clear that the case would come to trial, speculation about who was funding Madeline's suit reached a fever pitch. The "wonder has been all along how two such successful attorneys could be induced to take hold of a case where there was no money in site," noted the *Courier-Journal*, as such able and distinguished attorneys rarely take such cases "out of sympathy for their clients." The paper estimated that even without attorney's fees, the case had cost $2,500 so far and the "burning question is who is putting up the cash." There was no shortage of possible suspects: Breckinridge's political enemies back in the Ashland district; disgruntled Presbyterians who felt he had disgraced the church; a wealthy widower in Washington; a "well-known literary man"; even the *New York World* itself. The mystery only served to heighten interest in the trial, and the Ionic-columned portico of Old City Hall was thronged with hopeful spectators seeking entry into the courtroom.

Judge Bradley called the court to order at precisely 10:00 a.m. He was a precise man, a Republican, lean and taciturn, with his gray hair parted in the middle and a brown walrus mustache. The courtroom he was presiding over in the east wing of the building was known as the Old Criminal Court, and its dingy appearance, with tired olive paint rising from nondescript blue baseboards to a soiled white ceiling, belied the drama the chamber had seen. Francis Scott Key had defended Sam Houston here in 1832, when he was tried for assault after he beat Congressman William Stanbery with his cane for accusing him of defrauding the government. The abolitionist Daniel Drayton and Edward Sayres, the captain of a schooner called the *Pearl*, were tried here in 1849 for attempting to spirit seventy-seven runaway slaves out of the city, down the Potomac, up the Chesapeake, and to freedom in New Jersey through the Chesapeake & Delaware Canal. In one of the most famous antebellum scandals, Congressman Daniel Sickles was acquitted here in 1859 of murdering Philip Barton Key—Francis Scott Key's son, who, coincidentally, prosecuted Drayton and Sayres—despite having shot him on Pennsylvania Avenue in broad daylight after he found out Key was having an affair with his wife. John Surratt faced trial in the same room for his alleged role in the assassination of Abraham Lincoln, but avoided his mother's fate, being hung in the yard of the Washington Arsenal Penitentiary, because of an ironically "hung" jury. And most famously in the memory of those gathered that March morning, Charles Guiteau was convicted here in 1882 of assassinating President James Garfield.

Judge Bradley's bench, with its big red leather chair, was nestled under an arch on the front wall; the court clerks and the marshal were seated just below. The jury box, a platform with twelve chairs in two neat rows, was to the judge's right, with pegs for the jurors' hats and coats on the wall behind. There were two tables, one behind the other, in the front of the courtroom for the plaintiff and defense teams, over which hung two lamps "pulpit like." That, and what light streamed in from three large, arch-topped windows on each side of the courtroom, was the only illumination. The members of the press—which included reporters from the *New York Times*, and *World* and *Herald*; the *Washington Post* and *Evening Star*; the *Chicago Daily Tribune*; the Philadelphia and Boston papers; and the wire services—were off to one side of the courtroom, seated at an assortment of desks and tables procured for the occasion. The famous Washington correspondents of the great Ohio River cities—George Alfred Townsend of the *Cincinnati Enquirer*, known to all by his pen name of Gath; Fred Mussey of the *Cincinnati Commercial Gazette*; and O. O. Stealey of the *Louisville Courier-Journal*—ended up crammed together at a table of such diminutive proportions that they looked like hobbledehoy giants. The rest of the courtroom was taken up with rows of benches and cane chairs for the lucky spectators granted admission, who would soon include members of Congress, noted ministers, famous actors, and, rather inexplicably, the Princeton baseball team.

Jere Wilson and Calderon Carlisle arrived first and selected the table in front. The Breckinridge team drifted in in waves. First was Stoll and Totten's partner William Mattingly, who had agreed to assist with preliminary matters but warned Breckinridge he couldn't afford to work for free. Then came former congressman Benjamin Butterworth, most recently general counsel to the Chicago World's Fair, whom Breckinridge had hired only the day before. A few minutes later Desha Breckinridge, who looked like a younger, slighter version of his father, with close-cropped dark hair and a beard, entered the courtroom. Finally the defendant himself arrived. He looked, said the *Post*, like "a man who had slept well and enjoyed his breakfast." He went up and down the press row shaking hands and greeting reporters by name, then took his place with his counsel, his thumbs hooked casually under his armpits and one leg hoisted on his knee, with only the nervous jiggling of his foot suggesting anything other than total nonchalance. Gath thought he looked like a country parson: portly, in an old-fashioned vest and frock coat, with profuse, silky white hair, a bushy beard of the same color, and a florid face, "shrewd and roguish in expression—a snowy Cupid still shooting arrows out of his blue eyes and warm skin."

Phil Thompson hurried in late and the teams began wrangling over depositions, with Wilson arguing to block those he said were unrelated to the trial—namely those about Madeline's purported past relationships—and Breckinridge's team arguing to exclude depositions that they said had been taken without proper notice. Bradley said he would rule on the depositions later, and jury selection began. Twelve white men were selected from a pool of twenty-one white men and five black men: two carpenters, a housepainter, a paint dealer, a steamfitter, the owner of a produce stand, a farmer, two bookkeepers, a banker, a merchant, and one man who gave his profession as "agent." With the preliminaries over, Butterworth asked if the trial could be delayed until morning so he could familiarize himself with the case. When Carlisle didn't object, Bradley acquiesced and the onlookers began dispersing, resigned to having to wait one more day to hear from Madeline Pollard.

•

It's hard to know which would have been worse for Nisba: the silence in the house once Breckinridge and Desha had left for the courtroom, leaving her alone with Louise, or the raging when her stepmother became agitated, which tended to happen mostly when her father was around. It had been a precipitous decline for Louise. In the fall of 1892, Louise Rucks Scott Wing appeared to be a perfectly healthy forty-seven-year-old woman. She had been a widow for nearly twenty years. Her late husband, Edward Rumsey Wing, was the youngest-ever U.S. ambassador, taking charge of the U.S. mission in Ecuador when he was just twenty-four. He was, unfortunately, a disaster as a diplomat, best remembered for an ill-fated scheme to annex Ecuador, and drank himself to oblivion within four years, leaving twenty-nine-year-old Louise a widow in 1874. She returned to Washington and lived a comfortable life, a fixture in diplomatic social circles. When the Breckinridges first came to the capital in the mid-1880s, it was "Cousin Louise"—she was a distant Preston cousin of Willie's on her mother's side—who introduced the family around and saved them "from the drab existence that awaited the family of many unknown congressmen," recalled Ella.

Louise remained close to the family after Issa's death, writing to the Breckinridge children and seeing Willie in Washington. Sometime in the fall or winter of 1893, their relationship turned romantic. By mid-February 1893, she was regularly writing to "Cousin Willie" thanking him for wonderful evenings and anticipating their next outing. "I am in such a mood this morning—like champagne," she wrote in one. Her letters were effervescent; she wrote of "a time of new delight" in early March; soon after that she was "pining" for him.

It's not improbable, of course, that Breckinridge should have struck up a romance with a longtime friend after his wife's death, and Issa had been unwell for years. But the timing was awkward. Issa had passed away only the previous July, and becoming seriously involved with another woman so soon after her death was a transgression of protocol that, as Julia Blackburn noted, risked being seen as an insult to his dead wife. Only a man who had a passel of young children who needed a mother could be forgiven for replacing his wife so precipitously. And with the financial crisis looming and his prominent role in Congress, Breckinridge was especially hard-pressed for time. In early March, right about the time his courtship of Wing appears to have gone into high gear, he wrote to Nisba, "I have no leisure moments—my time is whole occupied and I am growing very tired." It seems that a new romance would have been the last thing on his mind—unless he hoped to replace Issa as quickly as possible to avert another woman who believed she was to be the next Mrs. W.C.P. Breckinridge. One of Louise's friends said that he was insistent, telling Louise that "no other woman had ever claimed his love as she had" and pressuring her to "promise him her hand" in marriage, a tempting prospect that Louise knew would "place her among the social queens of America."

By late March, however, Louise's notes take a dark turn. She tells Breckinridge that she has received a letter that has "disturbed her peace of mind"—perhaps a warning about Pollard. She seems distraught when she doesn't hear from him. By mid-April, she's under a doctor's care and confined to bed. She writes of an illness that came on "like a cyclone" and was like "a tempest while it lasted" but then seemed to subside. For a time after their July marriage, which came exactly one year and four days after Issa's death, she seemed better, but once the scandal broke, she was again unwell, and she declined throughout the fall and into the winter. In February, Breckinridge summoned her sister from Illinois, who stayed for ten days. Shortly before the trial started, he confided to Desha that Louise seemed "weaker instead of stronger."

Now, with the trial under way, the pressure on Louise was even greater; the papers were full of gossip about her marriage, most recently that her brother Preston had forced Breckinridge to marry her because their relationship "had aroused comment." Breckinridge claimed that he had made "a full statement to my wife prior to the trial," and, knowing that she likely would hear the details anyway from her gossiping friends, he probably had confessed the full extent of the relationship—at least to the degree he was planning to testify in court. The revelation of how thoroughly he had duped and betrayed her must have been devastating and destabilizing. She began lashing out. Nisba described a "nervous affliction that manifested itself sometimes in attacks of a hysterical character." Louise wrote of periods when her brain wasn't "clear."

Nisba said she found that if she could get to her in time, "by sheer will power and prayer" she could "carry her through" these attacks of hysteria. If she didn't, "the results were quite dreadful," she said, and "she became very abusive especially about my father." Dutiful as ever, Nisba took on the role of caretaker to her unhinged stepmother while her brother was where she likely wanted to be: in the courtroom with her father. The newspapers pressed, but she remained steadfastly loyal to her father and refused to comment on the trial or Pollard. Now just a month shy of her twenty-eighth birthday and still rudderless, it seemed that the family claim exerted more of a hold on Nisba than ever.

•

On Friday, March 9, men were lined up in front of the courtroom doors like "crowds before the box office of a theater," said the *Courier-Journal*. Madeline was among the first to arrive. She was tastefully attired in a plainly trimmed black dress with a perfectly tailored bodice with two neat little rows of buttons that converged at her waist, emphasizing her slender figure. The only jewelry she had on was a circular gold hatpin worn like a brooch on her stand-up collar, and she had added a demure dotted veil to her black velvet hat. She looked, most of the reporters thought, around thirty, not beautiful according to conventional standards—they judged her features not dainty enough; her nostrils too wide; her mouth too broad—but attractive enough in her way. "She is of the style a middle-aged man would be attracted to," opined Gath of the *Enquirer*.

Madeline was accompanied by Miss Ellis—who did sewing for the House of Mercy, although many assumed the elderly woman dressed in black was a nun—and Dr. Belle Buchanan, one of the doctors who had helped her after her first pregnancy in Cincinnati. She made her way to the plaintiff's table and took the seat closest to the jury box. Soon after, Breckinridge entered and threaded his way through the courtroom to the defense table. It was the first time they had been in the same room in almost a year; their last encounter had been the previous May, before Breckinridge left Washington for a speaking tour, when Madeline still hoped they might be married. Breckinridge took a seat diagonally behind Madeline, nonchalantly stuffing his red leather satchel under the table as he assiduously ignored her.

The court came to order. Calderon Carlisle stood before the jury and began outlining Madeline's case, pitting Breckinridge, "a man of family, of political prominence, high in the councils of the Presbyterian Church, famous throughout the country as an orator," against "a friendless young woman." As he spoke, Madeline turned in her seat to look at Breckinridge, raising her veil as she did so. She half rose and seemed on the verge of saying something when Miss Ellis touched her arm and stopped her. The movement caught Breckinridge's attention; he glanced up and flashed what Gath thought was a "careless, contemptuous, recognizing" smile before dropping his gaze.

Carlisle continued, unaware of the drama that was playing out steps away. "There are three credible witnesses who will testify that the promise to marry was made," he said. He told the story many already had read of Madeline's impoverished childhood, her desperate arrangement with Rhodes, the train ride when her sister was taken ill, and how "Col. Breckinridge brought a closed carriage to the college when it was nearly dark." Finally, he got to the seduction and described how "by wiles and artifices, the defendant lured her on, and eventually accomplished Miss Pollard's ruin in Lexington."

As he described her intimacy with Breckinridge, Madeline "trembled violently, while the tears burned their unceasing way down her cheeks," said the *Evening Star*. Carlisle told of the birth of her two children. He told of the last day of August 1892, after the death of Issa Breckinridge, when Breckinridge met Madeline at the train station and said he could finally fulfill his promise to marry her. And Carlisle revealed a detail that many newspapers had either omitted from their coverage of the lawsuit or so obscured with euphemisms that it was easily missed: Madeline had again become pregnant last spring, sometime around March, and Breckinridge had promised to marry her on May 31. Carlisle asserted that Breckinridge postponed the marriage, and Madeline subsequently had a miscarriage. After he wrapped up, Breckinridge's lawyer Phil Thompson said the defendant would reserve his opening statement for later.

The first witness was Julia Blackburn. Pale, plump, and steely, a pretty gray-haired woman in rich black silk and a plush black cape with feathery fur frizzes, she impressed everyone as a lady of substance and rank as she made her way to the witness stand. She gave essentially the same testimony she provided in her deposition. In a clear voice, staring directly at Breckinridge, she told how he and Madeline insisted on seeing her on Good Friday in 1893 and how Breckinridge said, "I shall make her Mrs. Breckinridge. I have brought this young lady with me to ask for your care and protection." She said Breckinridge asked her if she and her sister were going to Europe that summer "and if so, would we kindly take Miss Pollard with us," which she declined to commit to, although she said she did agree with Breckinridge that it might be best for Madeline to go away until they were married to avoid any hint of impropriety.

Blackburn also testified that Breckinridge denied to her face rumors that he was to marry Louise Wing and asked her to do something to counter Madeline's jealousy about the matter. She said when the Wing rumors persisted, she advised Madeline to give him up. "If

Mr. Breckinridge wishes to act the villain I think you are powerless to prevent him," she said she told her. Finally, she said, she saw Breckinridge and Madeline together one last time at her apartment. That's when Madeline placed her arms around "Willie" and asked him to tell Blackburn when they would be married. "Owing to present circumstances I cannot do it now, but I'll return and tell Mrs. Blackburn, and we will arrange the day, and my marriage will be with the girl I told Mrs. Blackburn I was engaged to," he said, according to Julia. Later, after Julia found out that they were in New York City together, she said she "scolded" Breckinridge about the potential damage to Madeline's reputation because of the way "in which he followed Miss Pollard around."

As evidence of the frequent communication between Breckinridge and Blackburn that spring regarding Madeline, Carlisle produced two telegrams from Breckinridge to Julia advising her where she could reach Madeline in New York, where Julia had gone on some financial business, and where Madeline was supposed to meet her.

Phil Thompson handled the cross-examination. He got off to a poor start, asking Julia if she was the widow of the late governor Luke Blackburn, to which she replied tartly, "You know that as well as I do." He asked her how she met Madeline, getting her to state that it was through her friend Mrs. Fillette, not Breckinridge, and that she had known Madeline for about three years. She said, however, that she had asked Breckinridge about her. "When I asked the Colonel who Miss Pollard was and he said she was from Kentucky, my feelings went out to her because she was from my own state," she said. "He said that her people were not what would be called fashionable, but they were industrious, upright, respectable people."

Thompson kept circling back to Madeline's behavior, probing the extent of Julia's closeness with her. "I extended to Miss Pollard only the protection I would extend to any unprotected woman from my own state of Kentucky," she insisted. "And always in my presence she acted like a perfect lady and I thought"—here she broke off and glared at Breckinridge—"that Col. Breckinridge was a gentleman." Still Thompson pressed, asking if Madeline had a nickname for her. Julia admitted that Madeline sometimes called her "the Duchess" but said that didn't mean they were particularly close. "Well, what were your relations?"

pressed Thompson. With tears in her eyes and quivering lips she shot back that she felt sorry for Madeline. "I am sorry for any woman who has to make her way alone in the world, just as I am sorry to have to come here. If I had my husband to defend me it would never have been necessary for me to be here," she spat. The courtroom grew very silent. Breckinridge flushed. Everyone knew what she meant. The insult he had given her by letting her chaperone Madeline around town was so great that her husband surely would have defended the Blackburn name in the traditional Kentucky manner—outside of any court of law.

Thompson barreled ahead, asking Blackburn if it was true that her friend Mrs. Fillette had said derogatory things about Pollard. She said that Mrs. Fillette told her that she disliked Madeline because she had stolen her friends and allowed Charles Dudley Warner to stay at her house without her permission. Thompson continued to grill Blackburn about dates and particulars of her various meetings with Breckinridge until she burst out: "I have told you everything I know about the case. It is only my sense of duty to God and man that has moved me in this matter," she said, again close to tears. "I have told you everything and spoken frankly through all this fearful ordeal." The last thing Thompson got her to admit before she stepped down was that she had told both Breckinridge and Madeline last May that she had "washed her hands" of them because she found them in New York together.

Blackburn's testimony had been widely expected, although delivered with a force and clarity that impressed the men in the courtroom, but the next two witnesses were a surprise. First came Mollie Desha, Breckinridge's estranged sister-in-law, dressed in green lizard silk with black trim, nervous and troubled-looking. Carlisle handed her a small wicker sewing basket and asked her if it was the basket she got for her sister in Nantucket, which Madeline claimed Breckinridge had given to her following Issa's death. "Yes," Desha said, "she used it all the time." When the time came for cross-examination, Breckinridge said sternly, "No cross-examination for her."

The next witness was Col. William Moore, superintendent of the Washington Metropolitan Police, who looked like a French marshal with his stupendous gray mustache and curled goatee. Referring to his shorthand notes, Moore said that on May 13 of last year the door of his office had burst open and in came Breckinridge and a young lady he identified as Pollard. Breckinridge told Moore he needed his protection as "the lady had threatened him with death." Moore said that the young woman was "very excited and insisted that they should be married at once." She then "held up her hands and said those were her only weapons." Breckinridge then promised to marry her on May 31 "if Providence in its wisdom should not intervene." Moore said he warned Madeline not to make any more threats, and they left his office.

Four days later the couple came back. Breckinridge told Moore what he had suspected from their last visit: that "Miss Pollard was in a delicate condition." Breckinridge said that Madeline was going to New York to "prepare for the event" and that he wanted Moore to witness an agreement to the effect that they would be married after the baby was born. "He and Miss Pollard clasped hands over it, and with his disengaged hand Breckinridge took mine," Moore said, noting it was one of the most solemn moments he had ever witnessed. After they had sworn to the agreement to marry, he said Madeline "drew from her bosom a revolver, and said should it be necessary she would use it on Col. Breckinridge and on herself." Moore said he took the gun from Madeline.

Moore said that beginning in late June he had received a series of letters and telegrams from Breckinridge asking him to intercede with Pollard to prevent a scandal because she had returned from New York after only a short time and was threatening to go public. Breckinridge sent him a check for one hundred dollars to give Madeline, but he was unable to deliver it because she had left town. A ripple went through the courtroom as the onlookers did the math and realized the date Breckinridge gave him the check—July 31—was two weeks after his marriage to Wing.

Thompson began his cross-examination. He asked Moore if it was true that Breckinridge had told him that Madeline couldn't accuse him of seduction. At that, Madeline sprang from her chair. "No, no—it is not so," she cried. Moore said that the first time they came to his office, Breckinridge told him, "Miss Pollard could not say he had seduced her, for on their first meeting he had taken liberties with her person, and the second night had intimate relations with her full consent." Madeline sobbed softly in her seat as he spoke. The question went to the heart not of the legal case against Breckinridge, which was whether or not he made a promise of marriage that he broke, but of the moral one. As Carlisle had noted in his opening argument, Madeline couldn't sue Breckinridge for seduction because women couldn't sue for seduction under District of Columbia law. But the language of her complaint, which charged that Breckinridge had taken advantage of Madeline's "youth and inexperience" through "wiles and artifices and protestations of affection" mirrored that of many states' seduction statutes and clearly was designed to suggest that Breckinridge had acted in a sexually predaceous manner.

The last witness was Nathan S. Lincoln, one of the city's best-known doctors. He testified that he also had received a visit from the couple in mid-May of last year—right between the two visits to Moore, it turned out—at which time he confirmed to Breckinridge that Madeline was indeed pregnant. Breckinridge, he said, told him that he "intended to make it alright with her." It was the capstone testimony of a day the press agreed was very favorable to Pollard. With the trial adjourned for the weekend, the capital was abuzz, especially regarding Blackburn's remark about her husband dealing with Breckinridge. Jennie wrote to Stoll aghast at what she thought was their too-gentle cross-examination of Blackburn about her relationship with Madeline, telling him that any woman "who volunteers to become the chief witness in a case of this kind" should not expect their social position to exempt them from rigorous questioning. She wrote to her mother, with whom she was increasingly less circumspect about her involvement in the trial, "The opening does not look very well for Mr. B . . . It was a good day for her case but the other side has not yet shown its hand."

That Sunday, when Jennie was leaving church, she ran into Sister Ella, one of the nuns from the House of Mercy. When she mentioned that she wanted to make a milk punch to build Madeline up for her ordeal of testifying, Jennie volunteered to contribute a bottle of whiskey to the cause as an excuse to come by. That evening she arrived at the House of Mercy with a bottle of bourbon she had procured from Breckinridge. She sat with Madeline as she drank the punch, helpfully adding more whiskey when she complained it was tasteless—"she evidently likes her punch to be clearly defined in its flavoring," Jennie noted. Madeline was thrilled with Blackburn. "She was dressed so perfectly and she looked the lady so thoroughly. Then her manner, and the way she gave her testimony, was so fine," Madeline told Jennie, adding that she had been with her lawyers all day Saturday, working through "things that might be brought up to confront us." Before she could ask for any specifics, Sister Ella hurried Jennie away so Madeline could get some sleep.

Monday morning brought more large crowds to the courtroom, and for the first time, some of the spectators were women. This surprised reporters; one noted that for "obvious reasons, the impression was general that the trial would be one which would attract few, if any, members of the gentler sex." At the time, women were a rarity in courtrooms as either lawyers or spectators, most especially so when matters of sex were dealt with. As Susan B. Anthony had complained nearly twenty years earlier, when it came to the "laws regulating . . . marriage and divorce, for adultery, breach of promise, seduction, rape, bigamy, abortion, infanticide—all were made by men. They, alone, decide who are guilty of violating these laws and what shall be their punishment, with judge, jury and advocate all men, with no woman's voice heard in our courts, saving as accused or witness."

On this day, about twenty women, young and middle-aged, had seated themselves at several benches near the front of the courtroom and were waiting expectantly for the proceedings to begin; one woman clutched a pair of opera glasses. As soon as the court was gaveled to order, however, Bradley turned to the marshal and said, "Mr. Marshal, I wish you to request these ladies to vacate their seats." With that the marshal intoned, "All ladies not witnesses in this case must leave the court room." They filed out, according to a reporter from the *Evening Star*, "with flushed faces . . . downcast eyes and an embarrassed manner."

With decorum thus restored, men immediately filled the open seats and the first witness was called. Claude de La Roche Francis took the stand. He gave his residence as New York City, where he said he was studying law. Ever since his name appeared on the witnesses list, Breckinridge had been pushing Jennie to find out who he was and what he would say. Mr. Francis, or "Frawncis" as he pronounced it, turned out to be a smooth-faced, bespectacled young man in a silk top hat and a purple-fur-lined overcoat. He said he had been in Washington last winter and had become acquainted with Miss Pollard when she lived at the home of his friend Mrs. Thomas, where he called several times a week. He said he frequently saw Breckinridge there with Madeline. On one occasion, he entered the drawing room, he said, and "Col. Breckinridge was holding Miss Pollard's hand and appeared to be leaving." He made to excuse himself, but Madeline insisted on introducing him to Breckinridge. Francis told her he recently had the pleasure of meeting the colonel at a reception at the Mexican legation with Mrs. Louise Wing. After he left the room, he heard Breckinridge tell Madeline he was worried that Francis might mention his attentions to her to Wing. Later Madeline told him that "it was Col. Breckinridge's desire that he should say nothing about [their] engagement."

Another time, he said Madeline broke down in tears because she said she feared that Breckinridge wouldn't keep his engagement with her because she had heard he was engaged to Wing. He said he told her there were many other "good and distinguished men in the world besides Mr. Breckinridge," but she told him that he had been "particularly good and kind to her and had shown her devoted attention."

The next witness was Dr. Tabor Johnson, who testified that on May 24 of last year he had been called to see Madeline at her boarding-house on H Street because she was miscarrying a fetus that he estimated to be a month or two old. He confirmed he had seen a number of telegrams and letters in her room signed by Breckinridge regarding arrangements for her to go to a sanatorium for her confinement. On cross-examination, Stoll asked the question that was on everyone's mind: whether the miscarriage had been "brought about by artificial means." Johnson said that "it might have been . . . as any one might, but there was no reason to believe that such was the case in this instance."

Johnson was followed by Dr. Mary Parsons, "a sensible looking woman of 45, in nice furs and respectable," who said she had been a physician in Washington for twenty years. She testified that she had attended Pollard when her second child was born in the winter of 1888 at a lying-in home on Second Street. She said a male child was born on February 3 and placed in the local Protestant foundling asylum. Jere Wilson, who had taken over the questioning from Carlisle, asked if she knew what had become of the baby. She said she had seen the baby once at the asylum and then in April at "an undertaker's." At the mention of her dead baby, Madeline moaned and threw herself forward, sobbing and shaking convulsively. "Oh, my God, pity me," she cried over and over. When Miss Ellis couldn't calm her, she was half led, half carried from the now-silent courtroom. As she crossed the threshold, she fainted and was caught by one of the bailiffs. After Madeline had been carried out, Dr. Parsons said she had seen Madeline and Breckinridge on the street together several times after the baby was born and that on Madeline's instruction she gave Breckinridge the bill for her services, which he paid.

With the witnesses done for the day, the lawyers turned to arguing over procedural issues. They had been sparring all day, and there was a barely suppressed energy crackling beneath the dry legal arguments. In the morning, Stoll had pulled a stunt with the disputed set of Washington Irving books that Madeline claimed she gave to the Norwood Asylum. Stoll had taken possession of the books after his visit there, but Judge Bradley had ordered them turned over to Madeline's lawyers for examination. Stoll brought the books, but had them done up in brown-paper wrapping, saying it was per Bradley's order, and suggested that Madeline be required to describe the books before they were released. Bradley said he made no such ruling and ordered the books turned over to Wilson.

Then in the afternoon, one of Madeline's lawyers, William Johnson, who was Carlisle's partner, accused the defense of "chicanery" over their efforts to suppress some of the Kentucky depositions. According to Johnson, when he showed up in Lexington to take the depositions of several critical witnesses—including Sarah Guess, who owned the Lexington assignation house where Madeline claimed Breckinridge deflowered her—all the notaries in town made themselves scarce, saying they feared reprisals from Breckinridge, so the depositions had to be postponed. Then, when a notary was secured and Johnson gave the defense counsel notice of the rescheduled depositions, Charles Stoll and Desha Breckinridge, who took the depositions in Cincinnati, suddenly claimed they weren't authorized to represent Breckinridge. Johnson said such "insolence" shouldn't be allowed to stand. When he finished speaking, Shelby rose to object, but Bradley adjourned the court before he could do so.

All the attorneys spilled into a small lobby leading to the hallway, everyone hot and prickly. Johnson was just behind Shelby, who spun to face him. "You have used language which is insulting to me, and I demand satisfaction," Shelby said to the younger man. "Well sir," replied Johnson. At that, Shelby slapped him across the face hard enough to knock his hat off. Breckinridge rushed between them as the lawyers began jostling each other. He put his hand on Calderon Carlisle's shoulder. "Take it off," Carlisle warned, as Desha rushed up from behind and caught Carlisle with his fist just behind his ear, sending his head jerking skyward. "Who struck me?" Carlisle demanded, as bailiffs took ahold of Shelby and Desha. Bradley stormed in and said their conduct was disgraceful, and he would deal with them in the morning.

That evening, Breckinridge's team gathered at his home, triumphant that Shelby's honor as a gentleman had been avenged, even though many attorneys present thought Johnson's accusations justified. To the reporters who stopped by, however, they expressed regret about the incident. Desha had already written an apologetic note to Carlisle, explaining that he mistakenly thought he was assaulting his father, and Carlisle had replied that he would let the judge deal with the incident.

There was another matter, however, that the team was anxiously huddled over out of earshot of the press. O. O. Stealey of the *Courier-Journal* had been poking around the Breckinridge-Wing marriage ever since he had been tipped off the previous week that Carlisle had sent to Louisville for a copy of the marriage certificate. What he had discovered was a bombshell: Breckinridge had secretly married Louise Wing in New York City some two and a half months before their marriage in Preston Scott's front parlor.

Stealey had asked Breckinridge to confirm the rumor, intending on breaking the story in the morning. Breckinridge refused to comment, but was now scrambling to rectify yet another secret that threatened to sink not only him but also his already fragile wife. The fact was, the Reverend John Paxton, an old friend, had performed a marriage ceremony for Breckinridge and Louise in his home on April 29 with Paxton's wife and her niece as witnesses. At Breckinridge's request, the reverend hadn't filed the marriage certificate with the New York City health department. Knowing it was now just a matter of time before the suppressed marriage was revealed, Breckinridge telegrammed Paxton and told him to register the marriage and authorized him to make a statement to the press. Now, he could only wait for the fallout.

•

The revelation of the secret marriage sheds further, painful insight into Louise's mental breakdown. Why the rushed marriage, especially when Breckinridge already had so many irons in the fire and when in a matter of months, with the one-year anniversary of Issa's passing, they could have been joyfully married with the Breckinridge children in attendance? A secret marriage was of no use in deterring Madeline; only a public marriage would do that.

One hint comes from a note Louise sent to Breckinridge in March: "I shall always cherish this Thursday, March 9 for bringing the dearest news," she wrote to him. Had she just found out about a surprise, late-life pregnancy? She didn't have any children and the news may well have been welcomed, despite the obvious dilemma it posed. A quick marriage before anyone knew would solve the problem. She even says in the letter that a friend commented on her looking "tired and pale."

By April, telegrams were flying back and forth between Breckinridge and Louise every few days. Preston was apparently concerned about the relationship and pressing for a face-to-face meeting with Breckinridge. The well-connected doctor may have heard rumors from Louisville or Lexington about Madeline and Willie and, possibly, about a long-ago carriage ride in Cincinnati. As the *Kentucky Leader* reported shortly after Madeline's suit was filed, it had "revived much of the gossip that had been current at various times regarding" she and Breckinridge. "Long before the congressman's wife died there was more or less talk about their intimacy," it noted in a stunningly frank tidbit. Louise cabled Willie on April 24 that she and Preston awaited him "impatiently." Apparently the meeting didn't take place, because four days later, one day before their secret wedding, Louise wired to Breckinridge in Philadelphia: "Preston very unhappy will come to NY."

By early May, Louise was sequestered in Atlantic City. The excuse Breckinridge later would give for her departure from Washington, and the hasty wedding, was that she was ill and her brother had recommended that she go east, while he needed to go west. He was hardly setting out cross-country in a covered wagon, however—only traveling through the southeast, lecturing for a few weeks, on what was an excellent and efficient network of trains. Preston cabled Breckinridge in Tennessee from Atlantic City, saying that he should send a telegram to Louise "every day without fail unless stronger," suggesting that her mental state was fragile. On May 14, two weeks after they had been married, Breckinridge wrote to Preston telling him that he intended to marry Louise: "That I should love and wish to marry Louise—your sister—will seem to you most rational. That she should consent to be my wife secures my future." He wrote that it was their "pleasure to confide this to you—asking you for the present to hold it a secret" until he could break the news to his children.

Louise was pleased, dashing off a note to Breckinridge that she liked his "manly letter" to her brother. Now she was in the position of having to lie to her brother, pretending that she wasn't Mrs. W.C.P. Breckinridge and, most likely, hiding a pregnancy. On May 18, Louise wrote to "My Husband" that she was ill and under a doctor's care; she speaks of a "want of sleep and peace of mind," and says that while she loves him, she fears she has become a "millstone" around his neck. On June 1 she cables, "Can't endure this alone," and seems desperate to see him. Did she have a miscarriage? By the time they are married in Louisville, she clearly isn't pregnant, and given her age and the stress she was under, a miscarriage wasn't unlikely.

Despite frantic letters and telegrams, Breckinridge still didn't come to her. He was, of course, also juggling Madeline, who was very definitely pregnant, and who also expected to be the next Mrs. Breckinridge. In her suit, Madeline asserted that Breckinridge had proposed dealing with her pregnancy through "the solemnization of a secret marriage to take place May 31" in New York. Apparently this was Breckinridge's go-to answer on such occasions, but it was Wing who had the social clout to ensure it happened.

On June 9, Louise arrived "exhausted" at the Midland Hotel in Kansas City, planning to meet up with Breckinridge. He didn't come; at this point, he probably didn't want to be seen with either woman in any city, as the comings and goings of well-known men from the busy downtown hotels that served as political and business hubs were regularly chronicled in the newspapers. As he lamented in one of his letters to Major Moore, "I pay the penalty of public life by having any reference to me published all over the country."

Louise cabled her brother: "Too weak [to] return home alone." Preston brought her to Cincinnati, where she finally met Breckinridge on June 15 at the Grand Hotel, where they took separate, but adjoining, rooms to preserve the fiction that they were unmarried, staying until June 17. The following day, rumors of Breckinridge's engagement to Pollard appeared in the *Cincinnati Commercial Gazette*. At least one of Breckinridge's acquaintances, a sharp-eyed judge, noticed his name, and Wing's below it, in the hotel register, although it was so scribbled he wasn't sure it was Breckinridge's "until I happened to meet him in one of the hallways," as he told the *Enquirer*. The judge thought it a "remarkable blunder" by a man who should have known better, as it subjected Wing "to the tongue of scandal." Had rumors of their arrival in town and their thinly disguised liaison sparked the gossip regarding his engagement to Madeline, which, in turn, forced Breckinridge's denials and set Madeline on the path that resulted in the suit?

Regardless, once her honor had been called into question by publication of rumors of the Breckinridge-Pollard engagement, Louise went immediately to her brother's home in Louisville. On July 1, she cabled to Breckinridge in Lexington that Preston wanted to see him that afternoon. Two weeks later, they were publicly married. A friend who was with Louise remembered her "nervous manner" on the day she was married. The friend told the *Courier-Journal*, a week after the secret marriage was revealed, "I am convinced she began to realize that she had been deceived. Col. Breckinridge vowed even then by all the saints that he hardly knew Miss Pollard." Less than a month later, Louise would learn just how well her new husband knew Miss Pollard.

•

On Tuesday morning, Bradley scolded the attorneys for yesterday's scrum in the vestibule, but said he would overlook it as it happened after adjournment. He also condemned "entirely reprehensible" reports that the defense had come to court armed, which prompted each attorney to stand in turn and empty his pockets to prove he was unarmed. Nonetheless, Bradley ruled in the defense's favor regarding the disputed deposition of Sarah Guess, saying that it couldn't be admitted under an obscure statute that banned typewritten depositions.

The trial resumed, and for the next two days Pollard's attorneys presented their evidence that Madeline had given birth to her first child in Cincinnati in the spring of 1885. The deposition of Dr. Street was read attesting that she had attended a woman who called herself Monica Burgoyne at the Norwood Asylum, but that she didn't recognize Pollard as that woman. The deposition of Dr. Perry was read identifying Madeline as a Louise Wilson, a "poor unfortunate girl from Kentucky" who was referred to a practice she shared with Dr. Buchanan by Dr. Street after supposedly suffering a miscarriage. Buchanan testified in person that she treated Madeline in the summer of 1885—at "the height of the strawberry season"—after she came from the Norwood Asylum and that she estimated she had given birth about ten weeks prior. On cross-examination, Stoll seemed determined to suggest there was some kind of "intimacy" between Buchanan and Street, asking Buchanan about her marriage and divorce, and how often she saw Street and the living arrangements of the women physicians.

Sister Cecilia, the nun who had been in charge of Norwood in 1885 and had been brought in from Pueblo, Colorado, to testify, confirmed there was a patient there who was visited by Dr. Street. She also said the patient had given her a set of Washington Irving books, and while she couldn't identify Pollard as that woman, she noted that two patients at the asylum at that time were veiled, as Madeline said she was.

With Sarah Guess's deposition disqualified, Madeline's lawyers brought Guess to Washington in person. She was the first witness to appear on Thursday morning. She said that she had been born a slave in Alabama around 1838 and had lived in New Orleans and Louisville before coming to Lexington and buying a cottage on Short Street. She said she had known Breckinridge for years. She said Breckinridge first brought "Miss Madeline" to her home about ten years ago around dusk on a Friday evening in August and asked her to keep her until Monday. She said she thought Madeline was about seventeen or eighteen and looked like a schoolgirl. "She had on a dress up to her shoe tops, and I said that she was too . . ." Before she could say "young," Stoll objected and she was cut off.

Guess said Breckinridge left and came back later in the evening and remained in the front bedroom with Madeline until about eleven o'clock. When he left, she said, Madeline was "undressed and in bed." He came again on Saturday night and then on Sunday night, each time "putting his arms about her and kissing her" when he returned. On Monday morning, she remembered getting Madeline an early breakfast so she could get to the train station to meet Rhodes.

After that first visit, Guess said Breckinridge brought Madeline back about a year later and then "about fifty times" over a period of three years and that sometimes she or someone else would see her back to Mrs. Ketchum's boardinghouse. She said that after the scandal broke, Breckinridge visited her and "said he didn't want me to have anything to say about the case." He also wanted to know if Colonel Swope had ever been to her house with Madeline, which she said he hadn't. She said she told him that Madeline "loved him and trusted him fully and that he ought to be good to her."

When she was asked if Madeline had ever been to her house before she came with Breckinridge, Guess said that she hadn't. When asked if Breckinridge had been there previously, she answered, "Yes, sir." Shelby objected, and his objection was sustained, but not before the jury heard the answer. On cross-examination, Shelby asked her how long she had run an assignation house, and she said for nineteen years but not in the last six. He asked her about Ed Farrell, the lawyer who had taken her deposition in Lexington and accompanied her to Washington, and she said she had known him since he was a young man. He seemed very interested in her travel and lodging arrangements and asked if she was being paid, and she said she was receiving $1.50 a day for her time, as well as her travel expenses. The sight of the dignified former slave, dressed all in black, in a black bonnet, testifying to the sexual perfidy of an esteemed ex-Confederate officer was remarkable—"the negress reproved to his face the Congressman who brought a schoolgirl there," said Gath.

The next witness was Lucretia Minear, who owned the Lafayette Square boardinghouse where Madeline lived for a time. She testified that

Breckinridge was a frequent visitor there. A woman named Kate Burt identified Madeline as a "Mrs. Foster," a pregnant woman who lived for two weeks in October 1887 in the same boardinghouse she did on Thirteenth and F Streets, where a man she recognized as Congressman Breckinridge frequently went to her room on the third floor. A deposition was read from Mrs. Hoyt of the Lexington boardinghouse where Madeline lived, saying Madeline had no older male visitors other than Rhodes, although some schoolboys called on her to "hear her sing and play" piano in the parlor.

As the first week of the trial drew to a close, Breckinridge appeared rattled by the "mass of testimony" produced by Madeline's lawyers and fretted to Desha about the "irregularity, insufficiency and inadequacy" of their defense preparation. Rumors of his secret wedding to Louise were now public and, if true, said the *Enquirer*, would show a "general duplicity of his character." To make matters worse, the *Enquirer* was reporting that several years ago, there had been some financial irregularities with Breckinridge's law practice. Apparently Breckinridge "collected certain moneys" in his capacity as a lawyer but "found himself unable to transfer the funds when required to do so." There was talk of disbarment proceedings, but "he was so highly esteemed by wealthy men at his home that they advanced cash" to cover the debt.

Nevertheless, Breckinridge continued to see himself as the victim of persecution. He fumed that the papers criticized him for building his defense around impugning Pollard's chastity yet "did not hesitate to publish every nasty and scandalous charge against me, wounding my wife and daughters." In a letter to one supporter, he complained that his enemies "have been hauling me around on a spike team"—a crude little team of a donkey and a cow used to break rough ground—"consisting of Sallie Guess and Ed Farrell." He mocked Farrell for having the temerity to bring Guess to Washington, telling one supporter he wished he had a camera to take a picture of him "meeting Sallie at the depot, driving her in a cab through the streets of Washington to a colored boardinghouse, and escorting her to introduce her to the family." The world seemed to be shifting under his feet, as were ideas about who was fit to sit in judgment of whom.

13

Somebody's Daughter

The "gusty spirit of Saint Patrick" blew into Washington a day early on Friday, March 16, rattling the still-bare trees and blowing away any hint of spring. Just after 10:00 a.m., word began spreading around town that Madeline Pollard had taken the stand. Many had doubted that she would, even up to the last minute. Some believed that her lawyers thought her too emotional to take a chance on letting her testify. Still others couldn't imagine a woman telling a story "that very few women would care to relate in public." As word spread, spectators packed into the old courthouse, filling the halls. They "struggled with the bailiffs in the corridor and told of their exalted government positions, their newspaper connections, or their personal relations to the participants or counsels." Those not lucky or connected enough to get in crowded on tiptoe around the windows in the hall that looked across the courtyard to the courtroom windows.

Madeline took the stand dressed in the same black dress and blue coat she had worn all along, her black velvet hat with its little feathered plume dancing like a question mark over her head. Miss Ellis sat stoically next to her. As Carlisle questioned her, she told about her father's death, how the family had been left destitute, and her years spent with her aunt in Pittsburgh and then with her other aunt outside of Lexington. She told about her arrangement with Rhodes and about meeting Breckinridge on the train and about how he came to Wesleyan and the paper he had in his hand and the concert in the heights and the closed carriage and the bad throat. She told how he brought her to Sarah Guess's and how she stayed until Monday morning and how she eventually went to Cincinnati "not because I wanted to, but because I had to." She told of the room over the mattress store and the Norwood Foundling Asylum and Drs. Perry and Buchanan. She said it was Breckinridge who told her to go to Cincinnati and find a woman doctor and Breckinridge who gave her money and Breckinridge who was the father of the baby born on May 29, 1885. "Had you ever before meeting Mr. Breckinridge had sexual relations with any man at any time or place?" asked Carlisle. "No, never," she replied emphatically. She told of more visits to Sarah Guess's and how Breckinridge came to her room at night when he boarded at Mrs. Ketchum's. "Were you ever at Sarah Guess's house with any other man than Mr. Breckinridge?" asked Carlisle. "Certainly not," she answered.

She was clear and direct as she spoke, recalling dates and facts without hesitation, discussing the details of her relationship with Breckinridge unflinchingly; she didn't blush or avert her eyes when she said "pregnant." The reporters in the courtroom were impressed by her testimony, "the rising and falling of her plaintive voice, the tone of her demure little acknowledgements about her early life," although the *World* thought her a bit "stagy . . . as if every word, action and gesture had been rehearsed."

Madeline then told how she had to leave Lexington a second time after Breckinridge's visits to her bedroom at Mrs. Ketchum's and how she came to Washington, where she stayed at a boardinghouse at Thirteenth and F as a "Mrs. Foster." She told how Breckinridge came there to see her, but someone recognized him and knew he wasn't her husband, so she had to leave. She told how she then went to St. Ann's Infant Asylum, but had to leave there too because she went out at night to meet Breckinridge, so she went to a private lying-in home, where Dr. Parsons delivered her second child. From there, Madeline filled in the story of the last few years of her life. After the baby was born and sent to an orphan asylum, she lived at the Academy of the Holy Cross, a Catholic girls' school on Thomas Circle, from March 1888 until the fall of 1890. From there, she went to live at Mrs. Fillette's boardinghouse, and then in the fall of 1891, after she lost the government job Breckinridge got for her, she went to Cambridge, Massachusetts, for six months. She came back to Washington in the spring of 1892, then spent six weeks at the Bread Loaf Inn in Vermont. Finally, she told how Breckinridge met her on the last day of August 1892, after his wife had died, at the Baltimore & Potomac Railroad station and on a carriage ride told her that his children were grown and settled and "he had thought it over and had determined to marry me if I would marry him, and I told him I would marry him." She said he thought a year was too soon after Issa's death to remarry—he had waited fourteen months after the death of his first wife—so she said she "told him we ought to wait two years."

Carlisle showed her tickets to the World's Fair and Issa Breckinridge's little willow sewing basket and asked if Breckinridge had given those to her, and she said he had. She identified the letters and the telegrams that had gone back and forth between them the previous spring regarding arrangements for her to leave Washington when she was again pregnant. He asked her to tell about arrangements they discussed for her to go to a lying-in establishment. For the first time, Madeline lost her composure. "I don't like to state these things before so many men," she said tearfully. Wilson chimed in and told her she didn't have to answer. Carlisle then read the spate of letters that had passed between her and Breckinridge when she was in Charlottesville, where she threatened to make their engagement public if he didn't make good on his promise to marry her and he begged her to avoid a scandal. Finally, she testified that from that first night at Sarah Guess's until he left her on May 17 of last year there was "never one single suggestion of discontinuing that miserable sin until he left me."

Ben Butterworth, big and beefy with muttonchops just going to gray, began the cross-examination with the air of a man handling a package he thought might contain nitroglycerin. It was when the fireworks were expected and when many people assumed that Madeline might crumble. But they underestimated just how much Madeline relished the opportunity to tell her story. When Jennie had visited her the previous evening, she had told her that she wasn't "one bit afraid" to take the stand and said that she told Carlisle not to try to stop the cross-examination, no matter how rough it got. "I wanted them to go ahead and ask all the questions they could think of," she told Jennie as she drank a hot toddy of whiskey, hot water, and lemon to prepare her for her big day. "People do not know what I can do, and I will surprise them all," she said.

Butterworth began by asking Madeline how old she was. She acknowledged there was some confusion about her age. She said she thought she was twelve when her father died in 1876, which would mean she was born in 1864. But later, her mother and her sister told her she was born November 30, 1866, and thereafter she used that date in good faith. She believed, she said, that she was seventeen when she met Breckinridge. Butterworth continued grilling her, asking how old she was when the family left Frankfort and when they lived in Crab Orchard and how many brothers and sisters she had and when they were born and how far apart in age from her they were, until finally she told him that if he "asked her forty thousand questions" she still couldn't say for sure how old she was. She also said that she hadn't been in doubt about her age until after the suit was filed and Breckinridge began questioning it, although, she noted with a smile, he signed her civil service papers attesting that she was born in 1866.

Butterworth asked her about her childhood and what she did with herself and about her education. He asked if she had ever studied history. "My father taught me some history," she said. "Of the United States or of Kentucky?" he asked. "Of both, but not as much of the history of Kentucky as Mr. Breckinridge afterward taught me," she said to laughter. He grilled her about meeting Breckinridge on the train. "I believe you spoke to him on the train," he asserted. "That is not true," she answered, saying that Breckinridge "came across the car to speak to me—and, by the way, that's quite a trick of his, to speak to young girls." He asked how she knew that. "Since the filing of this suit, when people have dared speak the truth about him," she said. Finally, he showed her a letter that he said she sent to Breckinridge regarding her difficulty with Rhodes and inviting him to come to Wesleyan, but she looked at the letter and denied she wrote it.

As Madeline spoke, Breckinridge became more and more fidgety— "now sitting well back in his chair, now sitting well forward, with his elbows on the table before him, his face resting in his hands," then whispering to Butterworth, then, as Madeline described the fateful carriage ride in Cincinnati, "nervously strok[ing] his beard first with one hand

and then with the other," said the *Evening Star*. Madeline's testimony for the day ended with the ride, and the trial adjourned for the weekend. With the papers all reporting on his secret marriage, Breckinridge returned home to deal with the effect of the latest revelations on Louise.

Jennie spent the weekend in what appeared to be an increasingly fruitless effort to get any useful intelligence out of Madeline. She spent most of Saturday at the House of Mercy doing sewing for the sisters, but Madeline was with her lawyers. She came in just as Jennie was leaving, exhausted from prepping her testimony and upset about a sensational article in the *Brooklyn Standard Union* by a woman named Helen Bridgman who knew her when she was in Cambridge and claimed she was an "opium eater." Jennie promised to hunt up a copy of the paper as an excuse to come back the next day. Like everyone on the defense team, she was putting great store in Charles Stoll's ability as a cross-examiner. "You can expect fire-works this week," she wrote to her mother. "They are scared to death of Mr. S. and his cross-examinations, if he gets after M.P. herself I expect there will be fun for they will both hit pretty hard and are well matched as to smartness." She was by now thoroughly invested in the case, both in her own sense of importance to the effort—she bragged that Butterworth had told Stoll that she had "more sense than you and I put together"—and in what she perceived to be her friendship with the principals. Her sister Maude was in the middle of an ugly divorce and she assured her mother that Stoll and Butterworth would be glad to take her case free of charge because "they are so pleased with my work." She seemed so friendly with everyone involved that her mother wrote to her sister, "I suppose Jane will come home engaged to Desha Breckinridge!"—Desha being a well-known bachelor about town.

On Sunday morning Jennie returned with a copy of the *Standard Union* and found Madeline in bed. Madeline read the article quickly, then declared it wasn't "as bad as I had feared." She said there was some truth to it, but that the author had provided her "own coloring." She told Jennie she "never made a confession to her of taking morphine, and I never had the habit." She also denied that she had ever claimed authorship of work by the popular poet Josephine Pollard, although she allowed that when she was at the Bread Loaf Inn she may have read aloud

"Love's Power," a poem of Josephine Pollard's, "as a poem of Miss Pollard's, but I did not tell them that it was mine or Josephine's."

•

The courtroom was packed almost to suffocation on Monday morning; the crowds surged against the doors, pressing to get in, as the bailiffs pushed them back; everyone knew what part of the story came next. The trial had, said the *Evening Star*, reached the "eminence of being the most sensational case ever reviewed in the District courts," a combustible mixture of sex and scandal and shame.

Breckinridge came in looking bleary-eyed and with a bit of rag wrapped around what appeared to be an injured index finger; apparently it had been a long weekend. Madeline took the stand immediately. Carlisle began the questioning. Had she ever been married? "No," answered Pollard. Had her sexual relations with Mr. Breckinridge continued after April 29, 1893, the date of the secret marriage? "Yes," she said. "How long did they continue?" asked Carlisle. "Up to the 17th of May," answered Madeline without blinking as her answer reverberated through the courtroom.

Ben Butterworth returned to the cross-examination, Stoll at his elbow. His tactic was immediately apparent, if not particularly subtle, as he ran through the Victorian markers of morality—religion, impure books. He asked Madeline if she was still an Episcopalian. "Once an Episcopalian, always an Episcopalian," she answered. He asked if when she lived with her aunt in Pittsburgh she ever read "anything that a pure-minded, virtuous girl should not read?" When Wilson objected, Butterworth countered that it was an appropriate question because Madeline had "put forth the claim of the purity of her character," which he said was the "soul" of the case. He asserted that there were "three great parties to the suit, the plaintiff, the defendant, and the community," implying, said the *Post*, "that a woman of Miss Pollard's character commits a crime against society in thus thrusting the story of her wrong-doing before the public."

Butterworth asked Madeline if when she was at Wesleyan she was "competent" to take care of herself. She answered yes, but Wilson again objected. "The question of whether a girl is able to take care of herself and resist temptation depends largely on the sort of people with whom she is thrown and the character and personality of the man who comes with a silver tongue to fill her mind with fair promises," he said, as the courtroom broke into snickers and scattered applause. Judge Bradley was having none of it. "I want it understood right now that we are not conducting a show," he said sternly, threatening to clear the courtroom if there were any more outbursts.

Rocking casually back in his chair like he was sitting on the front porch, Butterworth ran again over the ground of Madeline's teenage crushes. He asked her if Alex Julian had ever "made love" to her—in the nineteenth-century sense of wooing—or had ever caressed her. She said he hadn't, and that while she had liked him, he had liked her sister Mamie "very much." He read the letters she wrote to Owen Robinson, a student at the Kentucky Military Institute who used to call at her aunt Keene's. In one, she admitted to a "very unmaidenly bit of conduct," apparently referring to a Valentine's letter she wrote, and bemoaned the fact that Owen's friend Henry liked her sister, not her. Butterworth seemed to be trying to show that Madeline was a young temptress, but to most they sounded like the letters of a "sentimental young girl."

Butterworth again brought out the letter the defense claimed she had written to Breckinridge asking him to come to Wesleyan. Madeline read it over slowly. "I could have never written that letter," she said, declaring it a forgery. He asked if Breckinridge claimed to have business in the city when he came to see her. "No, sir," she answered. "He said he came to see me and he almost overpowered me with a glance as he said so." Butterworth made her walk again through the story of the carriage ride, how Breckinridge had "taken off her hat; had felt her hands; had kissed her while they were slowly driven through the suburbs." She tried to explain how even after she had fended off his advances she agreed to meet him the next day. "He was so apologetic for his conduct that he disarmed my fears," she said.

Again to the assignation house in Cincinnati, where Madeline said Breckinridge kept her locked in a room. She had threatened to "shriek," and he said, "Oh, come, come, come: don't be foolish. Don't scream." "How long were you there?" demanded Butterworth. "I don't know; perhaps it was two hours, surely more than one, and not quite three,"

Madeline said. Then she looked abruptly at Breckinridge: "Col. Breckinridge, how long was it?" There was dead silence as the whole courtroom
turned toward him. Breckinridge squirmed and looked away.

Then they were on the train to Lexington again and at Sarah Guess's
house three blocks from Breckinridge's own. Butterworth asked if she
knew she was at an assignation house. "I never heard that word before—
I did not know what it meant until Mr. Breckinridge had accomplished
his purpose. Then he told me of it and a great many other things I did
not know," she said. Madeline said when they got there, Breckinridge
took off her hat and stayed for half an hour before going home. "Didn't
you know whose house it was and what kind of house it was?" demanded
Butterworth again as Madeline dropped her head, flushing bright red
for the first time. She raised her head and said defiantly, "During that
half hour, sir, that I was with Col. Breckinridge I agreed to give myself,
heart and soul and body and life, to that man, and I had myself ready to
do that when he came back."

"Then you were not misled or disappointed as to the object of the
visit?" asked Butterworth. "Not after that, Mr. Butterworth," she said. "I
never claimed to be after that." Butterworth asked if she knew he had a
wife and children. "Yes, he told me," said Madeline. "What relation did
you propose to sustain with him?" he asked. "How could I know? How
could I think?" she replied, her voice tinged with desperation. "Didn't you
know this was wrong?" asked Butterworth. "Yes," she said, "but Mr. Breckinridge is such a man that he can make it all seem right to love in that way."

Butterworth persisted. "You of course appreciated all the dishonor
and disgrace the relations embraced?" he asked, less question and more
statement—didn't she know she would be ruined? "No, I did not, and
only now do I," said Madeline, looking at him "half fiercely, half sadly,"
according to the *Enquirer*. "What do you mean by only now?" he
demanded. "I have never realized it fully until now, when I am an outcast," said Madeline. Now her lips quivered and tears flowed down her
face; she clasped and unclasped her black-gloved hands. "Since he has
made it too hard for me to live. I was under his control then just as much
as I was years later. I loved him then with all my heart and soul, and a
single wish of his was religion to me," she sobbed.

Butterworth moved to the Norwood Foundling Asylum, asking if it was true that Sister Agnes had told her she was a bad woman. "She said to me 'Why on earth do you want to ruin that poor old man in his old age?'" Madeline said. "I asked her why should that poor old man have wanted to ruin me in my youth?" She said Sister Agnes pleaded with her to consider Breckinridge's daughters. "I said he did not consider me, and I was somebody's daughter, and that he did not consider the little daughter of his and mine whom he had compelled me to give away," she said, the words now coming in a torrent like some long-dammed stream had burst. "I said there was such a thing as justice, and it should be done. He should have his share and I should have my share, and I believed there was a principle involved as to whether a man had a right to do as he chooses without suffering the consequences, while the woman must be bowed down with her shame. I said I believed the time would come when there would be a change of feeling on that part, and I said the time was near and it must come."

Then, turning pointedly toward the jury, Madeline added, "I believe these men are going to help me." A murmur went through the court-room. The jurors looked at one another, then back at Madeline.

Still Butterworth persisted, even as the absolute stillness in the courtroom, the very change in the air, should have told him that something had shifted. "Had you no thought of your future?" he asked. "I knew I was always to be in Col. Breckinridge's life, for the night before I went to Norwood I promised him to give the baby up and he promised to marry me should he become a widower, and he said should he never become a widower he would keep me in his life and do all for me that could be done," she said.

With that, Bradley adjourned the court. The reporters rushed to file their stories. Madeline was a sensation. "Miss Pollard is probably as intelligent a witness as has sat in the old courtroom for many a day," said the *Evening Star*, crediting her "individuality" and a "remarkable story, told in a remarkable way" for the overwhelming interest in the trial. It wasn't just the story she told, but the way she handled herself that astounded. "More than once she turned the tables on the counsel and the distinguished defendant, which made everyone marvel that a lone woman in the presence of a roomful of men could conduct herself with such skill and daring," said the *Post*. Gath wrote that even lawyers "sat still in silent surprise and admiration at the soft, subdued, earnest, truthful little woman, who was fighting single-handed a crafty, powerful Congressman of the United States." The *Courier-Journal*, which initially dismissed the case as "the same old story of the discarded mistress," now praised Madeline's "intelligence, her quick perception, and her effective command of words." Madeline, it would seem, had just elevated the "ruined" woman, the "fallen" girl, from an outcast into a sort of heroine, intelligent and earnest, fighting the powers that be.

•

Tuesday was expected to be Madeline's last day on the stand. The hours of testimony were beginning to wear; she looked paler than before and a bit weary; her answers came more slowly. Butterworth began by reading a bundle of letters to Rhodes from Madeline that had been turned over to the defense by Rhodes's sister, who never forgave Madeline for the way she treated her brother. It was an area of obvious embarrassment for Madeline. The day before, Butterworth had asked her if it was true that after she came to live in Lexington, she was simultaneously being kept by Breckinridge, was engaged to Rankin Rossell, and was taking money from Rhodes, who believed he was to marry her. "Yes. As bad as it sounds, that was the condition," she said, adding that she always intended to pay Rhodes back until the relationship with Breckinridge made that impossible.

If Butterworth hoped to embarrass her further by reading the letters, he failed, as the contours of her relationship with Rhodes were already well understood and the letters, noted the *Evening Star*, seemed "very proper letters for a young lady to write." She did frequently ask him for money and usually made seeing her contingent on him bringing it. But she also put strict limits on when she would see him. "Please, dear, do let me have $40 by Saturday without fail, for Mrs. Hoyt has asked for it two or three times . . . Come Saturday evening about 7 o'clock and you can stay until half past eight," she wrote. Contrary to the defense's contention that she was running around assignation houses with Rhodes, he appeared to be paying dearly for the privilege of sitting in the parlor with her for an hour and a half. In one letter, she thanked him for the set of Washington Irving books he gave her for Christmas.

The letters also allowed her to explain how when she was in

Cincinnati having her first child, Breckinridge cooked up a scheme to make it appear she was traveling with an aunt through the southeast. She sent letters through her mother to Rhodes purporting to be from New Orleans and Mississippi, with the travelogue provided by Breckinridge, to explain her absence, painting Breckinridge as the author of the many deceptions, large and small, carried out over the years to hide their affair.

After lunch, Butterworth began questioning Madeline about her trip to New York around the time of Breckinridge's April marriage to Wing, apparently trying to establish that she had threatened Breckinridge's life as an excuse for his breach of contract. But he unwittingly set Madeline up to tell the story of the last tumultuous days of their relationship. "Even her own lawyers could not have brought forth before the jury such convincing testimony, such a startling recital," said Gath.

Madeline said she was supposed to meet Breckinridge at the Hoffman House in New York on April 29; she registered as his daughter, took a room adjoining his, and waited for him. He didn't come until the following day, at which point, unbeknownst to her, he was already married to Wing. Butterworth asked Madeline if it was true that when Breckinridge got to his room, she came through the adjoining door with a pistol in her hand and tried to shoot him. Madeline said that wasn't what happened at all. Taking a deep breath, she said Breckinridge showed up that Sunday very much excited and talking wildly about a big business deal. "He said Mr. William C. Whitney and ex-Secretary Fairchild, with others, had formed a big company with $30,000,000 in capital and that he was to be employed by them to visit Europe," she said. He told her he was going away with them that night on a private railroad car and left in a hurry, saying he would be back the next day. "He acted so queerly my suspicions were aroused," Madeline said. She phoned the offices of Whitney and Fairchild and found they hadn't seen Breckinridge. She sent a message to the manager of Grand Central Station, who replied back that there was no private railroad car on the sidetrack at Forty-Seventh Street, which is where Breckinridge said he was going.

Breckinridge returned on Monday, she said, and came and went several times over the next two days, claiming he was meeting his new partners. At one point, she said, he asked her how quickly she could be packed and ready to marry him, saying he might be sent abroad at any minute; at another, he "talked about going to Havana and then about going to Samoa." She said he "was nearly wild, having done what he had done, having made the promise that he had." It was while he was out and she was folding some of his clothes that, she said, she found a pistol in his bag, which she removed and put in her bureau drawer. When he came back, she confronted him about his lies, which he denied, and he told her it was never in his heart to marry anyone but her. She said she half believed him in the way that she always did. "If you break your promise to marry me I am going to kill you and myself," she said. That's when she told him about the pistol in her drawer and when he promised to marry her on May 31. She said he took the pistol and she never touched it. After that, he took her to meet Mrs. Blackburn, who was in New York on business, and they returned separately to Washington.

Madeline said that after Breckinridge came back she confronted him again because she had heard that Wing was with him in New York. She said she doubted that a "worthy woman" like Wing would do that without some "understanding"—meaning an agreement to marry. She said Breckinridge "denied indignantly" any intention to marry Wing and "maligned Mrs. Wing in the most abusive manner," telling Madeline that Wing was planning to marry someone else and that "she was not a woman he wanted to marry."

Butterworth asked if she had ever threatened to kill him before that, and she said she hadn't—but she said she had threatened to kill herself after she received anonymous letters "telling of his conduct with colored women." There were murmurs and titters in the courtroom at the seeming confirmation of rumors that had long circulated in Lexington that "the colonel does not draw the color line" and could sometimes be found chasing after a "good-looking colored girl." This, as well as the "revelations of the defendant's conduct after his secret marriage, his fervent promise to marry Miss Pollard, even when he was already married, caused a subdued surprise and even a sensation among the hardened lawyers," said Gath.

Butterworth pressed on: Hadn't they gone to see Major Moore the first time because she threatened to shoot Breckinridge? Again she said that's not what happened. Madeline said that a week after they returned from New York, she found out that Breckinridge was at Wing's residence on Jefferson Place. She went there and through a window saw them duck behind a curtain. When she went in, she found them huddled in a corner. "Come Willie, come with me. I want to see you," she said she told him. "Did he come?" asked Butterworth. "He did," she said, as a barely suppressed commotion swept the courtroom and the bailiff rapped desperately for order. It was then, she said, that they went to see Major Moore. "I did not have a thing in my hand except a parasol," she said. There were no threats, she said, but she was excited and had been crying a great deal. "My heart was broken that morning, for I had seen in that man that I had loved and trusted for nine years his absolute falsehood," she said.

Didn't Breckinridge beg you to break the relations off? asked Butterworth. Didn't he promise to give you $125 a month if you would go to Germany to study? he asked. "I should have liked the court to hear him plead for me to stay," she averred. "I made an absolute sacrifice of me and mine . . . He made his promise to marry me. I never released him from that promise." She continued, her voice growing tremulous, "On that last day that I talked with him, that 17th day of May 1893, he made me believe that he would keep his promise. He talked of our unborn child and what we would name it." Now her voice was choked with sobs: "I gave up my babies for him . . . A woman can't do more than that, she can't do more than give up her child. I laid my baby in its coffin because it needed a mother's care, which I had not been able to give it, because he made me put it away from me. I—never—let—him—see—me—cry—over—it. I—never . . ."

At that, Madeline broke off and collapsed on the rough boards of the desk in front of her, sobs shaking her slender frame. For a long minute, her crying was the only sound in the courtroom. Three of the jurors fumbled for handkerchiefs; Bradley stared at the ceiling. When it became clear she couldn't continue, he adjourned the court. "If there was a man among the curious hundred in the courtroom unmoved," said the *World*, "he was inconspicuous in the majority of sympathetic faces." Breckinridge left the courtroom ahead of his posse of counsel. He strode down the street, hat in hand, "head bent in a dejected way," said the *Enquirer*, "letting the cool breeze strike his silver locks" as the passersby stared.

14

A Man of Passion

Madeline was on the stand for only half an hour the morning following her dramatic breakdown over the death of her children before Butterworth concluded his cross-examination with a few desultory questions about Rhodes. When Carlisle announced that the plaintiff rested her case, satisfied with Madeline's testimony and seeing no need for redirect questioning to clarify anything, Breckinridge's team was caught off guard. They had to ask Bradley for time to prepare and hastily retreated to a nearby office, which caused one spectator to scoff, "The delegation from Kentucky retires for conference."

Anticipation had been building over Breckinridge's defense and the moment when the silver-tongued orator would take the stand. "It is evident that his attorneys place their principal reliance on the story he will tell," said the *Evening Star*, "and their sanguine state of mind indicates that they have in reserve resources which have not yet been made known." Breckinridge had been assuring his backers that he was preparing the case thoroughly and that "the testimony will be overwhelming that I am guiltless of the graver charges," although he did note he had been hampered by the absence of the lawyer Enoch Totten and "my own comparatively straitened pecuniary needs."

When the defense team filed back into the courtroom, it was Shelby, still glancing at the papers before him, who presented the defense. Pale and slight, with a sandy mustache and a shiny, balding pate, he seemed the inverse of his fodgel, florid partner. It soon became clear that he lacked his oratorical flourish as well, but Breckinridge thought him the most capable of his lawyers in laying out a defense. It was not the only antipode moment of the morning. Shelby proceeded to describe a version of the relationship in which Breckinridge was the hapless victim, entrapped by a persistent paramour, powerless to end the affair because he was terrified that Madeline would expose him, ultimately bullied by threats of violence into pretending they were engaged. "I am authorized to say," began Shelby, peering at the jury through his gold-rimmed glasses, "that he never did seduce this woman; that she never, at any time, until the filing of the suit last August, claimed or in any way apprised him of the fact that she had borne him any child." He said they would prove that Madeline was an "experienced woman" of nearly twenty-one when they met and that she had "enticed and tempted the defendant . . . and that even his first lascivious propositions were not repulsed, but passively encouraged."

According to Shelby, it was Madeline who pursued Breckinridge: "She would come to the door of his house; follow him to the House of Representatives; follow him to his rooms." Breckinridge was unable to resist, and time and time again "fell in with" the plaintiff and as a result "inappropriate relations were resumed"—the passive voice mirroring his supposed lack of agency. Shelby acknowledged that the relationship was wrong, but said that "many men had done the same thing and been forgiven," and that Madeline "had him more or less in her power and she used that in getting money from him and continuing their relationship." As a result, Breckinridge's "life was made an intolerable burden." He tried to get Madeline to go away, "to make something of herself," but she always returned to Washington. Finally, he said, by "such a pressure as designing women can use, Miss Pollard did induce him to go to Mrs. Blackburn and say to her they were engaged."

At first, every spectator was "on the tiptoe of expectation" to hear the defense, said the *Enquirer*. But once he finished summing up the defense, Shelby turned to the reading of depositions, most of which had already been reported on in the press. Soon, the mood of the spectators mirrored the weather: dank and gloomy. It was as if the "romantic character of the drama had left the stage," complained Gath. All that was left was the phlegmatic Shelby, reading depositions in his monotone.

And so it went, for the remainder of Wednesday and then all of

Thursday, when Stoll took up the reading. Sister Agnes and Sister Augustine said they didn't recognize Madeline as a former inmate of the Norwood Asylum; a nurse and doctor from Norwood said the same thing, although they confirmed there had been a patient there named Wilson. Orvin Brown, the son of the president of Wesleyan, said the other girls teasingly called Madeline "Madeline Vivian Bill-Breckinridge Joe-Blackburn Pollard" for her habit of claiming kinship with the prominent families of Kentucky. He said he found a record of her name as "Madeline V. B. Pollard" in the school's books. He concurred, however, with Madeline's account of Breckinridge's visit to the school and said he was "severely criticized" for letting them go out together in the carriage. He disputed Madeline's claim, however, that she received a telegram in August 1884 purportedly from her mother, but actually sent by Breckinridge, summoning her home. Brown said she left Wesleyan sometime in August because her tuition hadn't been paid.

As the depositions proceeded, the spectators thinned then dwindled to a few hardy souls. Gath thought some of the jurors looked like they were wondering, "What has this to do with the white-haired Kentucky Colonel's promise to marry Madeline Pollard?" The reliance on so many depositions was more necessity than strategy. Breckinridge simply didn't have the funds to bring more than a few well-chosen witnesses to Washington. The money crunch had only become more acute as the trial progressed and expenses for stenographers and other necessities piled up. Breckinridge's bank account was overdrawn. Jennie had to beg for money to pay her board. "My finances are in a state of total collapse," she wrote in desperation to Worthington.

Nonetheless, as the trial adjourned for the long Easter weekend, Breckinridge's team felt somewhat optimistic, finally having gone on the defensive and believing it had yet to play its strongest hand. Jennie wrote home that the trial was "the great topic everywhere at present." She thought "people have been a bit surprised at the evidence of the defense" so far and were more inclined to think Breckinridge may win. "Practically, I have won the case," Breckinridge assured a friend, saying that "whatever the technical verdict," he would win reelection because the people of his district wouldn't elect the "beneficiary of the blackmail suit brought by a wanton."

Breckinridge hinging his defense on painting Madeline as a "wanton," however, wasn't without risks, as the *Evening Star* warned. It noted that even if he "succeeds in blackening the reputation of the plaintiff it will convict the defendant of putting upon Mrs. Blackburn an affront such as could not be forgiven under the Kentucky . . . code of honor."

The *New York Herald* struck a darker note, reporting that Breckinridge was "politically dead." One prominent Kentuckian said that if Breckinridge had acknowledged his fault up front, he would have "fallen in public esteem for awhile" but bounced back: "Folks would have said, 'Oh, that is Breckinridge you know, but he was honest about it anyway.' But when he made a general denial, and was then forced into the sort of defense he has made, why, that kills him. Adam made that defense, you know. It didn't go in Eden then and it won't go today in Kentucky."

Breckinridge spent Good Friday writing to supporters to reassure them he was "as game as a game cock" and confident of success and reelection. William Owens, a former state legislator who had the backing of the powerful Blue Grass Hemp Trust, had announced he would challenge Breckinridge in the Democratic primary. Nevertheless, Breckinridge told supporters he wouldn't wage a "defensive canvas" and would campaign in his usual low-key manner. He already had compiled lists of Democratic voters from his cronies and appointees at the local post offices and sent some five hundred letters announcing he would be a candidate for reelection no matter what. He told one supporter that he believed the jury would see through Madeline's "acting" and "not lose sight of the fact that she has been [as] willing to live since 1883 on her shame as any woman does who lives in a bawdy-house." Above all else, he told them, despite the terrific ordeal he was undergoing, he was profoundly relieved, "for I have no secret of which I am afraid, no skeleton in my closet which chains me."

But at the same time, Breckinridge was writing other, more desperate letters. He, in fact, had no secret store of evidence, no bombshell revelation beyond a collection of smears and innuendo from a bevy of unsavory witnesses. There was only one place he could turn for rescue—to other men. Breckinridge had heard through a friend of a friend that Mississippi congressman John Allen had claimed that

Madeline had approached him after he made a speech on the House floor and "introduced herself and congratulated him over his able speech and gave him her card and insisted on him calling." When he didn't call on her, he said she came to his boardinghouse and summoned him to the parlor, where she chastised him for failing to visit her. Allen "put her off by agreeing to call" but supposedly "remarked to this friend that all she wanted was for him to take her to his room."

Breckinridge begged Allen to testify about the encounter. His colleague confirmed the story but insisted he not be dragged into the scandal. "Now you have my sympathy and I wish very much that I could be of service to you," Allen wrote, but said he doubted his testimony "would amount to anything." He said he mentioned the encounter with Madeline to friends only "in an effort to convince them you were not as bad as there was an effort to paint you," and he would be "very unhappy" if his attempt to support him resulted in "embarrassing notoriety."

There was one other man Breckinridge could turn to. But to do so was politically fraught, not only for himself, but for the entire Cleveland administration, which already was battered by the depression. Rumors had been bouncing around Washington since the previous summer— the fateful summer of 1893—that Madeline had "endeavored to make an assignation" with Treasury Secretary John Carlisle, the former House Speaker who had given his fellow Kentuckian Breckinridge a leg up in the House. Carlisle had gossiped to Breckinridge's partner John Shelby and his cousin Congressman Clifton Rhodes Breckinridge that Madeline had sent him a letter proposing a meeting "couched in such terms that it was evident that Miss Pollard's intentions were unduly kind," according to the *Enquirer*. "I can easily believe it," Breckinridge said when he heard the rumor at a Fourth of July picnic.

Carlisle was the most popular and influential member of Cleveland's cabinet and a critical component of sensitive negotiations over currency and tariffs; Cleveland "considered him a likely successor in 1896," according to the historian Hal Williams. Breckinridge had asked Carlisle several times to testify to Madeline's purported advances, which, coming after his promise of marriage, would automatically release him from any breach of promise claim since Madeline had already breached such promise. But Carlisle refused. The matter was apparently so sensitive to Carlisle that he had a go-between hand deliver a message to Breckin-ridge right after the scandal broke in August warning him that "this case must not come to a trial."

Now, Breckinridge wrote one last, desperate letter to Carlisle. "I need not say that it is with very sincere reluctance that I again insist upon you appearing as a witness," he wrote. "I would not do it if the exigencies of the case did not seem to me to require it." He assured Carlisle that such testimony would not damage him personally, since he had ignored Pollard's letter, but said it might be the only means of rescuing him "from the net which has been so assiduously and skillfully woven." He told him he wouldn't hesitate to help him if the circumstances were reversed and hinted at political revenge, telling Carlisle that his failure to testify might "subject you to adverse criticism" at home in Kentucky.

It wasn't an idle threat. Carlisle was believed to be eying a run for the presidency. But he was weak among Kentucky Democrats given his failure to attend to political patronage at home. The *Enquirer* reported that Breckinridge was promising to throw his considerable influence in the Kentucky Democratic machine behind Carlisle in exchange for his testimony. And, if Carlisle's presidential bid faltered, Breckinridge sup-posedly was offering to back him in a challenge to Joe Blackburn's Sen-ate seat—a seat that Breckinridge himself had been expected to eventually seek. Even the gubernatorial race was tied up in the machi-nations, with Cassius Clay, Jr., of the politically powerful Clay family, backing a bid for Blackburn's seat by the current governor John Young Brown in alliance with Breckinridge's primary opponent Owens so that Clay might ascend to the governor's office.

It appeared that the political fortunes of the three most powerful families in Kentucky—the Breckinridges, the Blackburns, and the Clays—as well as the upcoming presidential election—hinged on what Carlisle decided. But he didn't take the bait. In fact, according to the *Morning Transcript*, he said that if "Breckinridge forced him to testify in the sensational case he would resign his place in the Cabinet," poten-tially destabilizing the entire administration in the midst of a financial crisis. Breckinridge was forced to go without his testimony.

●

On Monday morning Breckinridge looked more chipper in court than he had in some time, maybe because his hair and beard had been trimmed in keeping with the old custom of cutting one's locks on "shere Thursday" during Holy Week. It was a good morning for the defense. Breckinridge's biggest concern was that Judge Bradley would rule out a majority of the depositions regarding Madeline's early life and supposed sexual antics because Pollard's lawyers claimed the depositions had been improperly taken. But Bradley ruled that most of the defense depositions could be submitted, with the exception of Dr. Lewis's about the abortion he was supposedly asked to procure for Colonel Swope, which was thrown out as hearsay. Bradley, however, noted rather pointedly that he would suppress some of the depositions if he could "on the grounds they were too filthy to be read" and implored the press to "suppress the disgusting details" for "the sake of the community and families."

In the morning, Stoll read a seemingly endless series of depositions attesting to Breckinridge's presence at various trials in Versailles, Winchester, and other places around Kentucky during the spring and summer of 1884, which were supposed to provide an alibi of sorts, but it wasn't made clear how they comported with Pollard's story. In the afternoon the depositions of William Wood, who was engaged briefly to Madeline when she lived with her aunt outside Lexington, and Alex Julian, the "groom" at the mock wedding at Squire Tinsley's Christmas party, were read.

Tuesday brought the first live witness—Major Moore, who was brought back to testify about his two encounters with the couple in May 1893. Shelby asked him if Breckinridge had admitted to fathering Madeline's children, calling the situation, as Madeline contended he did, "one of life's tragedies." Moore answered succinctly, "No." But on cross-examination, he admitted that Breckinridge could well have said such a thing but that he didn't record it in his shorthand notes.

Two handwriting experts testified that the disputed letter purportedly from Pollard to Breckinridge regarding her trouble with Rhodes appeared genuine. William Worthington, Breckinridge's stenographer, testified that he found the letter the previous September in a dusty old file case in Breckinridge's Lexington office. The letter was important because it appeared to show that it was Madeline who had invited Breckinridge to Wesleyan and that initially he declined to come. "I am glad you told me it would be inconvenient for you to come out here in the college, for if you had gone to even such a little trouble to listen to what sometimes overburdens a schoolgirl's mind you might be inclined to be provoked with yourself," it read. What Breckinridge's team thought the most damning was the part that read: "A preacher's opinion of my little affair of mine would cause premature gray hairs, when your opinion might clear away all doubts and fears . . . I think I have prepared you for a divorce case, but, listen: it is far worse than that."

But then the writer goes on to clearly state that she was referring to the deal she made with Rhodes, that he would advance her tuition for three years "under the promise that I marry him at the expiration of that time." What she wanted to know was if he could "do anything if I would not marry him, but teach and refund all he had advanced?" The letter closed with Madeline purportedly writing: "I liked your face and I am sure I would like you, and if at any future time you are in the city and would care to come around, remember that home faces are always welcome." It was signed Madeline B. Pollard. While the letter didn't appear particularly damaging, Madeline had denounced it as a fraud. Wilson disputed the credentials of both expert witnesses and got one, E. B. Hay, to admit the method he said he used to compare the handwriting in the letter to Madeline's handwriting was directly opposite the method he had used recently in a high-profile congressional investigation.

On Wednesday, Rankin Rossell appeared in the flesh to testify that Madeline had sat on his lap and allowed him to kiss her in the front parlor at Wesleyan and that he had broken his engagement to her because he "didn't like the way she allowed me to hug and kiss her." He claimed that Madeline told him she was born in November 1863 and provided five tintypes they had taken together in Cincinnati several months before she met Breckinridge. The pictures showed Madeline as a "very young and undeveloped girl" with frizzy bangs and a dress that reached only to her boot-tops. Kaufman's and Brand's depositions were read regarding Madeline's reported presence at Lena Singleton's house of ill repute.

On Thursday morning the crowds again had swelled in anticipation of seeing Breckinridge. It was standing room only; the weather had turned warm and the courtroom had an "unwholesome smell." Madeline's lawyers presented two rebuttal witnesses—out of order because they were in town only for a short time—who testified that no one named Lena Singleton occupied a house in the Lexington neighborhood where Madeline and Rhodes were said to be frequent visitors. Mollie Shindlebower, the former prostitute, testified in her deposition that she had known Madeline when she lived at her aunt Mary Stout's house in 1877 and said she was a fast girl who had gentlemen callers at irregular hours, wore long dresses, and appeared to be sixteen or seventeen.

After lunch, there was an expectant hum in the courtroom as the bailiff rapped the court to order. Stoll finished reading the Shindlebower deposition. Breckinridge took the stand at 1:47. The jurors roused themselves from their deposition-induced stupor; heads craned to get a better look at the snowy hair, the ruddy face, the black frock coat with the little white gull wings of Breckinridge's shirt peeping out as he solemnly swore his oath on a "fresh, new Bible." There was a moment of commotion as one of Carlisle's clerks ran out of the courtroom and across the street to fetch Madeline from his office and a collective intake of breath as she entered the room; all eyes followed her as she made her way to the plaintiff's table and sat right in front of Breckinridge. He stood as he testified, with one elbow propped casually on Bradley's bench, striking a "minor key of tenderness and pathos" as he spoke.

Breckinridge ran through his biography—college and law school, his first marriage, the Ninth Kentucky Cavalry, his second marriage, his law practice, his election to Congress. "When did you first meet the plaintiff?" Butterworth asked. Breckinridge said it was sometime in April 1884, on the train from Lexington to Frankfort. He said it was a cool morning and he had an overcoat with him that he left on the seat when he went forward on the train. When he returned to get it, a young woman called to him. He said he replied, "I suppose I ought to know you, but when people reach my time of life you find young folks growing up so around you that you don't recognize them." She said that he didn't know her, but that she knew him because "everybody knows you." She said that her name was Madeline Breckinridge Pollard and that her father, J.D. Pollard, was a great admirer of John Cabell Breckinridge. He told her he remembered her father and asked how he was, and apologized for his forgetfulness when she said he had died some years ago. She told him she was going "to the bedside of her sister at Frankfort, who was dying of consumption."

Breckinridge said the next time he heard from her was when he received a letter asking him to call on her regarding advice about some unnamed difficulty and then when he received a second letter giving more specifics of her problem. At that, Wilson objected to the admission of the disputed letter, and Breckinridge sat down while the lawyers hashed it out. Finally, Bradley ruled that the letter could be admitted. Breckinridge continued his story about having business in Covington, across the river from Cincinnati, that first Friday in August 1884 and staying overnight in Cincinnati, as Covington had no decent hotels, and deciding to call on Madeline in reply to her letter. He told about their discussion about Rhodes and his assurance that she couldn't be compelled to "marry a man if she did not want to." But then, he said, she told him there was another consideration that made the situation "much worse than a real marriage." He said Madeline told him that Rhodes was "anxious and jealous and very much in love" with her. Someone had warned him that Madeline wouldn't want to marry him once she was educated, so, Breckinridge said, she said that "she gave him higher proof of her intention to keep my contract"—meaning she had sacrificed her virginity. He said he told her she "ought to marry him" before "things come out" and she was ruined, but she told him that now that she was getting an education and had seen "what she was capable of," she couldn't imagine marrying him. He said he told her, "No young girl can afford not to marry after what you have told me, no matter the marriage be happy or unhappy." As he spoke, Madeline stared at him, at first resting her head in her hands and then "vigorously wield[ing] a fan" in the stuffy air.

Breckinridge told about the concert and the carriage ride, both of which he said were Madeline's idea. He said he hailed the first carriage in line at the hack stand near the old Post Office and made no excuse for the closed carriage because there was "no reason for any excuse." He said it was Madeline who suggested they skip the concert, saying she would "prefer to ride rather than go to a place where there is hot gas . . . so we took the road to the left." After they had driven about fifteen or twenty minutes, with Madeline "talking about her desires to be an authoress," he said she took off her hat and "I put my arm around her and drew her to me." He said, "There were no protestations on my part, no offer of love. What occurred then was—I was a man of passion, she a woman of passion. There was no outcry by her, no resistance. I, man as I was, took liberties with her person."

"Just a case of illicit love?" prompted Butterworth. "That was it, Butterworth," said Breckinridge. Breckinridge said Madeline made no objection to what happened and when they got back to the college, he put some money in an envelope and handed it to her, saying, "There are a great many little things you need." She refused the money, but he pressed it into her hand anyway as she got out of the carriage. Butterworth asked what was in the envelope. "My recollection of it is that it was a $10 bill," he said. At that, Bradley, who had sat through Breckinridge's entire testimony with his head averted toward the ceiling and his eyes closed, interjected, "Adjourn the court."

Breckinridge picked up the story on Friday morning. He said that after the carriage ride he went back to his hotel and had no further communication with Madeline. He denied that he met her at the Cincinnati Public Library or took her to Mrs. Rose's assignation house. He said he didn't arrange to return to Lexington with Madeline—that he wasn't even sure himself which train he would take home. He said when he got on the train on Saturday, he found Madeline already on it, and "their conversation resulted in an agreement to meet in Lexington that evening." According to Breckinridge, it was Madeline's idea to go to Sarah Guess's house. She said that she had gone there once as far as the front gate with Rhodes. He said when he returned to Guess's after having dinner with his family, he wasn't sure she would still be there and that it was her decision to spend the weekend there, instead of going to a "more respectable place." He said that she appeared to be a young woman who "understood matters pertaining to the sexes that a young girl would not know." Breckinridge said he thought Madeline was at the time a "young woman of twenty, or twenty-one, or twenty-two . . . She was a full grown young woman."

Breckinridge also said that Rhodes tracked him down at his office the following Monday morning to discuss Madeline, claiming that he—Rhodes—"ought to marry her—he not only intended, wanted, hoped, but that he ought to marry her." "I say he never did," Madeline suddenly interjected in a weak, half-broken voice as she rose from her seat. "He's not telling the truth about anything," she cried as Carlisle shushed her. Breckinridge denied that he arranged for Madeline to go to the Sayre Institute and said the first time he knew she was attending the school was when he saw her standing outside the gate. He said the next time he met Madeline was in October when he was going to Cincinnati to hear a speech and ran into her at the train station, and it was then that they arranged to go to Mrs. Rose's assignation house.

He denied knowing about Madeline going to the Norwood Asylum or paying her expenses or helping to deceive Rhodes. He said he had no idea at the time she was pregnant but that later she told him she'd had a miscarriage. He said that after the October visit to Mrs. Rose's house they had no further relations throughout 1884 or 1885. He claimed to have not seen Madeline at all in 1886 or to have had any communication with her. He said when he went to stay at Mrs. Ketchum's boarding-house in the spring of 1887 it was because the Phoenix Hotel was too noisy, and that while he might have known that Madeline was there, he was never in her room. He said their relations didn't resume until later that summer. He denied that he told Madeline to come to Washington in the fall of 1887, when she said she was again pregnant by him; he said that she came at the suggestion of the late Senator Beck.

He denied knowing that she had given birth in February 1888, although he admitted paying Dr. Parsons's bill. He said the relationship didn't resume until some time after Madeline went to live at the Academy of the Holy Cross in the spring of 1888, after which it continued until the fall of 1890, when he told her that they should separate because only "scandal and destruction" could come from their relationship. He said he got her to promise to leave Washington and agreed to pay her expenses to help fit her for some respectable employment. "The plaintiff I knew to be a woman of very considerable talent. I felt entangled with her to some extent through my belief in her statement that she had had an unfortunate miscarriage, caused by me, and again another miscarriage," he said. But when he returned from campaigning later that fall, he found that she had gotten a job with the Census Office and was still in the city.

In the fall of 1891, he said, Madeline agreed to go to Cambridge and went for a period of time, but returned to Washington "in distinct violation of our agreement." He said he tried to break it off with her, but she threatened him with "exposure" if he did. He denied Madeline ever helped him with his speeches or went with him to events, as she claimed she did. Finally, in the spring of 1892, he said, she went to Vermont, supposedly to work on a newspaper, but returned after the death of his wife. He denied that he had met with her at any time in August 1892, much less proposed marriage to her. He said he told her that "marriage between them was an impossibility" because he could not respect her since he "had not seduced her, and she had not come to me a maiden," which caused another half-broken outcry from Madeline. He denied he gave her Issa's sewing basket, which he said she took from his boarding-house without his knowledge. He denied begging her not to leave him, as Madeline said he did, and said she followed him about, haunting him with her demands: "She would come to the Capitol, to the rooms of the committee of which I was a member, and to the library. She would meet me on the street."

He claimed Madeline told Mrs. Blackburn that they were en-gaged because she was upset that Mrs. Fillette said that she was an adventuress who was inviting scandal by her behavior. He said Madeline told him that she would commit suicide and kill him "before she would allow the scandal to fall upon her alone." He said he told Blackburn that Madeline was an imprudent girl, and he and Blackburn finally convinced Madeline to go to New York. But, he said, Madeline was concerned that Blackburn was still suspicious. So he said he agreed to go to Blackburn's with her and "pretend that there was an engagement between us," and in return Madeline promised to "go away and gradually drop out of Mrs. Blackburn's life and not come into mine again."

He denied meeting Madeline at the Hoffman House after his mar-riage to Wing. He said he went back to his room to get some clothes and found Madeline there and that he narrowly averted getting shot by slamming the door between their rooms shut. The next time he saw her was the day she barged in on him and Louise. That's when they visited Major Moore, when, he said, Madeline again threatened to kill him, and then Dr. Lincoln, which was when he found out she was pregnant. He said he told Madeline, "If it is my child, I will know it when it is born. I will provide for it and will see that it is raised properly."

By the time the court adjourned for the weekend, Breckinridge had used every tool at his disposal—his famous, mellifluous voice, "silvery and soft-spoken but insinuating"; pointed denials stuffed with "high-sounding adjectives and nicely wrought sentences"; long soliloquies tinged with pathos. He name-dropped every name he could drop, from President Cleveland to "other great and good people," until, when he stepped down from the stand, there could be no doubt of his stature, of his importance to the affairs of the nation, of the estimable company in which he traveled. He had denied almost every aspect of Madeline's story, "save Madeline Pollard's existence," said Gath. The two stories, said the *Evening Star*, were so contradictory that there "was no possible way of harmonizing" them: "One is true and the other is not." But it remained to be seen whose version would be believed.

•

Breckinridge's testimony was not well received. Unlike Madeline's, little of it was corroborated by other witnesses. Many found it ridiculous that he, powerful and prominent as he was, claimed to be the victim of a designing young woman. "He was, to hear him talk to-day, a passive slave in her hands: he a man of 47, she a girl of 17," scoffed Gath. His defense also hinged on a remarkable string of coincidences, from just happening to choose a closed carriage, to just happening to find Madeline on the train to Lexington, to her just happening to know an assignation house blocks from his home. Just as remarkable was the string of miscarriages he asserted that Madeline had experienced, which conveniently absolved him from responsibility for any children.

It was his assertion that he knew of no "living children" born to Madeline that was his most desperate denial. As Breckinridge demonstrated when he said he promised to support the child Madeline was pregnant with in the spring of 1893, the rules about such things were very strict under Victorian morality, even within the context of an illicit relationship. A man was expected to take responsibility for children he conceived illicitly with all but the lowliest of women, such as prostitutes, where parentage was undeterminable. Madeline's charge that he failed to do this, that he compelled her to abandon their children, was damning. This was because, as the fate of Madeline's two children attested, leaving a newborn in a nineteenth-century infant asylum was often a death sentence. A combination of overcrowding, disease, a shortage of wet nurses—and only primitive, impure formula substitutes—and a sheer lack of affection, not to mention their shamed mothers' lack of prenatal care, contributed to an extraordinarily high death rate at these institutions.

St. Ann's Infant Asylum in Washington cared for 130 infants in 1895—74 died, for a death rate of nearly 60 percent. Thirty died before they reached one month, and the majority before they reached nine months. Summer was the deadliest time: seven or eight infants died per month in June, July, and August. And private Catholic asylums like St. Ann's, with a staff of nuns experienced in running such institutions, had better mortality rates than public asylums. In some large public asylums, like the Infants' Hospital on Randall's Island in New York, mortality rates were between 85 and 100 percent. "The babies die like sheep, many being deserted so young nothing can be hoped or done for them," reported Louisa May Alcott—now the successful author of *Little Women* and long removed from her days as a servant—when she visited Randall's Island. A doctor who had worked there thought it would be an "act of humanity if each foundling were given a fatal dose of opium on its arrival, since all of them died."

And for all Breckinridge's protestations about making provisions for his child, he told his lawyers in a confidential memo that when he and Madeline visited Dr. Lincoln on May 13 it was because "Lincoln had consented to perform an abortion if I would consent to ask him, and this is the reason why we went." He didn't record why he didn't go through with the request and he certainly didn't disclose this information during the trial. In the end, whether abortion or its functional equivalent, abandonment in an infant asylum, it was clear that Breckinridge, like many men of the era, preached a public morality denigrating women as "wantons" while taking advantage of a shadow system of infant asylums and secret abortionists that hid their sins—a system the trial was exposing to the light.

15

Hindered, Not Ruined

As Breckinridge struggled to present a credible defense, Jennie was "having a perfect circus" of a time getting into the House of Mercy to see Madeline. She had taken to stalking Pennsylvania Avenue on the streetcar route between the courthouse and the House of Mercy and jumping on the trolley if she saw Madeline. It worked, but it wasn't a particularly subtle tactic, especially when used repeatedly and especially since Madeline likely already had suspicions that Jennie was spying on her. "Why, Aggie, you are more devoted than a lover," Madeline exclaimed one morning when Jennie suddenly materialized in the seat behind her. "I never knew anyone to appear in such an astonishing manner. You must spend all your time waiting around on street corners for me."

Regardless, Jennie was having the time of her life running around Washington playing spy. One day she was instructed to come to Enoch Totten's house at precisely four o'clock—heavily veiled so she wouldn't be recognized. Another she was to meet a member of the defense team at "the statue in the circle when the clock strikes nine," most likely a reference to nearby Scott Circle, with its widely ridiculed statue of the towering Gen. Winfield Scott mounted on a petite mare—which was his mount of choice—to which male genitalia had been hastily appended after his relatives complained that a stallion was more appropriate for a man of his stature. It was all so cloak-and-dagger that Jennie imagined her life was in peril. She warned her family to keep her assignment secret: "[It] might cause me my life if the other side discovered my connection," she said of her link with Breckinridge, adding "the woman concerned in it would just hunt me up at the ends of the earth and kill me."

Jennie did manage to talk her way into the House of Mercy the Friday evening after Breckinridge wound up the bulk of his testimony. Jennie found Madeline in bed, happy that Breckinridge had "done so badly for his cause." She told Jennie that she had "lost all the old feelings" for him, "that sort of going out to him with my whole heart and soul whenever I saw him." She had another reason to be cheered beyond Breckinridge's poorly received testimony—she was getting an onslaught of public support. She had received some two hundred letters so far and had gotten fifty just that day. Some were offers for her to tell her story in print or on stage—the manager of a theater company offered her five hundred dollars a week. Some urged her to subscribe to the latest fads like mesmerism and clairvoyance. A number were offers of marriage. But most were applauding her for taking on Breckinridge and fighting what one woman called "this devilish business of seducing and betraying the pure and innocent."

Her supporters expressed faith in her vindication, which many said would be a victory for all women. An "ardent suffragist" from Baltimore assured Madeline that she "did perfectly right in bringing this hoary haired villain to court." She told Madeline that "every one of our sex who stands up for her rights, who refuses to be utterly trampled by men, and who determines that the man who had wrecked her life and blighted every thing for her in this world, *shall not, so far as she can prevent it,* pursue *his* pleasant career utterly unpunished and unscathed, is *helping the cause of women.*"

Some assured her that society was rethinking how it viewed ruined women. "I do believe every word you uttered on the witness stand is true. I firmly believe you are a virtuous woman to-day. I beg you hold yourself up, you are not a cast-out . . . These expressions are the expressions of thousands," said one anonymous supporter from Cincinnati. A man who had "caught a glance" of Madeline in Washington and hoped to open an "honorable" correspondence with her told her, "For past times it has been the rule when a girl went astray to keep her down, but the time for a change is at hand." A supporter who signed himself simply "A Poet" likewise assured her, "You are not 'ruined,' but hindered."

The letters to Madeline were only one aspect of a larger groundswell that was building against Breckinridge. On March 25, the National Christian League for the Promotion of Social Purity voted that Breckinridge "ought to be deposed from the high position he has attained." The following day, the Women's Rescue League of Boston passed a resolution asking the "chivalrous people of Kentucky to retire [Breckinridge] to a private life of obscurity and oblivion" because a "man old enough to be this school girl's grandfather, a man who stood high as an orator and lawmaker in legislative halls . . . a man with a silver tongue as well as silver hair . . . deliberately deceives, entraps, and betrays a poor, struggling girl," while "helping to fill up the asylums with his own offspring." They would soon be joined by a resolution from the Philadelphia Social Purity Alliance.

The Pollard-Breckinridge trial was a remarkable opportunity for social purity reformers, who for decades had been pushing without much success the idea of a single standard of morality for men and women. Dr. Caroline Winslow, a homeopathic physician who counted herself the fourth American woman to become a doctor, founded the Moral Education Society in Washington in 1877 and had become a national leader in early efforts to eradicate the double standard and the "ruined" woman. The journal she founded, the *Alpha*, was one of the first to discuss sex in frank terms and to argue that young adults should receive education about matters pertaining to sex. As early as 1878, the society tried to harness the power of the Washington elite when they voted that, due to "the disrespectful way that many men in power treat women," members would not "recognize socially . . . men who are known to be of impure life, and that where they are authentically informed of evil conduct of men towards women, they will endeavor by every means possible to make the character of such men known." Winslow and other social purity activists like Mrs. John Harvey Kellogg, the wife of the inventor of Kellogg's Corn Flakes, protested against Grover Cleveland's election in 1884. The Moral Reform Society passed a resolution calling "upon women in every station of life, high and low, rich and poor, the cherished wife and the betrayer's victim, to do all in their power to prevent Grover Cleveland being made the Chief Executive of the Nation."

Their call for solidarity among women fell on deaf ears, however, as did their crusade to end the double standard, hampered, no doubt, by their belief in "intercourse for procreation only"—which was known as the "Alpha Doctrine"—because they believed that sex depleted the vital forces and was best managed by abstinence. Even Susan B. Anthony, while sympathetic to the cause and friendly with Winslow, steered away from the issue after a brief foray in the 1870s because she feared anything related to sex was too controversial and might damage efforts to win the vote for women. By the early 1890s, Winslow had been eclipsed by male reformers like Aaron Macy Powell and Anthony Comstock, who focused less on frank discussions of sex and power and more on suppressing prostitution and information about birth control.

Suddenly, in Madeline Pollard, these women reformers had a visceral representation of the ideas they had been promoting for nearly twenty years: that the double standard not only allowed but encouraged men to prey on young women, and that the only way to end it was for men to be held to the same moral standard as women were. The resolutions against Breckinridge were widely covered in the press, which suggested a consensus coalescing around the issue, as did pointed condemnations from preachers like J. F. Carson of the Central Presbyterian Church in Brooklyn, who called for stamping out "that creeping worm of licentious doctrine" that the "man is not to be judged by the same high standard by which the woman is judged." No longer was it the disgraced woman who was a "creeping worm," but the mores that allowed men to prey on her.

The missing piece of the efforts to eradicate the curse of the fallen woman was getting a broad segment of women to publicly rebel against men who preyed on women. Now, this appeared to be happening—in the most unlikely of places. As Breckinridge was testifying, reports surfaced from Lexington that some of the most prominent women in the city—from the Clay, Hunt, and Goodloe families—had been "secretly circulating a petition praying Congress to impeach" Breckinridge. "The feeling against Breckinridge is rapidly changing," warned the *Enquirer*, which reported that if the petition failed, the women would "try to defeat his renomination."

•

When the trial resumed on Monday, Breckinridge looked tired, and the *Post* reporter thought he had "an unusual pallor on his countenance." It had been a long weekend. The newspapers had been merciless in their anti-Breckinridge editorials and cartoons. One showed the portly congressman trying desperately to keep a door shut while Madeline Pollard dragged a skeleton out of it. There were reports that his church in Lexington as well as his Mason lodge were looking to expel him. Someone had started a rumor as an April Fools' prank that he would be at the Burnet House in Cincinnati on Sunday to meet with supporters, and constituents showed up from far and wide only to go away angry when he wasn't there. He spent the weekend writing to supporters, railing about the "nefarious conspiracy" against him, which now included not only "unworthy and ignoble people" who "control the newspapers" but also "some most excellent ladies"—a reference to the petition circulating against him. He decried the failure of "cowardly" men "of whom better things ought to have been expected"—meaning Congressman Allen and Secretary Carlisle—to come to his aid and provide much-needed testimony.

There was more bad news for the defense. On Friday morning, Martha McClellan Brown, the wife of the former president of Wesleyan College, who was preparing to come to Washington to testify on Madeline's behalf, found the register for the school year of 1883–84 in an old sideboard. In it, Madeline Vivian Pollard, "aged sixteen," was recorded as entering as an irregular sophomore on November 20, 1883, which would confirm her contention that she was seventeen when she met Breckinridge the following April.

Breckinridge spent the closing hours of his testimony revisiting the final rocky weeks of his relationship with Madeline. He denied that he stayed at the Hoffman House with Madeline after he had married Louise. He also denied her story about his manic claims of big business deals or impending trips to Europe, and he claimed that he and Madeline didn't have any sexual relations after March 31. He asserted that he told

Major Moore he would marry Madeline only because she threatened to shoot him and later she promised to leave the city if he gave Moore the impression they were to be married to salvage her reputation.

Much of the story had been told already. The spectators seemed to have lost interest; there were a number of empty seats and those who were there read newspapers and talked among themselves. After lunch, the courtroom filled back up for Wilson's cross-examination. He had a reputation as a blunt, merciless interrogator. Clasping his hands behind his head, he began by having Breckinridge recite his church member-ships and the various Christian societies he had addressed over the years. He showed him an invitation addressed to Madeline inviting her to a reception in his honor at the Norwood Institute, an exclusive girls' school, in February 1893, which confirmed Madeline's contention that he in-cluded her in events he attended. He had Breckinridge tell again about the meeting at Wesleyan and his purported advice to Madeline to marry Rhodes because they'd had illicit relations. "What advice would you give a young man under the same circumstances?" asked Wilson. "I believe that the girl who had had improper sexual relations—and they have been made public—is ruined for the balance of her life; a young man under similar circumstances, who is young and unmarried, is injured, but he may recover," Breckinridge said.

Wilson asked him about the carriage ride and if Madeline had en-couraged him to make advances. "There was something internal that prompted me to put my arms around her. I could not have said that she encouraged me, but I would have been surprised if she had objected," he said. Breckinridge said that when Madeline talked of wanting to be an author, she mentioned the novelist George Eliot, who was known for her scandalous relationship with a married man, "as an example of all she would like to be."

"Up to that time you were a married man; a man who had unbounded advantages in life," said Wilson, the statement hanging in the air, half question. "There wasn't a man in America who had less excuse for it than I had under the domestic blessings with which I was surrounded," ad-mitted Breckinridge. He also confessed that he had "immoral relations" with other women during his marriage and had been to Sarah Guess's assignation house before going there with Madeline. Wilson asked him what such conduct on the part of a married man meant. "The act happened in the circumstances I have narrated, and the punishment I have received for it is the punishment I shall have to submit to," he said. "There is but one possible thing which I do not deserve for my punishment and which I did most positively refuse to accept, and that was to marry the woman with whom I had that transaction."

Wilson came back to Breckinridge's insistence that he hadn't seduced Madeline and asked him what he considered seduction. "I mean to say that I did not seduce her by any protestations of love or reward; that she did not come to me as a maiden or a virgin; that I did not seduce her in the physical sense," he answered.

Most observers thought Breckinridge had held his own with Wilson, whom some thought uncharacteristically flaccid in his questioning. The *Courier-Journal* believed that Wilson had embarrassed himself with his presumption that "the same standard of morality should be demanded of men as of women." Breckinridge, many deemed, had the bearing of a man who finally had made a clean breast of things. After the court adjourned, Breckinridge told his friends he hadn't covered up anything and "feared nothing from anything the prosecution could produce."

It turned out that he did have two things to fear. Wilson hinted at one as the day drew to a close, when he asked Breckinridge if he had a sister in Lexington named Louise or if he knew a woman in Washington named Louise Lowell. Breckinridge looked puzzled and not at all pleased. The other was on display in his answers to Wilson's subtle, leading questions. Breckinridge was relying on the legalistic definition of "seduction" to argue that he didn't seduce Madeline in the sense of a man promising a virgin that he would marry her if they had sex. But what if the idea of "seduction" was changing? What if a man of power and privilege who had sex with a younger, subordinate woman—especially one who was in financial or emotional distress—was now seen as predatory? Then, it seems, Breckinridge might find that it was he, not Madeline Pollard, who was ruined.

•

Jennie called on Madeline at the House of Mercy on Sunday, April 1, with the excuse of bringing her the *New York Herald*, which had some sketches of the trial she wanted Madeline to see. The day before, she had taken a boat trip down the Potomac with her friend Max Ihmsen, the Washington correspondent for the *Herald*, to visit Mount Vernon. Jennie was leveraging her friendship with Ihmsen to try to make inroads for the defense with the press. Through Ihmsen, she got Stoll introduced to several reporters and thought he had "won them over to Col. B's side," as she told her mother.

Stoll apparently was leaking details of the defense to Ihmsen to bolster Breckinridge's case in an increasingly skeptical press. On March 24, Ihmsen reported that the defense would provide evidence pertaining to "Miss Pollard's character." They would show that "while she was engaged to marry Mr. Rossell she was holding improper relations with Mr. Rhodes in return for her board and education" and that she was the resident of "a disreputable house for a time" before she went to college. On March 26, Ihmsen reported on the comments of a prominent "long time friend of Col. Breckinridge," who excused his behavior by saying that the congressman was a kind of Dr. Jekyll and Mr. Hyde who "can't help it [because] God gave him the nature. He struggled to control the evil side of it, and he couldn't."

Jennie also apparently encouraged Ihmsen to arrange a photo shoot for Madeline at the city's most fashionable portrait studio, most likely as an excuse to pump her for information, because on Wednesday, March 28, the *Herald* paid for a sitting for Madeline at the Charles Bell studio. Two days later, Ihmsen wrote a favorable story about Breckinridge's testimony regarding his visit to Wesleyan and what Ihmsen dismissed as "a silly adventure with a schoolgirl in a closed carriage" that was accompanied by a photo of the adult Madeline captioned to look as if it were taken when she was at Wesleyan.

After Jennie finished pumping Madeline for information about upcoming witnesses, she headed for Breckinridge's house near Dupont Circle, the need for expediency now trumping the need for secrecy. As she was leaving, Louise Wing Breckinridge stopped her, took her hand, and introduced herself. "I have been so anxious to know you, Miss Parker, and to tell you how thoroughly we appreciate what you have done for us all," she said. "You are helping to vindicate a good man." Jennie then met Nisba, who said she was equally grateful for her work on behalf of her father. It had been a brutal few weeks for Nisba and her stepmother. Anonymous letters arrived dripping with vitriol. "Oh, you pitiful cur—scoundrel & coward. Talk about Kentucky honor? Go kill yourself," read one scribbled on *New York World* letter-head.

Despite everything that had been reported, and the obvious way Breckinridge had deceived his family, they remained stubbornly loyal to him. A friend of Louise's shot down rumors that she intended to seek a divorce, saying that she remained "full of devotion" to her husband. So, too, did Nisba. According to a family friend, both Nisba's and Desha's "faith in their father was firm and unshaken," which was "a great com-fort to him" and allowed him to "bear up under his woes."

Still, with Louise largely confined to the house by her illness, it must have been painful for Nisba to be out and about doing the family's mar-keting, trying to avoid headlines about the man the press now deridingly referred to as "Papa Breckinridge." Everyone in Washington was talking about the trial; it had become absolutely unavoidable: "It is the talk of all the saloons and hotels. It is the ever renewed theme in the capitol lobbies, smoking rooms and committee rooms and, more than all else, it is the toothsome [morsel] of good society," reported the *Kentucky Leader*. Madeline Pollard had made what had been formerly unmention-able in polite society into the very thing that no one could stop talking about.

•

An air of expectation hung in the courtroom Tuesday morning. Wilson's questions at the close of the cross-examination Monday hinted that he had a surprise in store. Breckinridge had been combative and cocksure all day, until late in the afternoon, right after he finished asserting that all his assignations with Pollard in 1884 and 1885 were spontaneous, arising from accidental meetings, and insisting vehemently that he had no communications whatsoever with her in 1886. It was then that Wil-son asked him if he had ever taken a letter addressed to "My Dear Sister Louise" to a certain Capitol Hill typist named Louise Lowell. "In that letter did you not say that you were looking forward to the time when you would get home, and that you were anticipating with pleasure the meeting of this correspondent?" asked Wilson. And didn't you, he continued, comment on the disparity in your ages and warn the correspondent not to leave any of your letters lying around? Breckinridge had replied testily that he had "not the faintest recollection of any such letter, and I don't care to discuss it." He said he couldn't recall anyone named Louise Lowell, although "several women or females have done typewriting for me in Washington."

Now, all eyes were on a petite woman with gray-streaked hair when she entered the courtroom and sat next to Madeline, who, along with her lawyers, was early, as usual. Breckinridge hurried in at the last minute, it being the habit of the defense team to straggle in like they were going to a particularly poorly reviewed play. At first he didn't notice the little woman in the green dress and brown hat next to Madeline. When he did, he started whispering urgently to Butterworth. More than one observer thought the normally stern-looking Wilson, with his beaked nose and steel-gray hair and goatee, had a decided twinkle in his eye. Butterworth immediately objected to the admission of any new evidence, arguing that the plaintiff's case was already closed. Wilson countered that he should be allowed to question the witness in light of new evidence. Bradley ruled that the witness could be questioned to provide secondary evidence as to the existence of a letter that the defense had denied under cross-examination.

Lowell took the stand. She was so tiny that she was almost obscured by the witness box. At first she sounded timid as she told how she came to Washington from Maine in 1881 to live with her brother and was eventually forced to find employment, but she gained confidence as she went along. She said she got a job as a typist on Capitol Hill in 1886, her first job "in a public place." Her desk was located in a hallway in the Capitol; she took freelance work from whoever cared to hire her. She said Congressman Breckinridge first brought her work in February 1886—a handwritten letter to be typewritten addressed to "My Dear Sister Louise." Wilson tried to question her as to the contents of the letter, but Bradley sustained Butterworth's objections. The jury, however, had already gotten the drift from Wilson's questions. Lowell said that after she had typed two or three such letters, Breckinridge brought her a packet of small white envelopes, slightly yellowed with age, to address. Wilson asked what she had written on those envelopes. "Miss Pollard, 56 North Upper Street, Lexington, Ky.," she replied, giving the address of Mrs. Ketchum's boardinghouse as a murmur swept through the courtroom.

Wilson asked how she could be sure of the address. Lowell said she had written it on the flyleaf of the notebook she used to keep track of her accounts because it was an unusual request and she felt certain that "sooner or later, I would hear more of Miss Pollard," as she indicated a little red notebook in her hand. She said she did work for Colonel Breckinridge frequently, typing more letters and addressing more envelopes, until she got a job in the Treasury Department in 1890.

On cross-examination, Breckinridge said he now remembered Lowell and admitted giving her considerable work over the years, because, he said, she was convenient. But he denied giving her any "Dear Louise" letters to type or envelopes to Pollard to address, although he said he might have written to her once about a civil service exam. After lunch, Madeline was recalled to the stand. She said she had corresponded regularly with Breckinridge when he was in Washington in 1885 and 1886 and that she had received typewritten letters from him addressing her as "My Dear Sister Louise," "My Dear Sweetheart," and, in one, "My Little Spitfire." Breckinridge took the stand again and denied writing any such letters or telling Madeline to mail them from a certain train in Lexington so that they would reach the city in the morning and be delivered to his office at the Capitol instead of his home.

His protestations seemed to no avail in the face of the quiet certitude of the "little Yankee woman." It was, many thought, one of the most devastating days of the trial for Breckinridge. Lowell had flatly contradicted the key assertion of his testimony: that his relationship with Pollard was unplanned and unsought; not, as Pollard asserted, and the letters seemed to prove, an illicit but serious love affair that he ardently pursued. Lowell seemed an unimpeachable witness. She didn't know Madeline and she said she didn't even know how her lawyers found her. Savvy court watchers suspected that she was sniffed out by Wilson, who had a reputation as "a detective lawyer who goes deep into his cases and pulls out evidence of the most startling character." Now, said the *Enquirer*, "Everyone is conscious of the fact that an immense amount of mendacity has been brought into the case and no one seems to accuse the plaintiff of it."

The following morning, Wilson sprang another trap on Breckinridge. He asked him if he had ever used expressions of love and affection with Madeline. Breckinridge said he had used "expressions that a man would use toward a woman for whose condition he felt partly responsible." Wilson asked if he had ever done anything to give her the idea that he loved her. "Well," Breckinridge said, "I took her in my arms and kissed her and did those things which naturally resulted from our relationship." So, pressed Wilson, "Your expressions of affection and your relations were those of lust, then." Now trapped into either admitting he loved Madeline or merely used a girl thirty years his junior to sate his desires, Breckinridge admitted that they often met for reasons other than physical intercourse and that she was "a young woman of colloquial talents, sprightly and interesting."

Wilson read long passages of Julia Blackburn's testimony, daring Breckinridge to call her a liar. He denied telling Blackburn he would marry Madeline after sufficient time had elapsed from his wife's death or asking her to put Madeline under her protection. Wilson asked if that meant Blackburn's statements were untrue. "I was always leaving Mrs. Blackburn under the impression that I intended to marry the plaintiff," Breckinridge admitted, saying he was "honestly endeavoring to carry out" the pretend engagement. "You were honestly deceiving her, then?" asked Wilson. And so it went, with the silver tongue becoming more and more tarnished as Breckinridge twisted himself into ever-tighter rhetorical contortions. When asked about his promise to Major Moore that he would marry Madeline on May 31, he answered: "I did not promise to marry her—it was not a promise. I was in a frame of mind that was excited and I said 'yes, I'll marry you at the end of the month,' and I went right on talking."

Thursday morning opened to one of the smallest crowds since the trial started, with some no doubt put off by Judge Bradley's scorching rebuke of the spectators at the close of Wednesday's session, likening them to buzzards sitting on a fence waiting for a horse to die. Butterworth recalled Madeline to the stand and asked her about the baby she said was born in 1888. Madeline said the baby was born at noon on February 3 and two hours later the "old colored midwife named Aunt Mary" took him to the Protestant foundling asylum. She said she pinned a slip of paper to the baby with the name "Dietz Carlyle" on it because she was reading Thomas Carlyle and one of his heroes was named Dietz. Butterworth then called Susan Leidy, the matron of the Washington City Orphan Asylum, to the stand. She said the records showed that a colored woman had brought a newborn baby boy to the asylum on February 3, 1888, but that it had the name Dietz Downing pinned to it. She said the baby died on April 18. Shelby asked if any other child born in February died that month. "They die so fast and so rapidly that I cannot keep track of them," she answered flatly.

After a local health inspector testified that Dr. Parsons hadn't recorded any births in February 1888, which would be expected with an illicit pregnancy, the defense rested. The afternoon brought a devastating succession of rebuttal witnesses for Madeline. Dr. William Cowan, the superintendent of the Western Pennsylvania Hospital, who identified himself as Madeline's first cousin, said that Madeline had lived with his family near Pittsburgh continuously from just after her father's death in 1876 until the summer of 1880, which disproved Mollie Shindlebower's assertion that Madeline had been living a fast life in Bridgeport in 1877. Another cousin, Charles Sawyer, testified that he had lived with Madeline's aunt Keene from 1880 until 1883 and during all that time Madeline was away from home overnight only once, when she visited her uncle in Graefenburg for ten days over Christmas in 1882. Her cousin George Keene testified that Madeline went into Lexington only with other family members in a carriage, which meant she couldn't have frequented assignation houses, as testified to by Brand, before she left for school.

Then Martha McClellan Brown, the former vice president of Wesleyan College and a well-known suffrage and temperance leader, came to the stand escorted by Sarah La Fetra, the head of the local Woman's Christian Temperance Union. Taking the stand "as coolly as if about to deliver a temperance address," she removed her veil, handed it to La Fetra, and proceeded to demolish Rossell's testimony about kissing Madeline in the parlor. She said young women at the college were only allowed to receive visitors on Friday evenings and that they were never left alone with young men in the parlor, which often had up to twenty guests, so it would have been impossible for Rossell to visit several times a week and for Madeline to sit on his lap and let him kiss her as he claimed.

Louise Lowell was recalled as a rebuttal witness so she could be asked about the contents of the letters she typed. "The writer spoke of the great love between the two and the disparity in their ages; that no two persons in the same family with so great a difference in their ages could love each other so dearly," she said. Breckinridge also frequently wrote "in very glowing words" of "his pleasure in meeting with the person addressed" and his impatience with his duties that kept him away.

The last witness was Mary Yancey, a heavyset black woman who identified herself as the cook at Mrs. Thomas's house, where Madeline had lived in the winter of 1893 to 1894. Breckinridge had denied Pollard's claim that he was so pleased with a lunch that Yancey made for them that he asked her to be their cook when they got married. Yancey said the day after the luncheon, Colonel Breckinridge told her it was "one of the nicest lunches" he ever had and asked her to "come and cook for us when we go to housekeeping next fall." She said the colonel came frequently to visit Madeline, sometimes twice a day, often brought flowers or sent telegrams, and that he was very affectionate toward her. She said she had seen them sitting together in the parlor while Madeline had the willow sewing basket with the blue ribbon trim that Breckinridge had denied giving her on her lap.

The courtroom had a languid air on Friday morning, April 6, for what was expected to be the last day of testimony. Dr. Parsons identified the slip of paper found pinned to the infant with the name Dietz Downing on it as written in her handwriting. Mary McKenzie, the midwife known as "Aunt Mary," testified that Madeline was the "Mrs. Hall" who delivered a baby at her house in February 1888 and that she brought it to the foundling asylum. Madeline came back on the stand and denied knowing Mollie Shindlebower or Lena Singleton or John Brand or Hiram Kaufman. She emphatically denied having sexual intercourse with old Rhodes or telling Breckinridge about it, or accepting money from Breckinridge the night of their fateful carriage ride. She said that when Breckinridge stayed at Mrs. Ketchum's house, she crept into his room every night by a prearranged signal—he slammed the front door when he got in. She denied telling him she had miscarried her first two pregnancies. And she denied ever threatening to shoot him or agreeing to a sham engagement to fool Mrs. Blackburn.

Breckinridge, for his part, denied giving Madeline his wife's sewing basket or the ribbon to trim it, giving Louise Lowell any love letters to type, and Madeline being in his room at Mrs. Ketchum's. Just before three o'clock he stepped down from the stand, concluding the testimony in what was now being widely referred to as the celebrated case of *Pollard v. Breckinridge*. The trial had been going on for a solid twenty-one days; winter had turned to spring. The jury, and by extension the public at large, had heard accusations of abortion, and about lying-in homes and infant asylums and assignation houses, and steamy late-night rides through foothills in closed carriages with esteemed men—things that heretofore didn't make it into polite conversation or the newspapers. Maybe some wished they still hadn't. But it appeared that a page had been turned, and all anyone could do now was see where it would lead.

16

The Front Parlor and the Back Gate

To Willie Breckinridge, it must have seemed that the world had turned upside down. He found the women he had long taken for granted—the cook, the nameless typist in the hallway, the former slave who ran the assignation house where he had his trysts—not only aligned against him but also being taken seriously over his own word. To friends, he claimed that it was a pile of "perjured testimony . . . both black and white" manufactured to destroy him. He railed against "women doctors who are abortionists, women type-writers who are treacherous," the "fat conscienceless cook," and Martha McClellan Brown, one of those "ladies who attend conventions, deliver speeches and shriek for all sort of things which they call reform." How dare she swear to "what she knows is untrue, and in favor of a prostitute and against a man who is honest and clean."

This, for Breckinridge, was the crux. He thought that as a woman, Madeline should be defined and disgraced by her sins, but as a man, he should have his sins excused as just a blip in an otherwise blameless life. After all, he told a friend, he had atoned for his "secret sins" by "doing labors which knew no cessation" and by making the "lives of those who loved me as happy as I could." In his mind, he had suffered for his sins, had been crucified, and had died a kind of death; people would surely see, he thought, "my weakness, my sin, my punishment and my deliverance."

And now, as the lawyers prepared to make their case for the charges to the jury, his fate was in the hands of a man he believed to be against him. Indeed, people couldn't help noticing how Judge Bradley turned away whenever Breckinridge testified, like he had caught a whiff of something foul. But Bradley had made rulings that favored both sides; he had allowed most of Breckinridge's depositions to be admitted, as well as the disputed letter that Madeline claimed was a forgery. It seems that what the defense considered partiality was the fact that Madeline was being given a hearing at all. Butterworth told reporters the weekend after the testimony concluded that the judge should never have let such a case come to trial, saying that Madeline had "impregnated the homes of the land . . . where we have our pure wives and mothers and sisters" with "a foul, pestilence-breeding contagion."

At the hearing on Saturday about the charges for the jury, Carlisle argued that the burden of proof was on Breckinridge to show that Madeline was in on what he said was a pretend engagement, while Shelby argued that it was the plaintiff's responsibility to prove that the two parties had entered into a valid marriage contract. Beyond these dry legal questions, however, most of what the men on the jury were asked to examine poked deep into the intimate details of Madeline's life. Carlisle argued that it made no difference if Madeline had carnal knowledge of Breckinridge or any other man before she met him if he knew it when the marriage contract was made. Shelby asserted that if Pollard was guilty of "lewd and lascivious conduct" with other men, it would release Breckinridge from a contract to marry. Bradley asked exactly what he meant by "lewd and lascivious." Shelby said no man could be expected to marry a woman who wasn't chaste. "Suppose he knew of such conduct with five parties, and knowledge of it with a sixth afterward came to him?" asked Bradley, questioning whether that would change the legal aspect of the case, as Shelby fumbled to explain the exact mathematical calculation of a woman's chastity.

On Monday, Bradley ruled that while the burden of proof was on the plaintiff to show that a contract of marriage existed, the burden was on the defense to show that both parties were in on what Breckinridge said was an engagement ruse. Bradley also said that the only way Madeline's sexual conduct could be used as a defense was if Breckinridge found out after the marriage contract was made that she'd had illicit relations with men other than Rhodes.

For the rest of the day and into the next morning, Carlisle summarized the case. Standing before the jury in his white linen suit, a gold tiepin placed just so, he asked why, with all the knowledge Breckinridge had gained from being intimate with Madeline for nine years, the only depositions he could produce questioning her character were from disreputable people. He showed the jury the tintype of Madeline in her schoolgirl dress and asked if she appeared to be "the woman of experience on whom this defendant wishes to place more than half the burden of their intimacy."

Phil Thompson, portly and ruddy-faced, summarized for the defense in "florid Kentucky oratory," taking the tack that the "members of the jury would probably have done about what Mr. Breckinridge had done under the same circumstances." He called Madeline a "self-admitted wanton looking for revenge" and said that finding for her would "encourage every strumpet to push her little mass of filth into court." He appealed to deep-seated sentiments about women and purity, telling the jury that "every decent man knows the defendant was right in refusing to put [Madeline] at the head of the table with his daughters." He compared her to a dog in heat in a story an "old darky" used to tell. Even then, there was an audible gasp when Thompson, while discussing Dr. Belle Buchanan's testimony, said he didn't "take much stock in female physicians" because he "always noticed that whenever there is an abortion case, a secret birth or any case that a reputable and respectable physician will not touch, you will usually find the hand of a female physician in it somewhere."

Ben Butterworth's closing argument was tamer in rhetoric and better in oratory, with his sonorous voice that seemed to rattle the courtroom windows. He practically brought the spectators to their feet with his stirring testament to the manly bonds of friendship between himself and Breckinridge. He said that Madeline was no innocent country girl like those he had known back in the Miami Hills, "honest and virtuous" girls who went to spelling bees and log rollings. He said that if Madeline had been "high-minded," she would have repelled Breckinridge's advances and insisted that he drive her home. "And I say to you," he boomed, turning toward Breckinridge, "that you would not have taken her twenty feet further; I care not what they say of your blandishments, your silver tongue, your destructive eloquence and all that!"

He called Madeline an "unnatural" woman for abandoning the babies she claimed were "born along the way, and buried in unknown or forgotten places." He urged the jury to forgive Breckinridge for what many a great man had done, but to repudiate a woman who corrupted public morals when she "deliberately turned from everything that man or woman could desire, and proclaimed her shame." It was so late in the afternoon when Butterworth finished—with his words still reverberating through the old courtroom from what the *Enquirer* called "a superb effort," the kind of hair-tingling oratory that held people spellbound in the nineteenth century—that Wilson wisely asked the judge if he could begin his closing argument in the morning.

So it was on the morning of Friday, April 13, that Jere Wilson began the last address of the trial. It could, most agreed, hardly be called a speech like Butterworth's. There were no flights of oratory, "few pyrotechnic displays." Just scathing sarcasm and a dispassionate, point-by-point dismantling of the defense. Wilson stood close to the witness box; at first, his voice was low, as if forcing everyone to lean near, but it grew louder as he went on. He asked why, if Madeline was good enough to be Breckinridge's companion for nearly ten years, she wasn't good enough to be his wife. He told the jury to ignore the "clamor and howling" of the defense and focus on the facts: Madeline had proved that a contract of marriage existed. "Her word in this case is as good as his," Wilson said, noting that it was Breckinridge who had "lived a lie" and a "life of hypocrisy" by pretending to be a faithful husband to Issa and lying about his marriage to Louise. "How can you trust him?" Wilson asked, asserting that if anyone was to take the lion's share of the blame, it was Breckinridge, who was older, more experienced, and married.

Wilson said it was ridiculous to suggest that the case should have been suppressed to protect the community; only in "sunlight" could wrongs be redressed, especially the wrong of banishing a woman for immorality while sending "the man to Congress." Eyeing the jury, he declared, "I stand here for womanhood. This defendant proclaimed from the stand that while affairs of this kind only injured a man, they destroyed a woman. I am here to insist that social law should be equally distributed; I stand here to protest against allowing this man to enter my parlor and your parlor, while the basement door and the gate in the back alley are bolted against the woman."

He called Phil Thompson out for suggesting that women doctors were unsavory. "There was a time when women were drudges and the mere playthings for men. But women are pushing to the front in every walk of life, and the faster they come, the better for the land," he said, by now so hoarse he had to ask Bradley to adjourn until tomorrow.

By Saturday, spring had come to Washington; the courtroom windows were wide open as Wilson concluded his argument. He dismissed the defense's witnesses and their allegations about Madeline's character as disproven by their own more credible witnesses, and Breckinridge's assertion that he and Madeline had conspired to deceive Blackburn as a "clean-shaven, bald-headed, obese falsehood, manufactured to fit the exigencies of the case."

By lunchtime tempers were wearing thin. After Wilson insinuated that Stoll might have had a hand in the letter inviting Breckinridge to Wesleyan that Madeline claimed was a forgery, Desha tried to goad Stoll into challenging him to a duel, until Butterworth intervened and got Wilson to apologize. Just as that settled down, a delivery boy arrived with a towering basket of long-stemmed roses for Wilson. The attached note said they were in appreciation for the stand he took for "one code of morals for men and women, and also for the advancement of women in an active part in the world's affairs," particularly his support of women physicians. It was signed, rather mysteriously, "twenty-eight women," but among those who attached their cards to the basket were Mrs. Dan Waugh and Mrs. Nelson Trusler, both the wives of Indiana politicians; the pioneering stenographer Nettie White; Louise Lowell, who had typed Breckinridge's love letters; and, in a rebuff that was unmistakable, Mollie Desha, Breckinridge's sister-in-law.

After lunch Bradley reviewed the instructions to the jury and said that despite claims to the contrary, the only question they should concern themselves with was whether a contract to marry had been made, and if it had been broken, was there an excuse to do so. He said abstract principles shouldn't be vindicated, "nor the country girl, the home and the family."

The jury filed into the jury room a little after three o'clock and everyone dispersed, the feeling being that the verdict might take some time. Breckinridge's backers were predicting a hung jury; many of Madeline's thought they would find for her but award only a token sum. Breckinridge ambled down the courtroom steps just as Nisba and Louise, hoping for some news, drove up in an open barouche. Perhaps it was symbolic, a repudiation of the infamous closed carriage, perhaps their visibility was intended as a show of optimism, or perhaps they just wanted to enjoy the April sun after a long, dismal winter in which they had been stuck at home. Breckinridge chatted with them until they drove off, then stood in the courthouse portico and joked with the newsboys about bringing him the early editions.

Less than ninety minutes later, the jury gave word they had reached a verdict. They already had their hats in hand when Breckinridge, Desha, Thompson, and Butterworth spilled back into the courtroom; it was another ten minutes before Carlisle rushed in, red-faced and breathless. The clerk asked the jury if they had reached a verdict. "If it please the court," said the foreman, a piece of blue paper quivering in his right hand, "we find for the plaintiff." "For how much?" asked Bradley. "Fifteen thousand," he answered.

There was dead silence for a moment, then a shout echoed down the corridor like a shot: "Fifteen thousand for the plaintiff," setting off a roar from the crowd outside that sounded like breakers on rocks and a scrum among reporters rushing to file their stories. Breckinridge, who had been stretching and twisting an elastic band between his fingers like it was a little ribbon of time that could be made and unmade, turned to Thompson and asked, "How much?" Then he stood up slowly, his face nearly as white as his beard, and gave notice that he intended to file for a new trial before thumping back down and giving Desha a wan smile.

Wilson reached the courtroom just as Carlisle was leaving; they hurried out trailing a wake of reporters. When they got to the portico, Carlisle pulled out a handkerchief and waved it in the air. The reporters looked up and saw Madeline standing in the fourth-floor window of his office across the street. When she saw the signal, she threw her hands up. "Oh, isn't it good. Isn't it good," she said as she collapsed into a chair. Madeline refused all requests for interviews; she had already packed her trunk and taken leave of the House of Mercy. By the next morning, she was sequestered away in Providence Hospital, reportedly suffering from nervous exhaustion, although she had told Jennie a week ago that she had reserved a room there, where, for ten dollars a week, she could have "room, board, medical attendance, nursing and massage."

After the crowds had cleared, Breckinridge and Desha stood alone in front of the courthouse. The barouche pulled up, and Breckinridge clambered in beside Louise. They stopped at a grocer's and placed an order, then turned onto Pennsylvania Avenue and became caught in the late-afternoon swarm of theatergoers and shoppers and newsboys crying their "Extra!" editions. "Miss Pollard Wins!" proclaimed the *World*. The driver kept the team close to the sidewalk; pedestrians gaped at the famous silver-haired antagonist. Louise looked straight ahead, seeming to shrink in her seat. Breckinridge met their stares, smiling defiantly, now, said the *New York Sun*, the "observed of all the observers throughout the ride."

●

After nearly six long weeks, front-page coverage from coast to coast, and endless debates about whether Madeline Pollard was right or wrong to air her downfall for the world to see, the verdict was met with widespread approval. The conclusion of the trial "was to the satisfaction of the community generally," reported the *Evening Star*. Even in Kentucky, where news of the verdict swept Louisville just minutes after it hit the telegraph office, "not one person in the whole town has been heard to say that the plaintiff should not have recovered anything."

Feminist reformers hoped the verdict heralded an end to the double standard that had crippled so many women's lives, as well as a new day for women's rights. "All the efforts made by reformers and philanthropists to establish the same standard of morals for both sexes have been crystallized and expressed itself in the verdict of the jury in the Breckinridge case," wrote the suffragist Clara Colby in the *Woman's Tribune*. The suffragist Alice Stone Blackwell said in the *Women's Journal*, the official organ of the suffragist movement, that the trial showed not only the "perniciousness of the unequal standard of morality for men and women," but the need for women's suffrage because women "will not vote for candidates of notoriously bad moral character." She said she wondered how long Breckinridge would have lasted in office if "the mothers, wives and sisters of Kentucky had a vote."

Aaron Powell, the editor of the *Philanthropist*, the leading journal of purity reformers, marveled at the wholesale change in attitude regarding a "public man [who] hold[s] immoral relations with a young girl" and the fact that the "strategically indecent" addresses of Breckinridge's congressional friends Thompson and Butterworth had failed to sway the jury. "A decade or two ago such addresses by two well-known ex-members of Congress, in behalf of an eloquent, and hitherto an honored member of the present House of Representatives, would doubtless have sufficed to turn the scale in favor of the man and against the woman," he said.

But it wasn't just social reformers who hailed the victory. Kate Field, who had a broad audience for her *Kate Field's Washington* column, said the trial raised important questions about the "conventional morality" regarding sexually disgraced women and marriage. "Why should society discriminate between a man who has sinned and a woman who has sinned with him? If it is possible for a good woman to marry a man who is not good, why is it impossible for a woman who is not good to marry a man who is at least as culpable morally as herself?" she asked.

Most importantly, Edward Bok, the editor of the *Ladies' Home Journal*, which was the most popular magazine in the country and an influential arbiter of middle-class standards, hailed the verdict in the magazine. Saying that "the women of the world are suffering to-day from a code of morality which imposes on them all the responsibility for purity and all the penalty for wrong-doing," he called for a "different moral code among ourselves . . . a code which will hold a man as strictly accountable for the highest observance of moral principles as it does a woman." He said, "That which is wrong in a woman should be equally wrong in a man," and that what "is black for a woman should not be shaded into gray for a man."

•

For Breckinridge, the verdict wasn't the result of his slipshod defense, but of this "supposed popular sentiment," which he claimed had been inflamed by "the ceaseless clamor and lies and distorted reports of the daily papers." And he was right. A moral tide had turned, and he had been left stranded on the beach, fuming about "wantons." But his defense was poorly prepared and was obviously back-fashioned around Madeline's testimony. One of the jurors said the biggest strike against Breckinridge was his own testimony and his implausible excuse for lying to Blackburn. And there were a number of inconsistences in Madeline's story that the defense failed to exploit. Dr. Belle Buchanan testified in her deposition that Madeline first came to her in February 1885, months before Madeline said her first child was born, although she said she was unsure of the dates. But when she testified during the trial, she was quite sure Madeline came during "strawberry season," which was precisely ten weeks after she said she had given birth at the Norwood Asylum. What really happened that summer of 1884? Was Madeline just an innocent young girl when they met? Did Breckinridge actually promise to marry her?

Madeline was by all accounts a young, inexperienced woman when she met Breckinridge—the tintypes and the recollections of Wessie Brown Robertson and Sarah Guess all paint the same picture. And it's easy to see how she would have been swept away by meeting a larger-than-life figure like Breckinridge. And it's likely that he did approach her on the train. Two "reputable society women" in Lexington confirmed that "making mashes on the railroad train was one of his great grandstand plays," and, after the trial was over, a local professor who was sitting in front of Madeline on the train came forward and confirmed her version of the story, saying that "Breckinridge introduced himself to Miss Pollard."

But it's also likely that Breckinridge was telling the truth when he said he thought that she was a mature young woman—somewhere around twenty-one, not seventeen as she asserted. While Madeline still dressed like a young woman on the cusp of adulthood, the evidence suggests that she was significantly older. As Madeline testified, when her father died in June 1876, she thought she was about twelve, which means she would have been born in 1864. But she said that later, her mother told her she was born on November 30, 1866, which is why she gave her age as sixteen in the fall of 1884. Breckinridge tried to find some record of Madeline in the U.S. census, but was unsuccessful. The 1870 census, however, shows the Pollard family living in Crab Orchard with five children: Edward, born in 1859, nine months after his parents' marriage; Mary, born in 1861; Mattie, born in 1863; Rosalie, born in 1866; and John, born in 1869.

Why would Madeline's mother tell her she was born in 1866? The key to the mystery of Madeline's age appears to be her older sister, Mary, who went by Mamie. Mamie was born when the family still lived in Frankfort, and Franklin County birth records confirm that she was born March 18, 1861 (Madeline wasn't captured in county birth records, likely because of disruptions in recordkeeping due to the Civil War). In the 1880 census, however, when Mamie was living in Bridgeport with her mother and her aunt Mary Stout, she gave her age as eighteen when she was in fact nineteen. Three years later, when she was twenty-two, she married the Reverend Felix Struve, a Methodist minister, who was twenty-one. Given that twenty-two was about the upper age of desirable marriageability for southern brides, the country was still in the midst of the post–Civil War marriage panic, and it was unusual for Victorian grooms to marry women older than them, it seems likely that Mamie, in collusion with her mother, was systematically shaving years off her age to preserve her marriageability, which was probably a common thing to do before birth certificates and driver's licenses. In fact, Madeline's mother, Nancy, who may have hoped to remarry, claimed in 1880 that she was thirty-five when she was forty-two.

The original record of Mamie and Felix's marriage was destroyed in the Cincinnati Courthouse riots of 1884, so it's not possible to know what age she gave when she married. But the next time Mamie shows up in census records, in the 1900 census (the 1890 census records were damaged in a fire and eventually destroyed), she gives her age as thirty-six, two years younger than her husband, which means she was claiming to have been born in 1864. (Her 1920 death certificate gives her birthday as March 18, 1863.) It's reasonable to assume that when Madeline showed up in Bridgeport in 1880, Mamie was already passing herself off as a couple of years younger than she was, so Madeline couldn't have been born the same year. Therefore, her mother told her she was born in

1866, which was the year of Rosalie's birth. Frail little Rosalie, who spent most of her life in an orphanage, probably didn't know the difference.

So Madeline, who thought she was about sixteen in 1880, was told she was fourteen, when in fact she was seventeen. No wonder she had so much interest from men and created so much tension during her brief stay in Bridgeport. She had the rapidly maturing body of a seventeen-year-old, yet was dressing and passing herself off as a fourteen-year-old. That means when she met Breckinridge on the train in 1884, she was about twenty or twenty-one, which doesn't excuse his predatory behavior—but does make him technically correct about his perception of her age.

Mamie also explains the rumors about Madeline's purported "fast" behavior in Bridgeport. Madeline wasn't in Bridgeport at the time Mollie Shindlebower claimed she was causing disruptions in the family with her loose morals. But Mamie was, and even Madeline said that all the boys liked her best. When Shindlebower contacted Breckinridge, she wrote that "Miss Pollard . . . received company at unusual hours and went buggy riding the same." But she also wrote "at that time then (Mamie) Pollard claimed to be 17 years of age." Shindlebower was talking about Mamie, a fact that the defense misrepresented and that Wilson correctly surmised in his closing argument. In fact, a woman who knew the Pollards wrote to Breckinridge that "Mary Pollard was considered fast & did not bear a good reputation," and said she had to kick her out of the choir because she was "unladylike & I considered her a designing and untruthful girl."

What about the supposedly forged letter and the question of whether Madeline invited Breckinridge to Wesleyan? It seems unlikely that the letter was a forgery. If it was, it would have been an extremely clever one, not only because Madeline's handwriting was copied well enough to fool an expert, but because it was written on black-bordered mourning paper, which Madeline would have been using because of Rosalie's recent death, a touch that Breckinridge's team would have been unlikely to replicate. In a September 1893 letter to his father, Desha confirmed that Worthington found a letter from Pollard in Breckinridge's files and sent it on to Washington. It seems that Madeline was surprised by the letter and denied it at first blush—then had to stick to her guns. Some reporters thought it was her biggest misstep. And, the signature of "Madeline B. Pollard" seems to confirm that she was using Breckinridge as her middle name even then.

Madeline had demonstrated a penchant for soliciting prominent men. When she lived in Lexington, she gained a bit of notoriety for approaching James Lane Allen, the well-known local novelist, on the street and asking for advice about becoming a writer. Of course, if a young man had done the same thing it wouldn't have attracted notice, but it was considered improper for a young lady to approach a man she didn't know in public. Nor was she shy about contacting other famous men. She told Jennie that she met Charles Dudley Warner after he called a short story she sent him "remarkable" and insisted on meeting her. But he told a reporter that he "first heard from her while visiting Washington," when Madeline "invited him to call at the Convent of the Holy Cross" and "asked for instruction about writing for the press."

Warner wasn't the only well-known writer Madeline solicited for advice. In 1890, Madeline wrote to John Hay, statesman, author, and confidant of Henry Adams, with a similar request. "I wonder how impertinent you would think me if I were to ask you to come to the Convent to see me on Friday or Saturday evening next week?" she wrote. She told him there were "some questions I wish to ask you, and would go to you but do not know when I might disturb you least" and averred that they were questions best not asked in writing "for some things must be talked as 'slanting grass and snowy daisies' must be seen."

Madeline reaching out to Breckinridge for advice wasn't an invitation for a sexual encounter, although Breckinridge, steeped in the ways of southern women's respectability, seemed to think it was. It also seems inconceivable that she would have told Breckinridge that she had engaged in sexual intercourse with Rhodes; a girl was only "ruined" to the extent that her sexual activity became public. It's likely that her unconventional arrangement with Rhodes, her admiration of the equally unconventional George Eliot, and the fact that she didn't have a father to watch over her led Breckinridge to conclude that she wasn't a virgin and was sexually available. As for the carriage ride, Breckinridge never substantially disputed Madeline's account of what happened, including the fact that his advances were uninvited. The evidence also largely squares with Madeline's account of what happened in the days that followed. While there's no proof one way or another regarding Madeline's claim about his attempted seduction of her at Rose's assignation house, there's little doubt that they went to Lexington together by prearrangement and that it was he who took her to Sarah Guess's house.

It's unlikely, however, that Breckinridge was the reason Madeline left Wesleyan and went to Sayre, as she asserted. By the time Breckinridge came to Wesleyan in early August 1884, she already knew that she would have to leave because Rhodes hadn't paid her tuition—which only reinforces what a vulnerable position she was in at the time. It's likely she talked Rhodes into sending her to school in Lexington, which was cheaper and where he could see her more often. The former Wesleyan president William Brown told the *Courier-Journal* that Rhodes said the school was "too expensive for him" and "believed he would get his ward educated at Sayre Institute."

What about the other central claim of Madeline's story, that she gave birth to the two children that Breckinridge tried so hard to deny? There's little doubt given the testimony of Dr. Belle Buchanan and the other doctors that Madeline gave birth in the spring of 1885. The inconsistencies with their recollections appear to have had more to do with the various subterfuges she employed to hide the illegitimate pregnancy than whether it occurred. There was no reason for her to lie about going to the Norwood Foundling Asylum, because the records could be checked. She could have just as easily said she had the baby at one of the private lying-in homes that could be found in any city and were impossible to trace. And it does appear that she left the Washington Irving volumes there. In addition, both the principal of Sayre and Mrs. Ketchum testified that she was absent from Lexington from January 1885 until the following fall.

It's also possible that the nuns at Norwood went out of their way to not recognize her. Breckinridge had pulled some strings to get an introduction to Sister Mary Sebastian, the nun who was in charge, from the local archbishop. She told Breckinridge she would be "glad to do anything in her power that [he] may suggest" to help him. That the nuns would be eager to maintain conventional standards of sexual morality comes as no surprise. But there also appears to have been some animosity between Pollard and the sisters. One of Breckinridge's associates who was acting as a go-between told him that the "nuns are very careful what they write, but they cordially dislike Miss Pollard," and advised him to destroy the enclosed letter from Sister Sebastian. What was in that letter and why did the nuns so dislike Pollard if, as they claimed, they didn't know her? It seems likely that Pollard was there, but as was her wont, and much like she had at the House of Mercy, she had acted in such an imperious manner that she had made an enemy of the sisters.

If so, it was a trait she shared, and perhaps learned, from her female relatives. The same woman who wrote to Breckinridge with the intelligence that Mamie Pollard had been a fast girl also recounted that Madeline's mother had "tried hard" to get into the Louisville Masonic Widows and Orphans Home that took in the three youngest Pollard children. However, she "could not, as she was not liked by the Board of Directors, she being 'highly strung' and over-bearing." The woman also recalled Madeline's Pittsburgh aunt Mrs. Cowen visiting the home to see a grown daughter who presumably worked there and found her "very high toned . . . calling for delicacies & demanding as much attention as tho she was at a first class hotel," which echoed Sister Dorothea's description of Madeline's behavior at the House of Mercy. She concluded that the Pollard women were "designing" and "hot-blooded." Perhaps it was an inborn personality trait, but perhaps also the result of thwarted pride in situations where they were forced to rely on charity.

Nevertheless, it seems unlikely that Madeline would have been able to arrange for and finance her confinement, as well as dupe her mother and Rhodes about her real location, without Breckinridge's assistance when she was pregnant in 1884–85. And the timing of the birth in late May 1885 tracks exactly with the second of what she said were two sexual encounters with Breckinridge in August 1884. Indeed, Breckinridge's own investigation confirmed what he denied in court: that he had gone back to Cincinnati a second time that month, staying at the Burnet House on Saturday, August 23.

The apex of their relationship seems to date from the birth of this first child in 1885 through the spring of 1887. It's during this period that Breckinridge was writing Madeline impassioned love letters. It was the perfect relationship for him. He was busy in Washington, and Madeline was conveniently tucked away in Lexington, where Sarah Guess provided a secure, private place for their assignations. It's easy to imagine him, in the throes of infatuation, promising Madeline that he would marry her if he ever could. And it's just as easy to imagine her, as many women had before and after, believing that he meant it.

In early summer 1887, right after Breckinridge stayed in the same boardinghouse as Madeline, their relationship seems to have soured. That summer, Madeline worked for the *Lexington Gazette* and began a relationship with publisher Howard Gratz that culminated in an engagement to marry. It would have been the answer to all her problems. She would have been the wife of a man from a prominent Lexington family and could have dabbled in writing without being dependent on it for her livelihood. And, it would have legitimized the child that she was already carrying, which, if born in early February 1888, was conceived in early May 1887. But Breckinridge, who was at the time writing love letters to his "Little Spitfire," likely felt betrayed. When the engagement fell through after Gratz's daughter found out about Madeline's past—including, according to Breckinridge, a warning from the family's African American cook that Madeline "ain't a good woman" because she "goes to Sara Gess' [sic] house"—she was stranded. It was then that she took herself to Washington—not likely at Breckinridge's invitation, as she claimed—but because she needed to get away from Lexington and had nowhere else to turn. Breckinridge begrudgingly took responsibility for the pregnancy, paying Dr. Parsons's bill, but suspected that he wasn't the father, as he told Gratz in a letter he wrote just after the trial in which he acknowledged, despite his claims to the contrary, the birth of a "living child" in 1888. And his own investigation confirmed that Madeline did indeed enter St. Ann's Infant Asylum on November 10, 1887, but left on Christmas Eve because "she would not obey the rules."

The relationship didn't resume on a regular basis until sometime after Madeline moved to the Academy of the Holy Cross in March 1888. For a time, things were apparently good between them. Madeline was again sequestered away, and they saw each other three or four times a week, going to assignation houses on Indiana Avenue and H Street. Then something happened that not only altered the dynamic of their relationship but is essential to understanding how Madeline was eventually able to go toe-to-toe with Breckinridge. When Madeline first came to Washington in 1887, she was still "countrified," according to the *Leader*. Somewhere along the line, the country mouse turned into a social butterfly. It's Breckinridge who provides the key to understanding Madeline's unlikely rise through Washington society. While everyone was busy castigating him for introducing Madeline into society via Blackburn, he protested, to no avail, that Madeline "was not introduced into society by Mrs. Blackburn . . . but by Mrs. Admiral Dahlgren." Madeline herself said in her autobiography that Blackburn never introduced her "into other homes" until after Breckinridge asked for her chaperonage. Indeed, the rumor circulating about Madeline's multiple sets of visiting cards was that she "had become acquainted with Mrs. Admiral Dahlgren and ascertained that some of her ancestors were Vintons."

Mrs. Admiral Dahlgren was Madeleine Vinton Dahlgren, the author of *Etiquette of Social Life in Washington* and the most socially powerful woman in the city, a woman of substantial, seemingly contradictory accomplishments. The daughter of a congressman, she was the doyenne of society's labyrinthine rules of etiquette, but was nonetheless fiercely critical of high society, especially the "senseless waste of time involved in the tread-mill routine of social visits" expected of women— the almost daily round of perfunctory social calls that women made on one another, usually between two and five in the afternoon, unless a woman announced in the society column that she would receive on a particular day or at a particular time.

Dahlgren supported her children after her first husband died by writing and translating dense tomes on religion and civil society from French and Spanish, but was an outspoken opponent of suffrage. Her second marriage to Admiral John Dahlgren, the inventor of the famous Dahlgren gun that revolutionized naval ordnance during the Civil War, brought her wealth, but after he died, she kept on writing, most notably *A Washington Winter*, a satire of the high social season in the very society she policed. Bored with what passed for intellectual engagement in the capital, she established the closest thing Washington had to a French salon, inviting authors, diplomats, and intellectuals to her Thomas Circle mansion. One woman who received a coveted invitation recalled an endless evening in hard-back chairs discussing the "Metamorphosis of Negative Matter."

According to one reporter, Breckinridge said that Madeline met Madeleine at "a charitable institution" in Washington. If that's so, it's unlikely it was St. Ann's Infant Asylum. Although it was a Catholic institution and Dahlgren was one of the few Catholics in high society, Madeline was there only a short time, and Dahlgren was a deeply religious and fundamentally conservative woman; it's hard to imagine her admitting a fallen woman into her social circle. However, Dahlgren was also a patron of the Academy of the Holy Cross, which was just across Massachusetts Avenue from her home and which she visited frequently. In February 1888, right before Madeline entered, she took Baltimore's Cardinal James Gibbons, who was staying at her home, to the school to meet the students. However, another reporter at the same interview transcribed what Breckinridge said as "a charitable ball," which would mean that Madeline was already dipping her toe into high society and had wrangled an invitation to one of the many balls held in the capital, where she met Dahlgren.

Regardless of how they met, Dahlgren and Madeline shared a common interest: a love of literature. Dahlgren was a cofounder of the Literary Society of Washington and often hosted readings with well-known authors. It's not hard to imagine Madeline striking up a conversation with her about her ambition to be a writer and Dahlgren taking an interest in a bright young woman—who may have claimed to be a Vinton—and inviting her to attend a reading.

It was through Dahlgren, according to Breckinridge, that Madeline met one of the most socially connected young women in Washington: Florence Bayard, the daughter of former secretary of state Thomas Francis Bayard, who became ambassador to Great Britain in 1893. Madeline claimed to be about twenty-two at the time, which made her the same age as Bayard and Dahlgren's daughter Ulrica, one of the highest-profile debutantes of 1888. Riding on the coattails of these young women with impeccable social credentials, "Miss Pollard worked her way right in to Washington's best society," according to Breckinridge's account. She undoubtedly learned the finer points of etiquette from the Dahlgrens and the Bayards, like how to leave a calling card with the upper right corner turned down if you called on a woman but she wasn't home—or the lower right corner if you were leaving town and wouldn't be available to receive her return call.

Dahlgren was also Madeline's springboard into the literary elite. In the spring of 1890, Charles Dudley Warner visited Washington and gave a talk at one of Dahlgren's literary evenings, which is likely when Madeline met him. John Hay and his wife also often entertained Warner when he was in town, and Madeline used that connection to introduce herself to Hay. "If our good friend Mr. Warner were nearer than California I am sure he would give me a letter of introduction," she assured Hay when she wrote to him in May 1890.

The following spring, Madeline made her first appearance in the society columns, when the *Washington Post* reported that "Miss Madeline Pollard will sail for Europe July 1 with a party of friends for a brief stay on Richmond-on-the-Thames, where among the guests will be Charles Dudley Warner." The trip to England never happened and appears to be an early example of Madeline's social bragging gone awry. It's likely this is what she complained about to Jennie when she said she once told a society reporter something "in strict confidence" only to find it written up in the paper—unless, of course, she was referring to the news of her engagement to Breckinridge.

By the fall of 1890, Madeline found her living situation at Holy Cross too restricting. She went first to the fashionable Elsmere Hotel, where, Breckinridge told Jennie, Warner visited her. Then she went to the boardinghouse of Mrs. Fillette, through whom she met Blackburn, who introduced her into the southern circle of polite society. Madeline hired Miss Coffey the dressmaker and cultivated a distinctive style of rich, unembellished fabrics and muted tones that highlighted her figure. Madeline understood that for women in the Gilded Age, clothes were a form of currency; the right clothes enabled one to move around in certain social circles. "Clothes were really clothes then," remembered Julia Foraker about her years atop Washington's social hierarchy, and "ball-gowns were our poetry," she said.

Thus, Madeline Breckinridge Pollard, a refined young lady of somewhat hazy but seemingly respectable Kentucky antecedents, was born. Madeline thrust herself into the city's intellectual life with a fearless audaciousness. She told Jennie she knew Henry Adams "quite well." One afternoon, she said, she and Adams and Charles Dudley Warner and some friends drove out to Rock Creek Cemetery to see the allegorical bronze statue *Grief* that Adams had commissioned from the Beaux-Arts sculptor Augustus Saint-Gaudens after the suicide of his wife, Marian "Clover" Adams. Many believed Marian was the author of the anonymous, sensational political novel *Democracy* that was later credited to Adams and whose heroine—the formidable, wealthy widow Madeleine Lightfoot Lee, with her intellectual pretentions and impatience for receiving lines—many thought was modeled on Madeleine Dahlgren. Adams did like to visit the mysterious shrouded statue, which, he noted, "seemed to have become a tourist fashion, and all wanted to know its meaning." Madeline said Adams told her "it represented a figure wrapped in meditation on Chinese theosophy," although she told Warner it reminded her of "The Sphinx."

Madeline's Zelig-like social ascent posed a problem for Breckinridge, however. It became more difficult for them to hide their relationship; they tried renting a room in an out-of-the-way part of town, but quickly gave it up because they feared they had been recognized. It was around this time that Breckinridge apparently decided Madeline should leave Washington, contrary to her assertion that he never tried to end the relationship. The fact that Mollie Desha told Issa and Nisba about the affair in the fall of 1890 means it was current gossip in Washington. Especially after Madeline lost her government job, Breckinridge had to face the reality that she might remain dependent on him. Like a bird that hopes desperately its fledgling can fly, he pushed her into the world, first to Cambridge with some funding and the hope she would find gainful employment. That was wishful thinking. How could Madeline, with her spotty education and vague ambition to be a writer, earn a living when his own daughter, with a college education and a famous family name, could only get employment as a teacher? Madeline, who was more socially ambitious than Nisba, wasn't inclined to eke out a living as a spinster schoolteacher.

After a winter in Cambridge when she was supposed to be studying but apparently spent most of her time leveraging her relationship with Warner to expand her circle of literary acquaintances, she returned to

Washington. And for a time she did attempt to do some work as a writer. She wrote several articles about literary subjects for the *Washington Post*. One, a fawning profile of Ella Loraine Dorsey, the "pioneer of Catholic light literature," allowed her to not only insinuate herself with a well-known writer but also polish her own origin story. She wrote that she was first introduced to Dorsey's work "some years ago" when she was "one of those twenty girls who attended one of those very 'select' schools . . . where the elevating of one's brow can go just so far." Most of the genteel female writers, like Dorsey and Dahlgren, whom Madeline admired, however, had fortunes or husbands to fall back on. Few women earned a living as writers at the time, and Madeline remained dependent on Breckinridge.

Again in June 1892, Breckinridge got her to agree to go away, this time to work on a newspaper in Vermont. Then Issa died, and suddenly he was on the spot to make good on his promise. What really happened between them on the carriage ride in August when she returned to the city? It seems unlikely that he proposed, as Madeline claimed, although some of his friends thought he really did intend to marry her but backed away when it became clear that to do so would cause a scandal. "I honestly believe that he was infatuated with the Pollard woman, and that his intention and desire was to marry her," one of them told the *Enquirer*. It does seem likely, however, that Madeline, believing in his long-ago promise, came home and threw herself into his arms, thinking they would finally be together. Not knowing how to extricate himself, and knowing that Madeline had an excitable temper, Breckinridge played along.

Things were relatively calm until the rumors that Breckinridge was seeing Wing reached Madeline, who was pregnant, and she became increasingly distraught and more determined to push her claim. Eventually, she told Julia Blackburn they were engaged, partly to bolster her reputation in the wake of the Fillette scandal. This created a crisis for Breckinridge—but also an opportunity. When they went to see Blackburn on Good Friday, he knew he couldn't deny the engagement outright. Instead, he asked Blackburn to put Madeline under her chaperonage, with the idea of using Blackburn to get Madeline out of the way for the summer, preferably to Europe, so he could marry Wing, assuming that once the deed was done, Madeline would have no recourse but to slink away.

Shortly after, Blackburn asked Breckinridge to arrange an introduction for her and her sister to Frances Cleveland. Breckinridge arranged the visit to the White House, but then Madeline told him "she was to be one of the party." There was no way he could let that happen. He told her she couldn't go, which would have confirmed Madeline's suspicions that he didn't intend to marry her because she wasn't respectable enough. A certain pathos hangs over her entreatments at the time. She told Breckinridge that if she "went away and had the advantage of travel and refined society, she could return in two years and be fitted to become [his] wife."

It's surprising then that after their second visit to Major Moore, Madeline agreed to go to New York for the duration of her pregnancy. She came back to Washington after a couple of days though, and a few days after that, she miscarried. It's possible the miscarriage was brought on by stress. It seems just as likely that Madeline, now more knowledgeable about the ways of the world than the girl who allowed herself to be shuffled off to a room over a mattress store, went to New York for the purpose of obtaining an abortifacient potion from a pharmacist or someone else who sold such compounds illegally.

It turned out that Breckinridge's instincts that marrying Madeline would be political suicide were correct. As soon as news of the engagement became public, "scandal was current about him and Miss Pollard," according to one of Wing's friends. When an associate of Breckinridge's went to see President Cleveland about a government appointment, Cleveland told him: "I see you are endorsed by Col. Breckinridge; if he disgraces himself by marrying the woman to whom he is reported to be engaged, I can no longer respect him or a candidate he is backing." With his political career imperiled and Wing's brother pressuring him, Breckinridge had little choice but to move forward with the public marriage to Louise and to face the consequences.

Struggling with his own family drama and political problems, Breckinridge was blind to the relationships and depth of support that Madeline had amassed in the city. For instance, another person whom Madeline likely met through Dahlgren's circle was Dr. Nathan Lincoln, the doctor who confirmed her pregnancy to Breckinridge—and offered to perform an abortion. His wife, Mrs. Nathan Lincoln of the "pink and gold" Valentine's luncheon, was Jennie Gould Lincoln, a well-known author. She and her husband were frequent guests at Dahlgren's literary evenings—she read a poem the night in 1890 that Charles Dudley Warner was a guest and Madeline likely got her first taste of literary society. Jennie Lincoln was active on the board of Children's Hospital with her husband and Madeline's lawyer Calderon Carlisle. The Children's Hospital board had, in June 1893, just as the Pollard-Breckinridge-Wing engagement kerfuffle was blowing up, held a charity garden party that featured among its volunteer hostesses Julia Blackburn, who possessed the knowledge that Madeline and Breckinridge were supposedly affianced.

A week later, Mrs. Carlisle and Jennie Lincoln were at the Smith-Judson wedding. Then, as now, Washington was a small, gossipy town. "In Washington gossip and great men are the leading subjects," said Frank Carpenter. The Breckinridge-Pollard scandal had both. It's not hard to see how by the time the scandal exploded in mid-July 1893, a good slice of the upper class of the city had some idea what Breckinridge was up to and was inclined to take Madeline's side. "It is said that the story which was brought out in the suit has been in the possession of some persons in this city for some time," reported the *Evening Star*.

In the end, Breckinridge didn't present a coherent defense because he didn't have one. Madeline was largely telling the truth about the relationship, at least in its major contours, although she glossed over the periods of genuine contention between them and downplayed her own increasing agency. As one of Madeline's Wesleyan classmates summed it up: Madeline had her "faults—grievous ones—but that Colonel B. disappointed her there can be no doubt."

And it's likely Breckinridge didn't think he would need a particularly elaborate defense; he thought it was enough to make some smears about Madeline's purported sexual activity, assuming that the prevailing social mores, and the support of like-minded men, would get him off the hook. In not paying more attention to the details of his defense, however, he seems to have missed his only opportunity to save himself.

Right around the time the trial was starting, Breckinridge received a remarkable series of letters from individuals claiming to have intelligence about Madeline and other men. A Dr. Thomas Hershman, who had owned the St. Clair Hotel in Cincinnati, claimed a woman he thought was Madeline had come there three or four years earlier and stayed several nights with a man named Breckinridge who said he was her husband from Lexington. His wife, however, kicked them out when she found out the man wasn't her husband but a railroad conductor. A woman calling herself Nannie White said that she was a former chambermaid who worked at both the Gibson House and the Burnet House and that Madeline used to come to the Cincinnati hotels heavily veiled and spend nights there with a Cleveland businessman. She claimed Madeline had left a small purse behind with "Madeline V. Pollard" written on the inside, as well as "some of her visiting cards, 18 Cents, a Small Key and a note from the man." A salesman named Hall said he met Madeline at the Burnet House with a friend of his who was a traveling salesman for a Louisville liquor company and who bragged that the lady he was meeting was from one of the leading families of the South and was engaged to Congressman Breckinridge. He claimed his friend and Madeline shared a room as "man and wife" for two nights.

Taken individually, any one of the stories seems somewhat improbable, and not all the informants wholly reliable. The good doctor was in prison for stealing a horse and buggy in what he said was a mix-up and a miscarriage of justice. He may have hoped to enlist Breckinridge's aid in getting a pardon. The chambermaid wanted some money to come to Washington and Breckinridge's help in getting a job at a hotel, although that was hardly extortion, especially because she also said she had a letter of Breckinridge's in the forgotten purse. Taken together, though, they paint an intriguing pattern: All three incidences occurred in Cincinnati, two at the same hotel, and all with men who traveled for a living.

Dr. Sinclair got his sister Mrs. Ambrose to send Breckinridge a corroborating statement that only made the story more peculiar. She claimed that late one night she heard the woman "making a very loud noise" and she went to her room, where she delivered a very small, stillborn baby. She told Ambrose she had been "deceived" by a man who turned out to be married. Ambrose said this happened sometime during the Cincinnati Industrial Exposition, a landmark event for the city, which ran from July to late October 1888. This was during the time that Madeline was living at Holy Cross, but the nuns did tell Breckinridge that she was away three or four times for three or four days each. There also was apparently about a year, between the spring of 1888 and the spring of 1889, when she and Breckinridge weren't together. Breckinridge claimed their relations didn't resume until around the time of the Johnstown flood in May 1889, the memorable catastrophic failure of the South Fork Dam when some two thousand people died. More strikingly, Ambrose said the woman used the alias Josie Pollard, and the fact that Madeline purportedly tried to pass herself off as the poet Josie Pollard hadn't yet been published at the time she wrote to Breckinridge. And, Josie Pollard fancied herself a singer and "played piano and sang in parlor" for the guests. And, after the miscarriage, when Ambrose asked how she was feeling, she asked her to "get her a whiskey-punch."

Hall, the salesman, claimed that the incident with his friend happened about a year earlier, which was precisely when Madeline was in Cincinnati, on Breckinridge's dime, to visit the Cincinnati Conservatory of Music, one of the schools she was supposedly considering to take Breckinridge up on his offer to leave Washington. But Breckinridge hadn't yet testified to this fact when Hall wrote the letter, so there was no way he could have known this.

Hall also claimed he saw Madeline at a Chicago hotel the previous summer after the scandal broke and confirmed her identity, and one of Breckinridge's sleuths had reported that she was in Chicago at that time. It was the second time she had been in Chicago that summer. Mollie Desha testified that she met Madeline at the World's Fair with Treasury Secretary Carlisle, who was touring the fair in early July with his wife and some friends from Kentucky. It was on the Fourth of July, the day Carlisle left Washington, that Breckinridge first heard the rumor that Madeline had propositioned Carlisle. So if the rumor was true, it appears that Madeline was trying to arrange a liaison in conjunction with the trip, although it's not surprising it didn't come to fruition. Carlisle was a "shy, absent-minded, kindly man" who was "absolutely dominated by a forceful, ambitious wife." Taken with the claim of Congressman Allen, however, that Madeline was trying to arrange a rendezvous with him, it seems that she may have been trying to find a replacement for Breckinridge. And, it also seems that Madeline may have on several occasions traveled from Washington to meet with men in the anonymous hustle-bustle of busy hotels in the crossroad city of Cincinnati.

This would explain another enduring mystery. Where did Madeline get the money for the lifestyle that she led? Mrs. Fillette, in fact, first became suspicious about Madeline because she lived well but didn't have any visible means of earning a living. Her dressmaker Miss Coffey said she had given her a "good deal of work" over the past three years, and she charged forty dollars for a dress, which was a full month's board in Washington. Madeline showed Jennie an exquisite silk gown she said was from Mathilde of New York, a fashionable dressmaker. A young woman who visited Madeline after receiving a letter of introduction from Charles Dudley Warner said her closet was full of an "array of costly dresses and other finery," which she found suspicious because the boardinghouse she was living in was a dump.

Breckinridge said that he supported Madeline once she came to Washington but gave her only "irregular amounts," and Madeline appeared to be chronically short of money; she left Holy Cross owing two hundred dollars. Earlier that year, she wrote to Rhodes apologizing for not repaying him: "My expenses are very heavy and my salary so small that it is utterly out of the question to send even five dollars a month." And Breckinridge was in especially dire financial straits in the early 1890s, when he was simultaneously shelling out for all his children. This was around the time that one of his clients' money reportedly went missing, although he denied it.

Did Madeline occasionally entertain gentleman friends who would show their gratitude with some money for a new dress or other bit of finery? If she did, she wasn't alone; casual prostitution was not uncommon among women on their own in the cities at the time, whether to afford luxuries or to make ends meet. As Frank Carpenter noted, Washington was full of the "demimonde"—of women on the fringes; not quite prostitutes, but not wholly respectable either. "Many a female clerk, losing her position, devoid of family and friends, drifts into their ranks in order to keep body and soul together," he wrote.

Is that how Madeline kept body and soul together? If Breckinridge could have proved that she had liaisons with other men, it would have released him from his contract of marriage. But he had already spent much of the fall chasing down leads that didn't pan out and, immersed in trial preparation, didn't connect the dots, which, though circumstantial, suggest that while he may have started out as the exploiter, as time went on, it was unclear just who was using whom.

17

The Cavalier and the Puritans

As Breckinridge and Louise made their torturous way home along Pennsylvania Avenue the evening after the verdict was delivered, a group of women were headed in the opposite direction, rushing excitedly toward the Willard Hotel—the traditional political gathering place of men. The momentum had been building for weeks, ever since Judge Bradley had kicked a group of women out of the courtroom during the trial. It began as a "social conversation" among a few women in a Washington parlor. Why, the women asked, if they were being excluded as spectators from the trial in the name of morality, weren't men likewise excluded? They started talking with friends about public perceptions of women's sexual morality. Soon a dozen women who dubbed themselves the "Silent Jury" had convened. First they wrote to Bradley and asked him to "deal with men as he had dealt with women" and disallow male spectators from the trial. He replied that "he would be glad to do so if he could find an excuse for it," but left little hope he would find such an excuse. Then they wrote to Julia Blackburn, thanking her for appearing on Madeline's behalf.

The women, many whom had never been active in public life before, decided to address the larger issues raised by the trial and formed the Woman's Protective League to "combat the enforcement of the [words] uttered on the witness stand by Co. Breckinridge that social sins injure a man but destroy a woman" and to "secure equal rights for both sexes and aid women who have been wronged." They reached out to the major women's organizations in Washington: the District Woman Suffrage Association, the Woman's Christian Temperance Union, the Woman's National Press Association, and Pro Re Nata. "The Washington women have been quietly holding many indignant meetings," said Martha McClellan Brown, whose friend Sarah La Fetra of the local WCTU was one of the organizers. "The notorious conduct of congressmen and public men in Washington is a national disgrace and the women are now thoroughly awakened on the subject and are determined to demand a better order of things."

Now on the evening of the historic Pollard verdict, the "Silent Jury" and representatives of the city's women's organizations were gathering at the Willard in what was undoubtedly the first large-scale protest by women against the predatory sexual behavior of powerful men. A remarkable number of pioneering women were present. There was Dr. Caroline Brown Winslow, who had helped launch the crusade to end the double standard and founded the Homeopathic Free Dispensary, which was an important nucleus of the early women's rights movement in the city. Brown had helped organize both the District Woman Suffrage Association and the National Woman Suffrage Association. There was feisty Nettie White, one of the first stenographers to work for a congressional committee back in the 1870s and a mainstay of both the district and national suffrage associations, who was joined by Louise Lowell, who testified to typing Breckinridge's love letters. There was the botanist Carrie Harrison, one of the first women scientists to have a leadership position at the Smithsonian Institution, and Ellen Richardson, who was at the time pioneering the systematic study of home economics. There was the lawyer Ellen Mussey, one of the first women admitted to the District bar. There were two well-known women journalists, M. D. Lincoln, who wrote as "Bessie Beech," and Mary Smith Lockwood, who founded the Daughters of the American Revolution with Mollie Desha. They were the first and second presidents, respectively, of the Woman's National Press Association, which had been founded to fight for the right of women to sit in the House and Senate press galleries and now had sixty members, including Caroline Winslow and Carrie Harrison. There was Lucia Blount, the wife of millionaire plow manufacturer Henry Blount, who was a member of DAR, the founder of Pro Re Nata, and a devoted suffragist who served as the president of the District Woman Suffrage Association—through which she knew White, Mussey, La Fetra, and Brown. It was a remarkable cross section of women: old and young, northerners and southerners, secretaries, suffragists, and socialites.

The immediate concern of the Woman's Protective League was trying to force Congress to reprimand Breckinridge. Its members passed a resolution calling on Congress to "take some definite action" against Congressman Breckinridge to strike a blow "against the atrocious double standard which had cursed society so long." They also called for an end to the punishment of women for the sins of men: "We must have chastity for chastity, under one rule of right, bearing as rigidly in its application upon one sex as upon the other."

But even the most optimistic among them that evening at the Willard knew that the odds of Congress doing anything were long. They had no formal political power. All they could do was ask and hope.

•

Jennie was disappointed in the verdict; up until the very end, she thought that Breckinridge might be vindicated. "I do believe that if Mr. S. and I could have run this case it would have resulted very differently," she told her mother. And she was right about Stoll being underutilized. One of the big mysteries of Breckinridge's defense was why he didn't have Stoll, who was a feared cross-examiner, handle Madeline's cross-examination rather than Butterworth. "Butterworth's cross-examination of M.P. was something absurd," she complained to her mother. Jennie thought they should have "pulled [Blackburn] over the coals" and goaded Madeline "to get her furious" so she would lose "her self-control, but they all acted as if they were scared to death of her."

Nonetheless, Jennie was optimistic about her future. Breckinridge was planning to ask for a new trial, a request he assumed Bradley would deny, freeing him to appeal the decision, and she told her mother, "We are confident of success next time." And Stoll had a "scheme for some work" for her. Stoll suggested that Jennie use the notes she had taken of her encounters with Madeline to write a book, and she hoped to make "a good lot of money" from it. Jennie felt so upbeat about her future, with "enough money to my credit to more than pay my debts," that she had a new black silk dress made. Not only did she feel that she could afford the extravagance, but she had cause to need it. She was now staying with the Breckinridges, helping to get the "testimony and stuff boiled down" for the appeal, and, as she told her mother, "when you are visiting the quality you have to try and look a little respectable."

Jennie took to Nisba immediately, which wasn't surprising. They were the same age and both were struggling to make their way as single, professional women in a world that didn't seem quite ready for them. "Nisba and I have become great friends and she is such a perfectly lovely girl I do enjoy her," she told her mother. The family was kind to her, but reeling in the aftermath of the trial. Louise and Nisba "have been through a hard trial in every way and have born it bravely but they both show it now," she said. Louise was "very sick and I think they are afraid she will lose her mind," Jennie wrote. Nisba put on a brave face, although she was grateful for any "little kindness." The trial and public humiliation of her beloved father must have been devastating. It would overshadow the rest of her life, leaving a sort of rift in time, a before and after, that would never wholly mend.

Still the intrepid spy, Jennie tried to see Madeline at the Providence Hospital, but the nuns turned her away. Like much of the country, she was dying to know what Madeline planned to do next. Madeline herself seemed torn. One minute she told Jennie she would return to her original desire of being a writer. "I shall cut off my hair, wear flat heels and no corsets, and study and become a literary woman," she said, predicting that she would "write a great novel and become famous." But later she told Jennie that while she "might write in a little room away from the eyes of the public, and possibly make a living," chances were that she "would have to do without all the luxuries of life," which, she said, was an impossibility for her.

Feminist reformers wanted to claim Madeline for their own. Martha McClellan Brown urged her to go on the lecture circuit to advocate for women's rights. Others wanted her to devote herself to reforming her fallen sisters, as she already understood, as one woman told her, their "temptations and sorrows," but Jennie said she dismissed these women as "religious cranks." That left the stage. There was a great deal of speculation that Madeline would turn her talents to acting amid reports that several theater managers had offered her one hundred dollars a night. At first, Madeline told Jennie that she couldn't imagine facing the public and that Jene Wilson had told her she mustn't make an "exhibition" of herself because she was "a lady in spite of the past." More recently, she seemed tempted by the offers, telling Jennie she would have a "much easier life" and a "nice little flat in New York" if she went on the stage.

The Monday after the verdict, however, in a letter to her supporters on the front page of the *New York World*, she said she had no intention of "going on the stage or lecture platform . . . or otherwise accentuating the publicity which my unfortunate career has had in this trial." She said she was "deeply grateful for all the kind letters which have come to me and my counsel from all parts of the United States." And, she wrote, "If the future holds anything for me it cannot be in the direction of publicity and sensation, if my untrained literary ambition is to receive any reward or justification it must come with labor and patience." Even then, she said she would tell her story only if it could "point to the moral of my misguided life."

By Tuesday, Madeline felt well enough to sit up in bed and see a reporter from the *New York Sun*, dressed in a fluffy white peignoir and surrounded by flowers and congratulatory letters and telegrams. She said she would live quietly in Washington with her brother for the rest of her days and that "nothing can induce me to leave" this place— "I shall be buried in Washington cemetery." She said, "I will try to take up a new life. I shall study as I have never studied before, and then when I am equipped I will take up writing, always over a nom de plume."

But when Jennie finally got to see her the next day, Madeline told her that she thought she would accept one of the offers to go on the stage after all, as "forty cents is all I have at this moment in my pocketbook." When she dithered between going to New York to interview theatrical managers or starting work on her book, Jennie suggested she flip a coin. When the first flip didn't get the answer she wanted, Madeline flipped again—always the gambler and often the winner at a game of her own making.

•

Congress, as expected, ignored the petition from the Woman's Protective League. One of the members of the House Judiciary Committee told the *New York Times*, "You are safe in saying the House will do nothing. The public, as well as the House, have had all they want of it."

Many suspected that the men in Congress were reluctant to throw stones at their particular glass house. After all, hadn't Breckinridge testified that one evening when he and Madeline were having a heated argument at an assignation house someone knocked on the door and "said we were making a great noise; that my voice was particular, and that there was another member of Congress in the house who might recognize it."

Breckinridge plowed ahead with his plans to run for reelection, sure that if he submitted his case to the "generous people" of his district who had known him "as boy, soldier, lawyer, and congressman," they would vindicate him. And he wasn't a man to back down, no matter what the odds. When he commanded the Confederate forces at the Battle of Dug Gap near the end of the war, they had been outnumbered ten to one but managed to hold the rocky summit by raining fusillades of boulders on the Union troops below, causing massive casualties. Even at the very end, when most of his company surrendered at the Savannah River, Breckinridge mustered forty-seven volunteers to escort his cousin Gen. John Breckinridge in his flight southward and pledged to march on "until Mr. Davis or Gen. Breckinridge should order us to surrender or disband."

What he needed to do, he knew, was get back home and make the silver-tongued speeches he was famous for. Jennie now found herself with a front-row seat for the Breckinridge redemption tour. Stoll invited her to come to Lexington and stay with him and his family so he could oversee her work on the book, which no doubt he hoped would present a different version of Madeline Pollard in time for the appeal. With visions of herself cantering across the famed bluegrass with Nisba, she instructed her mother to get the green riding habit her sister Patty had given her down from the trunk in the attic and send it to her, as "I shall possibly get a chance for a ride on a good horse."

Jennie and Stoll arrived in Lexington on April 30. The dogwood and the tulip poplars were in bloom in the city that had been known as the "Athens of the West" since its days as a cultural mecca on a precarious frontier. The denizens of the Phoenix Hotel lobby should have been talking about the promising yearlings in the dazzling green pastures strung along Old Frankfort Pike like emeralds on a necklace and which might be the next Clifford—Clifford Porter's scrawny colt that astonished the country when he won eighteen of twenty-four races in 1893.

The talk, though, was of a horse race of a different kind, and the handicappers seemed uncertain as to the odds. On the one hand, Breckinridge controlled the political machinery of the Ashland district and the patronage appointments within. One newspaper calculated they alone accounted for eight thousand of the twenty thousand votes expected to be cast. Breckinridge's loyalists included his confidant Sam McChesney, who held the politically influential position of Lexington postmaster, and his partner Shelby's father, who was the even more influential Internal Revenue collector. He commanded the loyalty of the ex-Confederate soldiers within the district, as well as, ironically, of many African Americans, who hadn't forgotten the stand he took for them in his very first political race. He was also the favored candidate of local businessmen like bloodstock dealers and bourbon distillers, and of what were loosely termed the "public men"—the tax collectors, barkeeps, and hotel clerks who made up the political backbone of the city. On the other hand, Breckinridge was weak among farmers, especially those who grew hemp, because of his stand on tariffs, as well as among what the *Morning Transcript* termed "the masses"—he had never been much for retail politicking; by his own admission he didn't "buttonhole the voters, go to the country fairs, kiss the babies." In addition, the other elites of Lexington—the Clays, Blackburns, Deshas, and McDowells—were reportedly now opposed to him.

Even beyond these high-profile defections, there was something strange, indefinable, in the air. "I never saw a campaign in which public opinion was so difficult to gauge," wrote a reporter from the *Cincinnati Tribune*, adding, "There is something evasive and hidden about it." What seemed to be driving this undercurrent of reticence was an influence heretofore unknown in the Ashland district: women. "The women of the

Seventh District are united in their opposition to Breckinridge," the *Tri-bune* said, noting that in no political contest in memory had "the ladies of Lexington and the surrounding counties taken such an earnest part."

Women, it seems, were pressuring their husbands, sons, and suitors to reject Breckinridge. "I couldn't look my wife and daughters in the face if I were to vote for Breckinridge," one Lexington man told a reporter. "The womenfolk are determined in this matter," he avowed. These weren't just any women. They were the most prominent women of Lexington, women who heretofore concerned themselves only with the Women's Auxiliary of the Confederate Veterans' Association, whose main activity was organizing the laying of wreaths and flowers on Confederate graves for Decoration Day. When Kentucky's famed "Orphan Brigade," the Confederate brigade commanded by the late general John Cabell Breckinridge, held its annual reunion shortly before the trial began, Willie Breckinridge was disinvited from the event he had always attended as an honored guest at the insistence of "50 ladies—wives and sisters of the ex-soldiers, and many of them personal friends of Mrs. Blackburn," who threatened to boycott the reunion if he came.

The trial seemed to have awoken something in these women, something that went deep, beyond even the issues aired in Washington. It was a scar left by elite men and sexual predation that ran through the soul of southern women like the limestone that ran beneath Lexington. Even as the sexual folkways of the country evolved in the nineteenth century away from the permissive colonial attitudes and hardened into the Victorian double standard, the South remained in many ways a world apart, with its own folkways. While the descendants of the New England Puritans and the colonists who populated the mid-Atlantic states and eventually the Midwest looked to pure women to temper men's baser instincts, elite southerners "allowed the open expression of sexual desires"—by men—that "approximated the European libertine ideal," say the historians John D'Emilio and Estelle Freedman. While in theory these genteel southerners upheld religious proscriptions on premarital and extramarital sex, in reality "young white males of the planter class learned that they did not necessarily have to exert sexual control around female servants and slaves."

This white male sexual privilege predated slavery. The Royalist

English elite who colonized Virginia in the seventeenth century, the historian David Hackett Fischer's "distressed Cavaliers," brought it with them. These lesser sons of the rural gentry established a society that mirrored the aristocratic English families from which they sprang: insular, patriarchal, and fiercely hierarchical, with everyone under the patriarch's roof falling under his absolute authority. Women were wholly subservient to men and "held to the strictest standards of sexual virtue." Those found guilty of adultery or bastardy would be hog-tied, stripped to the waist, and flogged in public "until the blood flowed in rivulets down her naked back and breasts." Elite men, however, were rarely or only lightly punished and "were encouraged by the customs of the country to maintain a predatory attitude toward women." Almost any woman in their sphere was fair game: indentured servants, slaves, tavern maids, even relatives; one local folk saying defined "a virgin as a girl who could run faster than her uncle."

This culture of aggressive male sexuality spread throughout the Tidewater region as the Cavaliers ascended to economic and social prominence, a cluster of elite families interconnected by marriage, as obsessed with their own bloodlines as they were with those of their horses and dogs. Even before slavery was widespread, the sexual predation of female indentured servants, who were largely exclusive to the southern colonies, was common—between 1650 and 1700, one in five female servants in Maryland gave birth to an illegitimate child, not uncommonly that of her master or one of his sons. And, as D'Emilio and Freedman note, "Masters could abuse the law by impregnating a servant and enjoying not only sexual privilege but an extra year of servitude as well," which they were entitled to if a servant became pregnant. This provision was so widely abused that the law was changed to specify that "if the father of a bastard was the mother's master, her extra time was served under another master."

This rapacious sexual folkway was carried westward into Kentucky by the fortune-seeking descendants of the Cavaliers, including families like the Breckinridges who married into the Tidewater elite, and southward to the plantations of the Mississippi Delta, where the absolute authority southern planters held over enslaved women and the lack of even the modest civil protections afforded to indentured servants created a culture in which black female sexual victimization was rampant. Elite white women, while being held to exacting standards of female purity themselves, weren't allowed to complain, or even acknowledge this predation. Popular English advice books that were widely circulated in the Tidewater colonies told women their duties to their husbands were to be "humble, obedient, careful and thoughtful of his person, silent regarding his secrets, and patient if he is foolish and allows his heart to stray toward another woman."

For white southern women, then, sexual predation became what the diarist Mary Chesnut called "the thing we can't name." Privately she railed against the men who lived like "the patriarchs of old" surrounded by "their wives and concubines" on the prewar plantations. Publicly, women learned to remain silent, creating a kind of pathological incongruence around the fact that their husbands and sons preyed on women in their purview, both black and white. As Chesnut noted of southern women in the antebellum era, "Every lady tells you who is the father of all the mulatto children in everybody's household, but those in her own, she seems to think drop from the clouds or pretends so to think."

That the Breckinridge-Pollard scandal thrust into public view the elite southern male tradition of sexual predation was an irony that wasn't lost on African Americans. "If the countless thousands of beautiful colored girls who have been ruined in much the same way" as Madeline Pollard "at the South, just since the war, could speak all at once in an ordinary tone of voice, all the artillery in the country could not drown their voices," said the *Cleveland Gazette*, an African American newspaper. "None but Southerners and Afro-Americans have any idea as to the extent of this sort of crime, and for which the male 'chivalry' of the South will be held accountable at the final judgment."

Madeline Pollard gave these elite Kentucky women a chance to talk about what had been unmentionable. "Many prominent society women in Frankfort, Lexington and Louisville tell some racy anecdotes on the Colonel," reported the *Cincinnati Enquirer*. No one doubted that these tales had long been told. One society lady questioned why women were suddenly up in arms "when they knew as much about the private life of Colonel Breckinridge the first time he ran for Congress as they do now." But the code of silence was hard to break, and it took the public outing of Breckinridge to give women the confidence to speak up. Jennie was stunned by the level of opposition to Breckinridge she found among the women of Lexington; even Stoll's wife was against him. Internalizing Breckinridge's argument, she told her mother she thought the women opposed to Breckinridge were "fools" because everyone knew that Joe Blackburn "has lived just the same sort of life and yet because Col. B has been found out they do nothing but howl about his sin."

Breckinridge arrived in Lexington to much fanfare on Friday evening, May 4; a crowd of five hundred men greeted him at the train station. Breckinridge loyalists were predicting the largest crowd ever assembled in Lexington for his speech the next day. Desha and Shelby had been furiously working the local press, discounting reports of insurrection by the ladies of Lexington and downplaying Breckinridge's condemnation by local preachers under the banner of the Ministerial Union of Lexington. Their efforts were thwarted when an open letter signed "Many Women" appeared on the front page of the *Morning Transcript* the next day urging the men of the Democratic Party not to renominate Breckinridge. The women said they were "deeply humiliated" that men excused what Breckinridge had done and furious he was unapologetically asking "with smooth words and hypocritical tears" to remain in public life. "Let him sink in the oblivion" of his guilt, they urged, "let his voice be silent."

Smooth words and tears were exactly what the audience at the Opera House got that afternoon. "Clinching his hands with the most intense emotion, his nerves quivering, and tears coming to his eyes," Breckinridge gave the speech of his life. Looking over the audience of his comrades and constituents, he conjured the ghosts of the past, the "memories that cluster about me and surge upon me," as he denounced the men he said conspired to destroy him, metaphorically putting them on trial "in the presence of these witnesses and of this district." He said he had no defense for what he was guilty of; he had been, he explained, "entangled by weakness, by passion, by sin, by coils which it was almost impossible to break." But he dared them to find someone who could do the job better than he "whose life has been stainless, whose morals young men can imitate with profit, whose ability is ample, whose experience is wide." Wound up now, with the audience cheering, and some crying, he said: "For a hundred years this district had been represented by men.

They have not always been sinless men, and, whether you re-elect or reject me, hereafter when someone comes to write its history, whatever blame may attach to me, he will write of me . . . he loved the poor, he toiled for his fellow-man, he labored for good causes."

Breckinridge's allies were ecstatic with the speech; even some of his doubters were won over. "Every one says it was the finest speech ever heard and it won over lots to his side," Jennie told her mother. She spent the afternoon huddled in Desha's flat with Stoll, transcribing the final draft of the speech for the press. She would have liked to have heard it herself, but didn't go because she was "afraid there would not be any ladies there." And there weren't any ladies there, something the press was quick to note. Not only were there no women at Breckinridge's speech, but the crowd wasn't as large as many had expected. The lower level of the Opera House was full, but no one was turned away at the door, and there "was no great swarming of the aisles." Even some of the press seats were empty. One reporter noticed a great many sunburned faces and carelessly trimmed beards and said the "number of town folks was surprisingly small."

And the next day there was an unwelcome development: a *Courier-Journal* editorial denouncing Breckinridge's candidacy. It was an unexpected blow. Henry Watterson, the editor of the *Courier-Journal*, was not only a personal friend of Breckinridge's but also one of the most prominent supporters of the "New South" ideology. Breckinridge had complained bitterly about the paper's coverage of the trial, but Watterson had avoided any comment in his influential editorials. Now he called Breckinridge's plea for support in light of the revelations made during the trial an affront that no Kentuckian could countenance. He said Breckinridge was demanding absolution "upon the plea that his admission of guilt leaves him guiltless; that his sins are no worse than the sins of those to whom he appeals; that he should not be made a vicarious sacrifice for mankind."

The mail brought more bad news—a panicked letter from Nisba, who had stayed in Washington to care for Louise, who now appeared on the verge of a complete breakdown. She was "very feeble," wrote Nisba, and rarely lucid—she thought Nisba was her sister Rose; she couldn't finish a sentence; her eyes were crossed much of the time. The "cruel" things her friends had said to her about Breckinridge haunted her, and she uttered them in her delirium. But, loyal as ever, Nisba had high hopes for her father's canvas. "I do believe they will understand your position after your speech," she told him.

Breckinridge continued his whirlwind speaking tour. The following Monday in Paris, he cast the verdict as the result of public opinion inflamed by feminist purity reformers and a biased media. "Are you to choose your own representative or shall meetings in Boston and Philadelphia or editorials in the *Courier-Journal* decide for you?" he asked. It was clear that the battle lines had been drawn. Nominally the contestants were Breckinridge and his two primary opponents William Owens, who was a protégé of Watterson's, and Evan Settle, another former state legislator. The real combatants, though, were two worldviews about women and sex. One was the hierarchical, predatory southern ethic, which held that any woman who wasn't protected by her father and domestic isolation was fair game and became part of a debauched class necessary to protect the purity of respectable women. Breckinridge warned one of his friends that the "conspiracy to destroy me ought not be permitted to be successful" because it "exalted unchastity" and would tempt "every wanton and adventuress . . . to do what is possible to entangle a man." The other was the more egalitarian ethic of the eastern elite—the descendants of the pious but fair-minded Puritans—that increasingly saw men and women as equals and men as responsible as women for upholding high, and nonpredatory, standards of sexual morality. To them, fallen women weren't social necessities but victims of a skewed male sexuality.

Breckinridge was essentially asking his constituents to relitigate the trial and reject the more progressive ethic, lest it pollute their more traditional understanding of men, women, and sex. It was, as one of Breckinridge's friends told him, "a case of the Cavalier being tried by a lot of hypocritical Puritans," a "shining light in the Democratic firmament" under attack by the "short-haired women of Boston" and "that Willard Hotel gang of powdered, broken-down, she fanatics."

•

The rejoinders to Breckinridge came quickly. On May 8, the National Council of Women, which had been formed by activists like Susan B.

Anthony and Frances Willard of the Woman's Christian Temperance Union to unite reform-minded women's organizations under one umbrella, took time off from condemning corsets to declare that "there should be the same standard of moral purity for men and women." Three days later, the International Federation of Women's Clubs, which represented the local women's clubs that had exploded around the country in the past two decades, bringing middle-class women into contact with new ideas and allies, weighed in. They said that "moral purity should be equally binding on men and women, and that conduct which debars one from social life shall also debar the other."

In Lexington, word began circulating of an anti-Breckinridge rally planned for the following Monday afternoon at the Opera House. "Many Women" published another letter urging women to attend, telling them to put aside their housekeeping for the "higher obligation" they owed their family. They assured them that many of the city's most respectable women would be there, and warned women that by "your attendance or your non-attendance you are setting up your own history—a history to be stereotyped and preserved."

The anti-Breckinridge rally had been advertised for only a few days, but on Monday morning, trains into the city were packed. The Opera House was full to the balconies an hour before the rally began; the aisles were crammed and hundreds of latecomers were turned away. And although Breckinridge's backers had asserted that "outside a few women's suffrage cranks" no respectable women would be there, nearly half the seats were occupied by women. J. W. McGarvey of the Ministerial Union gave the main address. When he warned the audience that "just as the whole civilized world rendered a verdict" in the Pollard case, it would also judge them, "the ladies fairly shook the house clapping their hands and rapping on the floor with their umbrellas."

Not every woman was against Breckinridge. Mrs. Cuthbert Bullitt, who had recently married into the prominent Bullitt family, led the women's defense of Breckinridge and traditional morality where fallen women were concerned. "Miss Pollard knew from the beginning that Col. Breckinridge was married," she wrote to the *Louisville Times*, therefore, she was a "brazen brute" to become involved with him. Bullitt insisted that Breckinridge "was the victim of a smooth-tongued siren," and was not to blame because "with man's passion, which is different from women's he could not tear himself from her."

But Bullitt was in the minority, and the groundswell continued to build against Breckinridge. Despite this, he was nowhere to be found after the big women's meeting. He had returned to Washington, summoned by another desperate letter from Nisba, who warned him that Louise was "in grave danger, not of death, but worse than death." She was consumed with anxiety about her husband's well-being; even the telegram he sent every day no longer seemed to soothe her. Nisba was at her wits' end dealing with her increasingly deranged stepmother. "I fear I cannot stay here longer than this week," she warned her father, yearning to escape to Ella's house in Staunton for the summer, even as she knew there was no one to take her place.

Jennie remained in Lexington for another week and a half. She never did get a chance to ride a thoroughbred, discovering for herself that the last horse the Breckinridges owned was a fat white pony back in the days of crinolines. Although, right before she left on May 20, she did get "one great treat." Stoll took her to visit a stock farm in the Lexington countryside, where she marveled at a black stallion worth the unimaginable sum of thirty-seven thousand dollars. Jennie planned to stop in Washington only long enough to change trains for New York, but when she arrived in the city, she found Breckinridge snowed under with preparing documents for the new trial, so she stayed a few days to help out. Working side by side with Nisba, she told her mother, it "seems almost like home to come back here," and for Jennie it was the only home she had known in quite a while.

There was one last thing Jennie wanted to do before she left Washington. She went to see Madeline. It's not clear what more she thought she could discover; she seemed to be looking for answers to a riddle she couldn't quite solve. She found Madeline living in a cheap room in a small brick cottage on the same block as the House of Mercy. Madeline told Jennie she had taken up a "systematic course of English literature" to prepare herself to go abroad and study and that a sympathetic friend had lent her brother the money to pay her board. Her plans, as always, were up in the air, although she did tell Jennie she was having two new dresses made—a blue gown trimmed in white watered silk and a green linen one—which, she said, would have to do "unless she went away for the summer." She said she didn't care whether Breckinridge was re-elected or not, as he was "dead, practically, in Congress" and would "never amount to anything here in Washington." Jennie left feeling that Madeline "was as great a mystery to me as when I first saw her"—gifted and magnetic, yet by her reckoning, vain and idle.

It was Monday, May 28, when Jennie finally left Washington, reversing her hurried journey of what must have seemed the long-ago winter. She sent Breckinridge her bill of $191 for some five months of dogged work and asked him to send her check on to New York, where she planned to stay with a friend while she finalized her manuscript.

As Jennie's train steamed toward the Mason-Dixon Line, Breckinridge and his lawyers were meeting with Judge Bradley to present their bill of objections as grounds for their appeal. But there was a hitch. They were required to give the opposing counsel three days' notice, not counting Sundays. That meant they needed to get the bill to Madeline's lawyer Carlisle the previous Thursday. But they hadn't delivered it to his office until Friday, and Carlisle had refused to accept it. Shelby begged for an exception, explaining that Breckinridge had been delayed on account of his wife's illness, but Bradley was unmoved. Breckinridge had blown the appeal; there wouldn't be another trial. The case of *Pollard v. Breckinridge* was officially closed.

Jennie spent a week in New York working "like a gally [*sic*] slave." She was exhausted and eager to get home, but bursting with optimism. "I wish I could tell you that we would not need to take any more boarders all our lives," she told her mother, but assured her, "I am some shakes now." Her friend Max had arranged an interview with the Sunday editor of the *New York Herald*, and she thought she had "made a hit with him." But as she prepared to take the Fall River Ferry to Boston, she still hadn't gotten paid by Breckinridge, and she was about out of money. Getting desperate, she wrote to Nisba and asked her to intercede. Mortified, but deferential as always, Nisba wrote to her father in Kentucky and asked him to send at least partial payment right away, reminding him that Jennie was "very faithful and helpful that last week here" and saying she couldn't "bear to think of her out of money in New York."

As usual, however, Breckinridge was snowed under with bills. He owed Louise's cousin two months' rent on the house in Washington. He owed the stenographer who prepared the trial transcripts $250 and the handwriting expert who authenticated Madeline's letter $50. But his biggest balance of all, the debt he owed Nisba, continued to accrue; through some alchemy of firmness and love she seemed to be the only person who could manage Louise. Desperate to relieve her, he wrote to Louise's brother Dr. Scott and asked him to look after his sister while he campaigned. But Scott declined, saying that Kentucky wasn't the right place for Louise. He believed she needed "prolonged brain rest" and prescribed the "Rest Cure," a Victorian treatment for "hysteria" and other ill-defined nervous disorders thought to plague women that involved complete social isolation, strictly enforced inactivity, and the consumption of copious amounts of milk and other fatty foods—by force-feeding if necessary. He recommended a place nearby where she could "rest and hear and see nothing of the outside world," but fortunately for Louise, whether through compassion or his strained finances, Breckinridge didn't follow through. Now, both Nisba and Jennie were in limbo, waiting on Breckinridge for deliverance.

•

The battle of Ashland raged throughout the summer. It was like no primary contest anyone could remember. Newspaper correspondents from all over the country swarmed to Lexington to cover a campaign the *New York Herald* called the most famous political fight in the country. The *Washington Post* said it "had no parallel in our history"; in "intensity of feeling it was like a civil war." And indeed, many of the old loyalties of the war were tested and transposed. Basil Duke said he would stump for Major Henry McDowell—Nisba's friend Madge's father—who was a Republican and a former Union officer, if he sought the Republican nomination if Breckinridge won the Democratic primary. The vice president and the secretary of the Women's Auxiliary of the Confederate Veterans' Association resigned when the organization refused their request to boycott Decoration Day activities if the CVA didn't kick Breckinridge out, which was especially embarrassing since Issa Breckinridge had been president of the organization.

It was the active role that the normally reticent southern women took in the campaign that drove much of the interest. At first, many assumed the uprising against Breckinridge was the work of suffragists eager to prove the power of the women's vote. But Laura Clay said the Kentucky Equal Rights Association wasn't involved and that the anti-Breckinridge uprising was a spontaneous, grassroots effort largely driven by women who hadn't been active in progressive movements. "The women are aroused as never before, and the most conservative are those who are most active," she said.

The fervor of the anti-Breckinridge meeting at the Opera House gelled into a widespread, women-led economic and social boycott of anyone who supported Breckinridge. Female students at the Agricultural and Mechanical College announced they wouldn't accept the attentions of suitors who supported him, and the mothers of some of Lexington's most popular young women let it be known that Breckinridge men wouldn't be invited to the debutante dances come fall. Women refused to shake hands with men who wore Breckinridge buttons and boycotted the stores of merchants and fired doctors who backed him. A woman who ran the only hotel in New Liberty, Kentucky, refused to allow Breckinridge to stay there on a campaign swing.

The prominent role of women also attracted other, less desirable kinds of attention. The two women who emerged as leaders of the anti-Breckinridge effort, Mrs. Judge Jere Morton and Mrs. Colonel A. L. Harrison, received "insulting" anonymous letters that—in the nineteenth-century equivalent of trolling—had been routed from Lexington through Pittsburgh and back to make them impossible to trace. The letters demanded that the women cease their "detestable proceedings against Colonel Breckinridge" and contained "insulting insinuations and obscene innuendoes" and threats of a "bloody character." Morton, however, assured the press that the women were not intimidated and would redouble their efforts.

As the women organized, Breckinridge hopscotched across the Ashland district, focusing on his strongholds of Woodford and Bourbon Counties, carrying a little notebook in his pocket in which he scribbled the names of the men in each city and town and hamlet who were for him. In mid-July, he got another grim letter from Nisba. Stuck with

Louise in a city that now felt like someone had thrown a wet rag over it, Nisba decided it was time to level with her father, who believed that Louise eventually would recover from the ordeal of the last eighteen months. But Nisba told him that Louise was a "feeble woman, feeble in body" and in mind. Nisba believed her "brain has certainly suffered from a long use of sedatives," most likely laudanum, a tincture of opium that was a popular nerve tonic for women. Nisba told her father that he needed to make long-term plans for Louise. "I don't believe . . . that you can hope for these attacks to cease," she said, essentially confirming that Louise had gone mad under the strain her father had put her through.

As the summer wore on, the primary contest turned rancorous. "The Breckinridge business floats in the air like a buzzard," complained a Chicago reporter. Desha almost got into a duel with an Owens supporter after he called Owens a coward, traitor, liar, and gambler. Breckinridge lashed out publicly at the men he thought had betrayed him. He accused Judge Jere Morton, whose wife had emerged as a leader of the anti-Breckinridge effort, of using his friendship with him to dissuade him from compelling Morton's father-in-law Howard Gratz to testify about his relationship with Madeline. When Gratz published an editorial in the *Gazette* savaging his candidacy, Breckinridge threatened a retaliatory attack, saying he knew "what your relations with Miss Pollard were when you had her as the guest of your own daughter under your roof; when she was nominally in your office in your employ, when you were together late at night."

By the last, languishing days of August, the contest had boiled down to Breckinridge and Owens. Women formed their own Owens clubs in Lexington and Frankfort, a first in Kentucky politics. On August 23, the Lexington club, under the direction of Julia Hunt of the local Hunt-Morgan dynasty, organized and financed a huge picnic and rally for Owens. After a brass band led a gigantic parade snaking through the streets of Lexington, Owens banners flapping in the breeze, some thirty thousand people, nearly a third of them women, packed into Woodland Park to dip tin cups into vast kettles of burgoo, a stew that was a staple of Kentucky political gatherings and into which went "eighty sheep, eleven [cows], forty hogs, besides two immense wagon loads of corn, twenty bushels of potatoes, six bushels of onions and 1,000 tomatoes." After everyone had feasted, they heard speeches from Jere Morton and Owens, but the real point was standing publicly against Breckinridge and marveling at the fact that women "who all through the course of their lives have left politics and all such public matters to their husbands and have had a horror of being before the public" had organized it all.

Into this boiling political cauldron stepped Mollie Desha with a letter to the people of the Ashland district "to tell you some truths which it is necessary for you to know." She said that the "truth is that of all the immoral delegations in Congress, that of Kentucky has the reputation of being the worst." She urged the election of a "clean, pure man, with brains enough to know that it is a man's actions and not his religious twaddle that make for righteousness." She said that if Breckinridge were reelected, the men of Kentucky would endorse his position that "all men are libertines," which would "announce to the world the unchastity of your women."

The letter was the talk of the town. It was a further reminder, as if anyone needed it, that the same men who zealously policed women's sexuality ran rout with their own. The fact that Washington was a sexual playground for men was no secret. Frank Carpenter had called it "one of the wickedest cities" in the country because of the large number of "married men away from their wives." He said that every afternoon the demimonde "parade Pennsylvania Avenue" in "sealskins and silks," and even sat in the boxes reserved for members' families in the congressional galleries. Martha McClellan Brown said at the time of the women's meeting at the Willard Hotel, "It is an open secret in Washington that there are women . . . whose relations with Congressmen or other public men high in the councils of the nation are either perfectly understood or suspected, who are met at every turn at the most fashionable functions, often in the receiving line [or] presiding over the tea-room . . . Society knows all this, but so powerful has been the influence of the names [in] back of them that no one has had the courage to drop the woman or rebuke the man."

Yet Mollie's letter wasn't without risk. Her outspokenness about Breckinridge had already cost her the only family she had and she acknowledged that she risked "shocking her friends"; nonetheless, she persisted. But her friends were anything but shocked. They congratulated

her on a much-needed takedown not only of Breckinridge but also of
Kentucky's particular sexual mores. "It has been greatly complemented
by all who have read it," her good friend Julia Blackburn assured her.

That, as one of Mollie's friends told her, the feeling in Kentucky
"against Breckinridge is so bitter that one is reminded of the condition
of things during the war" became apparent just a few days later when
the campaign saw bloodshed. John King, a young man from Clay's Ferry
who backed Breckinridge, met on the road near Boonsboro a tobacco
farmer named George Cook, who supported Owens. The conversation,
inevitably, turned to politics. Cook told King, "Any woman who would
go to hear Breckinridge speak is no better than a Megowan Street
woman," referring to Lexington's red-light district. King replied that his
wife and daughters had gone to hear Breckinridge, at which both men
sprang from their horses and went at each other with knives. Within minutes, Cook lay dead.

By now, Lexington was delirious with talk of the race. It began at
6:00 a.m. at the Phoenix Hotel and went on well past midnight. "Everyone looks like he has lost three hours of sleep, and men say 'no' and mean
'yes,' and forget their umbrellas and canes, and in some cases their
names," said the *Courier-Journal*. The primary was the talk of the country as well. "What a time you have been having in the old Henry Clay
district," Susan B. Anthony wrote to Laura Clay. "I do hope exposed and
confessed unchastity will not win." Theodore Roosevelt, who had urged
his friend Henry McDowell to jump into the race, said he wanted to see
Breckinridge retired from public life. "I feel it would be an infamy and
something to make every American hang his head to have him continued in public service," he told McDowell. Julia Blackburn wrote excitedly to Mollie Desha just days before the election, "Like myself I suppose
you are watching with intense interest the result of" the race. She thought
it "sheer madness" that anyone could "support such filthy immorality."

On September 8, some two hundred women packed into the Capital Hotel in Frankfort for an anti-Breckinridge rally. A reporter marveled
that the local women were so immersed in the campaign that they had
given up their "social duties" and were even leaving their homes on their
traditional receiving days. The day before the election, women who just
six months earlier would have blanched at seeing their name in the

paper began the morning with a ten o'clock organizing meeting at the Opera House. Then they got in their carriages and went door-to-door campaigning for Owens; all day long, the streets of Lexington were thronged with politicking women. Women announced they would be at the polls the next day serving coffee and rolls, an extraordinary declaration at a time when election days were so filled with public drunkenness, swearing, and fighting that women took care to stay home.

Despite predictions of violence, election day itself was surprisingly quiet. The polls closed at four. Breckinridge awaited the results with Desha at his cramped headquarters on the third floor of a downtown building. Women circled Owens's headquarters like buzzards well past the hour when respectable ladies should have been home. Crowds gathered around the bulletin board outside the *Post*'s office in Washington, cheering as each update was posted. The tension was almost unbearable. When someone mistakenly told Maria Hunt that Breckinridge won, she fainted. But it wasn't so. When the results were tallied, Owens had defeated Breckinridge by some 250 votes out of nearly 20,000 cast. The biggest upset came from Fayette County, the home of Lexington and the place where the Breckinridge name burned brightest. Breckinridge had expected to run up a margin of 1,000 votes or more, but he beat Owens there by fewer than 200 votes, rejected by the very men he spent his life among.

The headlines trumpeted the defeat: "The Silver Tongue Is Silenced," said the *Leader*; "Decency Wins in Kentucky," said the *Times*; "The Wages of Sin Paid to the Silver-Tongued Breckinridge," said the *Knoxville Journal*; "The Women Triumphant," proclaimed the *Transcript*. No one doubted that it was women who made the difference; Owens wasn't a spectacular candidate and issues hadn't been important. "Never before in any canvas have the women interpreted the leading role," marveled the *Cincinnati Enquirer*, as many wondered what the campaign foretold for the role that women would play in politics in the coming century. Indeed, the slow-burning spark of suffrage had been lit in the South. Julia Hunt, the president of the women's Owens club in Lexington, became a member of the Kentucky Equal Rights Association, convinced that "there is a place for women in politics." The women's uprising also bolstered Laura Clay's contention that the South was the "most promising" place in the country for suffrage organizing. She organized a southern speaking tour for Susan B. Anthony and other suffrage leaders that kicked off in Lexington in January 1895.

Reporters tracked down Madeline to where she was living on East Thirty-First Street in New York under the name of Mrs. Higgins, but she didn't want to talk about Breckinridge or the election. She had decided over the summer to go on the stage after all, in a play described as a "comedy-drama with a strong emotional role," saying it was the only way she could make a living. She was reticent when a reporter asked how her training was coming along, leaving it to her manager to brag that her acting instructor said she was "a finished actress already." Madeline's plans were scuttled, however, when professional actors formed the Actors Protective Union of New York to keep her and any other celebrities by dint of notoriety who had visions of going on the stage from dinging their hard-won, and still nascent, respectability. She would, however, shortly assure a reporter that she had "a novel nearly completed, which a leading New York publishing house will put on the market."

What no one doubted was that Breckinridge, who had bet his political redemption on the ruin of Madeline Pollard, was now himself ruined. He was "a ruin that is complete and irremediable," said the *Kentucky Leader*, condemned by all: "by the religious for his hypocrisy, by the moral for his vice, by good society for what they call his odious treachery to Mrs. Blackburn, by his colleagues in Congress for his folly." With his cousin Clifton Rhodes Breckinridge having resigned his congressional seat to become the minister to Russia, there would be no Breckinridge in Washington for the first time in living memory. The shock of this, combined with the admission from even those who opposed him that the state was unlikely to see another public servant of his caliber, reverberated with unexpected resonance. "The fall of Breckinridge," said two noted Kentucky historians, "was like that of an archangel."

Nisba would never quite get over her father's loss to a man she considered "a mediocre representative of certain special interests." She blamed not only his political enemies in the Hemp Trust, but also the "many women who wished to punish my father for his marriage and for the scandal involving [Madeline] Pollard." She never could bring herself to hold her father accountable for his downfall. By the time the votes were counted, Nisba was in Staunton, having taken a job teaching at a girls' school for the year. The pay was poor and the work promised to be boring, but she didn't want to burden her father and knew she needed to make a path for herself. "It is a step toward making a profession of teaching," she said, assuring him, "I already have quite a schoolmarmish air."

Jennie was home in Maine when the news of Breckinridge's downfall reached her, her optimism of the previous spring tempered by the realities of the summer and fall. Her family, her brother in particular, was shocked when they learned the details of her mission in Washington. Her book *The Real Madeleine Pollard: A Diary of Ten Weeks' Association with the Plaintiff in the Famous Breckinridge-Pollard Suit* had been overshadowed by two other quickie books about the trial. One, a sensationalized recounting of the trial cobbled together from newspaper coverage by a woman calling herself "Fayette Lexington," better mirrored the public mood in its sympathy for Madeline. "To say she did right to call him to account in the way that she chose is only to state the opinion of all fair-minded people," Lexington wrote. Jennie, influenced by what she believed to be her friendship with the Breckinridge family and her relationship with Stoll, had written a dramatized account of her friendship with Madeline, that while true in its basic facts—Jennie was not one for fabrication—was heavily shaded toward the portrait of Madeline the defense had tried to paint. With no new legal proceedings slated, there was little interest in revisiting the question of Madeline's character, and Jennie's hopes for financial success were dashed. By the fall, she still hadn't been paid by the man she now dismissed as "old Breck," as she realized she was just another woman to be used, another hireling to be stiffed.

Despite it all, Jennie's taste for adventure remained undiminished. Two weeks before the election, she had donned a diving suit, screwed the big brass helmet in place, and descended forty feet under the Sheepscot River. She was, they said, only the second woman to ever do so. She stayed there for fifteen minutes, simultaneously terrified and thrilled, suspended in the murky depths, unable to see a way forward but unwilling to surrender to the surface.

18

Refusing to Behave

As Jennie's friend Max Ihmsen wrote in the *Herald*, the emergence of Madeline Pollard "startled the whole country." This seemingly powerless woman from a backwater in Kentucky took on one of the nation's most powerful men—and by extension much of Washington—and won. By having the nerve to tell her story in public, she broke the conspiracy of silence that allowed powerful men like Breckinridge to prey on younger and less powerful women. She led Victorian America on a front-row tour of the various subterfuges—the lying-in homes, the orphan asylums, the homes for fallen women—that men used to maintain an underclass of "ruined" women. She showed how men like Breckinridge manipulated their power and social conventions to ensure that it was women, and their unwanted children, who took the fall for men's behavior. In doing so, Madeline inspired a generation of women to demand change and presaged conversations about powerful men and sexual privilege that resonate into the twenty-first century.

The Pollard-Breckinridge trial didn't end the double standard, but it did begin its transition to a more realistic sexual ethic that flowered in the twentieth century. Indeed, one of the great ironies of the episode is that the more equal standard of sexual morality wished for so fervently by purity reformers would come to pass—only in the direction of more premarital sexual freedom for women. By asserting that a woman who had lost her virginity outside of marriage should still receive the consideration of society, Madeline Pollard helped break the taboo around women and premarital sex and pave the way for what would be a series of sexual revolutions in the century to come.

How did Madeline Pollard manage to bring down Col. W.C.P. Breckinridge? For one, the timing of her suit was critical. Societies often are only able to confront deeply embedded, systemic issues—like the sexual predation of women—at times of cultural change and instability. The historian and ambassador James Bryce called the period during which the Breckinridge-Pollard scandal took place the "shattering Nineties"—and shattering they were, as economic and culture pressures created fissures that allowed for the exploration of new ideas about women, sex, and shame. Madeline Pollard came along at a moment of profound cultural transition, as women flooded into formerly all-male workplaces and public spaces and society was forced to grapple with new questions about women's respectability. The widespread entry of women into the workforce between 1880 and 1900 was "the most significant event in the modern history of women," says the feminist historian William O'Neill. By the early 1890s, even well-off families had daughters and sisters working outside the home. They were worried about them being taken advantage of by predatory men, but were ready to rethink old rules about women, sexual respectability and were the responsibilities and standards held by men.

One of the most significant things Madeline Pollard accomplished was making it acceptable to talk openly about sex, which was necessary to confront sexual predation. There was a marked increase in public discourse related to sex in the years following the trial—so much so that in 1913, one editor famously declared it "Sex o'clock in America." William Marion Reedy wrote, "A wave of sex hysteria and sex discussion seems to have invaded the country. Our former reticence on matters of sex is giving way to a frankness that would even startle Paris." A year later, the essayist Agnes Repplier complained in *The Atlantic* about "The Repeal of Reticence," saying that the open discussion of sex had gone too far, with "teachers, lecturers, novelists, story-writers, militants, dramatists, social workers, and magazine editors" now "chatt[ing] freely" about sex and sexual vice.

Just as timing was essential to Madeline's success, so, too, was the awakening among women and the explosion of new networks for women, especially in Washington, that helped build a groundswell of public opinion against Breckinridge. Organizations like the Daughters of the American Revolution, the Woman's Christian Temperance Union, and the various reform and professional societies lifted women beyond their traditional segregated domestic spheres and allowed them to voice their displeasure with the status quo about men and sex across class and sectional lines. The rich networks undergirding the women who staged the Willard protest illustrate the new ways that women were interacting with one another, as working women, society leaders, reformers, and organizers all came together.

One woman stood at the intersection of all these groups and the Lexington women who delivered the final blow to Breckinridge: Mollie Desha. Her testimony, brief as it was, was a powerful rebuke of her brother-in-law and an early sign that polite society was massing against him. She likely helped foment the anti-Breckinridge sentiment that percolated throughout Washington during the trial into a broader movement—she knew not only the truth about his relationship with Madeline, but nearly half the women at the Willard gathering knew Desha through either the Daughters of the American Revolution or Wimodaughsis, the networking organization she founded. Her letter about Kentucky men in Washington landed at exactly the right moment during the Battle of Ashland and helped push the pendulum over the edge. When Breckinridge was looking for someone to blame for his downfall, he should have looked to his own family.

Only one other woman used her social capital as effectively on Madeline's behalf, and that was the indomitable Julia Blackburn. Breckinridge himself knew it was Blackburn he had to blame for his ruination. As he wrote to a friend, "There would have been no scandal but for Mrs. B. The girl would have gone away from Washington and behaved herself." That Madeline refused to behave was due partly to her own anger at being discarded by Breckinridge in favor of a woman of higher social standing and in part to what Breckinridge called her "insane belief in Mrs. B's power and influence." As it turned out, Madeline's belief in Julia's influence wasn't so crazy after all. As the *Washington Post* noted even months after the trial, Blackburn's "testimony as a woman of social standing and unimpeachable character went far to influence the jury in awarding damages to the plaintiff," not to mention that her letter to Basil Duke helped Madeline reframe the narrative of the predatory fallen woman at a critical time.

What Breckinridge called the "support and encouragement" Madeline got from Julia likely was critical in another way. Madeline was with Julia in Charlottesville when Breckinridge's marriage to Wing was announced, and it was clear Madeline had been jilted. Madeline said she told Julia that her "honor was involved," and she would remove herself from her protection as she prepared to head back to Washington. It's likely that it was Julia who convinced her to see a lawyer and pursue a legal settlement, not knowing the full extent of her relationship with Breckinridge. Calderon Carlisle was exactly the type of society lawyer to whom Julia would refer Madeline; likely, he was the only lawyer she knew. Carlisle's wife and mother were members of the Women's Auxiliary of the Ex-Confederate Aid Society along with Julia Blackburn and Mollie Desha—who, naturally, had helped organize the society when it became clear there were a number of destitute Confederate veterans in the capital. Madeline told Jennie that Carlisle was "the first one I talked to about my suit." Because Carlisle specialized in international law, he had reason to bring in Jere Wilson for his skills as a litigator. If Madeline had talked to Wilson first, he wouldn't have had any reason to bring in Carlisle. After the trial, when a *Washington Post* reporter was chasing down ultimately false rumors that Madeline's lawyers would try to attach the proceeds of Breckinridge's speeches to pay for her settlement, Wilson referred him to Carlisle, averring that "he had the case in his charge."

Given the legalistic language that suddenly appeared in Madeline's July 15 letter to Breckinridge—and the fact that her lawsuit was filed less than a month later—it seems likely that she first consulted Carlisle on her mid-July trip to Washington. Once Carlisle heard the details of her relationship with Breckinridge, he could have easily walked away. No one had ever successfully argued a breach of promise case in which the plaintiff couldn't claim she had been seduced under the promise of marriage. Madeline was obviously able to convince him that she had the evidence to back her claims, including letters from Breckinridge and Blackburn's avowal of the engagement.

It was likely Jere Wilson, however, who decided to turn the suit into a test case about the double standard and a society that punished women for men's predation. It's clear from his impassioned closing argument that he was aligned with the thinking of social reformers about the issue. Wilson appears to have been part of a circle of progressive Indiana Republicans who were committed to moral reform. Three of the women prominent in the anti-Breckinridge efforts hailed from Indiana: Lucia Blount; Mrs. Nelson Trusler, the wife of a former U.S. district attorney for Indiana; and Mrs. Dan Waugh, the wife of Congressman Dan Waugh.

The enduring mystery of the great Breckinridge-Pollard scandal remains: Who paid for Madeline's lawsuit? Even if Carlisle and Wilson donated their services, which seems likely as both were wealthy men, the expenses for the trial ran in excess of $3,500—some $100,000 today. Most people assumed that Breckinridge's political enemies were behind the suit; Breckinridge himself believed it to the end. This seems unlikely. Wilson's closing argument shows that the suit was brought to make a point about women and the double standard, not to destroy Breckinridge politically. Madeline's case was just too audacious for a conventional political interest like the Hemp Trust to have attached itself to, although the trust was happy to back his opponent once he was crippled politically.

The evidence points to more unconventional backers: It's likely that the shadowy figures behind Madeline's suit wore corsets. One of the most persistent rumors was that Madeline was financed by a wealthy widow. Many people assumed it was Blackburn, but she explicitly denied giving Madeline money "directly or indirectly." The *Evening Star*, however, reported that the money was provided by a woman who was "a widow, a Kentuckian and a near relative of one of the plaintiff's female witnesses," which describes Blackburn's sister Emily Zane, who also was wealthy and who never denied providing any money. If she did, however, she left no record of her involvement. Likewise, there's no record that another wealthy widow, Madeleine Dahlgren, gave Madeline any money, although she was well known for her views about the sanctity of marriage. By the early 1890s, with her youngest daughter married off, she spent most of her time at her estate in the mountains of western Maryland.

There are three women who, based on motive, means, and proximity, almost certainly aided Madeline. The *New York World*, which had the best intelligence on the case, said that Caroline Fellows Morgan, the widow of David P. Morgan, a Wall Street wizard—who hailed from a different branch of the family tree that produced J. P. Morgan and who had made a fortune in Suez Canal and railroad stocks—was Madeline's primary backer. She reportedly provided five thousand dollars for trial expenses because she didn't think "a man who made such a profession of Christianity as did Breckinridge during the years he was living a double life should go unrebuked." Morgan never denied her involvement, and before she and her husband relocated from New York City to Washington because of his health, they attended St. Thomas's Episcopal Church, where Caroline was known as "an enthusiastic church worker." As such, she would have been familiar with the New York Episcopal Church's interest in purity reform. She was also a Kentucky girl, hailing from Louisville, and may have had a natural sympathy toward Madeline.

Another New Yorker who loomed large in Madeline's life was Margaret Thorne, the daughter of the wealthy businessman Samuel Thorne. Samuel, along with his wife, was well known for his charitable works, and Margaret was similarly philanthropic-minded. She also was passionate about rescuing morally imperiled working girls. In 1885, when she was just twenty-one, she founded the Columbia Working Girls' Club as part of the wave of clubs for working girls started by wealthy, civic-minded young women. In December 1893, she folded it into another organization she founded, Hephzibah House, which trained young women to be Christian missionaries—Thorne herself had already gone to China and Japan as a missionary. In February 1894, just as the trial was about to start, Hephzibah House was offering lectures such as "How a Girl's Life Can Be Transformed." A year after the trial concluded, Madeline sailed for Europe as the "traveling companion of a wealthy and charitable woman who has taken an interest in her case." As she and Thorne (who was later Margaret Thorne Tjader, the wife of a big-game hunter turned missionary) would be lifelong friends and travel together, this likely was Thorne.

Lucia Blount was another wealthy woman whose motive and means suggest she almost certainly backed Madeline. She and her husband, Henry, had, like many midwesterners with Gilded Age industrial fortunes, relocated to Washington. Nonetheless, Blount was "one of the few rich society women who are entirely liberal and progressive" and "holds advanced and independent views," noted the *Washington Post*. She was committed to feminist ideals and had hosted Susan B. Anthony at the Oaks, her estate in Georgetown. In addition to being active in the national and local suffrage groups, one of the reasons Blount founded Pro Re Nata was so that women could educate themselves about the legislative process and advocate for social policies to protect the rights of women and children. She was one of the women at the Willard meeting, so she was clearly committed to ending the double standard and was energized by the Pollard case. She even may have been the "noted philanthropist" the *Star* noticed peeking into the courtroom one day during the trial. Most important, she and her husband were elite Indianans who would have certainly known Jere Wilson. It's likely that once he decided to proceed with the suit as a test case challenging the double standard, it was Blount who provided the seed money. She was also friendly with Nettie White, the pioneering stenographer who was a mainstay of the National American Woman Suffrage Association and District suffrage groups. White appears to be the link between her friend Louise Lowell, the typist who spilled the beans on Breckinridge's love letters, and Wilson, who clearly knew White, because that's whom he sent his thank-you note for the flowers to.

The *Cincinnati Tribune* reported after the trial concluded that the suit was organized by women connected to the Woman's Christian Temperance's White Cross social purity program, including Mrs. Carlisle; Clara Colby, the editor of the *Woman's Tribune*; and Mrs. James R. Hobbs, the wife of the former president of the Chicago Board of Trade, who convinced Madeline to sue as a test case of the double standard. There's no evidence that any of these women played a role, and of the three, only Hobbs was active in the WCTU. Carlisle's wife was involved only with proper southern causes like the ex-Confederates. Colby was busy in the summer of 1893 covering the Chicago World's Fair for the *Women's Tribune*, and a review of her extensive correspondence gives no indication she was involved in the suit. If the WCTU had been involved, it would have almost certainly stashed Madeline in its Home for Fallen Women, not the rival House of Mercy. Madeline herself wasn't sympathetic to activists' organized efforts to challenge the double standard. She said after the trial that while the motive of the women who formed organizations like the Protective League was good, "Nothing has ever yet been accomplished by such radical movements, and nothing ever will be. The matter must be handled in an entirely different way."

A wealthy widower also likely played a role. Jennie told Stoll in March that Madeline's brother Dudley had met with Woodbury Lowery, "one of the richest men in the city." Lowery was indeed rich and hailed from an old cave-dweller family. He had the money to assist Pollard, but what was his motive? Love, or long-thwarted love, it seems.

In 1880, Lowery's sister Virginia was one of the city's most desirable debutantes, a tall, brunette beauty. Virginia fell in love with Count Brunetti, the secretary of the Spanish legation. He asked her to marry him, but her parents objected because they didn't want their daughter to leave the country, and Virginia refused to marry without their permission. So she and the count waited. He was assigned another post and left the country; and then another and another. She turned down numerous offers of marriage, including one from Commodore (later Admiral) George Dewey. The 1880s turned into the 1890s and still they waited, corresponding faithfully.

By the time Madeline brought her lawsuit, Woodbury's sister had been waiting thirteen years for her beloved. Did he see in Madeline's decade-long wait for the day she could marry Breckinridge an echo of his sister's devotion? He certainly would have known Carlisle, another high-society cave dweller. Furthermore, Carlisle was the attorney for the Spanish legation, which meant that he knew Count Brunetti, who was now, with the death of his father, the Duke of Arcos. And it appears that the duke and Woodbury also maintained a relationship. In the spring of 1895, after the death of the objecting Archibald Lowery, the duke came to Washington and stayed with Woodbury and Virginia. When the duke was appointed the minister to Mexico, Woodbury accompanied him to Mexico, and shortly thereafter, in October 1895, he and Virginia were finally married.

One hundred and twenty-five years later, no cashed checks, no receipts exist to prove exactly who gave what to Madeline's cause. Because so many of those involved were women, who at the time left a scant trace in the official historical record, inferences of their involvement must be made by tracing relationships, circles of influence, motive, and means. All the evidence suggests that Belle Buchanan was on the mark when she said that Madeline told her that the "expenses incurred by my witnesses in this trial are all paid by a fund raised for me in Washington" and that the key contributors were Morgan, Blount, Lowery, and perhaps Thorne. Guy Mallon, the Cincinnati attorney who handled some of the depositions, confirmed to Buchanan that "some society people of Washington had quietly raised a fund for [Madeline] to carry on her case with." Madeline herself told Sister Dorothea the money for her travel expenses was "furnished her by lady friends who were interested in her case," although it's likely that she didn't know who her benefactors were since the money went through her lawyers. It appears that this fund was overwhelmingly raised by women to make a statement about Breckinridge's behavior. How many of them had seen young women "ruined" under similar circumstances and felt powerless to do anything? How many were tired of seeing hypocrites like Breckinridge parade around Washington while their mistresses sat in the House galley?

The women who supported Madeline didn't need her to be the perfect victim; they just needed her to do what no other woman in her shoes had done—not be ashamed to tell her story. Maybe Madeline was a fabulist; maybe every word she said wasn't the absolute truth. But who wasn't hustling in the hurly-burly world of the crashing Gilded Age? Breckinridge, who was living on his august family name while he fleeced the people who brought his ice and typed his letters? Jennie, with her mothballed riding habit and her new dress for the "quality"? The daughters of the broke cave dwellers, who were selling their services as "social secretaries" to the ambitious wives and daughters of the nouveaux riches who flooded Washington looking to make a splash in high society? Everyone was on the make in one way or another. Madeline, who had more to gain and more to lose, was just more audacious. It was a unique confluence of timing, networks, and, above all else, determined and impassioned women, that made Madeline's unlikely victory possible. In the end, it wasn't one woman who brought down Colonel Breckinridge. It was all of them.

19

Redemption

In the years following the Breckinridge-Pollard scandal, most of the participants, like the rest of the depression-bound country, struggled. Coxey's march to Washington to demand a public works program for the unemployed fizzled. A ragtag army of five hundred men reached the Capitol two weeks after the conclusion of the trial and was met by a phalanx of mounted police under the command of Major Moore. The marchers were beaten and Coxey was arrested for trespassing on the Capitol's grass. Still unrest percolated, exploding into the violence of the Pullman railroad strike in the summer of 1894.

Under the weight of the depression and grasping for solutions, the Democratic Party splintered into a populist silverite faction and an old-guard Bourbon faction and went into eclipse. The 1894 midterms and the 1896 presidential election ushered in an era of progressive Republican ascendancy. The country had changed; the Panic of 1893 showed that it needed complex solutions to modern problems. Politics had changed as well. Willie Breckinridge had warned about the rise of a new class of "troublesome voters upon whom party ties sit lightly"—of political independents unmoved by the parades and picnics and hoopla of nineteenth-century politics and more concerned with issues. "We lost zest after that for explaining everything with silver-tongued oratory and brass bands," explained Julia Foraker.

For the Breckinridges, the years after the trial were an exercise in humility, as they learned to do with less—less prestige, less money, less certainty in the future. Willie Breckinridge tried, and failed, to reclaim his seat in 1896 by running as the Gold Democrat candidate, part of the short-lived National Democratic Party of Bourbon Democrats who opposed William Jennings Bryan, who would nab the Democratic presidential nomination on the strength of his famous pro-silver "Cross of Gold" speech and send the Bourbons into political oblivion.

In 1897, Desha Breckinridge took over the *Lexington Herald* and made his father the chief editorial writer, where Breckinridge continued to espouse his Bourbon politics while criticizing the increasing disenfranchisement and segregation of African Americans as Jim Crow overspread the South. Still hustling to make a living at age sixty-seven, he was on a speaking tour of the Great Lakes region in September 1904 when he caught a bad cold. He suffered a stroke after he returned home but insisted on returning to his law office within weeks. He suffered a second stroke on November 16 as he sat at his desk. He died on November 19.

After their father's death, Desha and Nisba sent Louise, who had never fully recovered her mental equilibrium, back to her family, having recommended that she be institutionalized, although she apparently never was. Louise died in 1920 and was buried not with her husband in Lexington but in Frankfort Cemetery near her brother.

As he must have feared, Breckinridge was forever linked to Madeline Pollard in his obituaries. As the *New York Times* noted after recapping his illustrious career, "He was defeated for renomination, largely owing to the notorious Madeline Pollard case, which involved his name in much scandal."

The damage he inflicted to the storied family name must have haunted him as his life drew to a close, because just two years earlier he warned Nisba, "The [Breckinridge] name has been connected with good intellectual work for some generations—for over a century—you must preserve this connection." And he was prescient, because it was the women of the family who ultimately would redeem it.

•

Jennie Tucker never did get paid by Breckinridge. She wrote to Stoll, and then to his wife, to give "old Col. Billie the devil," but to no avail. By

November 1894, with a bitter cold winter closing in and cash scarce in a frozen economy, she and her parents moved into a few downstairs rooms of Castle Tucker to economize. A brief romance with her friend Max had ended badly. By 1897, she was selling a rose-leaf balm she had concocted to department stores in Boston and New York. When that venture failed, she got a job as a secretary for Mary Morton Kehew, a wealthy Bostonian who was the president of the Women's Education and Industrial Union, which focused on improving conditions for working women. Despite her own struggles with low wages and her proximity to a pioneering labor reformer, Jennie remained apathetic about organized activity to improve the lot of women. She had dismissed "some woman's rights gang" she saw when she was in Washington as an "awful queer looking lot." She referred derisively to Kehew as "Madam Kehew," and although Kehew was known as a bit of a snob, Jennie's assessment seemed to stem more out of her own discomfort with her position, and she didn't take the opportunity to make a career with an organization that was a "regular hotbed" for Wellesley girls like Nisba looking to do good and make a living.

By 1902, Jennie was again in New York City, living in bedbuggy rooms and using her dressmaking know-how to sell corsets to corpulent matrons trying to squeeze into the latest silhouettes. That lasted until she got into a fight with the management over the quality of the corsets, which she claimed had declined—her customers were literally busting out of them. Her next job as a traveling pattern consultant for McCall's took her all over the East Coast and Midwest, which was groundbreaking at a time when few women traveled for business. She was often harassed on the road, again finding herself at the intersection of women's expanding economic opportunities and traditional expectations of respectability.

Jennie was in Wilmington, Delaware, when she got word that Breckinridge had died. "I'll bet they were glad to 'plant' him every one of his relatives—surely Pollard killed him—didn't she," she wrote to her mother. She saw Stoll when her route took her through Lexington in 1905. She found the man who had been mentioned as a possible Republican gubernatorial candidate during the trial "terrible stupid and prosy," his wife dead, and "out of all his deals" as a result of his involvement with Breckinridge.

In 1906, she was assigned a territory out West and traveled through Wyoming and Montana. Like Mollie Desha many years before, she found the West a revelation and reveled in the freedom she found there. She was never "sassed" in her travels, she said, as "they enjoyed a woman with brains enough to get around and do that sort of work." She learned to ride astride and even considered staking a claim and homesteading. But reality drew her back east. She worked for a time selling wholesale for A. A. Vantine & Co., a popular importer of decorative goods from China and Japan, but business was slow—the economy again went into a tail-spin in the Knickerbocker Panic of 1907, when the failure of New York's third largest bank set off a wave of bank failures. Eventually, Jennie re-turned to Maine and Castle Tucker. She hatched a plan to raise squab for the commercial market and spent three hundred dollars on 150 pairs of supposedly superior breeding stock only to end up with crates full of sickly birds and "such pigeons as one might pick up in the streets of any of our cities or towns." But through it all, she remained fiercely inde-pendent and proud of her ability to make a living. "The world is wide and I have always been able to support myself," she boasted to her mother during one of their frequent spats.

When her mother died in 1922, Jennie inherited Castle Tucker, an expensive white elephant with few modern conveniences. But with the advent of the automobile, the once-isolated town of Wiscasset took on new life as a tourist destination. Jennie updated the house with elec-tricity and indoor plumbing and ran Castle Tucker as a popular summer tourist hotel from 1924 until just after the Second World War. Some-where along the way, Jennie Tucker became a local legend, a flinty sur-vivor of Maine's seafaring past who credited her longevity to a "hard head" and plenty of food and sleep. She lived to be ninety-seven, dying on April 28, 1964. She left Castle Tucker to her niece Jane Tucker, who lived in it largely untouched until her death in 2003, when she left it to Historic New England. Sitting on a bluff overlooking the Sheepscot River, Castle Tucker is still a perfectly preserved Victorian home where visitors can almost imagine Jennie rushing around the corner, a telegram from Charles Stoll fluttering in her hand.

•

Nisba Breckinridge lasted one year teaching; she quit at the end of the spring 1895 term. She was twenty-nine, still frail, and still searching. That summer, with "the question of my health and my future" having become "acute," Nisba went to visit a former Wellesley classmate, May Cook, in Oak Park, Illinois. May took Nisba to see her friend Marion Talbot, who was now the dean of women at the University of Chicago. "I'm not sure how it came about," said Nisba, but somehow the money was found and by the fall she was enrolled at the university as a graduate student in political science. Despite being "very poor" and having "almost no clothes," she had a "wonderful year" studying under the eminent legal scholar Ernst Freund, who was exploring cutting-edge questions about the role of the government in providing for the public welfare—although she was so petite that she had to have a janitor shorten the legs of one of the chairs in Cobb Hall because her feet couldn't touch the floor.

Unfortunately, when Willie Breckinridge decided to run for reelection in 1896, Nisba wasn't able to return to finish her degree because the family "did not have the money." Nisba spent a year at home, keeping house, studying law in her father's office, and working on her master's thesis on the evolution of Kentucky's judicial system. One day in January 1897, when Desha was going to Frankfort, Nisba decided to go along and ask the chief justice of the Court of Appeals, who had been a "mess mate" of her father's during the war, to give her a bar examination—which was done orally at the time. "He assembled two other justices and we sat in one of their chambers in the beautiful old court building," she remembered. The exam lasted "three or four hours." Nisba passed with flying colors. Three days later, on January 25, 1897, after swearing that she had "never fought a duel with deadly weapons," Nisba Breckinridge became the first woman admitted to the bar in Kentucky—an accomplishment that was remarkable enough to warrant coverage in the *New York Times*, which noted she "inherits her love for the law from the Breckinridge family." (The *Times* had reported erroneously in 1892 that Nisba had taken the bar exam, but according to the records of the Kentucky Bar Association, the only exam Nisba took was on January 22, 1897.)

Nisba spent the spring trying to build a law practice and going to

Chicago to defend her master's thesis. She handled a few cases of "special women's interests" steered her way by friends of her father, but work was scarce. Then, out of the blue, deliverance. Marion Talbot offered her a doctoral fellowship that a male student had given up. Nisba packed her bags for Chicago and never looked back. In 1901, she became the first woman to receive a Ph.D. in political science from the University of Chicago, and in 1904, the first woman to graduate from the University of Chicago Law School. "I am growing quite famous as your father," Willie wrote proudly, just months before he died. His remarkable daughter had made him rethink his views on women and work. In a 1902 editorial, he questioned why an intelligent, capable young woman like Nisba shouldn't be able to enter any field she wanted. He called "the system which differentiates so sharply between the activities of a man and a woman" a "perverted one," and said he had come to see "the strange new demands made by women" not as an upending of the social order, but "part of the development of the new social conscience."

It was as part of this new social conscience that Nisba Breckinridge would make her mark as a pioneering feminist social scientist. Along with her colleagues Edith and Grace Abbott and working in tandem with an influential circle of Chicago social reformers, she forged a new field that combined social science and social activism, a "social politics" that provided the impetus for many progressive-era reforms involving women and children. For the rest of her remarkable life she straddled academia and the real world, as at home in a classroom, where she taught a generation of social service professionals, as she was at Hull House, where Jane Addams was now a good friend. Her work on the economic status of women in the first decade of the 1900s was groundbreaking, shining a light on entrenched patterns of inequality in women's employment. She criticized legal restrictions on women's work as serving states' interest in limiting women "to the bearing and raising of children" and advocated for a minimum wage to lift women from poverty. She studied juvenile delinquents in Chicago, highlighting the role of poverty and social conditions rather than inherent immorality in bringing young adults into conflict with the law, and was especially concerned about helping young women whose "virtue is in peril." She campaigned against "moral courts" that entrapped and humiliated prostitutes and spearheaded the transformation of the Chicago Orphan Asylum into a more modern, noninstitutional social service agency. It was as if, even unconsciously, Nisba was trying to undo many of the conditions that helped create her father's downfall.

Nisba was especially consumed with the question of how women could reach full equality in society, especially economically, while meeting their demands as mothers. Her work on juvenile delinquency led her to advocate for the establishment of "mother's pensions"—state-sponsored aid for impoverished widows—laying the intellectual groundwork for what would become Aid to Families with Dependent Children, or "welfare," and epitomizing a new approach to alleviating the root causes of poverty. Nisba supported Margaret Sanger and her efforts to provide women with access to birth control and was a vice president of the National American Woman Suffrage Association, noting the link "between lack of political equality and this double under-payment of women workers." She was active in labor reform activities through the Women's Trade Union League and helped organize a garment workers' strike in Chicago. The daughter of Willie Breckinridge studied race-based housing discrimination in Chicago and helped found the Chicago Urban League. The granddaughter of Robert Breckinridge studied substandard housing in the city's teeming immigrant slums and founded the Immigrants Protective League. To Nisba, it was all interconnected in a great web of social justice: "An attempt to give a course on the subject of the legal and economic status of women raised questions of trade union organizations, of the immigrant girl, of the working mother."

Somewhere along the way, Nisba's ill health disappeared, her life "a hectic round of meetings, conferences, interviews, campaigns and causes." She didn't take vacations and she didn't mind. "I came to the university in poor health and without professional equipment and found here a situation so democratic with reference to sex, age, and color," she remembered in an address at an alumni dinner in 1938, that she decided never to leave Chicago without "a round-trip ticket in [my] pocket."

Still, Nisba fought her own battles with discrimination. Despite graduating at the top of her classes, the prestigious academic appointments that flowed to her male classmates didn't come her way. For years she was employed only part-time by the University of Chicago. When she engineered the affiliation of the Chicago School of Civics and Philanthropy—where she was dean and created a pioneering curriculum for the training of social workers—with the University of Chicago in 1920 to create the School of Social Service Administration, she was made only an assistant professor despite a half-dozen influential publications to her credit; she wouldn't be made a full professor until 1925.

When the Great Depression came around, however, Nisba's work was vindicated, as the need for social welfare programs became clear and the social service professionals she had trained were in demand to staff newly created social welfare agencies. Still, she saw much work to be done, especially in ensuring an adequate living wage for families and child care for working women. "If we come out of the depression with a truly national program of adequate relief and skillful service, a truly national insurance of child care and child welfare," she said, "we shall have wrung something infinitely precious from the experience." It was the capstone of her career when in 1933, President Franklin Delano Roosevelt appointed her as a delegate to the seventh Pan-American Conference, making her the first woman to represent the United States at an international conference.

Nisba would be the last of the prominent Breckinridges. Nevertheless, eight decades later, when the U.S. government scholar Stephen Hess ranked the top ten American political dynasties for the *Washington Post*, the Breckinridges came in at number eight, not far below the Adamses and above the Tafts and Bayards.

Nisba wasn't the only Breckinridge woman who changed the world for other women. Sometime during the brutal primary campaign of 1894, her prickly, hotheaded brother Desha fell in love with her friend Madeline McDowell. It was an unlikely pairing. Desha was known as a swell, albeit one so charming that the daughter of a wealthy senator and the niece of a Supreme Court justice pursued him, and was vehemently opposed to suffrage and progressive politics. Madge McDowell was, according to Nisba, "able, eloquent and public spirited," enraptured with suffrage and socialism. She had hoped to join Nisba at the University of Chicago, but had to give that dream up after her foot was amputated to cure long-simmering tuberculosis of the bone. More fox than hound, she led Desha on a merry chase for four years, going to country club dances with other beaux and teasingly sending him *A Bachelor's Christmas* as a gift one year.

When Desha and Madge finally married in 1898, the transformation was unmistakable: Desha was converted to Madge's politics. The *Herald* became the most prominent southern voice for progressive reform. Drawing on Nisba's work and her connections in Chicago, Madge became the leading progressive reformer in Kentucky, undertaking an exhausting succession of "municipal housekeeping" projects: kindergartens and playgrounds for the poor, industrial schools for black and white students, a model school for the "Irishtown" slum of Lexington, laws to ensure that children went to school instead of work.

But it was as the most prominent southern suffragist that Madeline McDowell Breckinridge became best known. Even after tuberculosis moved into her lungs, she rose to a leadership position in the National American Woman Suffrage Association and undertook a grueling succession of speaking tours. A pro-suffrage pamphlet titled *A Mother's Sphere* that she wrote for the General Federation of Women's Clubs, which represented one million middle-class women, helped convince that organization to officially endorse suffrage in 1914, which was a major turning point in the mainstreaming of the movement. When Kentucky ratified the Nineteenth Amendment in January 1920, it was Madge who was standing behind Governor Edwin Morrow as he signed the resolution in recognition of her decade-long effort to promote suffrage in Kentucky. On November 2, 1920, she cast her first vote for president of the United States. Three weeks later, she died of a stroke at age forty-eight, her frail body worn out by incessant work and her indomitable spirit perhaps dimmed by the revelation that her beloved Desha had been having an affair with her friend Mary LeBus, which had long been the gossip of Lexington—especially after Desha made a hasty exit down the fire escape of the Phoenix Hotel in his pajamas after LeBus's husband showed up—the lessons of the father, apparently, not having been learned by the son.

Nisba memorialized her beloved "sister" in a book about her work "toward a more modern, a juster, nobler life." It was one of more than ten books she wrote in her lifetime, including *Marriage and the Civil Rights of Women* and *Women in the Twentieth Century*.

Nisba never slowed down. Students recalled her hurrying to her office every day well into her seventies, a sprightly Victorian specter in a long, dark dress. She was nearly eighty when she finally sat down to write about her life. For all her accomplishments, she seemed torn about the choices she had made. She wondered if she would have had a "more honest and simpler" life if she had never left Kentucky, as if she could have changed her family's fate by stifling her own abilities. Having lived most of her adult life in the "women's halls" of the university and outlived all her immediate family, including Desha, Ella, Curry, and Robert—who spent twenty years wandering the globe after he jumped ship and didn't return home until 1914—she seemed to regret never having had a family and home of her own. She mused about her long-ago beaux and the women they married who "made happy gracious homes." The question of whether "the access of women to the satisfactions of life must either require celibacy or continue to be vicarious or indirect through a husband" haunted her. Neither the social conditions nor the technology—in the form of modern methods of birth control—had existed throughout much of her life to make combining marriage and a professional career possible, but Nisba worried that she had been "afraid of life," and indeed it seemed that she never allowed herself to believe she was good enough, either in her work or her personal life.

Time and again she tried to tell the story of her life, and time and again she stopped and restarted—fragments on paper, the years between Wellesley and the University of Chicago a confused blur. She could remember the long-ago buttonholes her Grandma Desha made her practice, but little of what happened in those painful years between 1890 and 1895. She was ashamed that she never reconnected with her aunt Mollie, although, she noted, she "died in a way she would have liked, 'with her boots on.'" And Mollie Desha did drop dead on the street in Washington in 1911 as she was hurrying between meetings, and was buried not by her family, but by the Daughters of the American Revolution, who honored her profusely—her remains were the first to lie in state in DAR's Memorial Continental Hall in Washington.

For Nisba, it seemed, her own story was inextricably linked to that of her father. "I have wanted to write an account of my father, but I seem unable to make a beginning of a biography of him, while I cannot speak of myself without speaking at length of him," she wrote. Again and again she began: "W.C.P. Breckinridge . . . , My father . . . ," only to cross it out or divert the story to some illustrious ancestor, as if writing the words would unearth truths too painful to bear. She tried to reach some understanding of what had happened, of the betrayal, the deceit, of what a lifetime's work must have told her was exploitation. "As I look back, now, I see how complicated and difficult a burden my father carried," she wrote, with the family's money woes and Issa's frail health. But still the story would not come. For Nisba, who died on July 30, 1948, at the age of eighty-two, and was hailed by the *New York Times* as an "outstanding figure in the field of social service," her father would always be the circle that would not square, the hole in her heart that would not heal.

•

Madeline Pollard, it turned out, was neither friendless nor ruined. She said after the trial that she would show that a "thoroughly disgraced woman can, by true penitence and absolute reform, succeed in getting and retaining the respect of the people about her," and it seems she was right. Madeline, who now styled her name as "Madeleine," returned to New York in the fall of 1896 after her first sojourn to Europe. As expected, she hadn't received any money from Breckinridge. By the spring of 1897, the *Washington Post* reported that she was living in London "in good circumstances" and "studying with the view of engaging in literary work." By 1901, she was living in Oxford, where she told census takers she was a "writer of fiction." It was in Oxford that she met a wealthy Irish-born widow named Violet Hassard. By 1911, the two friends were living together, with Madeline calling herself Madeleine Urquhart Pollard, appropriating the name of a Scottish clan that hailed from near Loch Ness. The two would be friends and traveling companions for the rest of her eventful life, which continued on its Zelig-like romp through history.

Madeline spent a good part of the mid-1920s in the Paris of Ernest Hemingway and Ezra Pound and Gertrude Stein and F. Scott Fitzgerald and just about anyone else who was worth knowing in the literary world. She traveled to Egypt as the "Tutmania" craze gripped the western world following the discovery of King Tutankhamun's tomb. She visited

Italy, Switzerland, Holland, Spain, and Algeria, always returning with Hassard to their home in London. She traveled home to the United States every few years, returning to New York in 1928 with Margaret Thorne Tjader, who was now widowed and provided Madeline with a home base at her estate in Darien, Connecticut.

Madeline never wrote her book. She also never lost her taste for reaching out to well-known men. In 1936, she wrote to Nobel Peace Prize–winner Nicholas Murray Butler, the president of Columbia University and the head of the Carnegie Endowment for International Peace, to thank him for his support of Anglo-American friendship at a time when some Americans were criticizing the growing ties between the United States and Great Britain. "I am sure that it is providential that you should be in England just now," she told him. "I thank God for you in the heart of our national life and the world movement towards the better understanding between nations." She did not, however, invite him to come see her.

"I have asked a question with my life, it cannot be answered in a day," Madeline said when the dust from the trial was still settling. Had she ever answered it? We will never know. One thing is certain: Madeline Pollard lived life wholly on her own terms, neither afraid nor ashamed, and in her own way helped create a new world for women as surely as Nisba Breckinridge did. She died on December 9, 1945, in Devon, just six months after her friend Violet. According to the records, she was seventy-nine at the time of her death, which meant she was still claiming to have been born in 1866, although on one of her voyages to the United States she gave her birth year as 1867.

Except for one time. On one of Madeline's very last transatlantic trips, on the S.S. *Olympic* from Southampton to New York in 1931, the original entry of her name on the passenger list is crossed out and reentered. Maybe it was an overly persistent immigration officer, maybe it was the forgetfulness of age, maybe it was karma, but the corrected birthday that appears on one of the last official vestiges of Madeline Pollard's existence: November 30, 1863.

Notes

Sources are given for direct quotations, which are identified by their opening words, for numbers and statistics, and for the attribution of key historical theories. Direct quotations not sourced individually can be cited to the preceding source in that paragraph or, for multiple sources within one paragraph, to the first source in that paragraph. Ephemeral sources cited only once are not listed in the bibliography, nor are newspaper articles. Abbreviations used for newspapers and manuscript collections can be found in the bibliography.

1. GOLD TO BE MADE

3   *severe coastal storms*: Monthly Weather Review 22, no. 1, U.S. Department of Agriculture, Washington, D.C., 1894.

4   *"the bottom had dropped out"*: Jane Armstrong Tucker (*JAT*) to Mary Tucker, Dec. 27, 1893, *TFP*.

4   *"feeble and [grew] childish"*: JAT to Richard Tucker, Dec. 15, 1893.

4   *"I'm so tired"*: JAT to Maude Tucker, Nov. 20, 1893, TFP.

4   *"I think the shock"*: JAT to Mary Tucker, Jan. 5, 1894, TFP.

4   *"bleeding piles"*: Mary Tucker to Maude Tucker, Jan. 17, 1894, TFP.

5   *"old duds"*: JAT to Mary Tucker, Nov. 15, 1893, TFP.

5   *"Why you, of all persons"*: Charles Stoll to JAT, Jan. 21, 1894, TFP.

5   *"pretty, tasteful dress"*: Mary Tucker to Maude Tucker, Jan. 17, 1894, TFP.

5   *"My surprise and the feelings"*: JAT to Charles Stoll, Jan. 27, 1894, in Tucker, TRMP, 18.

5   *"in the line of detective work"*: Charles Stoll to JAT, Jan. 22, 1894, in Tucker, TRMP, 10.

6   *"I leave for Washington Monday"*: JAT to Charles Stoll, Jan. 27, 1894, in Tucker, TRMP, 18.

6   *"My lifelong friend"*: Charles Stoll to JAT, Jan. 22, 1894, in Tucker, *TRMP*, 10–11.

6   *"silver-tongued"*: "For Breach of Promise," WP, Aug. 13, 1893.

6 *"the brilliant achievements of its statesmen"*: "Breckinridge Defeated," *Louisville Commercial*, Sept. 16, 1894.

7 *"Everybody who knows"*: "Both Kept Out of View," *WP*, Aug. 14, 1893.

7 *"the real motive"*: Charles Stoll to JAT, Jan. 22, 1894, in Tucker, *TRMP*, 12.

7 *"created such a sensation"*: Ibid., 13.

7 *"be in a position"*: Ibid., 15.

7 *"pitiful tale"*: Ibid., 16.

7 *"lying and living a lie"*: JAT to Charles Stoll, Jan. 27, 1894, in Tucker, *TRMP*, 21.

7 *"If I could be the means"*: Ibid., 20.

8 *"I have undertaken"*: JAT to Mary Tucker, Jan. 28, 1894, TFP.

2. A BRIGHT AND BRAINY WOMAN

9 *virgin forest*: Michael Bednar, "Nicholas Lewis House—Charlottesville, Virginia," University of Virginia, Feb. 2002, http://www.people.virginia.edu/~mjb6g/LewisHouse/nicolaslewishouse.htm.

9 *narrowly escaped*: Robert Brickhouse, "University Architects Restore Historic Gem," (Charlottesville, VA) *Daily Progress*, July 12, 1995.

9 *sneak home in civilian clothes*: Ian Zack, "Couple Buys 'The Farm' and a Window to the Past," *WP*, Sept. 23, 1995.

9 *Confederate spy, renowned*: See Horan, *Confederate Agent*.

10 *wave of Scotch-Irish Presbyterians*: Klotter, *Breckinridges of Kentucky*, 6.

10 *Mary Hopkins Cabell*: Ibid., 11.

10 *six-hundred-acre farm near Lexington* and *thirty thousand acres*: Ibid., 3.

10 *"greater prestige for unborn generations"*: Ibid.

10 *"serve[d] the commonwealth"*: Ibid., 17.

10 *Kentucky Resolutions of 1789*: Ibid., 20.

11 *"They were governors and senators"*: Charles Davenport, quoted in Abbott, "Sophonisba Preston Breckinridge," *Social Service Review*, 417.

11 *"Breckinridges of Kentucky"*: *Lexington Herald*, March 1, 1914, quoted in Klotter, *Breckinridges of Kentucky*, ix.

11 *"a reminder of past glories"*: Klotter, *Breckinridges of Kentucky*, 11.

11 *Ann Sophonisba Preston*: Ibid., 43.

11 *"Prestons and Breckinridges have intermarried"*: Chalkley, *Magic Casements*, 49.

11 *graduating from Centre College*: Klotter, *Breckinridges of Kentucky*, 140–41.

11 *seventeen-year-old Issa Desha*: Ibid., 141.

12 *"I think to lose Kentucky"*: Lincoln, *Collected Works*, 532.

12 *"a bloody repulse"*: Klotter, *Breckinridges of Kentucky*, 141.

12 *"a loving, kind, indulgent father"*: Ibid., 139.

12 *John Cabell Breckinridge*: Ibid., 117–19.

12 *"I shall never forget your kindness"*: Ibid., 142.

12 *"Morgan on the loose"*: Foraker, *I Would Live It Again*, 18.

13 *"the war was over"*: Walmsley, "The Last Meeting of the Confederate Cabinet," 341.

13 Lexington Observer and Reporter *as editor*: Klotter, *Breckinridges of Kentucky*, 146.

13 *"all the elements"*: Ibid., 150.

14 *House Ways and Means Committee*: Ibid., 156.

14 *"thick growth of silver-gray hair"*: Ibid., 154.

14 *"the most gifted and attractive orator"*: Ibid., 153.

14 *"vacillated between the law and theology"*: Ibid., 141.

14 *Evangelical Alliance of the United States*: "Meeting of the Evangelical Alliance," *WP*, Sept. 26, 1887.

14 *Eastern Presbyterian Church*: "Calvinistic Philosophy," *WP*, Feb. 2, 1891.

14 *"the Bible, book by book"*: "The Bible Society," *WP*, May 3, 1886.

14 *"monogamic marriage"*: "The Pilgrim Fathers," *WP*, Aug. 2, 1889.

14 *"the foundation, the corner-stone"*: Klotter, *Breckinridges of Kentucky*, 160.

14 *"useless hand-shaking, promiscuous kissing"*: Ibid.

14 *"two days of oratory"*: Nevins, *Cleveland*, 391.

15 *"The money in the Treasury"*: "The Tariff Reform Issue," *NYT*, Jan. 28, 1888.

15 *"the galleries were filled"*: Nevins, *Cleveland*, 391.

15 *"The surplus continues to grow"*: The Tariff Speech of Hon. W.C.P. Breckinridge of Kentucky, in the House of Representatives, May 18, 1888, in *Comparison of Existing Tariff with Bills Submitted to Ways and Means Committee, House of Representatives, Fiftieth Congress First Session*. Washington, D.C.: Government Printing Office, 1888.

15 *"eternal quality that set them"*: Wiebe, *Search for Order*, 33.

16 *possible Speaker of the House*: "Breckinridge Holds Off," *WP*, Nov. 8, 1890.

16 *"Colonel Breckinridge is an idol"*: "Will Be a Battle of Legal Giants," *New York Herald*, March 20, 1894.

16 *"remarkably bright girl"*: "Was Known in Pittsburgh," *LCJ*, March 20, 1894.

16 *"A Bright and Brainy Woman"*: "A Bright and Brainy Woman," *WP*, June 24, 1893.

16 *"At last, the devil has got his own!"*: Ibid.

17 *"was as careful of me"*: Tucker, *TRMP*, 64.

17 *"There is an apparently well authenticated rumor"*: CCG, June 18, 1893.

18 *"I am sorry to have announced"*: Madeline Pollard to WCPB, June 23, 1893, as reported in "Miss Pollard Is a Wonder," *NYW*, March 17, 1894.

18 *"I cannot go to Charlottesville"*: WCPB to Madeline Pollard, June 27, 1893, as reported in "Miss Pollard Is a Wonder," *NYW*, March 17, 1894.

18 *"denied that there had ever been a possibility"*: "Fooled the Newspaper Man," *NYW*, March 18, 1894.

19 *"Written [Maj.] Moore"*: Cable from WCPB to Madeline Pollard, July 9, as reported in "Miss Pollard Is a Wonder," *NYW*, March 17, 1894.

19 *"Col. W.C.P. Breckinridge"*: *Lexington Gazette*, July 13, 1893, as reported in "Miss Pollard Is a Wonder," *NYW*, March 17, 1894.

19 *"said what was false"*: Madeline Pollard to WCPB, July 15, 1893, as reported in "Miss Pollard Is a Wonder," *NYW*, March 17, 1894.

19 *"engagement is announced"*: *LCJ*, July 16, 1893.

20 *"rather testily"*: "Fooled the Newspaper Man," *NYW*, March 18, 1894.

20 *"created a sensation in the capital"*: "A Congressman in Trouble," *NYT*, Aug. 13, 1893.

20 *"a great deal of gossip"*: "Tongues Wagged," *CE*, Aug. 13, 1893.

20 *"quiet in the extreme"*: "Col. Breckinridge Wedded," *LCJ*, July 19, 1893.

20 *"spent the past three months"*: Ibid.

21 *"clear-cut"*: *LCJ*, July 19, 1893.

21 *"ruined about eight months ago"*: "Unparalleled. Mrs. Henry Delaney, a Bride of an Hour," *KL*, April 6, 1893.

21 *"he had reason to believe"*: "Afraid of Miss Pollard," *WES*, Aug. 14, 1893.

22 *"He betrayed no sign"*: "Is It Blackmail?," *WES*, Aug. 14, 1893.

22 *"a married man of 47 years of age"*: "Is It Blackmail?," *NYW*, Aug. 13, 1894.

22 *"completed his seduction of her"*: *Celebrated Trial*, 10.

23 *"repair the injury"*: "Is It Blackmail?," *NYW*, Aug. 13, 1894.

23 *"Victorian Americans obsessively feared"*: Ireland, "The Libertine Must Die," 42, note 20.

23 *"The fallen woman"*: Bushnell, *The Women Condemned*, 10.

23 *"a complete riddle"*: Charles Stoll to JAT, Jan. 22, 1894, in Tucker, *TRMP*, 11.

23 *"any woman, whose reputation"*: Ibid., 13.

3. A BASTARD CATCH'D

24 *"a steady succession of trials"*: Demos, *Little Commonwealth*, 152.

24 *"seen upon the ground together"*: D'Emilio and Freedman, *Intimate Matters*, 21.

24 *"seven months" rule*: Stiles, *Bundling*, 80.

25 *"for committing carnall coppulation"*: Demos, *Little Commonwealth*, 158.

25 *"a fine of nine lashes"*: D'Emilio and Freedman, *Intimate Matters*, 22.

25 *men and women were punished*: Fischer, *Albion's Seed*, 89.

25 *"judged the 'reputed father'"*: Ulrich, *Midwife's Tale*, 149.

25 *"Massachusetts during the seventeenth century"*: Fischer, *Albion's Seed*, 89.

25 *"bundled"*: See Stiles, *Bundling*.

25 *"The lover steals"*: Ibid., 29.

26 *namzat bezé*: Ibid., 43.

26 *"If she blows out the light"*: Ibid., 42.

26 *"family is supposed to be"*: H. Ling Roth, *Natives of Sarawak and British North Borneu*, quoted in Stiles, *Bundling*, 44–45.

26 *"districts in New England"*: Aurand, *Little Known Facts About Bundling*, 5.

26 *"women of a shady reputation"*: Ibid., 24.

26 *"prevailed among the young"*: Stiles, *Bundling*, 7.

26 *"having sat up as long"*: Ibid., 71.

27 *"pursue his wooing"*: Ibid., 73.

27 *"frolicking" and "night walking"*: Godbeer, *Sexual Revolution*, 237–39.

27 *"very frequently get together"*: Ibid., 239.

27 *one-fifth of births in Somerset County*: Daniel Scott Smith, "The Long Cycle in American Illegitimacy," in *Bastardy and Its Comparative History*, 370.

27 *fewer than 10 percent and more than 20 percent*: Smith and Hindus, "Premarital Pregnancy," 561.

27 *"the only social condition"*: Wells, "Illegitimacy and Bridal Pregnancy," in *Bastardy and Its Comparative History*, 351.

28 *nearly two-thirds of cases*: Godbeer, *Sexual Revolution*, 23.

28 *prosecutions practically disappeared*: Wells, "Illegitimacy and Bridal Pregnancy," in *Bastardy and Its Comparative History*, 352.

28 *"fertility testing"*: Laslett, "Comparing Illegitimacy," in *Bastardy and Its Comparative History*, 8.

28 *"hand-fasting"*: James Browne, *A History of the Highlands, and the Highland Clans*, London, 1853, quoted in Stiles, *Bundling*, 18.

28 *"a high proportion"*: Laslett, "Comparing Illegitimacy," in *Bastardy and Its Comparative History*, 54.

28 *"to make its appearance"*: Stiles, *Bundling*, 30.

29 *the standard fine for fornication*: Demos, *Little Commonwealth*, 158.

29 *"There is no evidence"*: Ulrich, *Midwife's Tale*, 149.

29 *"such liberties in company-keeping"*: Marsden, *Jonathan Edwards*, 130.

30 *"Persons of Rank and figure"*: Adams, *Diary*, vol. 1, 196.

30 *one-third of all brides*: Smith and Hindus, "Premarital Pregnancy," 561.

30 *In one Massachusetts parish*: Stiles, *Bundling*, 80.

30 *Just under 40 percent*: Ulrich, *Midwife's Tale*, 155.

30 *"Was called . . . to go"*: Ibid., 156.

30 *"Sally declard [sic] that my son"*: Ibid., 147.

30 *percentage of truly illegitimate births*: Wells, "Illegitimacy and Bridal Pregnancy," in *Bastardy and Its Comparative History*, 353.

30 *"rise to profound and widespread anxiety"*: Godbeer, *Sexual Revolution*, 265.

31 *"disintegration of the traditional"*: Smith and Hindus, "Premarital Pregnancy," 558–59.

31 *"a favorite custom"*: Stiles, *Bundling*, 78–79.

31 *"virtuous domesticity"*: Godbeer, *Sexual Revolution*, 289.

31 *widespread reports of sexual assaults*: Ibid., 293.

32 *"A New Bundling Song"*: Stiles, *Bundling*, 83–89.

32 *"no girl had the courage"*: Ibid., 82.

32 *"The Forsaken Fair One"*: Godbeer, *Sexual Revolution*, 264.

32 *"ruined female"*: Ibid., 265.

32 *"By the late 1700s"*: Ibid., 266.

33 *"superstitious rite"*: Washington Irving, *A Knickerbocker's History of New York*, quoted in Stiles, *Bundling*, 52.

33 *"to have had a child before marriage"*: *Yankee* (Portland, ME), Aug. 13, 1828, quoted in Stiles, *Bundling*, 120–21.

33 *"an object of disgust and loathing"*: From the *Middlesex Washingtonian*, reprinted in the *Advocate for Moral Reform* 10 (1844).

33 *about 20 percent of brides*: Smith and Hindus, "Premarital Pregnancy," 561.

33 *innately less sexual desire*: See Cott, "Passionless-ness: An Interpretation of Victorian Sexual Ideology," 219–36.

33 *"the majority of women"*: William Acton, *Functions and Disorders of the Reproductive Organs*, quoted in Degler, "What Ought to Be and What Was," 1467.

34 *"priceless jewel"*: *Middlesex Washingtonian*, reprinted in the *Advocate for Moral Reform* 10 (1844).

34 *"who is not engaged"*: Deuteronomy 22:29.

34 *"goes with a man clandestinely"*: Stiles, *Bundling*, 35.

34 *seduction lawsuits could be filed*: Gonda, "Strumpets and Angels," 36.

34 *"in the eyes of this law"*: Dall, *Women's Rights*, 44.

35 *"engaging herself to another"*: Demos, *Little Commonwealth*, 157.

35 *"materially affected by the treachery"*: Grossberg, *Governing the Hearth*, 36.

35 *"the delicacy of the sex"*: Ibid., 38.

35 *"woman who falls from virtue"*: Ibid., 41–42.

36 *"It is enough to say"*: Ibid., 42.

36 *"without sexual fault"*: "Is It Blackmail?," *NYW*, Aug. 13, 1894.

4. THE LEFT-HAND ROAD

37 *"A Sensational Suit"*: "A Sensational Suit," *WES*, Aug. 12, 1893.

37 *"A Congressman in Trouble"*: "A Congressman in Trouble," *NYT*, Aug. 13, 1893.

37 *"Was Wicked of Him"*: "Was Wicked of Him: Breckinridge of Kentucky Sued for Breach of Promise," *San Francisco Morning Call*, Aug. 13, 1893.

37 *"The Breckinridge-Pollard case was discussed"*: "Rhodes Was Not Breckinridge," *CDT*, Aug. 14, 1893.

37 *"Nothing in recent years"*: "Romance with Bitter Realities," *CE*, Aug. 13, 1893.

37 *two dozen a day*: Williams, *Years of Decision*, 76.

37 *six hundred banks and fifteen thousand businesses*: Ibid., 77.

37 *The great railroads*: Ibid., 76–77.

38 *15 percent*: Ibid., 77.

38 *"famine is in our midst"*: Ibid., 77.

38 *"Men died like flies"*: Adams, *The Education of Henry Adams*, 265.

38 *"suspended, for several months"*: Ibid., 264.

38 *"was the worst month"*: Williams, *Years of Decision*, 76.

38 *"Mills, factories, furnaces"*: Ibid., 76–77.

38 *"the symbol of the country's ingenuity"*: Ibid., 77.

38 *"reshaped ideas, altered attitudes"*: Ibid.

38 *"the financial situation which had engrossed"*: "Is It Blackmail?," *WES*, Aug. 14, 1893.

38 *"These charges are the result of vindictiveness"*: "Is It Blackmail?," *WES*, Aug. 14, 1893.

39 *"Miss Pollard is not the woman"*: "Much Excitement Here," *LCJ*, Aug. 13, 1893.

39 *"indirectly"*: Ibid.

39 *"prominent gentleman"*: "Romance with Bitter Realities," *CE*, Aug. 14, 1893.

40 *"well educated, a constant student"*: "Miss Pollard's Story of Col. Breckinridge," *NYW*, Sept. 17, 1893.

40 *popular New York weeklies*: (Frankfort, KY) *Daily Commonwealth*, Sept. 12, 1861.

40 *appointed as a local police judge*: Journal of the Senate of the Commonwealth of Kentucky, 1863; Civil Appointments by Governor Thomas E. Bramlette, 1863–1867, Kentucky Department for Libraries and Archives, Frankfort, KY.

40 *"full of books"*: "Miss Pollard's Story of Col. Breckinridge," *NYW*, Sept. 17, 1893.

40 *resigned his position*: J.D. Pollard to Gov. Thos. E. Bramlette, May 27, 1865, Kentucky Department for Libraries and Archives, Frankfort, KY.

41 *"always held some public office"*: "Miss Pollard's Story of Col. Breckinridge," *NYW*, Sept. 17, 1893.

41 *"If you are absolutely determined"*: Quoted in Allen, *The Law as a Vocation*, 25.

41 *"refined influence"*: "Miss Pollard's Story of Col. Breckinridge," *NYW*, Sept. 17, 1893.

41 *earnest and active member*: Journal of the Proceedings of the Right North Grand

Lodge of the United States of the I.O.O.D., 1821–1878, Baltimore, MD: James Ridgeley Publisher, 1879, 7044.

42 *"took cold"*: Ibid.

42 *"that the King of Terrors"*: Ibid.

42 *"almost on the verge of starvation"*: Effie E. Knight to WCPB, Nov. 25, 1893, BFP.

42 *she asked her mother*: "Madeline's Story," *WES*, March 16, 1894.

43 *"advantages of a Northern education"*: "A Romantic Story Has Little 'Madge,'" *CCG*, Aug. 15, 1893.

43 *"seminaries"*: See Jabour, *Scarlett's Sisters*, 54.

43 *"charmed with my young, widowed auntie"*: "A Romantic Story Has Little 'Madge,'" *CCG*, Aug. 15, 1893.

44 *"jealously guards every penny"*: Ibid.

44 *"old, gray-faced rough-looking customer"*: Ibid.

44 *read her letters*: "Miss Pollard's Story of Col. Breckinridge," *NYW*, Sept. 17, 1893.

44 *"the liberal education of women"*: Shotwell, *A History of the Schools*, 494.

45 *five hundred students*: Ibid., 495.

45 *"I never saw a person who studied"*: "Miss Pollard's Suit," *LCJ*, Aug. 16, 1893.

45 *"before a large and brilliant audience"*: "Romance with Bitter Realities," *CE*, Aug. 14, 1893.

45 *"poor, ambitious, delicate girl"*: "A Romantic Story Has Little 'Madge,'" *CCG*, Aug. 15, 1893.

45 *"nervous temperament"*: "Will She Kill Him?," *LMT*, March 15, 1894.

46 *"always looking downward"*: *Celebrated Trial*, 2.

46 *"She had never lived in a city"*: "Sister Cecilia Resumes and Finishes Her Testimony," *LMT*, March 15, 1894.

46 *"always seemed anxious to raise"*: "Will She Kill Him?," *LMT*, March 15, 1894.

46 *"When I think of the debt of gratitude"*: "Romance with Bitter Realities," *CE*, Aug. 14, 1893.

46 *"Your face is very familiar"*: "Miss Pollard's Story of Col. Breckinridge," *NYW*, Sept. 17, 1893.

47 *"man of his standing should come to her"*: "Sister Cecilia Resumes and Finishes Her Testimony," *LMT*, March 15, 1894.

47 *"compel"*: "Miss Pollard's Story of Col. Breckinridge," *NYW*, Sept. 17, 1893.

48 *Her face flushed*: "Miss Pollard Corroborated," *CCG*, Aug. 15, 1893.

48 *"higher proof"*: "His Story in Detail," *WP*, March 31, 1894.

48 *"I do not want to be like Aunt Lou"*: "Breckinridge Testifies," *NYW*, March 30, 1894.

48 *"get up some kind of relationship"*: "Madeline's Story," *WES*, March 16, 1894.

48 *"he was a relative"*: "Miss Pollard's Suit," *LCJ*, Aug. 16, 1893.

49 *"protested about a student"*: "Gossip's Tongue," *KL*, Aug. 17, 1893.

49 *"Are we going in a closed carriage"*: "Madeline's Story," *WES*, March 16, 1894.

49 *"being an ignorant Kentucky country woman"*: "Mr. Breckinridge Testifies," *NYT*, March 30, 1894.

49 *"such an act on his part"*: "Miss Pollard's Story of Col. Breckinridge," *NYW*, Sept. 17, 1893.

49 *"further liberties"*: "Miss Pollard's Story of Col. Breckinridge," *NYW*, Sept. 17, 1893.

49 *"wrenched"*: "More About Her Life," *WP*, March 20, 1894.

50 *"conduct had not been improper"*: "Miss Pollard's Story of Col. Breckinridge," *NYW*, Sept. 17, 1893.

50 *"nervous and excited"*: "Miss Pollard's Story of Col. Breckinridge," *NYW*, Sept. 17, 1893.

50 *"uncouth farmer"*: "Her Autobiography," *LCJ*, Aug. 15, 1893.

50 *"a penchant for rich and gay old men"*: "Miss Pollard," *CE*, Aug. 13, 1893.

50 *"lady clerk in the Treasury Department"*: "Breach of Promise," *NYT*, Feb. 9, 1877.

50 *"improper meeting"*: "The Oliver-Cameron Suit: Candid Avowals by the Widow," *NYT*, March 20, 1879.

50 *"say whether or not he had made the promise"*: "The Oliver-Cameron Suit: Closing Events of the Long Trial," *NYT*, April 1, 1879.

51 *"disgustingly and without shame"*: "The Oliver-Cameron Suit: Candid Avowals by the Widow," *NYT*, March 20, 1879.

51 *"Mrs. Oliver was easily shown"*: "Breach of Promise Cases," *NYT*, April 3, 1879.

51 *"Gentlemen of the jury"*: "Mr. Cameron Vindicated," *NYT*, April 2, 1879.

5. THE WANTON WIDOW

52 *Halpin was a young widow*: The 1868 Jersey City, New Jersey, City Directory lists Maria as the widow of Frederick Halpin. *U.S. City Directories, 1822–1995* (database online). Ancestry.com.

52 *Her husband, Frederick*: Frederick Thomas Halpin was the son of Frederick William Halpin, who emigrated from England and became a naturalized citizen in 1858. According to Maria's father, Robert Hovenden, her husband, Frederick, died of "consumption." Frederick T. Halpin died on July 27, 1865, and was buried in Cypress Hills Cemetery in Brooklyn. Frederick William Halpin, Petition for Naturalization, June 23, 1858, *New York, Index to Petitions for Naturalization filed in New York City, 1792–1989* (database online). Ancestry.com. "Poor Old Hovenden," *CDT*, Aug. 18, 1884. Frederick Thomas Halpin, *U.S. Find a Grave Index, 1600s–Current* (database online). Ancestry.com.

52 *Her son, Frederick, was six*: Frederick T. Halpin was born Aug. 27, 1862. *Pennsylvania Death Certificates, 1906–1964* (database online). Ancestry.com.

52 *her daughter, Ada, was four*: Ada Elise Halpin was born Oct. 6, 1864. *New Jersey Episcopal Diocese of Newark Church Records, 1809–1816, 1825–1970* (database online). Ancestry.com.

52 *twenty-five thousand in Boston alone*: "Report on the Condition of Women and Child Wage-Earners," vol. 9, 16.

52 *"a mere pittance"*: Penny, *The Employments of Women*, vi.

52 *"about $2 a week"*: "Report on the Condition of Women and Child Wage-Earners," vol. 9, 23.

52 *The majority of the 533 jobs for women*: See Penny, *The Employments of Women*.

53 *the overwhelming majority of women*: Women's employment as household servants peaked in 1870, when 58 percent of working women were employed as servants. "Report on the Condition of Women and Child Wage-Earners," vol. 9, 18.

53 *"going into service"*: Alcott, "How I Went Out to Service," in *Louisa May Alcott*, 806–19.

53 *fifty cents more*: Kessler-Harris, *Out to Work*, 57.

53 *six months or so*: "120 Years of American Education: A Statistical Portrait," Fig. 8: Average number of days per year attended by public school students: 1869–70 to 1980–81, 28.

53 *drove down wages and working conditions*: Kessler-Harris, *Out to Work*, 46.

53 *"vests at 18 cents apiece"*: Quoted in "Report on the Condition of Women and Child Wage-Earners," vol. 9, 148.

54 *experience working as a seamstress*: The 1860 census lists Maria, along with her mother and sisters, as a "dressmaker." *1860 U.S. Federal Census* (database online). Ancestry.com.

54 *lived near her in-laws*: The 1868 Jersey City Directory lists Maria as living at 62 Montgomery and Frederick and Elizabeth Halpin as living at 48 Montgomery. *U.S. City Directories, 1822–1995* (database online). Ancestry.com.

54 *the first department store*: Christopher Gray, "The A.T. Stewart Department Store; A City Plan to Revitalize the 1846 'Marble Palace,'" *NYT*, March 20, 1994.

54 *"tasteful frescoes"*: Haven, "A Morning at Stewart's," 431.

54 *nine hundred other seamstresses*: Resseguie, "Alexander Turney Stewart and the Development of the Department Store," 301.

54 *"flock of women and girls"*: Haven, "A Morning at Stewart's," 432.

54 *"responsible position"*: "The Cleveland Scandal," *CDT*, July 30, 1884.

54 *"careful matrons"*: Haven, "A Morning at Stewart's," 432.

54 *"lowest market rate"*: "Alexander Turney Stewart," *Frank Leslie's Popular Monthly*, 647.

54 *one-third to one-half*: Kessler-Harris, *Out to Work*, 59.

54 *possibly with some of her late husband's family*: Maria's father, Robert, who apparently didn't have much contact with her after she married, seemed to think she had gone to Buffalo with Frederick and Elizabeth Halpin, who was a milliner, to work in a millinery establishment, but there is no record of the Halpins ever leaving Jersey City, so it may have been other Halpin kin. "Poor Old Hovenden," *CDT*, Aug. 18, 1884.

54 *leaving Ada with her in-laws*: In the 1870 census, Ada is living with her paternal grandparents, Frederick and Elizabeth Halpin, in Jersey City. *1870 U.S. Federal Census* (database online). Ancestry.com.

54 *making mourning collars*: Maria appears in the Buffalo City Directory for the first time in 1871, listed as a widow and "mourning collar manf.," *U.S. City Directories, 1822–1995* (database online). Ancestry.com.

54 *promoted to sales clerk*: The 1872 *Buffalo City Directory* lists Maria as a "clerk." *U.S. City Directories, 1822–1995* (database online). Ancestry.com.

54 *320 or so sales clerks at Stewart's*: Resseguie, "Alexander Turney Stewart and the Development of the Department Store," 301.

55 *"inferior class position"*: Benson, *Counter Culture*, 24.

55 *"the confidence and esteem"*: "Politics for All; Maria Halpin's Pitiful Story of Her Acquaintance with Grover Cleveland," *CDT*, Oct. 30, 1884.

55 *"ladylike, intelligent and fine appearing"*: "The Cleveland Scandal," *CDT*, July 30, 1884.

55 *"unusual intelligence, modesty, neatness and business tact"*: "Is It Gov. Cleveland's Boy?" *CDT*, July 22, 1894.

55 *"no longer owed her sexuality"*: Wood, *Freedom of the Streets*, 16.

55 *"You have to dress well"*: Kessler-Harris, *Out to Work*, 104.

55 *"remarkable sweetness of manner"*: "Is It Gov. Cleveland's Boy?" *CDT*, July 22, 1884.

56 *"persistently sought"*: "What Widow Halpin Says," *CDT*, Aug. 16, 1884.

56 *"honorable"*: "Politics for All," *CDT*, Oct. 30, 1884.

56 *in her early thirties*: Various census records give different birth years for Maria, which wasn't unusual at a time with no birth certificates, but the most accurate appears to be the 1865 New York State Census, which lists her birth as "about 1842," which comports with her father's recollection that she was "but 19 years old" when she was married. If earlier censuses are correct, she may have been in her mid-thirties at the time. New York State Census, 1865 (database online). Ancestry.com. "Poor Old Hovenden," *CDT*, Aug. 18, 1884.

56 *"very marked attention"*: "Politics for All," *CDT*, Oct. 30, 1884.

56 *"to go with him to dinner"*: "The Strife of Parties; Maria Halpin Relates the Story of Her Ruin by Grover Cleveland," *CDT*, Oct. 31, 1884.

56 *"by the use of force and violence and without my consent"*: Ibid.

56 *"accomplished my ruin"*: Ibid.

56 *"sensible, domestic American wife"*: Grover Cleveland to Mary Cleveland Hoyt, March 21, 1866, Nevins, *Letters*, 103–4.

56 *"told him that I never wanted to see him again"*: "The Strife of Parties," *CDT*, Oct. 31, 1884.

56 *"What the devil are you blubbering about?"*: Ibid.

57 *"made it virtually impossible for a mature, healthy woman"*: Bock, "An Accusation Easily to Be Made," 112.

57 *"utmost resistance"*: Ibid., 105.

57 *"consummation meant consent"*: Ibid., 119.

57 *"there was a general assumption"*: Ibid., 20.

57 *"notwithstanding the defendant treated the girl"*: Ibid., 88–89.

57 *"without an excitation of lust"*: Farr, *Elements of Medical Jurisprudence*, 42–43.

58 *"ordinarily it is impossible"*: Storer, "The Law of Rape," 55.

58 *"was willing to socialize alone"*: Lindemann, "To Ravish and Carnally Know," 68.

58 *"promised that he would marry me"*: "The Strife of Parties," *CDT*, Oct. 31, 1884.

58 *"irritated, rude and rebellious"*: Merrill, *Bourbon Leader*, 9.

58 *"man's man"*: Nevins, *Cleveland*, 71–72.

58 *"the circumstances of her intimacy"*: "Maria Halpin; A Buffalo Clergyman Speaks His Mind," *Boston Globe*, Oct. 31, 1884.

58 *"was excusable and understandable"*: Grossberg, *Governing the Hearth*, 48.

58 *"the act of a male person"*: Humble, "Seduction as a Crime," 144–45.

59 *"to compel an unmarried man"*: Ibid., 151.

59 *"He must marry you"*: "Maria Halpin," *Boston Globe*, Oct. 31, 1884.

59 *"would be impossible"*: Ibid.

59 *"of good repute"*: Humble, "Seduction as a Crime," 146.

59 *"agree to provide for the child"*: "Maria Halpin," *Boston Globe*, Oct. 31, 1884.

59 *"friend, employé and father confessor"*: "Is It Gov. Cleveland's Boy?," *CDT*, July 22, 1884.

59 *"would pay me . . . and told me several times"*: "Maria Halpin's Terrible Experience Related by Her Child's Nurse," *CDT*, Oct. 1, 1884.

60 *"I begged Cleveland"*: "What Widow Halpin Says," *CDT*, Aug. 16, 1884.

60 *"very much depressed and broken down"*: "The Cleveland Scandal," *CDT*, July 30, 1884.

60 *"They came to me in a hurry one day"*: "Maria Halpin's Terrible Experience," *CDT*, Oct. 1, 1884.

60 *"overjoyed"*: Ibid.

60 *"apprehensive that she might attempt some injury"*: "The Cleveland Scandal," *CDT*, July 30, 1884.

60 *"in which he demanded that she give the baby up"*: "Is It Gov. Cleveland's Boy?," *CDT*, July 22, 1884.

60 *"appealed to the Chief of Police"*: "The Cleveland Scandal," *CDT*, July 30, 1884.

60 *"could do nothing with her"*: "A Terrible Tale," *Evening Telegraph*, July 21, 1884.

61 *pay for his care and establish her in a dressmaking business*: Nevins, *Cleveland*, 165.

61 *on April 28 she spirited him from the orphanage*: According to the records of the Buffalo Orphan Asylum, Oscar was "stolen" by Maria. "The Charges Swept Away," *NYT*, Aug. 12, 1884.

61 *"old crony"*: Lynch, *Grover Cleveland*, 70.

61 *"the assistance of Mr. Baker"*: "Is It Gov. Cleveland's Boy?," *CDT*, July 22, 1884.

61 *"It was a hell of a time"*: "A Terrible Tale," *Evening Telegraph*, July 21, 1884.

61 *"was drunk at the time"*: "Is It Gov. Cleveland's Boy?," *CDT*, July 22, 1884.

61 *"without warrant or form of law"*: "A Terrible Tale," *Evening Telegraph*, July 21, 1884.

61 *"boozy"*: "The Cleveland Scandal," *CDT*, July 30, 1884.

61 *"abduction and false imprisonment"*: Ibid.

61 *"had plotted the abduction"*: "A Terrible Tale," *Evening Telegraph*, July 21, 1884.

61 *"anxious to avoid public scandal"*: Ibid.

62 *"fair lawyer in the host of average lawyers"*: "Is It Gov. Cleveland's Boy?," *CDT*, July 22, 1884.

62 *"remarkably unreceptive to new ideas"*: Merrill, *Bourbon Leader*, 25.

62 *"frustrated, uneasy retreat into conservatism"*: Ibid., 29.

63 *"much-despised Jay Gould"*: Ibid., 27.

63 *"class legislation"*: Ibid., 31.

63 *"refreshing moral correctness"*: Ibid., 35.

63 *"We do not believe that the American people"*: *New York Evening Post*, quoted in "A Clean Candidate," *CDT*, Aug. 5, 1884.

64 *"The issue of the campaign"*: "Character and Candidates," *CDT*, Aug. 4, 1884.

64 *"serious stampede"*: "The Presidential Race," *CDT*, Aug. 7, 1884.

64 *"tell the truth"*: Nevins, *Cleveland*, 163.

64 *"I don't think there is an intelligent man"*: "A Methodist Minister on Cleveland," *CDT*, Aug. 13, 1884.

64 *"formed an irregular connection with a widow"*: "An Amazing Confession," *New York Evening Post*, Aug. 5, 1884.

64 *"Is he fool enough to suppose"*: Nevins, *Cleveland*, 168.

65 *let political associates do his dirty work*: Merrill, *Bourbon Leader*, 17.

65 *"a little bit of detective work"*: "Cleveland's Vindication," *NYW*, Aug. 8, 1884.

65 *"call[ing] on some of Gov. Cleveland's friends"*: "Beecher; He Flops to Back Cleveland," *CDT*, Aug. 7, 1884.

65 *He blamed the Reverend George Ball*: "Beecher Means Business," *Boston Globe*, Aug. 7, 1884.

65 *"The facts seem to be that many years ago"*: "Cleveland's Vindication," *NYW*, Aug. 8, 1884.

66 *"made a habit of visiting every man"*: Ibid.

66 *"much esteemed"*: "A Terrible Tale," *Evening Telegraph*, July 21, 1884.

66 *"dead and the child is his perfect image"*: "Cleveland's Vindication," *NYW*, Aug. 8, 1884.

66 *"It is perhaps worthy of note"*: "The Defense," *CDT*, Aug. 13, 1884.

66 *"vile wretch"*: "Politics for All," *CDT*, Oct. 30, 1884.

67 *"vile slander"*: "Beecher Means Business," *Boston Globe*, Aug. 7, 1884.

67 *"committed an error"*: "Beecher Supports Cleveland," *NYT*, Aug. 7, 1884.

67 *"primary offense"*: "The Charges Swept Away," *NYT*, Aug. 12, 1884.

67 *"plump, pretty and decidedly attractive"*: "Cleveland; History of Wicked Maria Halpin," *New York Mercury*, reprinted in *CDT*, Aug. 13, 1884.

67 *"and to say otherwise is infamous"*: "What Widow Halpin Says," *CDT*, Aug. 16, 1884.

67 *"quiet, decorous, unobtrusive housekeeper"*: "Widow Halpin's Narrative," *CDT*, Aug. 16, 1884.

67 *under cover of night*: "The Cleveland Scandal," *CDT*, Aug. 13, 1884.

68 *"urging [him] to make a statement"*: "Cleveland's Shame," *CDT*, Sept. 30, 1884.

68 *"said she would die"*: "Cleveland's Shame," *CDT*, Sept. 30, 1884.

68 *"uniform kindness and courtesy"*: "Politics for All," *CDT*, Oct. 30, 1884.

68 *"the scandal business is about wound up"*: Nevins, *Cleveland*, 168–69.

68 *"vast audience"*: "Beecher's Great Speech," *CE*, Oct. 25, 1884.

69 *"gladly remain silent"*: "Politics for All," *CDT*, Oct. 30, 1884.

69 *"circumstances under which my ruin was accomplished"*: Ibid.

69 *"accomplished my ruin by the use of force and violence"*: "The Strife of Parties," *CDT*, Oct. 31, 1884.

69 *"good, plain, honest-hearted man"*: "Contraction of the Maria Halpin Story," *NYW*, Nov. 2, 1884.

69 *"Me make a statement"*: "What Widow Halpin Says," *CDT*, Aug. 16, 1884.

70 *"blowing hitherto undecided Catholic voters"*: Merrill, *Bourbon Leader*, 67.

70 *by 1,149 votes*: Ibid., 67–69.

70 *"I'm only waiting for my wife to grow up"*: Nevins, *Cleveland*, 72.

70 *"tall, pretty and pleasing in manner"*: Ibid., 164–65.

71 *"King's intrusion made me trouble"*: Ibid., 168–69.

71 *"did not question [Maria's] charge"*: Ibid., 165.

71 *"woman scrape"*: Ibid., 167.

71 *"If a scapegoat was to be chosen"*: Lynch, *Grover Cleveland*, 72.

71 *"preliminary offense"*: "The Charges Swept Away," *NYT*, Aug. 12, 1884.

71 *the book review editor of the* Independent: "Dr. Kinsley Twining," *Independent*, 2727.

71 *"transient weakness"*: Nevins, *Cleveland*, 164–65.

71 *was popularized in the 1894 novel*: McHatton, "The Honorable Peter Stirling," 247.

72 *"spare the feelings of his partner's daughter"*: Lynch, *Grover Cleveland*, 72.

72 *Oscar Folsom was alive and well*: Folsom died on July 23, 1875.

72 *only ten at the time*: Frances Folsom Cleveland was born July 21, 1865.

72 *"Half a dozen of us floated down the river"*: Andrew, "Sea and River Fishing," 411.

73 *"leading the chubby little girl"*: Nevins, *Cleveland*, 76.

6. NOT SO EASILY HANDLED

74 *"Col. Breckinridge's friends say"*: "Both Kept Out of View," *WP*, Aug. 14, 1893.

74 *"a liberal allowance"*: Charles Stoll to JAT, Jan. 22, 1884, in Tucker, *TRMP*, 11.

74 *"many warm, devoted friends"*: Ibid., 14.

74 *"No members of the legal fraternity"*: "For Breach of Promise," *WP*, Aug. 13, 1893.

75 *Mary Oliver had tried to hire*: "The Oliver-Cameron Suit: Candid Avowals by the Widow," *NYT*, March 20, 1879.

75 *"men of their reputation"*: "A Philadelphia View," *Philadelphia Press*, Aug. 13, 1893.

75 *"corroborated by a number of students"*: "Miss Pollard Corroborated," *CCG*, Aug. 15, 1893.

75 *"stylish ecru-colored"*: "Miss Pollard Talks," *WES*, Aug. 16, 1893.

75 *"My position is public enough"*: Ibid.

76 *"Anyone can see from the character"*: Ibid.

76 *"not exactly a beautiful girl"*: Ibid.

76 *"bastions of old tradition and culture"*: Richardson, "What on Earth Was a 'Bourbon Democrat'?"

77 *"interfere, beyond the very minimum"*: Merrill, *Bourbon Leader*, 25.

77 *"cheap resources, business opportunities"*: Woodward, *Origins of the New South*, 6.

77 *"They might look like Southern colonels"*: Edward F. Prichard, quoted in Woodward, *Origins of the New South*, 6.

77 *"a helpless, inept air"*: Williams, *Years of Decision*, 19.

77 *"disappearing quorum"*: Ibid., 20.

77 *"I deny the power of the Speaker"*: Ibid., 23.

77 *slate of landmark bills*: Ibid., 40–41.

78 *"force bill"*: Ibid., 31.

78 *"paid peddlers to sell household goods"*: Ibid., 44.

78 *"we are coming back"*: Ibid., 16–17.

78 *"close friend of President Cleveland"*: "Congressman Sued by a Pretty Clerk," *CCG*, Aug. 13, 1893.

78 *"shared common traits"*: Klotter, *Breckinridges of Kentucky*, 156.

79 *"I do not believe that the power"*: Grover Cleveland to U.S. House of Representatives, Feb. 16, 1887.

79 *"system [that] must be wrong"*: "The Tariff Reform Issue," *NYT*, Jan. 28, 1888.

79 *"looks very much as if Congressman Breckinridge"*: Undated clip, WCPB papers, 1892 folder, BFP.

80 *"running very smoothly"*: *KL*, March 30, 1893.

80 *"There is one distinguished member"*: Quoted in "The Philadelphia Times Rather Sides with the Plaintiff," *KL*, Aug. 17, 1893.

81 *"undiminished confidence"* and *"spotless honor"*: Daniel Bedinger to WCPB, Aug. 13, 1893, BFP.

81 *"would not be further annoyed"*: Campbell Carrington to WCPB, Aug. 15, 1893, BFP.

81 *"told her of his engagement"*: "Outraged Feels Mrs. Blackburn," *CE*, Sept. 2, 1893.

81 *died in infancy*: Baird, *Luke Prior Blackburn*, 19.

81 *knew Madeline's aunt Mary Stout*: WCPB to W. J. Lewis, Feb. 1, 1894, BFP.

82 *put out a call for volunteers*: Baird, *Luke Prior Blackburn*, 48.

82 *"He sat with his hand on the key"*: "Miss Pollard's Story of Col. Breckinridge," *NYW*, Sept. 17, 1893.

82 *circumstantially damning*: Baird, *Luke Prior Blackburn*, 22–31.

82 *"Hero of Hickman"*: Ibid., 49–50.

82 *told Julia about the Sunday school*: WCPB to W. J. Lewis, Feb. 1, 1894, BFP.

82 *Julia was well known*: "In- and out-of-state newspapers lauded the first lady's activities," says Baird, in *Luke Prior Blackburn*, 97.

82 *"Black Hole of Calcutta"*: Ibid., 78.

83 *"keen, penetrating eyes"*: Foraker, *I Would Live It Again*, 70.

83 *"Mrs. Zane received in a gown"*: "Society's Endless Rounds," *WP*, Jan. 28, 1893.

83 *"those utterances of Mrs. Blackburn"*: Shelby to WCPB, Sept. 3, 1893, BFP.

84 *"a scandalous report"*: William S. McChesney to WCPB, Aug. 17, 1888, BFP.

84 *"not true in many essential particulars"*: Joseph S. Blackburn to James F. Robinson, Aug. 21, 1888, BFP.

84 *"had not treated her well"*: James B. Beck to James F. Robinson, Aug. 24, 1888, BFP.

84 *"It seems that the publication"*: William McChesney to WCPB, Sept. 5, 1893, BFP.

84 *"on the best of authority"*: "Will Come Home," *KL*, Sept. 14, 1893.

84 *which Shelby had seen*: "I have seen the letter of Mrs. Blackburn to Duke," Shelby wrote to Breckinridge. John Shelby to WCPB, Sept. 3, 1893, BFP.

85 *"utterly depraved"*: "Will Come Home," *KL*, Sept. 14, 1893.

85 *"vigorously deny that he is the father"*: "Col. Breckinridge's Defense," *LCJ*, Sept. 13, 1893.

85 *"has touched womankind"*: "Gossip's Tongue," *KL*, Aug. 17, 1893.

85 *"thousands of dead newborns"*: Gordon, "Law and Everyday Death," in *Lives in the Law*, 63.

85 *"horrible crime of infanticide"*: "Apologies for Infanticide," *NYT*, Dec. 1, 1868.

85 *young servant named Hester Vaughn*: Gordon, "Law and Everyday Death," in *Lives in the Law*, 56–57.

85 *"laws of infanticide"*: Quoted in Anthony, "Social Purity," in *"The Life and Work of Susan B. Anthony*," 1005.

85 *"seduced deserted unfortunates"*: Ibid.

85 *looking for a scoop*: William McChesney to WCPB, Sept. 5, 1893.

85 *"chief effort of the defense"*: "Col. Breckinridge's Defense," *NYW*, Sept. 14, 1893.

86 *"glided to and fro"*: "Miss Pollard's Story of Col. Breckinridge," *NYW*, Sept. 17, 1893.

86 *"in the weary interval"*: Ibid.

86 *"very much wanted to study"*: Ibid.

87 *"claimed to be engaged in literary work"*: Ibid.

87 *"Mr. Breckinridge knew each day"*: Ibid.

87 *"he had succeeded in fascinating me"*: Ibid.

88 *"stating that the school was as good"*: Ibid.

88 *"as a result of this course"*: Ibid.

89 *"begged in every way"*: Ibid.

89 *"by his invitation"*: Ibid.
90 *"I have been told many things"*: "A Romantic Story Has Little 'Madge,'" *CCG*, Aug. 15, 1894.
90 *"My purpose in entering"*: "Revenge Not Her Motive," *WP*, Oct. 2, 1893.
90 *"Revenge!"*: Ibid.

7. WHAT SHALL WE DO WITH OUR DAUGHTERS?

91 *"relics and historic treasures"*: Shaw, *World's Fair Notes*, 21.
91 *"Old Cairo"*: Ibid., 58.
91 *"260 feet above terra-firma"*: Ibid., 59.
91 *"caged lightning"*: Ibid., 44–45.
92 *some twenty-seven million people attended*: Ibid., 6.
92 *"I am very glad I did go"*: JAT to Richard Tucker, Nov. 8, 1893, TFP.
92 *"It has been hard to get along"*: JAT to Mary Tucker, Nov. 1, 1893, TFP.
92 *Her family made a fortune*: "Historical/Biographical Note," TFP.
92 *"I used to climb"*: JAT autobiography, TFP.
93 *"Quaker jail"*: JAT to Patty Tucker, Nov. 2, 1879, TFP.
93 *"high-maintenance, high cost"*: "Historical/Biographical Note," TFP.
93 *"I am very much anxious"*: JAT to Richard Tucker, Dec. 10, 1883, TFP.
93 *"The old folks have numerous fights"*: JAT to Maude Tucker, Feb. 3, 1884.
94 *for women the mean age of marriage was twenty-three*: See Table 1, "Nuptiality Measures for the White Population of the United States, 1850–1880," in Hacker et al., "The Effect of the Civil War on Southern Marriage Patterns."
94 *nearly a third*: Ibid.
94 *"Married life has lost"*: Quoted in Chudacoff, *The Age of the Bachelor*, 73–74.
94 *250,000 "surplus" women on the East Coast*: Quoted in Kessler-Harris, *Out to Work*, 98.
94 *"the popular belief"*: "The Domestic Millennium," *WP*, May 22, 1881.
94 *"if women do not marry"*: Quoted in "Bad Advocate of a Good Cause," *NYT*, July 23, 1882.
95 *"no longer a career"*: Kessler-Harris, *Out to Work*, 98.
95 *"Girls are being prepared daily"*: Quoted in Livermore, "What Shall We Do with Our Daughters?," 1883.
95 *"Who are the women whom the social scientists"*: Ibid.
96 *"Five years ago the typewriter"*: Quoted in Davies, *Woman's Place*, 37.
96 *"six women shorthand writers"*: "The First Woman Stenographer," *National Stenographer*, vol. 3, 1892.
96 *"In every large down-town building"*: *Catalogue of the Albany Business College*, Albany, NY, 1890.
96 *upward of five dollars an hour*: Davies, *Woman's Place*, 64.
96 *"I have no objection"*: Aron, *Ladies and Gentlemen*, 211, note 32.
97 *"the gentleman whose initials are I.B."*: Stern, *So Much in a Lifetime*, 140.
97 *"to accompany her to keep her"*: Willard, *A Woman of the Century*, vol. 2, 767.
97 *"Treasury courtesan" scandal*: Aron, *Ladies and Gentlemen*, 166.
97 *"all female clerks (innocent or guilty) now behaved"*: Ibid., 169.
98 *"rather quietly, on high-buttoned shoes"*: Davies, *Woman's Place*, 55.

98 *fewer than 5 percent*: Ibid., Appendix, Table 1.

98 *"office is an awfully hard place"*: JAT to Mary Tucker, n.d., TFP.

98 *"I suppose you have noticed"*: JAT to Mary Tucker, March 1892, TFP.

99 *"going all the time"*: JAT to Mary Tucker, June 1891, TFP.

99 *"I stood it as long as I could"*: JAT to Mary Tucker, Nov. 12, 1892, TFP.

99 *"I have at last 'found location'"*: JAT to Mary Tucker, Nov. 28, 1892, TFP.

100 *"The money market has been very high"*: JAT to Mary Tucker, March 31, 1893.

100 *"I do hope Patty will get through"*: JAT to Maude Tucker, Nov. 23, 1893, TFP.

100 *"I hardly know what I want to do"*: JAT to Mary Tucker, Jan. 4, 1894.

8. FOR THE LIKES OF ME

101 *"Mr. Breckinridge never"*: "Silver-Tongued Oratory," *WP*, Sept. 29, 1893.

101 *"growing opinion that the Congressman"*: *The Frankfort Roundabout*, Oct. 21, 1893; *The Frankfort Call*, Sept. 29, 1893.

101 *"I did not believe"*: WCPB to Desha Breckinridge, Dec. 18, 1893, BFP.

102 *"most important session"*: WCPB to J. H. Cunningham, Dec. 23, 1893, BFP.

102 *"Keep Bob locked up"*: NYT, Sept. 22, 1894.

102 *"no apparent aim in life"*: WCPB to SPB, Oct. 31, 1891, BFP.

102 *"sleep all morning"*: WCPB to SPB, Nov. 13, 1891, BFP.

102 *"notorious"*: WCPB to SPB, Nov. 19, 1891, BFP.

102 *"over the hand of a Blue Grass beauty"*: "At the Governor's Ball," *NYT*, Nov. 15, 1891.

102 *"more or less under the influence"*: WCPB to SPB, March 31, 1892, BFP.

102 *"We are making a mighty effort"*: WCPB to SPB, April 4, 1892, BFP.

102 *"This is the damnedest mess"*: WCPB to SPB, April 26, 1892, BFP.

103 *"Lock father up"*: NYT, Sept. 22, 1894.

103 *he jumped ship in Savannah*: Klotter, *Breckinridges of Kentucky*, 184.

103 *"Happiest Woman in Washington"*: Louise Wing Breckinridge to WCPB, March 2, 1893, BFP.

103 *"right serious attack"*: WCPB to Desha Breckinridge, Sept. 7, 1893, BFP.

103 *"She does not sleep well"*: WCPB to Desha Breckinridge, Jan. 23, 1894, BFP.

103 *"I am somewhat nervous"*: Ibid.

104 *"keeper of her husband's secrets"*: May Estelle Cook, "Notes and Comments," *Social Service Review*, 93.

104 *"liked all kinds of people"*: SPB Autobiography, SBP.

104 *"missed the point of every joke"*: SPB Autobiography, SBP.

104 *"peace baby"*: WCPB to SPB, March 30, 1886, BFP.

105 *childbearing patterns remained*: Lewis and Lockridge, "Sally Has Been Sick," 5.

105 *"There was no doctrine of birth control"*: SPB Autobiography, SBP.

105 *"My father was wonderfully skillful"*: Ibid.

105 *"I learnt my letters"*: Ibid.

106 *"coveted and forbidden joys"*: Chalkley, *Magic Casements*, 62.

106 *"Long before it was time for me"*: Ibid., 4.

106 *"a favorite playground"*: Ibid., 9.

107 *"She looks somewhat like"*: SPB Autobiography, SBP.

107 *"a sword in one hand"*: Chalkley, *Magic Casements*, 26.

107 *"ready reference bureau"*: Ibid., 22.

107 *young woman's neat progression*: Censer, *Reconstruction of White Southern Womanhood*, 32.

108 *widespread fear about a generation of spinsters*: Hacker et al., "The Effect of the Civil War on Southern Marriage Patterns," 39.

108 *"hang[ing] like a locket"*: Chalkley, *Magic Casements*, 14.

108 *"when a great number of planters"*: Breckinridge, "Mary Desha," 3.

108 *"If we cannot teach"*: Scott, *The Southern Lady*, 125.

108 *"it was humiliating for a lady"*: Chalkley, *Magic Casements*, 14.

108 *"We were very poor"*: SPB Autobiography, SBP.

108 *"dresses were like"*: Chalkley, *Magic Casements*, 63.

108 *"coming in swift succession"*: SPB Autobiography, SBP.

109 *"We will be coming back"*: Chalkley, *Magic Casements*, 13–14.

109 *"You ought to look squarely"*: WCPB to SPB, Oct. 22, 1884, BFP.

109 *"brain a fair chance"*: WCPB to SPB, March 30, 1885, BFP.

109 *"established for me or the likes of me"*: SPB Autobiography, SBP.

110 *"The system never does two things well"*: Clarke, *Sex in Education*, 55–56.

110 *"his college life was spent"*: SPB Autobiography, SBP.

110 *first two black students*: Perkins, "Racial Integration of the Seven Sisters Colleges," 104.

110 *one of the largest slave owners*: Klotter, *Breckinridges of Kentucky*, 24.

110 *"Purchase all the negroes"*: Ibid.

111 *"surely mistaken the price necessary"*: Quoted in Martin, *The Anti-Slavery Movement in Kentucky Prior to 1850*, 26.

111 *"by one experiment emancipate our slaves"*: Harrison, *The Anti-Slavery Movement in Kentucky*, 24.

111 *"Kentucky would have been made a free state"*: William Birney in *James G. Birney and His Times*, quoted in Martin, *The Anti-Slavery Movement in Kentucky Prior to 1850*, 32, note 69.

111 *"void, and of no force"*: Klotter, *Breckinridges of Kentucky*, 21.

111 *"where powers are assumed"*: Ibid.

111 *"would form a stepping-stone"*: Ibid., 22.

112 *"Domestic slavery cannot exist forever"*: Martin, *The Anti-Slavery Movement in Kentucky Prior to 1850*, 101, note 8.

112 *"to allow for the gradual prospective emancipation"*: Ibid., 101.

112 *"considerable money and supplies"*: Ibid., 59, note 45.

112 *"Platform of Emancipation"*: Ibid., 133.

112 *"a leading spokesman"*: Klotter, *Breckinridges of Kentucky*, 83.

113 *"unchristian"*: Ibid., 68.

113 *"aggressive, exclusive and intolerant"*: Breckinridge, *Papism in the XIX Century, in the United States*, 6.

113 *"most degraded and brutal white population"*: Ibid., 25.

113 *"take arms in their hands"*: Ibid., 163.

113 *three days of rioting*: Peter Kumpa, "The Case of the Crazy Nun," *Baltimore Sun*, Feb. 19, 1991.

113 *"had been for centuries"*: Brown, *The Presbyterians*, 84.

114 *"took her by the hand"*: Chalkley, *Magic Casements*, 12.

114 *"almost despised"*: Klotter, *Breckinridges of Kentucky*, 87.

114 *"sees fit to ask it in writing"*: Quoted in ibid.

114 *"accepted the verdict of the Confederate failure"*: SPB Autobiography, SBP.

114 *"I am aware that this avowal"*: Klotter, *Breckinridges of Kentucky*, 148.

114 *helped several up-and-coming*: Ibid., 180.

114 *"loco-foco" Democrat*: Ibid., 103.

114 *"he was always for fair play"*: SPB Autobiography, SBP.

115 *"handsomely dressed couple"*: Fitzpatrick, *Endless Crusade*, 7.

115 *"Well, Colonel"*: Abbott, "Sophonisba Preston Breckinridge," 418.

115 *"She got on all right with the boys"*: Fitzpatrick, *Endless Crusade*, 7.

115 *"temporary"*: WCPB to SPB, Oct. 3, 1884, BFP.

115 *"hard for people raised with our prejudices"*: Issa Breckinridge to SPB, Sept. 19, 1884, BFP.

115 *"nothing of the colored girls"*: SPB to Issa Breckinridge, Sept. 26, 1884, SPB.

115 *"proud, even haughty"*: Klotter, *Breckinridges of Kentucky*, 142.

115 *"uncomfortable at their house"*: Ibid., 150.

115 *some southern women cultivated*: Lewis and Lockridge, "Sally Has Been Sick," 5.

115 *"I have loved you Willie"*: Issa Breckinridge to WCPB, Oct. 24, 1884, BFP.

115 *"You know you are"*: Issa Breckinridge to SPB, Sept. 20, 1884, BFP.

116 *"I know it is inevitable"*: WCPB to SPB, March 30, 1884, BFP.

9. THE NEEDLE, THE SCHOOL ROOM, AND THE STORE

117 *"quicksilver—ever active, amazingly fluid"*: Wright, "Three Against Time," 41.

117 *"the most brilliant student"*: Cook, "Notes and Comments," 94.

117 *"keen Southern wit"*: Ibid.

117 *"an ease and grace of manner"*: Ibid.

117 *"We hear pleasant and sweet things"*: WCPB to SPB, Oct. 22, 1884, BFP.

117 *"dutiful"*: WCPB to SPB, March 30, 1885, BFP.

118 *"my own food"*: SPB Autobiography, SBP.

118 *"the problem of racial relationships"*: SPB Autobiography, SBP.

118 *"heavy dresses and things"*: SPB to Issa Breckinridge, Feb. 1, 1887, BFP.

118 *"I ache to get out and work"*: SPB to WCPB, March 20, 1887, BFP.

118 *"The great contradiction"*: Fitzpatrick, *Endless Crusade*, 8.

118 *"in chemistry, botany and such sciences"*: WCPB to SPB, Oct. 22, 1884, BFP.

119 *208 women lawyers*: *Report on Population of the United States at the 11th Census: 1890*. Washington, D.C.: U.S. Government Printing Office, 1895.

119 *Ada Kepley*: Norgren, *Rebels at the Bar*, 36.

119 *state bar associations, however, that proved*: Ibid., 36–38.

119 *"feminine wiles"*: Ibid., 109.

119 *"were designed by God"*: Ibid., 39.

119 *"natural and proper timidity"*: Ibid., 42.

119 *"mix professionally with all the nastiness"*: Ibid., 65–66.

120 *Ada Hulett*: Ibid., 36–37.

120 *Belva Lockwood*: Ibid., 87–92.

120 *only two women practicing law*: Ibid., 156.

120 *"I wish you would be very clear"*: SPB to WCPB, March 9, 1887, BFP.

120 *"good girl"*: SPB to WCPB, June 10, 1887, BFP.

120 *"She would be a valuable acquisition"*: Quoted in Klotter, *Breckinridges of Kentucky*, 198.

120 *"penchant for a professional career"*: "Congressman Breckinridge's Daughter's Legal Studies," *NYT*, Nov. 28, 1892.

120 *"I had expected to study law"*: SPB Autobiography, SBP.

121 *"I had promised myself"*: Ibid.

121 *"did a good deal of the housework"*: Ibid.

121 *"incredible number"*: Chalkley, *Magic Casements*, 105.

121 *"at homes"*: Ibid., 107.

121 *"fashionable"*: Ibid., 95.

121 *"welsh rabbits"*: Ibid., 112.

121 *"I fear in my scamper"*: Ibid., 97–98.

122 *"family claim"*: Addams, *Twenty Years at Hull House*, 71.

122 *"hard years"*: SPB Autobiography, SBP.

122 *"The salary was"*: Ibid.

122 *"it was hard enough"*: Ibid.

122 *"I don't expect Sodom and Gomorrah"*: Mary Desha to Breckinridge family, Sept. 16, 1888, BFP.

123 *"muskets instead of shears"*: Aron, *Ladies and Gentlemen of the Civil Service*, 70.

123 *"The truth is"*: Ibid., 71.

123 *"war smitten and impoverished South"*: Ibid., 46.

123 *"pay such miserable prices"*: Ibid., 45.

123 *"special center"*: Quoted in Moldow, *Women Doctors in Gilded Age Washington*, 10.

123 *"heroines and pioneers"*: Chalkley, *Magic Casements*, 89.

124 *"plan her conferences"*: SPB Autobiography, SBP.

124 *"colored and white ladies"*: "Women's War Still On," *WP*, March 9, 1891.

124 *"colored men to the entertainments"*: "No Color Line Drawn," *WP*, March 7, 1891.

125 *"the executive ability of a Yankee"*: "Women of High Rank," *WP*, Feb. 8, 1891.

125 *"Were there no mothers"*: *WP*, July 13, 1890.

125 *"determined that the contribution"*: SPB Autobiography, SBP.

125 *"daring feat of horsemanship"*: "Women of High Rank," *WP*, Feb. 8, 1891.

125 *"brought in members by the thousands"*: Foraker, *I Would Live It Again*, 137.

125 *"quite ill for some time"*: SPB Autobiography, SBP.

125 *"One word suffices abundantly"*: "'88 Class Letters: 1890–1891," Wellesley College Archives.

126 *"I am glad that you are studying law"*: WCPB to SPB, July 19, 1891, BFP.

126 *asked for a study the organization had done*: SPB to Marion Talbot, Jan. 3, 1882, BFP.

126 *"I have seen young girls suffer"*: Addams, *Twenty Years at Hull House*, 70.

126 *"The law practice"*: WCPB to SPB, Sept. 4, 1891, BFP.

127 *"more wholesome"*: WCPB to SPB, June 28, 1891, BFP.

127 *"you will find"*: WCPB to SPB, June 4, 1892, BFP.

127 *"gives me a better idea"*: WCPB to SPB, Nov. 7, 1891, BFP.

127 *"entirely herself"*: WCPB to SPB, Nov. 30, 1891, BFP.

127 *"better today than she had been"*: WCPB to SPB, June 9, 1892, BFP.

127 *"I hardly know exactly"*: WCPB to SPB, July 5, 1892, BFP.

128 *"made up his mind"*: WCPB to SPB, June 4, 1892, BFP.

128 *"veracity, courage, affection"*: WCPB to SPB, Nov. 13, 1891, BFP.

128 *"advantages of college"*: Addams, *"Twenty Years at Hull House,"* 71–72.

128 *"Bowery boys can be found"*: Quoted in Fitzpatrick, *Endless Crusade*, 10.

129 *"day to day was often so exhausting"*: SPB to Madeline McDowell, Sept. 20, 1893, in Hay, *Madeline McDowell Breckinridge*, 33.

129 *"Neither really loved me"*: SPB Autobiography, SBP.

129 *"more pulled down"*: Desha Breckinridge to WCPB, Aug. 31, 1893, BFP.

129 *"But when she tried"*: SPB Autobiography, SBP.

129 *"do some work along"*: SPB to Madeline McDowell, Sept. 20, 1893, in Hay, *Madeline McDowell Breckinridge*, 37.

130 *"I shall do some work"*: SPB to WCPB, Sept. 6, 1893, BFP.

130 *"seems a great deal"*: SPB to WCPB, Jan. 11, 1894, BFP.

130 *"I am very anxious"*: WCPB to Desha Breckinridge, Jan. 22, 1894, BFP.

130 *"To tell the truth"*: SPB to WCPB, Jan. 27, 1894, BFP.

130 *"until some time"*: Enoch Totten to WCPB, Nov. 24, 1893, BFP.

131 *"I wrote to you some little"*: Lydia M. Fox to WCPB, June 5, 1893, BFP.

131 *"sent several letters"*: Hoffman House to WCPB, Aug. 6, 1893, BFP.

131 *"very worthy liveryman"*: James Moore to WCPB, July 27, 1893, BFP.

131 *"was not adequate"*: SPB Autobiography, SBP.

131 *"would take the best part"*: Carpenter, *Carp's Washington*, 2.

131 *six live-in servants*: *1870 U.S. Federal Census* (database online). Ancestry.com.

132 *"the advantages he had enjoyed"*: Chalkley, *Magic Casements*, 23.

132 *"I am thoroughly convinced"*: Charles Stoll to WCPB, Jan. 16, 1894, BFP.

10. A HOUSE OF MERCY

133 *"wide formal avenues"*: Hall, *Travels in North America*, vol. 3, 1.

133 *"a great, sprawling country village"*: Stern, *So Much in a Lifetime*, 99.

133 *a quarter million*: Table 12, "Population of the 100 Largest Urban Places: 1890, U.S. Bureau of the Census," June 15, 1998, https://www.census.gov/population/www/documentation/twps0027/tab12.txt.

133 *"fairy-tale sense of instability"*: Carpenter, *Carp's Washington*, 4.

133 *"it has sprung up in a morning"*: Ibid., 5.

134 *"capital's various charms"*: Jacobs, *Capital Elites*, 168.

134 *"beautiful homes with large ballrooms"*: Ibid., 147.

134 *"rootless rich"*: Ibid., 171.

134 *"it is the fashion"*: Quoted in Jacobs, *Capital Elites*, 168–69.

134 *"the season"*: Ibid., 178.

134 *"Houses had been opened up"*: Adams, *The Education of Henry Adams*, 251.

134 *"brilliant"*: Foraker, *I Would Live It Again*, 6.

134 *"rich, spectacular New York-crowd-with-the-names"*: Ibid., 7.

134 *"There is enough silk worn here"*: Carpenter, *Carp's Washington*, 91.

134 *"monumental floral decorations"*: Ibid., 88.

134 *"pink and gold" Valentine's luncheon*: "St. Valentine Luncheons," *NYT*, Feb. 15, 1891.

135 *"drifting in the dead-water of the* fin-de-siècle*"*: Adams, *The Education of Henry Adams*, 259.

135 *"a vast army of unemployed"*: "Helping the Destitute," *WES*, Nov. 30, 1893.

135 *"pitiful tale"*: Charles Stoll to JAT, Jan. 22, 1894, in Tucker, *TRMP*, 16.

135 *"Don't you know"*: JAT to Charles Stoll, Jan. 27, 1884, in Tucker, *TRMP*, 21.

135 *"delighted"*: Ibid., 20.

136 *"carefully curtained windows"*: JAT to Charles Stoll, Jan. 30, 1894, in Tucker, *TRMP*, 23.

136 *"overcoming a strong desire"*: Ibid.

136 *"My child"*: Ibid., 24.

136 *"going to tell a lie"*: Ibid., 24–25.

137 *"could not stand it"*: Ibid., 25.

137 *"this resolve on your part"*: Ibid., 25–26.

137 *"appalling proposition"*: Ibid., 26.

137 *"miserable sinking feeling"*: Ibid., 28.

138 *"in a false position"*: Ibid.

138 *"a teacher"*: Ibid., 29.

138 *"seems determined to tell"*: Ibid., 30.

138 *"the woman's ward of a prison"*: Ibid., 31.

138 *"The tea certainly was"*: Ibid., 31–32.

139 *"None of them seem"*: Ibid., 32.

139 *Sisters of the Good Shepherd*: Wood, *The Freedom of the Streets*, 190.

139 *"millionaire evangelist"*: Kunzel, *Fallen Women, Problem Girls*, 14.

139 *"social purity"*: Pivar, *Purity Crusade*, 111–13.

139 *Working Girls Society*: Ibid., 108–9.

140 *"grandeur of womanhood"*: "The Welfare of Women," *NYT*, April 16, 1890.

140 *"a house of refuge"*: "The House of Mercy," *Annual Report of the Commissioners of the District of Columbia*, Sept. 18, 1884.

140 *"deserving indigent and unprotected females"*: "'Infant Asylum' Undergoes Renovations," *WP*, March 22, 2011.

140 *"The Maiden Tribute of Modern Babylon"*: Pivar, *Purity Crusade*, 133.

140 *WCTU also started campaigning*: Ibid., 104–5.

140 *"Please accept this little outcast"*: "Notes pinned to babies at the Foundling Asylum," in Ephemeral New York, records from the New York Foundling Hospital from a collection at the New-York Historical Society, https://ephemeralnewyork .wordpress.com/2012/10/01/the-notes-pinned-to-babies-at-the-foundling -asylum.

141 *"fancy dress" and "excitement"*: Kunzel, *Fallen Women, Problem Girls*, 31, 28.

141 *"disproportionate number of the fallen women"*: Deutsch, *Women and the City*, 59.

141 *"dissipation and degradation"*: "Reclaiming Fallen Women," *WP*, May 2, 1887.

141 *"taught to sympathize"*: Tucker, *TRMP*, 19.

141 *"the necessity of suspending judgment"*: "Discussing Society Purity," *WP*, May 2, 1887.

142 *"that this woman was really ruined"*: Tucker, *TRMP*, 21.

142 *"very well indeed"*: Ibid., 35.

142 *"Her face is almost repulsive"*: Ibid., 33–34.

142 *"When she smiles"*: Ibid., 34.

143 *"no idea beds"*: Ibid., 31.

143 *"cold, cheerless"*: Ibid., 36.

143 *"and generally had whatever she wanted"*: Ibid., 38.

143 *"stood all the time"*: Ibid., 39.

143 *"the luxury of"*: Ibid., 43.

144 *"small, weak voice"*: Ibid., 40–41.

144 *"the soft side of a pine board"*: Ibid., 31.

144 *"fairy tales"*: Ibid., 41.

144 *"real prisoner"*: Ibid., 42.

144 *"hardly keep back the tears"*: Ibid., 44.

144 *"quite confidential"*: Ibid., 45.

144 *"begin life anew"*: Ibid., 46.

145 *"the pleasantest sort of Bohemian life"*: Ibid., 47.

145 *"vexed and disappointed"*: Ibid., 55.

145 *"sort of a household drudge"*: Ibid., 56.

145 *"vexed her by some little impertinence"*: Ibid., 56–57.

145 *"too ill to get up"*: Ibid., 63.

145 *"gave him all her girlhood"*: Ibid., 64.

145 *"how she had discovered his infidelity"*: Ibid., 66.

145 *"strength giving out"*: Ibid., 71.

145 *"I am getting out of prison"*: Ibid., 68.

146 *"in a sort of stage whisper"*: Ibid., 69.

146 *"marble calm"*: Ibid., 69.

146 *"a very bitter fight"*: Ibid., 69.

146 *"like an Arctic explorer"*: Ibid., 71.

146 *"I was simply starved"*: Ibid., 71.

146 *"due to a lack of courage"*: Ibid., 75.

146 *"the sisters objected to me"*: Ibid., 71.

146 *"I think a cold chill"*: Charles Stoll to WCPB, Jan. 31, 1884, BFP.

147 *"contemptuous authority"*: Tucker, *TRMP*, 70.

147 *"It is like a jail there"*: Ibid., 79.

147 *"I did the best"*: Ibid., 79.

147 *"out of the question"*: Ibid., 73.

147 *"a certain quick wit"*: Ibid., 72.

147 *"a very good actress"*: Ibid., 73.

147 *"parents were Kentuckians"*: Ibid., 48.

148 *"I thought you were one of those dreadful reporters"*: Ibid., 61.

148 *"Mr. S's associates seem to think"*: JAT to Mary Tucker, Feb. 6, 1894, TFP.

11. A GOOD WOMAN

149 *"a little icy"*: Tucker, *TRMP*, 81.

149 *"The day my suit"*: Ibid., 98.

149 *"had gone about among Madeline's"*: Ibid., 86.

149 *"would not have to be stared at"*: Ibid., 83.

150 *"the money to square"*: WCPB to Charles Stoll, Feb. 21, 1894, BFP.

150 *"How are you for money"*: Desha Breckinridge to WCPB, Feb. 17, 1894, BFP.

150 *"tried to employ him to produce an abortion"*: Robert J. Breckinridge to WCPB, Oct. 10, 1893, BFP.

150 *"letting her get sick on their hands"*: Charles Stoll to WCPB, Feb. 8, 1894, BFP.

151 *"did some work"*: D. Robertson to Charles Stoll, Feb. 15, 1894, BFP.

151 *"absolute falsity of all the more serious"*: WCPB to Al Core, Jan. 9, 1894, BFP.

151 *"disorder consequent upon child-birth"*: "Madeline Helped by Lady Doctors," *CE*, Feb. 11, 1894.

152 *"The name Louise Wilson means nothing"*: Charles Stoll to WCPB, Feb. 10, 1894, BFP.

152 *"she and the Buchanan woman had performed"*: Charles Stoll to WCPB, Feb. 3, 1894, BFP.

152 *"went into hysterics"*: "Scenes Shift in the Famous Case," *CE*, March 22, 1894.

152 *"took therefrom a copy of Washington Irving"*: "Here in Cincy the Pollard Case Is to Be," *CE*, Feb. 27, 1894.

152 *"she must be a bad woman"*: Sister Sebastian to Miss Todd, Dec. 28, 1894, BFP.

152 *"Oh no. I was a bad girl"*: "Fair Madeline and Colonel Billy," *LMT*, Feb. 15, 1894.

153 *"decidedly in favor of Colonel Breckinridge"*: "Madeline Pollard," *LMT*, Feb. 13, 1894.

153 *"She could not bear to talk of it"*: Tucker, *TRMP*, 102.

153 *"I cannot give this up now"*: Ibid., 100.

153 *"unsophisticated"*: Ibid., 82.

153 *"by no means able"*: Enoch Totten to WCPB, Feb. 23, 1894, BFP.

153 *"rather the best lawyer"*: WCPB to "Hinton," Feb. 22, 1894, BFP.

154 *"I am in a hole"*: WCPB to Enoch Totten, Feb. 25, 1894, BFP.

154 *"a mock marriage"*: "A Bad Woman," *LCJ*, Feb. 17, 1894.

154 *"formerly a sporting woman"*: Ibid.

154 *"caused frequent family disturbances"*: Ibid.

154 *"the mistress of James Rhodes"*: Ibid.

155 *"she told her that her father"*: "They Came Near Fighting," *LMT*, Feb. 16, 1894.

155 *"a sensation of great magnitude"*: "Dead Involved; The Late Col. A. M. Swope Dragged into the Breckinridge Case," *LCJ*, Feb. 20, 1894.

156 *"bombshell"*: "Scandalized the Name of Col. Swope," *CE*, Feb. 20, 1894.

156 *"intensely favorable to Miss Pollard"*: "'Willie,' That's What Miss Pollard Called the Colonel," *CE*, Feb. 19, 1894.

156 *"came into the parlor"*: Ibid.

156 *"looked shocked"*: Ibid.

156 *in the spring of 1857*: Baird, *Luke Pryor Blackburn*, 18.

156 *"This seems to me*: "'Willie,' That's What Miss Pollard Called the Colonel," *CE*, Feb. 19, 1894.

157 *"she was a woman"*: "'Willie,' That's What Miss Pollard Called the Colonel," *CE*, Feb. 19, 1894.

157 *"appalled"*: Ibid.

157 *"terrible denouement"*: "Mrs. Blackburn's Deposition," *LCJ*, Feb. 21, 1894.

157 *"star-chamber"*: "'Willie,' That's What Miss Pollard Called the Colonel," *CE*, Feb. 19, 1894.

157 *"Blackburn put things into my mouth"*: WCPB to "Hinton," Feb. 22, 1894, BFP.

158 *"a gang in Lexington"*: WCPB to John Andrew Steel, Dec. 13, 1893, BFP.

158 *"those who have been disappointed"*: WCPB to Al Core, Jan. 9, 1894, BFP.

158 *"unqualifiedly false"*: "Mock Marriage," *LCJ*, Feb. 21, 1894.

158 *"very drunk"*: "More Testimony," *LMT*, Feb. 21, 1894.

158 *"that he had pulled up the plaintiff's"*: Notes to file, Breckinridge case file, n.d., BFP.

158 *"I mean no disrespect"*: "Mock Marriage," *LCJ*, Feb. 21, 1894.

159 *"on account of the reputation"*: Ibid.

159 *"had attended Mrs. Pollard"*: "Mrs. L. P. Blackburn," *LMT*, Feb. 21, 1894.

159 *"generally quarreled all the time"*: "He Loved Her," *LCJ*, Feb. 23, 1894.

159 *"saying that he had an important case"*: Ibid.

160 *"friendship led to an engagement"*: Ibid.

160 *"a double life"*: "Madeline Pollard Accompanied by Her Attorney," *LMT*, Feb. 13, 1894.

160 *"he said he was educating"*: "Her Character," *LCJ*, Feb. 24, 1894.

160 *"his girl"*: Ibid.

160 *"soon fell in love"*: Ibid.

161 *"prove every thing"*: Desha Breckinridge to WCPB, Feb. 23, 1894, BFP.

161 *"At no time in the course of the examinations"*: "Madeline Pollard Again Visits Cincinnati," *LMT*, Feb. 11, 1894.

161 *"already absorbing interest"*: "Mud, Slathers of It Thrown," *CE*, Feb. 24, 1894.

161 *"claim he attempted to take advantage of her"*: "Charges of Conspiracy," *CE*, Feb. 19, 1894.

161 *"The character of the Immaculate Son of God"*: "Another Name of National Note," *CE*, Feb. 22, 1894.

162 *"your friend and admirer"*: Squire M. Tinsely to WCPB, n.d., 1893 folder, BFP.

162 *"unmitigated, contemptible lie"*: "Mock Marriage," *LCJ*, Feb. 21, 1894.

162 *"one of the most sober"*: "Dead Involved," *LCJ*, Feb. 20, 1894.

162 *"aroused a storm of indignation"*: "Another Name of National Note," *CE*, Feb. 22, 1894.

162 *December 10*: "A Mistake That Col. Swope Story," *CE*, Feb. 25, 1894.

162 *"I can not find anybody"*: "His Brother's Honor," *LCJ*, Feb. 16, 1894.

162 *"she was on illicit relations"*: WCPB memo to file, n.d., BFP.

163 *"was heartbroken"*: "Madeline Pollard Accompanied by Her Attorney," *LMT*, Feb. 13, 1894.

163 *"such a fall would have"*: Desha Breckinridge to WCPB, Feb. 23, 1894, BFP.

163 *"approached right"*: WCPB to John Shelby, Feb. 12, 1894, BFP.

163 *"he couldn't prove anything"*: Charles Stoll to WCPB, Feb. 24, 1894, BFP.

163 *"was in her room at the Elsmere"*: WCPB to JAT, March 2, 1894, BFP.

163 *"You don't know how discouraged"*: JAT to Charles Stoll, Feb. 24, 1894, BFP.

163 *"delicate and difficult undertaking"*: WCPB to JAT, Feb. 26, 1894, BFP.

163 *"sinking ship"*: WCPB to JAT, March 2, 1894, BFP.

164 *"unnatural state of mind"*: WCPB to SPB, March 7, 1894, BFP.

12. MISS POLLARD'S RUIN IN LEXINGTON

165 *"mired in outdated doctrine"*: Williams, *Years of Decision*, 84.

165 *"reincarnated spirit of Andrew Jackson"*: "Coxey's Army Soon to March," *NYT*, March 24, 1894.

165 *"Everywhere"*: Williams, *Years of Decision*, 78.

166 *"wonder has been all along"*: "The Trial Begun," *LCJ*, March 9, 1894.

166 *Old Criminal Court*: See "Historic Courthouse/Old City Hall," https://www.dccourts.gov/sites/default/files/pdf-forms/HistoricCourthouse_CityHall.pdf.

167 *"pulpit like"*: "Started; Opening of the Great Trial," *CE*, March 9, 1894.

167 *"a man who had slept well"*: "Breckinridge on Hand," *WP*, March 9, 1894.

168 *"shrewd and roguish"*: "Started; Opening of the Great Trial," *CE*, March 9, 1894.

168 *disaster as a diplomat*: Jett, *American Ambassadors*, 19.

169 *"from the drab existence"*: Chalkley, *Magic Casements*, 75–76.

169 *"I am in such a mood"*: Louise Wing Breckinridge to WCPB, Feb. 20, 1893, BFP.

169 *"a time of new delight"*: Louise Wing Breckinridge to WCPB, March 2, 1893, BFP.

169 *"pining"*: Louise Wing Breckinridge to WCPB, March 7, 1893, BFP.

169 *"I have no leisure moments"*: WCPB to SPB, March 10, 1893, BFP.

169 *"no other woman had ever claimed"*: "Mrs. Breckinridge Remains Loyal," *LCJ*, March 20, 1894.

169 *"disturbed her peace of mind"*: Louise Wing Breckinridge to WCPB, March 20, 1893, BFP.

170 *"like a cyclone"*: Louise Wing Breckinridge to WCPB, April 16, 1893, BFP.

170 *"weaker instead of stronger"*: WCPB to Desha Breckinridge, March 1, 1894, BFP.

170 *"had aroused comment"*: "The Women of Breckinridge's District," *CE*, March 3, 1894.

170 *"a full statement to my wife"*: Statement to *Washington News* from W.C.P. Breckinridge, April 15, 1894, BFP.

170 *"nervous affliction"*: SPB Autobiography, SBP.

170 *"clear"*: Louise Wing Breckinridge to WCPB, May 5, 1894, BFP.

170 *"crowds before the box office"*: "Date Was Fixed," *LCJ*, March 10, 1894.

171 *"She is of the style"*: "A Smile Played on the Features of Col. Breckinridge," *CE*, March 10, 1894.

171 *"a man of family"*: "The Date Was Fixed," *LCJ*, March 10, 1894.

171 *"careless, contemptuous, recognizing"*: "A Smile Played on the Features," *CE*, March 10, 1894.

171 *"There are three credible witnesses"*: "Miss Pollard's Side," *WP*, March 10, 1894.

172 *"trembled violently"*: "Madeline in Tears," *WES*, March 9, 1894.

172 *"I shall make her Mrs. Breckinridge"*: "If I Had My Husband," *NYW*, March 10, 1894.

172 *"If Mr. Breckinridge wishes to act"*: Ibid.

173 *"You know that as well"*: "Madeline in Tears," *WES*, March 9, 1894.

173 *"When I asked the Colonel"*: "If I Had My Husband," *NYW*, March 10, 1894.

173 *"I extended to Miss Pollard"*: Ibid.

174 *"I have told you everything"*: Ibid.

174 *"Yes . . . she used it"*: Ibid.

174 *"No cross-examination"*: "Miss Pollard's Side," *WP*, March 10, 1894.

175 *"the lady had threatened him"*: "If I Had My Husband," *NYW*, March 10, 1894.

175 *"very excited and insisted"*: "Madeline in Tears," *WES*, March 9, 1894.

175 *"if Providence in its wisdom"*: "If I Had My Husband," *NYW*, March 10, 1894.

175 *ripple went through*: "Madeline in Tears," *WES*, March 9, 1894.

175 *"No, no—it is not so"*: Ibid.

176 *"intended to make it alright"*: Ibid.

176 *"who volunteers to become the chief witness"*: Tucker, *TRMP*, 133.

176 *"The opening does not look"*: JAT to Mary Tucker, March 10, 1894, TFP.

176 *"she evidently likes her punch"*: Tucker, *TRMP*, 136–38.

177 *"obvious reasons, the impression"*: "Women Excluded," *WES*, March 12, 1894.

177 *"laws regulating . . . marriage and divorce"*: Anthony, "Social Purity," in *The Life and Work of Susan B. Anthony*, 1009.

177 *"Mr. Marshal, I wish you"*: "Women Excluded," *WES*, March 12, 1894.

178 *"Col. Breckinridge was holding Miss Pollard's hand"*: Ibid.

178 *"good and distinguished men"*: Ibid.

178 *"brought about by artificial means"*: Ibid.

178 *"a sensible looking woman"*: "Upper Cuts, Not of the Legal Caste," *CE*, March 13, 1894.

178 *"an undertaker's"*: "Gave Way to Emotion," *WP*, March 13, 1894.

179 *"chicanery"* and *"insolence"*: "Upper Cuts, Not of the Legal Caste," *CE*, March 13, 1894.

180 *"You have used language"*: "Bad Blood and Blows," *WP*, March 13, 1894.

181 *"I shall always cherish"*: Louise Wing Breckinridge to WCPB, March 9, 1894, BFP.

181 *"revived much of the gossip"*: "Miss Pollard's Attorneys," *Kentucky Leader*, Aug. 17, 1893.

181 *"impatiently"*: Telegram from Louise Wing Breckinridge to WCPB, April 24, 1894, BFP.

181 *"Preston very unhappy"*: Telegram from Louise Wing Breckinridge to WCPB, April 28, 1894, BFP.

182 *"every day without fail"*: Telegram from Preston Wing to WCPB, May 1, 1894, BFP.

182 *"That I should love and wish"*: WCPB to Preston Wing, May 14, 1894, Green Family Papers, Western Kentucky University.

182 *"manly letter"*: Louise Wing Breckinridge to WCPB, n.d., 1893, BFP.

182 *"want of sleep"*: Louise Wing Breckinridge to WCPB, May 18, 1893, BFP.

182 *"Can't endure this alone"*: Telegram from Louise Wing Breckinridge to WCPB, June 1, 1893, BFP.

182 *"the solemnization of a secret marriage"*: "Miss Pollard's Petition," *Celebrated Trial*, 12.

182 *"exhausted"*: Telegram from Louise Wing Breckinridge to Preston Scott, June 9, 1893, BFP.

183 *"I pay the penalty"*: "If I Had My Husband," *NYW*, March 10, 1894.

183 *"Too weak [to] return home alone"*: Telegram from Louise Wing Breckinridge to Preston Scott, June 9, 1893, BFP.

183 *"until I happened to meet him"*: "Colonel Breckinridge and Wife Visited Cincinnati Before Their Public Marriage," *CE*, March 24, 1894.

183 *"nervous manner"*: "Mrs. Breckinridge Remains Loyal," *LCJ*, March 20, 1894.

183 *"entirely reprehensible"*: "Sister Celia Proves a Stumbling Block," *CE*, March 14, 1894.

184 *"poor unfortunate girl from Kentucky"*: "Tilts Over Testimony," *WP*, March 15, 1894.

184 *"She had on a dress"*: "Miss Pollard's Witness," *New York Herald*, March 16, 1894.

185 *"undressed and in bed"*: Ibid.

185 *"about fifty times"*: "Tilts Over Testimony," *WP*, March 15, 1894.

185 *"loved him and trusted him"*: Ibid.

185 *"Yes, sir"*: Ibid.

185 *"the negress reproved to his face"*: "Shifts the Scene to Lexington," *CE*, March 16, 1894.

186 *"hear her sing and play"*: "Miss Pollard's Witness," *New York Herald*, March 16, 1894.

186 *"mass of testimony"*: WCPB to Dr. J. J. O'Mahoney, March 15, 1894, BFP.

186 *"irregularity, insufficiency and inadequacy"*: WCPB to Desha Breckinridge, March 1, 1894, BFP.

186 *"general duplicity of his character"*: "Sister Celia Proves a Stumbling Block," *CE*, March 14, 1894.

186 *"collected certain moneys"*: "The Women of Breckinridge's District," *CE*, March 3, 1894.

186 *"did not hesitate to publish"*: WCPB to "Bean," March 3, 1894, BFP.

186 *"have been hauling me around"*: WCPB to Dr. J. J. O'Mahoney, March 15, 1894, BFP.

13. SOMEBODY'S DAUGHTER

187 *"gusty spirit of Saint Patrick"*: "Miss Pollard a Wonder," *NYW*, March 17, 1894.

187 *"struggled with the bailiffs"*: "Told Her Sad Story," *WP*, March 17, 1894.

188 *"not because I wanted to"*: "Miss Pollard a Wonder," *NYW*, March 17, 1894.

188 *"the rising and falling of her plaintive voice"*: "Told Her Sad Story," *WP*, March 17, 1894.

188 *"stagy . . . as if every word"*: "Miss Pollard a Wonder," *NYW*, March 17, 1894.

189 *"he had thought it over"*: "Madeline Tells Her Own Story," *CE*, March 17, 1894.

189 *"told him we ought to wait"*: "Miss Pollard a Wonder," *NYW*, March 17, 1894.

189 *"I don't like to state"*: Ibid.

189 *"one bit afraid"*: Tucker, *TRMP*, 149.

190 *"People do not know"*: Ibid., 151–52.

190 *"asked her forty thousand questions"*: "Miss Pollard a Wonder," *NYW*, March 17, 1894.

190 *"My father taught me some history"*: "Madeline Tells Her Own Story," *CE*, March 17, 1894.

190 *"I believe you spoke to him"*: "Madeline's Story," *WES*, March 16, 1894.

190 *"now sitting well back"*: Ibid.

191 *"You can expect fire-works"*: JAT to Mary Tucker, March 17, 1894, TFP.

191 *"I suppose Jane will come home"*: Mary Tucker to Maude Tucker, n.d., March 1894, TFP.

191 *"as bad as I had feared"*: Tucker, *TRMP*, 167.

192 *"as a poem of Miss Pollard's"*: Ibid., 169.

192 *"eminence of being the most sensational"*: "Madeline's Story," *WES*, March 19, 1894.

192 *"How long did they continue?"*: "Madeline's Story," *WES*, March 19, 1894.

192 *"Once an Episcopalian"*: "More About Her Life," *WP*, March 20, 1894.

192 *"The question of whether"*: "Madeline's Story," *WES*, March 19, 1894.

193 *"made love"*: "More About Her Life," *WP*, March 20, 1894.

193 *"very unmaidenly bit of conduct"*: "Madeline's Story," *WES*, March 19, 1894.
193 *"I could have never written that letter"*: Ibid.
193 *"He said he came to see me"*: "More About Her Life," *WP*, March 20, 1894.
193 *"taken off her hat"*: "An Outcast, in Tear-Broken Tones," *CE*, March 20, 1894.
193 *"Oh, come, come, come"*: Ibid.
194 *"I never heard that word before"*: "More About Her Life," *WP*, March 20, 1894.
194 *"Then you were not misled"*: "Miss Pollard at Bay," *NYW*, March 20, 1894.
194 *"You of course appreciated"*: "An Outcast, in Tear-Broken Tones," *CE*, March 20, 1894.
194 *"Since he has made it"*: "Miss Pollard at Bay," *NYW*, March 20, 1894.
195 *"She said to me"*: Ibid.
195 *"I believe these men"*: Ibid.
195 *"Had you no thought"*: Ibid.
195 *"Miss Pollard is probably"*: "Madeline's Story," *WES*, March 19, 1894.
195 *"More than once she turned"*: "More About Her Life," *WP*, March 20, 1894.
195 *"sat still in silent surprise"*: "An Outcast, in Tear-Broken Tones," *CE*, March 20, 1894.
196 *"the same old story"*: "Life of Shame," *LCJ*, March 17, 1894.
196 *"Yes. As bad as it sounds"*: "More About Her Life," *WP*, March 20, 1894.
196 *"very proper letters"*: "Deluded Mr. Rhodes," *WES*, March 20, 1894.
196 *"Please, dear, do let me"*: "An Abrupt Question," *WP*, March 21, 1894.
197 *"Even her own lawyers"*: "Tears, Smiles and Tears Again," *CE*, March 21, 1894.
197 *"He said Mr. William C. Whitney"*: Ibid.
197 *"talked about going to Havana"*: Ibid.
198 *"worthy woman"*: Ibid.
198 *"telling of his conduct"*: Ibid.
198 *"the colonel does not draw"*: Lexington, *The Celebrated Case*, 38.
198 *"revelations of the defendant's conduct"*: "Tears, Smiles and Tears Again," *CE*, March 21, 1894.
199 *"Come Willie"*: "Whole Court in Tears," *NYW*, March 21, 1894.
199 *"I should have liked the court"*: "Tears, Smiles and Tears Again," *CE*, March 21, 1894.
199 *"If there was a man among the curious"*: "Whole Court in Tears," *NYW*, March 21, 1894.
199 *"head bent in a dejected way"*: "Tears, Smiles and Tears Again," *CE*, March 21, 1894.

14. A MAN OF PASSION

200 *"The delegation from Kentucky"*: "Scenes Shift in the Famous Case," *CE*, March 22, 1894.
200 *"It is evident that his attorneys"*: "Madeline's Story," *WES*, March 19, 1894.
200 *"the testimony will be overwhelming"*: WCPB to A. W. Hardin, Jan. 9, 1894, BFP.
200 *"my own comparatively straitened"*: WCPB to Dr. L. B. Woolfolk, March 23, 1894.
201 *"I am authorized to say"*: "Scenes Shift in the Famous Case," *CE*, March 22, 1894.
201 *"She would come to the door"*: "The Other Side," *WES*, March 21, 1894.
201 *"fell in with"*: "Says She Led Him On," *WP*, March 22, 1894.

201 *"life was made an intolerable burden"*: "The Other Side," *WES*, March 21, 1894.

201 *"on the tiptoe of expectation"*: "A Lull in the Pollard Trial," *CE*, March 23, 1894.

202 *"severely criticized"*: "Attacking Her Story," *WP*, March 23, 1894.

202 *"What has this to do with"*: "A Lull in the Pollard Trial," *CE*, March 23, 1894.

202 *"My finances are"*: JAT to William Worthington, March 9, 1894, BFP.

202 *"the great topic everywhere"*: JAT to Mary Tucker, March 22, 1894, TFP.

202 *"Practically, I have won"*: WCPB to "Lucas," March 22, 1894, BFP.

203 *"succeeds in blackening"*: "Madeline's Story," *WES*, March 19, 1894.

203 *"politically dead"*: "Kentucky Men Are Agitated," *New York Herald*, March 24, 1894.

203 *"as game as a game cock"*: WCPB to "Lucas," March 23, 1894, BFP.

203 *"defensive canvas"*: WCPB to J.D. Lillard, Jan. 9, 1894, BFP.

203 *"acting"*: WCPB to "Ben," March 23, 1894, BFP.

203 *"for I have no secret"*: WCPB to "Myall," March 23, 1894, BFP.

204 *"introduced herself and congratulated him"*: G. M. Miller to WCPB, March 5, 1894, BFP.

204 *"Now you have my sympathy"*: John M. Allen to WCPB, March 28, 1894, BFP.

204 *"endeavored to make an assignation"*: "A Meeting Which Miss Pollard Tried to Make with a Member of the President's Cabinet," *CE*, Jan. 1, 1894.

204 *"couched in such terms"*: "Queer Are the Latest Stories," *CE*, March 27, 1894.

204 *"I can easily believe it"*: H. S. Sutton to WCPB, n.d., BFP.

204 *"considered him a likely successor"*: Williams, *Years of Decision*, 73.

205 *"this case must not come to a trial"*: A man named Williams wrote to Breckinridge asking for his help in getting an appointment and reminded him of the note he delivered from Carlisle "last August . . . in regard to the scandal" and repeating its contents. E. L. Williams to WCPB, Dec. 23, 1893, BFP.

205 *"I need not say"*: WCPB to John G. Carlisle, March 24, 1894, BFP.

205 *reported that Breckinridge was promising*: "Queer Are the Latest Stories," *CE*, March 27, 1894.

205 *"Breckinridge forced him to testify"*: "He Sounds Public Sentiment Regarding the Status of Col. Breckinridge," *LMT*, April 19, 1894.

206 *"on the grounds they were"*: "When She Was Young," *WP*, March 27, 1894.

207 *"I am glad you told me"*: "The Disputed Letter," *WP*, March 28, 1894.

207 *"under the promise"*: Ibid.

207 *"didn't like the way"*: "Romeo Rossell Was Coy," *NYW*, March 29, 1894.

208 *"unwholesome smell"*: "Denials from the Silver-Tongued," *CE*, March 30, 1894.

208 *"fresh, new Bible"*: Ibid.

208 *"minor key of tenderness and pathos"*: "Breckinridge Testifies," *NYW*, March 30, 1894.

208 *"When did you first meet"*: Ibid.

209 *"much worse than a real marriage"*: Ibid.

209 *"no reason for any excuse"*: Ibid.

209 *"There were no protestations"*: "Denials from the Silver-Tongued," *CE*, March 30, 1894.

210 *"Just a case of illicit love?"*: Ibid.

210 *"their conversation resulted"*: "His Story in Detail," *WP*, March 31, 1894.

210 *"young woman of twenty"*: "Breckinridge Testifies," *NYW*, March 30, 1894.

210 *"ought to marry her"*: "His Story in Detail," *WP*, March 31, 1894.

211 *"scandal and destruction"*: Ibid.

211 *"in distinct violation"*: Ibid.

212 *"She would come to the Capitol"*: "That Is Not True," *NYW*, March 31, 1894.

212 *"before she would allow the scandal"*: "His Story in Detail," *WP*, March 31, 1894.

212 *"If it is my child"*: Ibid.

213 *"silvery and soft-spoken"*: "Smoothly the Silver Tongue Wagged," *CE*, March 31, 1894.

213 *"One is true"*: "More of His Story," *WES*, March 30, 1894.

213 *"He was, to hear him talk"*: "Denials from the Silver-Tongued," *CE*, March 30, 1894.

214 St. Ann's Infant Asylum in Washington: *Report of the Joint Select Committee to Investigate the Charities and Reformatory Institutions in the District of Columbia* (Washington, D.C.: U.S. Government Printing Office, 1897).

214 *85 and 100 percent*: Miller, *Abandoned*, 163.

214 *"The babies die like sheep"*: Quoted in Miller, *Abandoned*, 158.

214 *"act of humanity"*: Miller, *Abandoned*, 161.

214 *"Lincoln had consented"*: WCPB memo to attorneys, n.d., Pollard Case File, BFP.

15. HINDERED, NOT RUINED

215 *"having a perfect circus"*: JAT to William Worthington, March 20, 1894, BFP.

215 *"Why, Aggie, you are more devoted"*: Tucker, *TRMP*, 191.

215 *"the statue in the circle"*: LBD to JAT, March 29, 1894, BFP.

216 *"might cause me my life"*: JAT to Maude Tucker, March 28, 1894, TFP.

216 *"done so badly"*: Tucker, *TRMP*, 229.

216 *"this devilish business"*: Mrs. Frances to Madeline Pollard, in Tucker, *TRMP*, 199.

216 *"did perfectly right"*: J. B. Moore Bristor to Madeline Pollard, in Tucker, *TRMP*, 212.

216 *"I do believe every word"*: A Friend to Madeline Pollard, in Tucker, *TRMP*, 223.

216 *"For past times"*: J. H. Winter to Madeline Pollard, in Tucker, *TRMP*, 228.

217 *"You are not 'ruined'"*: "A Poet" to Madeline Pollard, in Tucker, *TRMP*, 201.

217 *"ought to be deposed"*: "Congress No Place for Him," *NYT*, March 25, 1894.

217 *"chivalrous people of Kentucky"*: "Boston Women Indignant," *NYT*, March 27, 1894.

217 *Moral Education Society*: Pivar, *Purity Crusade*, 80–83.

217 *"the disrespectful way that many men"*: "Resolved," *The Alpha*, April 12, 1878.

217 *"upon women in every station"*: "A Woman's View of Cleveland," *CDT*, Sept. 13, 1884.

218 *"intercourse for procreation only"*: "The Alpha Doctrine," *The Alpha*, Dec. 1, 1883.

218 *"that creeping worm of licentious doctrine"*: "Colonel Breckinridge Roasted in a Sermon by a Brooklyn Divine," *CE*, March 26, 1894.

218 *"secretly circulating a petition"*: "The Colonel's Scalp Threatened by the Ladies of Lexington," *CE*, March 29, 1894.

219 *"an unusual pallor on his countenance"*: "Judge Wilson's Hint," *WP*, April 3, 1894.

219 *"nefarious conspiracy"*: WCPB to "Myall," March 30, 1894, BFP.

219 *"cowardly"*: WCPB to "Ab," March 31, 1894, BFP.

219 *"aged sixteen"*: "Miss Pollard's Age," *WP*, March 31, 1894.

220 *"What advice would you give"*: "Judge Wilson's Hint," *WP*, April 3, 1894.

220 *"There was something internal"*: Ibid.

220 *"Up to that time"*: "The Colonel Repeats His Oft-Told Tale," *CE*, April 3, 1894.

220 *"There wasn't a man"*: "Judge Wilson's Hint," *WP*, April 3, 1894.

220 *"immoral relations"*: Ibid.

221 *"I mean to say"*: "The Colonel Repeats His Oft-Told Tale," *CE*, April 3, 1894.

221 *"the same standard"*: "A Living Hell," *LCJ*, April 3, 1894.

221 *"feared nothing"*: Ibid.

222 *"won them over"*: JAT to Mary Tucker, April 1, 1894, TFP.

222 *"Miss Pollard's character"*: "Kentucky Men Are Agitated," *New York Herald*, March 24, 1894.

222 *"can't help it"*: "Will Be Battle of Legal Giants," *New York Herald*, March 26, 1894.

222 the Herald *paid for a sitting for Madeline*: C. M. Bell Studio Log Books, vol. 4, sitting #41108, Miss Madeline Pollard, paid *New York Herald*, March 28, 1894.

222 *"a silly adventure"*: "Breckinridge on the Stand," *New York Herald*, March 30, 1894.

222 *"a photo of the adult Madeline"*: *New York Herald*, March 30, 1894.

222 *"I have been so anxious to know you"*: Tucker, *TRMP*, 240.

223 *"Oh, you pitiful cur"*: Undated letter in May 1894 file, n.d., BFP.

223 *"full of devotion"*: "Mrs. Breckinridge Remains Loyal," *LCJ*, March 20, 1894.

223 *"faith in their father was firm"*: "Not a Line Does Mrs. Breckinridge Read," *CE*, March 28, 1894.

223 *"It is the talk of all the saloons"*: "Falls Like Lucifer," *KL*, March 29, 1894.

223 *"In that letter did you not say"*: "Judge Wilson's Hint," *WP*, April 3, 1894.

224 *"not the faintest recollection"*: "The Colonel Repeats His Oft-Told Tale," *CE*, April 3, 1894.

224 *"several women or females"*: "Letters to Louise," *WES*, April 3, 1894.

224 *"in a public place"*: Ibid.

224 *"My Dear Sister Louise"*: Ibid.

225 *"sooner or later, I would hear"*: "Firm in His Denials," *WP*, April 4, 1894.

225 *"little Yankee woman"*: "Letters and the Writer of 'Em," *CE*, April 4, 1894.

226 *"expressions that a man"*: "Witness Steps Down," *WP*, April 5, 1894.

226 *"a young woman of colloquial"*: "Jere Let's the Colonel Go," *CE*, April 5, 1894.

226 *"I was always leaving Mrs. Blackburn"*: "Witness Steps Down," *WP*, April 5, 1894.

227 *"old colored midwife"*: "Constant the Shifting of Scenes," *CE*, April 6, 1894.

227 *"as coolly as if about to"*: Ibid.

228 *"The writer spoke of the great love"*: "Crowning Her Story," *WP*, April 6, 1894.

228 *"one of the nicest lunches"*: "Constant the Shifting of Scenes," *CE*, April 6, 1894.

16. THE FRONT PARLOR AND THE BACK GATE

230 *"perjured testimony"*: WCPB to E. P. Holly, April 6, 1894, BFP.

230 *"women doctors who are abortionists"*: WCPB to George O. Graves, April 24, 1894, BFP.

230 *"ladies who attend conventions"*: WCPB to Kerry M. Lawson, April 6, 1894, BFP.

230 *"secret sins"*: WCPB to "Myall," April 6, 1894, BFP.

231 *"impregnated the homes of the land"*: "Miss Pollard Is a Wonder," *WP*, April 8, 1894.

231 *"a foul, pestilence-breeding contagion"*: "Legal Points Argued Pro and Con," *CE*, April 8, 1894.

231 *"lewd and lascivious conduct"*: Ibid.

232 *"the woman of experience"*: "Lawyers Now Talk," *WES*, April 9, 1894.

232 *"florid Kentucky oratory"*: "Hard Words Used," *WES*, April 10, 1894.

232 *"every decent man"*: "Madeline Under Fire," *WP*, April 11, 1894.

232 *"old darky"*: "Hard Words Used," *WES*, April 10, 1894.

232 *"honest and virtuous"*: "More Eloquence," *WES*, April 12, 1894.

233 *"unnatural"*: Ibid.

233 *"deliberately turned from everything"*: "Butterworth Closes His Superb Effort," *CE*, April 13, 1894.

233 *"few pyrotechnic displays"*: "Jere Wilson's Plea," *WP*, April 14, 1894.

233 *"sunlight"*: Ibid.

233 *"I stand here for womanhood"*: Ibid.

234 *"There was a time"*: "Sarcasm That Cut to the Quick," *CE*, April 14, 1894.

234 *"clean-shaven, bald-headed"*: "Damages Awarded Madge Pollard," *CE*, April 15, 1894.

234 *"one code of morals for men"*: "Seeking a New Trial," *WP*, April 17, 1894.

235 *"nor the country girl"*: "Damages Awarded Madge Pollard," *CE*, April 15, 1894.

235 *"If it please the court"*: "Miss Pollard Wins," *NYW*, April 15, 1894.

235 *"Fifteen thousand for the plaintiff"*: Ibid.

236 *"Oh, isn't it good"*: Ibid.

236 *"room, board, medical attendance"*: Tucker, *TRMP*, 255.

236 *"observed of all the observers"*: "Victory for Miss Pollard," *New York Sun*, April 15, 1894.

236 *"was to the satisfaction"*: "'To Fight It Out," *WES*, April 16, 1894.

236 *"not one person"*: "Any Verdict a Just One," *LCJ*, April 15, 1894.

236 *"All the efforts made"*: "A White Life for Two," *Woman's Tribune*, April 21, 1894.

237 *"perniciousness of the unequal standard"*: *Woman's Journal*, April 7, 1894.

237 *"public men [who] hold immoral"*: "The Breckinridge Scandal," *The Philanthropist*, May 1894.

237 *"conventional morality"*: *Kate Field's Washington*, April 11, 1894.

237 *"the women of the world"*: "At Home with the Editor," *Ladies' Home Journal*, June 1894.

238 *"supposed popular sentiment"*: "For Miss Pollard," *WP*, April 15, 1894.

238 *"the ceaseless clamor"*: WCPB to John A. Lewis, April 15, 1894, BFP.

238 *"reputable society women"*: "Not a Line Does Mrs. Breckinridge Read," *CE*, March 28, 1894.

238 *"Breckinridge introduced himself"*: "Sustains Miss Pollard," *Cincinnati Tribune*, April 18, 1894.

239 *1870 census*: *1870 U.S. Federal Census* (database online). Ancestry.com.

239 *Franklin County birth records*: *Kentucky Birth Records, 1847–1911* (database online). Ancestry.com.

239 *1880 census*: *1880 U.S. Federal Census* (database online). Ancestry.com.

239 *married the Reverend Felix Struve*: *Semi-Weekly Bourbon News* (Paris, KY), Sept. 25, 1883.

239 *thirty-six*: *1900 U.S. Federal Census* (database online). Ancestry.com.

239 *1920 death certificate*: *Kentucky Death Records, 1852–1963* (database online). Ancestry.com.

240 *"Miss Pollard . . . received company"*: Mollie Shindlebower to WCPB, Nov. 25, 1893, BFP.

240 *"Mary Pollard was considered"*: Effie Knight to WCPB, Nov. 25, 1893, BFP.

240 *Desha confirmed*: Desha Breckinridge to WCPB, Sept. 6, 1893, BFP.

241 *"remarkable"*: Tucker, *TRMP*, 122.

241 *"first heard from her"*: "Breckinridge Guarded," *NYW*, Aug. 15, 1893.

241 *"I wonder how impertinent"*: Madeline Pollard to John Hay, May 20, 1890, John Hay Papers, Brown University.

242 *"too expensive for him"*: "Miss Pollard's Suit," *LCJ*, Aug. 16, 1893.

242 *"glad to do anything"*: McTodd to WCPB, Dec. 2, 1893, BFP.

243 *"nuns are very careful"*: Ibid.

243 *"tried hard"*: Effie Knight to WCPB, Nov. 25, 1893, BFP.

243 *he had gone back to Cincinnati*: Burnet House to WCPB, Aug. 23, 1884, BFP.

244 *"ain't a good woman"*: "Another Assault," *LCJ*, Sept. 11, 1894.

244 *"living child"*: WCPB to H. H. Gratz, May 11, 1894, BFP.

244 *"she would not obey"*: Note in Trial Folder, BFP.

245 *"countrified"*: "Gossip's Tongue," *KL*, Aug. 17, 1893.

245 *"was not introduced into society"*: "Will Come Home," *KL*, Sept. 14, 1893.

245 *"into other homes"*: "Miss Pollard's Story of Col. Breckinridge," *NYW*, Sept. 17, 1893.

245 *"had become acquainted"*: "Believe Him Innocent," *LCJ*, Aug. 14, 1893.

245 *"senseless waste of time"*: Dahlgren, *Etiquette of Social Life*, 35.

246 *"Metamorphosis of Negative Matter"*: Jacob, *Capital Elites*, 217.

246 *"a charitable institution"*: "Will Come Home," *KL*, Sept. 14, 1893.

246 *February 1888*: "Society," *WP*, Feb. 14, 1888.

246 *"a charitable ball"*: "Col. Breckinridge's Defense," *LCJ*, Sept. 13, 1893.

246 *"Miss Pollard worked her way"*: "Will Come Home," *KL*, Sept. 14, 1893.

246 *upper right corner*: Dahlgren, *Etiquette of Social Life*, 58.

247 *spring of 1890*: "Mrs. Dahlgren's Party," *WP*, March 6, 1890.

247 *"If our good friend"*: Madeline Pollard to John Hay, May 20, 1890, John Hay Papers, Brown University.

247 *"Miss Madeline Pollard"*: "Personal Paragraphs," *WP*, June 3, 1891.

247 *"in strict confidence"*: Tucker, *TRMP*, 58.

247 *"Clothes were really clothes then"*: Foraker, *I Would Live It Again*, 158.

248 *"quite well"*: Tucker, *TRMP*, 113.

248 *modeled on Madeleine Dahlgren*: Jacob, *Capital Elites*, 216.

248 *"seemed to have become a tourist fashion"*: Adams, *Education of Henry Adams*, 258.

248 *"it represented a figure wrapped in meditation"*: Tucker, *TRMP*, 113–14.

249 *"pioneer of Catholic light literature"*: "Ella Loraine Dorsey," *A Woman of the Century*, 254.

249 *"some years ago"*: "Writing Boys' Stories," *WP*, April 12, 1891.

249 *"I honestly believe"*: "The Women of Breckinridge's District," *CE*, March 3, 1894.

250 *"she was to be one of the party"*: WCPB, note to file, BFP.

250 *"went away and had the advantage"*: "His Story in Detail," *WP*, March 31, 1894.

250 *"scandal was current"*: "Mrs. Breckinridge Remains Loyal," *LCJ*, March 20, 1894.

250 *"I see you are endorsed by Col. Breckinridge"*: Ibid.

251 *charity garden party*: "Social and Personal," *WES*, June 1, 1893.

251 *Smith-Judson wedding*: "Social and Personal," *WES*, June 7, 1893.

251 *"In Washington gossip"*: Carpenter, *Carp's Washington*, 9.

251 *"It is said that the story"*: "Is It Blackmail?," *WES*, Aug. 14, 1893.

251 *"faults—grievous ones"*: "Miss Pollard Corroborated," *CCG*, Aug. 16, 1893.

252 *"some of her visiting cards"*: Nannie White to WCPB, March 5, 1894, BFP.

252 *"man and wife"*: A. L. Hall to WCPB, March 17, 1894, BFP.

252 *"making a very loud noise"*: Mrs. J. Ambrose to WCPB, March 3, 1894, BFP.

253 *Johnstown flood*: Note from WCPB, 1893, Pollard case file, BFP.

253 *"shy, absent-minded"*: Chalkley, *Magic Casements*, 84.

254 *"good deal of work"*: "Now for Her Scrub Woman," *CCG*, Aug. 18, 1893.

254 *"array of costly dresses"*: "Miss Pollard's Story of Col. Breckinridge," *NYW*, Sept. 17, 1893.

254 *"irregular amounts"*: "Letters and the Writer of 'Em," *CE*, April 4, 1894.

254 *"My expenses are very heavy"*: Madeline Pollard to James C. Rhodes, Jan. 30, 1890, BFP.

254 *casual prostitution*: Stansell, *City of Women*, 180.

254 *"Many a female clerk"*: Carpenter, *Carp's Washington*, 3–4.

17. THE CAVALIER AND THE PURITANS

256 *"social conversation"*: "Pure Men in Congress," *WP*, April 16, 1894.

256 *"combat the enforcement of"*: "For Expulsion," *LCJ*, April 16, 1894.

257 *"The Washington women"*: "Declare War on Gay Congressmen," *CDT*, April 16, 1894.

258 *"take some definite action"*: "Pure Men in Congress," *WP*, April 16, 1894.

258 *"I do believe"*: JAT to Mary Tucker, April 22, 1894, TFP.

258 *"We are confident of success next time"*: Ibid.

258 *"scheme for some work"*: JAT to Mary Tucker, April 1, 1894, TFP.

259 *"enough money to my credit"*: JAT to Mary Tucker, April 22, 1894, TFP.

259 *"Nisba and I have become"*: Ibid.

259 *"have been through a hard trial"*: JAT to Mary Tucker, May 7, 1894, TFP.

259 *"I shall cut off my hair"*: Tucker, *TRMP*, 153.

259 *"might write in a little room"*: Ibid., 293.

259 *"temptations and sorrows"*: Ibid., 273.

259 *"religious cranks"*: Ibid., 270.

260 *"exhibition"*: Ibid., 232.

260 *"much easier life"*: Ibid., 293.

260 *"going on the stage"*: "Miss Pollard Speaks," *NYW*, April 16, 1894.

260 *"nothing can induce me"*: "Madeline Pollard's Hope," *New York Sun*, April 18, 1894.

260 *"forty cents"*: Tucker, *TRMP*, 314.

261 *"You are safe in saying"*: "House Will Do Nothing, It Is Said," *NYT*, April 17, 1894.

261 *"said we were making"*: "He Talked Kindly," *LMT*, April 5, 1894.

261 *"generous people"*: WCPB to S. L. Yager, April 6, 1894, BFP.

261 *"until Mr. Davis"*: WCPB to Robert Tucker, Dec. 21, 1893, BFP.

261 *"I shall possibly get"*: JAT to Mary Tucker, April 1, 1894, TFP.

262 *"Athens of the West"*: Hollingsworth, *Lexington*, 26.

262 *eight thousand of the twenty thousand*: "Mr. Breckinridge," *Cincinnati Tribune*, April 19, 1894.

262 *"buttonhole the voters"*: WCPB to C. H. Reed, Jan. 31, 1894, BFP.

262 *"I never saw a campaign"*: "Mr. Breckinridge," *Cincinnati Tribune*, April 19, 1894.

263 *"I couldn't look my wife and daughters in the face"*: Ibid.

263 *"50 ladies—wives and sisters"*: "The Women of Breckinridge's District," *CE*, March 3, 1894.

263 *"allowed the open expression"*: D'Emilio and Freedman, *Intimate Matters*, 19.

264 *"distressed Cavaliers"*: Fischer, *Albion's Seed*, 213.

264 *"held to the strictest"*: Ibid., 300.

264 *"until the blood flowed"*: Ibid., 299.

264 *"a virgin as a girl"*: Ibid., 303.

264 *one in five female servants*: Carr and Walsh, "The Planter's Wife," 548.

264 *"Masters could abuse the law"*: D'Emilio and Freedman, *Intimate Matters*, 33.

264 *"if the father of a bastard"*: Wells, "Illegitimacy and Bridal Pregnancy in Colonial America," 357.

265 *"humble, obedient, careful and thoughtful"*: Scott, *The Southern Lady*, 15, note 40.

265 *"the thing we can't name"*: Woodward, *Mary Chesnut's Civil War*, 28.

265 *"Every lady tells you"*: Ibid.

265 *"If the countless thousands"*: "Miss Madeline Pollard Giving Breckinridge and South Hard Time," *Cleveland Gazette*, March 24, 1894.

265 *"Many prominent society women"*: "Not a Line Does Mrs. Breckinridge Read," *CE*, March 28, 1894.

265 *"when they knew"*: "Women Up In Arms," *LMT*, March 29, 1894.

266 *"fools"*: JAT to Mary Tucker, May 15, 1894, TFP.

266 *"deeply humiliated"*: "They Take a Hand," *LMT*, May 5, 1894.

266 *"Clinching his hands"*: "Col. Breckinridge Pleads in Public," *NYT*, May 6, 1894.

267 *"Every one says"*: JAT to Mary Tucker, May 7, 1894, TFP.

267 *"was no great swarming of the aisles"*: "Confession and Defiance," *LCJ*, May 6, 1894.

267 *"upon the plea"*: "The Breckinridge Candidacy," *LCJ*, May 7, 1894.

267 *"very feeble"*: SPB to WCPB, May 4, 1894, BFP.

268 *"Are you to choose"*: "In Ashland," *LCJ*, May 8, 1894.

268 *"conspiracy to destroy me"*: WCPB to Henry S. Halley, April 24, 1894, BFP.

268 *"a case of the Cavalier"*: John Phillips to WCPB, April 16, 1894, BFP.

269 *"there should be the same"*: "Dress and Divorce," *CDT*, May 9, 1894.

269 *"moral purity should be"*: "Women's Clubs Adjourn," *WP*, May 12, 1894.

269 *"higher obligation"*: "Not Women Alone," *LMT*, May 13, 1894.

269 *"outside a few women's suffrage cranks"*: "Breckinridge Is Denounced," *LCJ*, May 15, 1894.

269 *"Miss Pollard knew from the beginning"*: "She Defends Breckinridge," *New York Sun*, March 30, 1894.

270 *"in grave danger"*: SPB to WCPB, May 7, 1894, BFP.

270 *"one great treat"*: JAT to Mary Tucker, May 22, 1894, TFP.

270 *"seems almost like home"*: JAT to Mary Tucker, May 22, 1894, TFP.

270 *"systematic course of English literature"*: Tucker, TRMP, 335.

271 *"unless she went away"*: Ibid., 334.

271 *"dead, practically, in Congress"*: Ibid., 335.

271 *"like a gally [sic] slave"*: JAT to Mary Tucker, May 31, 1894, TFP.

271 *"very faithful and helpful"*: SPB to WCPB, June 7, 1894, BFP.

272 *"prolonged brain rest"*: Preston B. Scott to WCPB, June 13, 1894, BFP.

272 *"had no parallel"*: "Col. Breckinridge's Defeat," WP, Sept. 17, 1894.

273 *"The women are aroused"*: "Pollard, Another Story of the Source of the Funds," KL, May 24, 1894.

273 *"insulting"*: "Villainous Threat," *Cincinnati Tribune*, June 11, 1894.

274 *"feeble woman"*: SPB to WCPB, July 20, 1894, BFP.

274 *"The Breckinridge business floats"*: "A Chicago Woman," KL, Aug. 23, 1894.

274 *"what your relations"*: WCPB to H. H. Gratz, May 11, 1894, BFP.

274 *"eighty sheep, eleven [cows]"*: Fuller, "Congressman Breckinridge and the Ladies," 7.

275 *"who all through the course"*: "Owens, Owens, Owens," KL, Aug. 23, 1894.

275 *"to tell you some truths"*: "Miss Desha's Appeal," WP, Aug. 28, 1894.

275 *"one of the wickedest"*: Carpenter, *Carp's Washington*, 3.

275 *"parade Pennsylvania Avenue"*: Ibid., 110.

275 *"It is an open secret in Washington"*: "Declare War on Gay Congressmen," CDT, April 16, 1894.

275 *"shocking her friends"*: "Miss Desha's Appeal," WP, Aug. 28, 1894.

276 *"It has been greatly complemented"*: Julia C. Blackburn to Mary Desha, Aug. 30, 1894, Mary Desha Papers, the University of Kentucky.

276 *"against Breckinridge is so bitter"*: Mary Mitchell Foster to Mary Desha, Aug. 29, 1894, Mary Desha Papers, the University of Kentucky.

276 *"Any woman who would"*: "Cut to Death," LMT, Aug. 31, 1891.

276 *"Everyone looks like"*: "Ready to Snap," LCJ, Sept. 14, 1894.

276 *"What a time"*: Susan B. Anthony to Laura Clay, Sept. 21, 1894, Laura Clay Papers, University of Kentucky.

276 *"I feel it would be"*: Quoted in Hay, *Madeline McDowell Breckinridge*, 35.

276 *"Like myself I suppose you"*: Julia Blackburn to Mary Desha, Sept. 11, 1894, Mary Desha Papers, the University of Kentucky.

276 *"social duties"*: "She's All Right," LCJ, Sept. 11, 1894.

277 *"Never before in any canvas"*: "Silver Tongue Silenced," CE, Sept. 16, 1894.

277 *"there is a place"*: Anthony and Harper, *The History of Woman Suffrage*, 667.

277 *"most promising"*: Fuller, *Laura Clay*, 57–59.

278 *"comedy-drama"*: "Miss Pollard's Plans," KL, Aug. 16, 1894.

278 *"a novel nearly completed"*: "Madeline Pollard's Plans," WP, Oct. 24, 1894.

278 *"a ruin that is complete"*: "Falls Like Lucifer," KL, March 29, 1894.

278 *"The fall of Breckinridge"*: Tapp and Klotter, *Kentucky*, 337.

278 *"a mediocre representative"*: SPB Autobiography, SBP.

279 *"It is a step toward"*: SPB to WCPB, Sept. 8, 1894, BFP.

279 *"To say she did right"*: Fayette Lexington, *The Celebrated Case*, 18.

279 *the second woman*: (Lewiston, ME) *Weekly Journal*, Oct. 4, 1894.

18. REFUSING TO BEHAVE

280 *"startled the whole country"*: "Kentucky Men Are Agitated," *New York Herald*, March 24, 1894.

281 *"shattering Nineties"*: Foraker, *I Would Live It Again*, 7.

281 *"the most significant event"*: O'Neill, *Everyone Was Brave*, 148.

281 *"Sex o'clock in America"*: Reedy, "Sex O'Clock in America," 1.

281 *"teachers, lecturers, novelists"*: Repplier, "Repeal of Reticence," 298.

282 *"There would have been no scandal"*: WCPB to A. W. Macklin, Feb. 26, 1894, BFP.

282 *"testimony as a woman of social standing"*: "Our Wealthy Widows," *WP*, Dec. 9, 1894.

283 *"support and encouragement"*: WCPB to A. W. Macklin, Feb. 26, 1894, BFP.

283 *"honor was involved"*: "Miss Pollard's Story of Col. Breckinridge," *NYW*, Sept. 17, 1893.

283 *Women's Auxiliary*: "The Women's Auxiliary Ex-Confederate Aid Society," *WP*, Nov. 16, 1891.

283 *"the first one I talked to"*: Tucker, TRMP, 262.

283 *"he had the case"*: "They May Follow Breckinridge," *WP*, Dec. 27, 1894.

284 *"directly or indirectly"*: "Motion Filed," *LCJ*, April 18, 1894.

284 *"a widow, a Kentuckian"*: "For the Defense," *WES*, March 22, 1894.

285 *"a man who made such a profession"*: "Miss Pollard's Backers," *NYW*, March 27, 1894.

285 *Columbia Working Girls' Club*: "Home for Working Girls," *NYT*, Dec. 14, 1893.

285 *"How a Girl's Life Can Be Transformed"*: "The Social World," *NYT*, Feb. 8, 1894.

285 *"traveling companion"*: "Madeline Pollard to Go Abroad," *Sentinel* (Fort Wayne, IN), April 25, 1895.

286 *"one of the few rich"*: "Women at the World's Fair," *WP*, Oct. 23, 1892.

286 *"noted philanthropist"*: "Under Fire Today," *WP*, April 3, 1894.

286 *suit was organized*: "The Pollard Fund," *Cincinnati Tribune*, May 20, 1894.

287 *"Nothing has ever yet been"*: "Madeline Pollard's Hope," *New York Sun*, April 18, 1894.

287 *"one of the richest"*: JAT to William Worthington, March 9, 1894, TFP.

287 *one of the city's most desirable debutantes*: "The New Spanish Minister," *NYT*, June 11, 1899.

287 *In the spring of 1895*: "Days of Romance Not Past," *Lewiston (ME) Daily Sun*, June 24, 1895.

288 *"expenses incurred"*: "Money for Trial Expenses," *LCJ*, March 21, 1894.

288 *"furnished her by lady friends"*: Tucker, TRMP, 86.

19. REDEMPTION

289 *"troublesome voters upon whom"*: Breckinridge, "Issues of the Presidential Campaign," 274.

289 *"We lost zest after that"*: Foraker, *I Would Live It Again*, 151.

290 *caught a bad cold*: Klotter, *Breckinridges of Kentucky*, 184.

290 *suffered a stroke* and *suffered a second*: "W.C.P. Breckinridge Ill," "Col. Breckinridge Stricken Again," *NYT*, Sept. 30 and Nov. 17, 1904.

290 *November 19*: *Kentucky Death Records, 1852–1964* (database online). Ancestry .com.

290 *Louise died in 1920*: *U.S. Find a Grave Index, 1600s–Current* (database online). Ancestry.com.

290 *"He was defeated for renomination"*: "W.C.P. Breckinridge Dead," *NYT*, Nov. 20, 1904.

290 *"The [Breckinridge] name has been connected"*: WCPB to SPB, Nov. 16, 1902, BFP.

291 *"some woman's rights gang"*: JAT to Mary Tucker, March 2, 1894, TFP.

291 *"regular hotbed"*: Deutsch, *Women and the City*, 104.

291 *"I'll bet they were glad"*: JAT to Mary Tucker, Dec. 11, 1904, TFP.

291 *"terrible stupid and prosy"*: JAT to Mary Tucker, Dec. 7, 1905, TFP.

292 *"sassed"*: JAT Obituary, April 29, 1964, TFP.

292 *"such pigeons as one"*: JAT to Arthur Warren, Dec. 22, 1908, TFP.

292 *"The world is wide"*: JAT to Mary Tucker, June 28, 1898, TFP.

292 *"hard head"*: JAT Obituary, April 29, 1964, TFP.

293 *"the question of my health"*: SPB Autobiography, SBP.

293 *"did not have the money"*: SPB Autobiography, SBP.

293 *"He assembled two other justices"*: SPB Autobiography, SBP.

293 *"inherits her love for the law"*: "Miss Breckinridge a Lawyer," *NYT*, Jan. 26, 1897.

293 *reported erroneously in 1892*: "Congressman Breckinridge's Daughter's Legal Studies," *NYT*, Nov. 28, 1892.

293 *only exam Nisba took*: 1897 Kentucky Court of Appeals Order Book 73, 376.

294 *"special women's interests"*: SPB Autobiography, SBP.

294 *"I am growing quite famous"*: WCPB to SPB, June 17, 1904, BFP.

294 *"the system which differentiates"*: quoted in Klotter, *Breckinridges of Kentucky*, 194–95.

294 *"social politics"*: Goodwin, *Gender and the Politics of Welfare Reform*, 6.

294 *"to the bearing and raising of children"*: Ibid., 94.

294 *"virtue is in peril"*: Fitzpatrick, *Endless Crusade*, 185.

295 *Chicago Orphan Asylum*: Wright, "Three Against Time," 47.

295 *"mother's pensions"*: See Goodwin, *Gender and the Politics of Welfare Reform*.

295 *"between lack of political equality"*: Fitzpatrick, *Endless Crusade*, 194.

295 *"An attempt to give a course"*: Travis, "Sophonisba Breckinridge," 112.

295 *"a hectic round of meetings"*: "Sophonisba Preston Breckinridge," *Notable American Women, 1607–1950*, vol. 1.

295 *"I came to the university"*: Travis, "Sophonisba Breckinridge," 112.

296 *"If we come out of the depression"*: Lenroot, "Sophonisba Preston Breckinridge," 89.

296 *seventh Pan-American Conference*: "Roosevelt Limits Montevideo Talks," *NYT*, Nov. 10, 1933.

296 *ranked the top ten American political dynasties*: Stephen Hess, "America's Top Dynasties," *WP*, Nov. 13, 2009.

296 *"able, eloquent and public spirited"*: SPB Autobiography, SBP.

297 *"municipal housekeeping"*: See Porter, *Madeline McDowell Breckinridge*.

297 *pro-suffrage pamphlet*: Breckinridge, *Madeline McDowell Breckinridge*, 22.

297 *had been having an affair*: Porter, *Madeline McDowell Breckinridge*, 209.

297 *"toward a more modern"*: Breckinridge, *Madeline McDowell Breckinridge*, viii.

298 *long, dark dress*: Fitzpatrick, *Endless Crusade*, 215.

298 *"more honest and simpler"*: SPB Autobiography, SBP.

298 *"the access of women"*: Breckinridge, *Women in the Twentieth Century*, 107.

298 *"afraid of life"*: SPB Autobiography, SBP.

298 *"died in a way"*: Ibid.

298 *"I have wanted to write"*: Ibid.

299 *"outstanding figure"*: "Miss Breckinridge Dies in Chicago," *NYT*, July 31, 1948.

299 *"thoroughly disgraced woman"*: "Madeline Pollard's Hope," *New York Sun*, April 19, 1894.

299 *"in good circumstances"*: "Madeline Pollard in London," *WP*, June 20, 1897.

299 *"writer of fiction"*: *1901 England Census* (database online). Ancestry.com.

299 *Madeleine Urquhart Pollard*: *1911 England Census* (database online). Ancestry.com.

299 *good part of the mid-1920s*: *U.S. Passport Applications, 1795–1925* (database online). Ancestry.com.

300 *returning to New York*: "Paris" from Plymouth to New York, May 23, 1928, *New York, Passenger Lists, 1820–1957* (database online). Ancestry.com.

300 *"I am sure that it is providential"*: Madeline Pollard to Nicholas Murray Butler, July 3, 1936, Nicholas Murray Butler Papers, Columbia University.

300 *"I have asked"*: "Miss Pollard Speaks of Her Past, Present, and Future," *The News* (Frederick, MD), Dec. 29, 1894.

300 *December 9, 1945*: *England and Wales Civil Registration Death Index, 1916–2007* (database online). Ancestry.com.

300 *November 30, 1863*: *Olympic* from Southampton to New York, May 12, 1931, *New York, Passenger Lists, 1820–1957* (database online). Ancestry.com.

Bibliography

The primary sources for *Bringing Down the Colonel* are contemporaneous newspaper coverage of the Breckinridge-Pollard scandal and trial in ten major newspapers, the letters of the Breckinridge and Tucker families, Sophonisba Breckinridge's unpublished autobiography, Eleanor Breckinridge Chalkley's autobiography *Magic Casements*, and Jennie Tucker's account of her time at the House of Mercy and friendship with Madeline Pollard, *The Real Madeleine Pollard: A Diary of Ten Weeks' Association with the Plaintiff in the Famous Breckinridge-Pollard Suit*.

The trial records of the five-and-a-half-week trial in the Supreme Court of the District of Columbia are not extant, although they are listed as being in the records of the court held at the National Archives. According to the Federal Judicial Records archivist Robert Ellis, this is not the first instance of files from high-profile cases like sex scandals or divorces mysteriously disappearing before the records are accessioned into the National Archives. And Willie Breckinridge did have friends in high places. Fortunately for historians, both the *New York World* and the *Cincinnati Enquirer* had stenographers present in the courtroom and provide detailed transcriptions of much of the testimony, which, when cross-referenced with the other newspaper coverage, provides an accurate account of the proceedings. All newspaper articles referenced are on file with the author.

A key source for understanding the complex history of the Breckinridge family and its politics and the political rise of Willie Breckinridge is James Klotter's essential *The Breckinridges of Kentucky: 1760–1981*. The most important works about the legacy of Sophonisba Breckinridge are Ellen Fitzpatrick's *Endless Crusade: Women Social Scientists and Progressive Reform* and Joanne Goodwin's *Gender and the Politics of Welfare Reform*. Melba Porter Hay's *Madeline McDowell Breckinridge and the Battle for the New South* provides key insights into both Nisba and Desha Breckinridge's politics and the social milieu in which the scandal occurred.

MANUSCRIPT COLLECTIONS

Breckinridge Family Papers (BFP). Library of Congress, Washington, D.C.
Breckinridge, Sophonisba Papers (SBP). University of Chicago.
Butler, Nicholas Murray Papers. Columbia University, New York.
Clay, Laura Papers. University of Kentucky, Lexington.
Desha, Mary Papers. University of Kentucky, Lexington.
Green Family Papers. Western Kentucky University, Bowling Green.
Hay, John Papers. Brown University, Providence, RI.
Tucker Family Papers (TFP). Historic New England, Boston.

NEWSPAPERS

Chicago Daily Tribune: CDT
Cincinnati Commercial Gazette: CCG
Cincinnati Enquirer: CE
Kentucky Leader: KL
Lexington Morning Transcript: LMT
Louisville Courier-Journal: LCJ
New York Times: NYT
New York World: NYW
Washington Evening Star: WES
Washington Post: WP

BOOKS, ARTICLES, AND DISSERTATIONS

Abbott, Edith. "Sophonisba Preston Breckinridge over the Years." *Social Service Review* 22 (Dec. 1948): 417–23.
Adams, Henry. *The Education of Henry Adams: A Centennial Version*. Edited by Edward Chalfant and Conrad Edick Wright. Boston: Massachusetts Historical Society, 2007.
Adams, John. *Diary and Autobiography of John Adams*. Vol. 1, edited by Lyman Butterfield. Cambridge, MA: Harvard University Press, 1961.
Addams, Jane. *Twenty Years at Hull House*. New York: Macmillan, 1910.
Alcott, Louisa May. "How I Went Out to Service." In *Louisa May Alcott: Work, Eight Cousins, Rose in Bloom, Stories and Other Writings*, edited by Susan Cheever, 806–19. New York: Library of America, 2014.
Allen, Frederick James. *The Law as a Vocation*. Cambridge, MA: Harvard University Press, 1924.
Andrew, Charles B. "Sea and River Fishing: The President as an Angler." *Forest and Stream*, June 17, 1886, 411.
Anthony, Susan B. "Social Purity." In *The Life and Work of Susan B. Anthony*. Vol. 2, edited by Ida Husted Harper, 1004–12. Indianapolis, IN: Bowen-Merrill, 1898.
Anthony, Susan B., and Ida Harper, eds. *The History of Woman Suffrage*. Vol. 4. Rochester, NY: Susan B. Anthony, 1902.
Aron, Cindy Sondik. *Ladies and Gentlemen of the Civil Service: Middle-Class Workers in Victorian America*. New York: Oxford University Press, 1987.

Aurand, A. Monroe. *Little Known Facts About Bundling in the New World*. Harrisburg, PA: Aurand Press, 1938.

Baird, Nancy Disher. *Luke Pryor Blackburn: Physician, Governor, Reformer*. Lexington: University Press of Kentucky, 1979.

Benson, Susan Porter. *Counter Cultures: Saleswomen, Managers, and Customers in American Department Stores, 1890–1940*. Urbana: University of Illinois Press, 1996.

Block, Mary R. "An Accusation Easily to Be Made: A History of Rape Law in Nineteenth-Century America." Ph.D. diss., University of Kentucky, 2001.

Bowen, William, ed. "Dr. Kinsley Twining." *Independent*, vol. 53, 2727.

Brands, H. W. *The Reckless Decade: America in the 1890s*. Chicago: University of Chicago Press, 1995.

Breckinridge, Robert J. *Papism in the XIX Century, in the United States*. Baltimore: David Owen and Son, 1841.

Breckinridge, Sophonisba Preston. *Madeline McDowell Breckinridge*. Chicago: University of Chicago Press, 1921.

———. "Mary Desha." *New York State News Sheet*, Oct. 1942, 1–4.

———. *Women in the Twentieth Century: A Study of Their Political, Social and Economic Activities*. New York: McGraw Hill, 1933.

Breckinridge, W.C.P. "Issues of the Presidential Campaign." *North American Review* 154 (March 1892): 257–80.

Brown, Richard C. *The Presbyterians: Two Hundred Years in Danville, 1784–1984*. Danville, KY: Presbyterian Church, 1983.

Bureau of Labor. "Report on the Condition of Women and Child Wage-Earners in the United States," vol. 9. Washington, D.C.: Government Printing Office, 1911.

Bushnell, Kate. *The Woman Condemned*. New York: Funk and Wallace, 1886.

Carpenter, Frank G. *Carp's Washington*. New York: McGraw-Hill, 1960.

Carr, Lois Green, and Lorena S. Walsh. "The Planter's Wife: The Experience of White Women in Seventeenth-Century Maryland." *William and Mary Quarterly* 34 (Oct. 1977): 542–71.

The Celebrated Trial: Madeline Pollard vs. Breckinridge. New York: American Printing and Binding Company, 1894.

Censer, Jane Turner. *The Reconstruction of White Southern Womanhood, 1865–1895*. Baton Rouge: Louisiana State University Press, 2003.

Chalkley, Eleanor Breckinridge. *Magic Casements*. Frankfort: Kentucky Historical Society, 1982.

Chudacoff, Howard P. *The Age of the Bachelor: Creating an American Subculture*. Princeton, NJ: Princeton University Press, 1999.

Clarke, Edward H. *Sex in Education; or, a Fair Chance for Girls*. Boston: James R. Osgood, 1873.

Cook, May Estelle. "Notes and Comments by the Editor." *Social Service Review* 23 (March 1949): 93–96.

Cott, Nancy F. "Passionless-ness: An Interpretation of Victorian Sexual Ideology." *Signs* 4 (Winter 1978): 219–36.

Dahlgren, Madeleine Vinton. *Etiquette of Social Life in Washington*. Philadelphia: J. B. Lippincott and Co., 1881. Reprint, London: Forgotten Books, 2015.

Dall, Caroline Wells Healey. *Women's Rights Under the Law*. Boston: Walker, Wise, and Company, 1861.

Davies, Margery W. *Woman's Place Is at the Typewriter: Office and Office Workers, 1870–1930*. Philadelphia: Temple University Press, 1982.

Degler, Carl N. "What Ought to Be and What Was: Women's Sexuality in the Nineteenth Century." *American Historical Review* 79 (Dec. 1974): 1467–90.

D'Emilio, John, and Estelle B. Freedman. *Intimate Matters: A History of Sexuality in America*. 2nd ed. Chicago: University of Chicago Press, 1997.

Demos, John. *A Little Commonwealth: Family Life in Plymouth Colony*. New York: Oxford University Press, 1970.

Deutsch, Sarah. *Women and the City: Gender, Space and Power in Boston, 1870–1940*. New York: Oxford University Press, 2000.

Duffield, Isabel McKenna. *Washington in the 90's*. San Francisco: Press of Overland Monthly, 1929.

Farr, Samuel. *Elements of Medical Jurisprudence*. London: T. Becket, 1788.

Fischer, David Hackett. *Albion's Seed: Four British Folkways in America*. New York: Oxford University Press, 1989.

Fitzpatrick, Ellen. *Endless Crusade: Women Social Scientists and Progressive Reform*. New York: Oxford University Press, 1990.

Foraker, Julia. *I Would Live It Again: Memories of a Vivid Life*. New York: Harper and Brothers, 1932.

Fuller, Paul. "Congressman Breckinridge and the Ladies, or Sex, Politics, and Morality in the Gilded Age." *Adena* 2 (1977): 1–13.

———. *Laura Clay and the Women's Rights Movement*. Lexington: University Press of Kentucky, 1975.

Glazer, Penina Migdal, and Miriam Slater. *Unequal Colleagues: The Entrance of Women into the Professions, 1890–1940*. New Brunswick, NJ: Rutgers University Press, 1987.

Godbeer, Richard. *Sexual Revolution in Early America*. Baltimore: Johns Hopkins University Press, 2002.

Gonda, Susan. "Strumpets and Angels: Rape, Seduction, and the Boundaries of Consensual Sex in the Northeast, 1789–1870." Ph.D. diss., University of California, Los Angeles, 1999.

Goodwin, Joanne L. *Gender and the Politics of Welfare Reform: Mother's Pensions in Chicago, 1911–1928*. University of Chicago Press, 1997.

Gordon, Michael, ed. *The American Family in Social-Historical Perspective*. New York: St. Martin's Press, 1973.

Gordon, Sarah Barringer. "Law and Everyday Death: Infanticide and the Backlash Against Women's Rights After the Civil War." In *Lives in the Law*, edited by Austin Sarat, Lawrence Douglas, and Martha Umphrey, 55–81. Ann Arbor: University of Michigan Press, 2002.

Grossberg, Michael. *Governing the Hearth: Law and the Family in Nineteenth-Century America*. Chapel Hill: University of North Carolina Press, 1985.

Hacker, David J., Libra Hidle, and James Holland Jones. "The Effect of the Civil War on Southern Marriage Patterns." *Journal of Southern History* 76 (Feb. 2010): 39–70.

Hall, Basil. *Travels in North America*. Vol. 3. Edinburgh: Cadell and Co., 1829.

Harrison, Lowell H. *The Anti-Slavery Movement in Kentucky*. Lexington: University Press of Kentucky, 1978.

Haven, Alice B. "A Morning at Stewart's." *Godey's Lady's Book and Magazine*, May 1863, 429–33.

Hay, Melba Porter. *Madeline McDowell Breckinridge and the Battle for a New South*. Lexington: University Press of Kentucky, 2009.

Hollingsworth, Randolph. *Lexington: Queen of the Bluegrass*. Charleston, SC: Arcadia Publishing, 2004.

Horan, James D. *Confederate Agent: A Discovery in History*. New York: Crown Publishers, 1954.

Humble, H. W. "Seduction as a Crime." *Columbia Law Review* 21 (Feb. 1921): 144–54.

Ireland, Robert. "The Libertine Must Die: Sexual Dishonor and the Unwritten Law in the Nineteenth-Century United States." *Journal of Social History* 23 (Autumn 1989): 27–44.

Jabour, Anya. *Scarlett's Sisters: Young Women in the Old South*. Chapel Hill: University of North Carolina Press, 2007.

Jacob, Kathryn Allamong. *Capital Elites: High Society in Washington After the Civil War*. Washington: Smithsonian Institution Press, 1995.

Jett, Denis. *American Ambassadors: The Past, Present, and Future of America's Diplomats*. New York: Palgrave Macmillan, 2014.

Johnson, Joan Marie. *Southern Women at the Seven Sister Colleges: Feminist Values and Social Action, 1875–1915*. Athens: University of Georgia Press, 2008.

Kessler-Harris, Alice. *Out to Work: A History of Wage-Earning Women in the United States*. New York: Oxford University Press, 1982.

Klotter, James C. *The Breckinridges of Kentucky: 1760–1981*. Lexington: University Press of Kentucky, 1986.

Kunzel, Regina G. *Fallen Women, Problem Girls: Unmarried Mothers and the Professionalization of Social Work, 1890–1945*. New Haven, CT: Yale University Press, 1993.

Laslett, Peter. "Comparing Illegitimacy over Time and Between Cultures." In *Bastardy and Its Comparative History*, edited by Peter Laslett, Karla Oosterveen, and Richard M. Smith, 1–65. London: Edward Arnold, 1980.

Leach, William. *True Love and the Perfect Union: The Feminist Reform of Sex and Society*. Middletown, CT: Wesleyan University Press, 1980.

Lenroot, Katharine F. "Sophonisba Preston Breckinridge, Social Pioneer." *Social Service Review* 23 (March 1949): 88–92.

Lewis, Jan, and Kenneth Lockridge. "'Sally Has Been Sick': Pregnancy and Family Limitation Among Virginia Gentry Women, 1780–1830." *Journal of Social History* 22 (Autumn 1988): 5–19.

Lexington, Fayette. *The Celebrated Case of Col. W.C.P. Breckinridge and Madeline Pollard*. Chicago: Current Events Publishing, 1894.

Lincoln, Abraham. *Collected Works of Abraham Lincoln*. Vol. 4. Ann Arbor: University of Michigan, 2001.

Lindemann, Barbara. "To Ravish and Carnally Know." *Signs* 10 (Autumn 1984): 63–82.

Livermore, Mary A. *What Shall We Do with Our Daughters? Superfluous Women, and Other Lectures*. Boston: Lee and Shepard, 1883.

Lynch, Denis Tilden. *Grover Cleveland: A Man Four Square*. New York: Horace Liveright, 1932.

Marsden, George. *Jonathan Edwards: A Life*. New Haven, CT: Yale University Press, 2003.

Martin, Asa Earl. "The Anti-Slavery Movement in Kentucky Prior to 1850." Ph.D. diss., Cornell University, 1918.

McHatton, Thomas A. "The Honorable Peter Stirling by Paul Leicester Ford." *Georgia Review* 7 (Fall 1953): 247–49.

Merrill, Horace Samuel. *Bourbon Leader: Grover Cleveland and the Democratic Party*. Boston: Little, Brown, and Co., 1957.

Meyerowitz, Joanne J. *Women Adrift: Independent Wage Earners in Chicago, 1880–1930*. Chicago: University of Chicago Press, 1988.

Miller, Julie. *Abandoned: Foundlings in Nineteenth-Century New York*. New York: New York University Press, 2008.

Moldow, Gloria. *Women Doctors in Gilded-Age Washington: Race, Gender, and Professionalization*. Urbana: University of Illinois Press, 1987.

Nevins, Allan. *Grover Cleveland: A Study in Courage*. New York: Dodd, Mead and Company, 1962.

Nevins, Allan, ed. *Letters of Grover Cleveland, 1850–1908*. Boston: Houghton Mifflin, 1933.

Norgren, Jill. *Rebels at the Bar: The Fascinating, Forgotten Stories of America's First Women Lawyers*. New York: New York University Press, 2013.

Odem, Mary E. *Delinquent Daughters: Protecting and Policing Adolescent Female Sexuality in the United States, 1885–1920*. Chapel Hill: University of North Carolina Press, 1995.

O'Neill, William L. *Everyone Was Brave: A History of Feminism in America*. Chicago: Quadrangle Books, 1969.

Peiss, Kathy. *Cheap Amusements: Working Women and Leisure in Turn-of-the-Century New York*. Philadelphia: Temple University Press, 1986.

Penny, Virginia. *The Employments of Women: A Cyclopaedia of Woman's Work*. Boston: Walker, Wise, and Company, 1863.

Perkins, Linda M. "Racial Integration of the Seven Sisters Colleges." *Journal of Blacks in Higher Education* 19 (Spring 1998): 104–8.

Pivar, David J. *Purity Crusade: Sexual Morality and Social Control, 1868–1900*. Westport, CT: Greenwood Press, 1973.

Reedy, William Marion. "Sex O'Clock in America." *Current Opinion* 55 (Aug. 1913): 1–7.

Repplier, Agnes. "The Repeal of Reticence." *The Atlantic Monthly*, March 1914, 297–304.

Resseguie, Harry E. "Alexander Turney Stewart and the Development of the Department Store, 1823–1876." *Business History Review* 39 (Fall 1965): 301–22.

Richardson, Heather Cox. "What on Earth Was a 'Bourbon Democrat'?" Historical Society, March 15, 2011, http://histsociety.blogspot.com/2011/03/what-on-earth-was-bourbon-democrat.html.

Rothman, Ellen K. *Hands and Hearts: A History of Courtship in America*. Cambridge, MA: Harvard University Press, 1987.

Scott, Anne Firor. *Natural Allies: Women's Associations in American History*. Urbana: University of Illinois Press, 1993.

———. *The Southern Lady: From Pedestal to Politics, 1830–1930*. Charlottesville: University Press of Virginia, 1970.

Shaw, Marian. *World's Fair Notes: A Woman Journalist Views Chicago's 1893 Columbia Exposition*. St. Paul, MN: Pogo Press, 1992.

Shotwell, John B. *A History of the Schools of Cincinnati*. Cincinnati, OH: School Life Company, 1902.

Smith, Daniel Scott. "The Long Cycle in American Illegitimacy and Prenuptial Pregnancy." In *Bastardy and Its Comparative History*, edited by Peter Laslett, Karla Oosterveen, and Richard M. Smith, 362–78. London: Edward Arnold, 1980.

Smith, Daniel Scott, and Michael S. Hindus. "Premarital Pregnancy in America." *Journal of Interdisciplinary History* 4 (Spring 1975): 537–70.

Smith-Rosenberg, Carroll. *Disorderly Conduct: Visions of Gender in Victorian America*. New York: Oxford University Press, 1985.

Stansell, Christine. *City of Women: Sex and Class in New York, 1789–1860*. Urbana: University of Illinois Press, 1987.

Stern, Madeleine B. *So Much in a Lifetime: The Story of Dr. Isabel Barrows*. New York: Julian Messner, 1964.

———. *We the Women: Career Firsts of Nineteenth-Century America*. Lincoln: University of Nebraska Press, 1962.

Steward, Frank, ed. "Alexander Turney Stewart: The Story of a Hundred Millions." *Frank Leslie's Popular Monthly*, June 1876, 641–56.

Stiles, Henry Reed. *Bundling: Its Origin, Progress and Decline in America*. Reprint, Sandwich, MA: Chapman Billies, 1999.

Storer, Horatio. "The Law of Rape." *Quarterly Journal of Psychological Medicine and Medical Jurisprudence* 2 (1868): 47–66.

Tapp, Hambelton, and James Klotter. *Kentucky: Decades of Discord, 1865–1900*. Lexington: University Press of Kentucky, 2008.

Travis, Anthony R. "Sophonisba Breckinridge, Militant Feminist." *Mid-America: An Historical Review* 58 (April 1976): 111–18.

Tucker, Jane [Agnes Parker]. *The Real Madeleine Pollard: A Diary of Ten Weeks' Association with the Plaintiff in the Famous Breckinridge-Pollard Suit* [TRMP]. New York: G. W. Dillingham, 1894.

Ulrich, Laurel Thatcher. *A Midwife's Tale: The Life of Martha Ballard, Based on Her Diary, 1785–1812*. New York: Vintage Books, 1990.

VanderVelde, Lea. "The Legal Ways of Seduction." *Stanford Law Review* 48 (April 1996): 817–901.

Walmsley, James Elliot. "The Last Meeting of the Confederate Cabinet." *Mississippi Valley Historical Review* 6 (Dec. 1919): 336–49.

Wells, Robert V. "Illegitimacy and Bridal Pregnancy in Colonial America." In *Bastardy and Its Comparative History*, edited by Peter Laslett, Karla Oosterveen, and Richard M. Smith, 349–61. London: Edward Arnold, 1980.

Wiebe, Robert H. *The Search for Order, 1877–1920*. New York: Hill and Wang, 1967.

Willard, Frances E., and Mary A. Livermore, eds. *A Woman of the Century*. Vol. 2. New York: Gordon Press, 1893.

Williams, R. Hal. *Years of Decision: American Politics in the 1890s.* New York: John Wiley and Sons, 1978.

Wood, Sharon E. *The Freedom of the Streets: Work, Citizenship and Sexuality in a Gilded Age City.* Chapel Hill: University of North Carolina Press, 2005.

Woodward, C. Van. *Origins of the New South, 1877–1913.* Baton Rouge: Louisiana State University Press, 1951.

Wright, Helen R. "Three Against Time: Edith and Grace Abbott and Sophonisba P. Breckinridge." *Social Service Review* 28 (March 1954): 41–53.

Acknowledgments

Bringing Down the Colonel represents a ten-year project of historical excavation. The Breckinridge-Pollard scandal was all but forgotten by history, dismissed as a tawdry sex scandal. But the history of women is inextricably tied up with the history of sex, and from the moment I discovered the scandal I knew it was an important chapter in the history of the social, political, and sexual emancipation of women. I have incurred many debts along the road of restoring the Breckinridge-Pollard scandal to history. I am especially indebted to the staff at the Library of Congress, particularly the staff at the Manuscript Reading Room, which holds the Breckinridge Family Papers, and the staff at the Newspaper and Current Periodical Reading Room, whose vast resources allowed me to access newspaper coverage from key nineteenth-century newspapers from Washington, New York, Cincinnati, Kentucky, and beyond. The staff in the Microform Reading Room helped me track down and access one of the few extant copies of Jennie Tucker's *The Real Madeleine Pollard*. I am also indebted to Janice Ruth of the Manuscript Division, one of the conveners of the Library of Congress Women's History and Gender Studies Discussion Group, for the invaluable suggestion to track Madeline Pollard's post-trial life through immigration records, which allowed me to build a picture of her vibrant life abroad from the late 1890s until her death in 1945.

I am also indebted to the staff at Historic New England, especially

Abigail Cramer and Stephanie Krauss, for their assistance with the Tucker Family Papers and photos. I would also like to thank Jennifer Cole at the Filson Historical Society for her assistance with Julia Blackburn's letters; Matthew Harris and Gordon Hogg of the Special Collections and Research Center at the University of Kentucky for their assistance with the Madeline McDowell Breckinridge letters and various other resources; and Jonathan Jeffrey at Western Kentucky University's Library of Special Collections for assistance with the Green Family Papers. I am also indebted to Tara Craig at Columbia University's Rare Book and Manuscript Library, and to the archivists at the John Hay Library at Brown University, the Manuscript and Archives Division at the New York Public Library, the Historical Society of Washington Reading Room, the Booth Family Center for Special Collections at Georgetown University, the Friends Historical Library at Swarthmore College, the Wright State University Libraries, and the Huntington Library.

I would like to thank the Reverend Jim Stewart of the Presbyterian Church in Danville, Kentucky, for providing me with a copy of *The Presbyterians: Two Hundred Years in Danville*, and Lois Ewald of Hephzibah House in New York for answering my questions about Margaret Thorne's founding of Hephzibah House and her activities in the 1890s.

I am indebted as always to my friend and mentor Kristin Luker for our regular chats that helped me shape *Bringing Down the Colonel*, her support and encouragement during the long course of this project, and her as always helpful reading of my manuscript. I would also like to thank Susan Rabiner for graciously reading and commenting on an early draft of the proposal for this book. My gratitude also goes to my friend Dan Sterenchuk for his helpful comments on the first draft of the manuscript.

My thanks especially to my agent, Geri Thoma, for believing in this project as much as I did and for bringing me to the wonderful Sarah Crichton at Farrar, Straus and Giroux, whose skillful editing, insight, and encouragement have been invaluable, and to Kate Sanford for her editing and support of this project. I would also like to thank Maureen Klier for her meticulous copyediting of the manuscript, and the first-rate design, production, and publicity staff at Farrar, Straus and Giroux for their work in bringing this book to fruition.

And as always, my deepest thanks and gratitude to my most faith-

ful companions in life and over the course of this book: my always wonderful and supportive husband, Anthony Spadafore, who has heard more
about Willie Breckinridge and Madeline Pollard than anyone deserves
and yet always encouraged me to soldier on, and my lovely dog Rosie,
who always reminded me when it was time to put the past down and
go for a walk.

Index